DATE

Upbeat: Nine Lives of a Musical Cat

Amram conducting the Houston Symphony, 1968. Photo by Tom Bywaters. Used with Permission.

♪

Upbeat:
Nine Lives
of a Musical Cat

David Amram

Paradigm Publishers
Boulder • London

Paradigm Publishers is committed to preserving ancient forests and natural resources. We elected to print *Upbeat: Nine Lives Of A Musical Cat* on 30% post consumer recycled paper, processed chlorine free. As a result, for this printing, we have saved:

    16 Trees (40' tall and 6-8" diameter)
  6,852 Gallons of Wastewater
  2,756 Kilowatt Hours of Electricity
   755 Pounds of Solid Waste
 1,484 Pounds of Greenhouse Gases

Paradigm Publishers made this paper choice because our printer, Thomson-Shore, Inc., is a member of Green Press Initiative, a nonprofit program dedicated to supporting authors, publishers, and suppliers in their efforts to reduce their use of fiber obtained from endangered forests.

For more information, visit www.greenpressinitiative.org

All rights reserved. No part of this publication may be transmitted or reproduced in any media or form, including electronic, mechanical, photocopy, recording, or informational storage and retrieval systems, without the express written consent of the publisher.

Copyright © 2008 Paradigm Publishers

Published in the United States by Paradigm Publishers, 3360 Mitchell Lane, Suite E, Boulder, CO 80301 USA.

Paradigm Publishers is the trade name of Birkenkamp & Company, LLC, Dean Birkenkamp, President and Publisher.

Library of Congress Cataloging-in-Publication Data

Amram, David.
   Upbeat : nine lives of a musical cat / David Amram.
     p. cm.
   Includes index.
   ISBN-13: 978-1-59451-424-1 (hardcover : alk. paper)   1. Amram, David. 2. Composers—United States—Biography.   I. Title.
   ML410.A534A3 2008
   780.92—dc22

                                                                2007032936

Printed and bound in the United States of America on acid-free paper that meets the standards of the American National Standard for Permanence of Paper for Printed Library Materials.

Designed and typeset in 11-point Garamond 3 by Straight Creek Bookmakers.

12 11 10 09 08   1 2 3 4 5

Dedicated to those who gave me these words of wisdom

"I named my song 'Now's the Time' because Now is what it was, what it is today, and what Now will always be. The right time!"

> Charlie Parker in a conversation with me in my basement apartment in Washington, DC, 1952.

"You must always love the music more than you love yourself"

> New York Philharmonic's conductor Dimitri Mitropolous in a conversation with me in New York, 1955

"Why don't you guys just calm down once in a while?"

> Advice from artist Dody Muller to Jack Kerouac and myself in New York, 1960.

"Your job as a composer is not just to please yourself. You should add something the repertoire."

> Leonard Bernstein to me in New York, 1978.

"Sincere musicians playing all types of music together like we're doing this weekend will bring the world together."

> Drummer Max Roach in a conversation after a concert in Prospect Park, Brooklyn, 1982.

"Music heals, and folk music is the root of the musical tree.

> Folksinger Odetta to me in Greenwich Village, 1994

"Write the way you talk."

> Advice to me from Kurt Vonnegut in New York, 2004

"Always follow your heart. It will tell you the right thing to do."

> Floyd Red Crow Westerman in a conversation with me in Venice Beach, California, 2007

David Amram conducting the Austin Symphony in a performance of Amram's "Theme and Variations on Red River Valley," July 2001. Photo by Jim Dirden. Used with permission.

Contents

Foreword by Frank McCourt		ix
Acknowledgments		xi
	Introduction: At Home Around the World	1
1	Merrymaking and Mayhem in the Mountains: Hunter S. Thompson's Final Blastoff	5
2	Kenya, Africa: The Mother of Us All	41
3	Natural Ambassadors	83
	Photo Section	following page 98
4	Kokopelli: Walking the Native American Trail of Beauty	99
5	Bouquets and Bombs on Broadway: Agony and Ecstasy on the Great White Way	133
6	The Dutch Treat: The Genesis of *Offbeat: Collaborating with Kerouac*	163
7	Words and Music: Scat and Make-up Songs, the Art of One-Time-Only Rap Reporting	177
8	Postcards from the Road, 2002–2007	227
9	Fond Farewells: Honoring Six Old Friends	291
Index		309
About the Author		322

David Amram composing at his home. Courtesy of David Amram.

Foreword by Frank McCourt

Let us bend an elbow and raise a glass to that great moveable feast—David Amram. Better still, and more appropriate, let us reach for whatever instrument we play and serenade him.

All this, of course, after we've read his latest memoir, *Upbeat: Nine Lives of a Musical Cat.* Nine lives? Oh, the man is modest. He has led at least fifty lives and touched the lives of millions. It may be a bit of cliché to say it but he is—and has been—Pied Piper to those millions.

The book's first chapter is an account of David's experiences at the memorial service of Hunter Thompson. You're barely into the chapter when you encounter the likes of Doug Brinkley, Johnny Depp, Lyle Lovett, and Ed Bradley.

A memorial service or, in the case of Hunter Thompson, a celebration, is the cue for a massive series of Amram reminiscences. Does the man know a billion people? Look at the names. In his seventy-odd years on this planet David seems to have met anyone who tooted a horn, plucked a stringed instrument or banged on a drum. He has hung out with Jack Kerouac, George Plimpton, Bob Dylan, Leonard Bernstein, and Dizzy Gillespie.

Musically, he is at home everywhere.

Everywhere, man!

Drop him in Lithuania and he's tootling on some local flute. Slip him into Carnegie Hall and he's conducting an orchestra. Hell, he conducts orchestras everywhere. He's the one you'll see supplying heavenly background music on judgment day—though not if anyone is turned away from the gates of Heaven. Oh, no. David Amram is all joy. David Amram is all music, and the music can be made with instruments or with language itself.

Yeah, man, he's into his eighth decade but he'd exhaust fourth graders in a playground. You can dip into this book at any page and find yourself breathless with wonder, music, and laughter. That is his magic. He moves through life and music with an openness that makes the rest of us look worn. He praises and praises and loves and loves. He personifies that dictum of Thomas Carlyle's, "Happy is the man who has found his work."

Work? Well, I don't know if David Amram even thinks of work. His life is music and music is his life. It's as natural as his breathing, though he breathes with a mighty gusto.

This is a cosmic and a microcosmic memoir. It is leavened, not with just love of music, but of life itself, of family, of language, of gusto.

Don't try reading this book in one sitting.

And leave your critical tendencies at the door.

David Amram is beyond criticism, and if you say otherwise I'll invite you out that door.

You're in for a treat, pilgrim!

Acknowledgments

I would like to thank my three children, Alana, Adira, and Adam for the inspiration they gave me to write these stories for them to share with their children some day. And my gratitude to their mother, Lora Lee, who made them a home, gave them love, understanding, and the confidence to be creative people in their own right and grow up to be strong, compassionate, and gracious to others.

To my sister, Mariana, who has been a soul mate my entire life, and my parents Emilie and Philip Amram, and my uncle David, who gave me a foundation of basic values for building a life.

Also, to David Stanford, who gave me the idea when we spoke in 1994 of writing a book which would recount the many lives I have lived and the numerous adventures I have experienced through my work in many genres of music.

For Dean Birkenkamp, who was not only interested in publishing this book and reissuing my other two books, but who also gave me invaluable ideas of how to structure this book. And this would not have been possible without the support of sociologist Dr. Audrey Sprenger, who was an enormous help in putting *Upbeat: Nine Lives of a Musical Cat* into a cohesive form. Also, her organizing of trail-blazing academic events throughout the United States and London, England, which she invited me to co-teach with her, gave me a whole new perspective on the way the social sciences and the fine arts can relate to one another in the academy.

To five of the literary luminaries of our time: Joyce Johnson, Lawrence Ferlinghetti, Herb Gold, Kurt Vonnegut, and Frank McCourt, who encouraged me to dare to put words on paper and to try to tell my stories in my own way. They all treated me in the same generous fashion that they always have with so many other writers, young and old, who, like myself, admire their collective mastery.

To my two dear friends and neighbors, Jean Sweezey, who put in twelve years of editing and organizing mountains of materials for this book, and her husband,

Tom, who allowed me to share the great talents of his wife, Jean, for endless hours and who encouraged me to persevere.

To my production editor, Dianne Ewing, whose painstaking work and patience would make any author grateful.

To Nikoletta Skarlatos, who was by my side during the worst crisis in my life, and who has remained a steadfast friend, showing me how to always deal with adversity in a positive way, always remembering the divine gift of laughter and the importance of consideration for others. She was also responsible, with the help of David Helfant, for bringing my score for *The Manchurian Candidate* out of obscurity after forty-two years, and facilitating it finally being released as a recording for the first time.

To Johnny Depp, whose selfless love and support of the work of both Hunter S. Thompson and Jack Kerouac helped to bring both of these authors to the attention of new audiences. Playing music with him, as well as accompanying his readings of both authors, was an experience I'll always treasure.

And to John Sampas, the executor of Kerouac's estate, and his late sister, Stella, who were keepers of the flame for Jack, years before he was finally recognized solely for his artistic merits.

And all the volunteers of "Lowell Celebrates Kerouac," who have shown the world for the past twenty years how to honor an artist in their own hometown.

To Sir James Galway, who by his own example, teaches all of us how to be better than we dreamed of being in whatever line of work we choose to pursue in life, and how to become ambassadors of music by sharing your gifts with everyone, young and old, in a joyous way. Sir James also gave me the chance to compose one of my best pieces for him, made possible by violinist Fred Horwitz, who brought us together. His performances of my music were all any composer could dream of. And his friendship included making me aware of many books I had never read or heard of before.

To Sterling Lord, the legendary literary agent who has kept the legacy of Jack Kerouac alive for more than a half century and guided and helped me in my own writing, as well as sharing camaraderie and advice since 1956.

To Floyd Red Crow Westerman and Vine Deloria Jr. for companionship and collaborations since the 1960s, allowing me the honor of participating with them in the many forms of Native American music that enriches our continent.

To Dizzy Gillespie, whose genius for music was equaled by his genius for living, who took me under his wing when I was twenty years old, and who remained a friend and mentor for forty-two years until he left us.

To photographers Tom Bywaters, John Cohen, Jim Dirden, Chris Felver, Henry Grossman, Fred McDarrah, Ebet Roberts, and Arnold J. Smith for their decades of friendship and superlative pictures, all of which capture a moment in time and give everyone who sees them a sense of what it was like to be there.

And finally to every person I mentioned in this book, all of whom have had something special to offer the world.

Upbeat: Nine Lives of a Musical Cat

Introduction: At Home Around the World

It was springtime 1978. I lay on the ratty-carpeted floor of the New Delhi Airport in India, leaning against my instrument cases and bags, hungry and thirsty. I was supposed to be in Tehran, Iran, performing that evening in a symphonic concert, conducting the orchestra, as well as playing my instruments from around the world. Instead, I was stuck in No Man's Land, the nickname given to the isolated room in the New Delhi Airport where travelers whose connecting flights were canceled or delayed for more than twenty-four hours were housed and not allowed to leave the airport since they had no visa for India (my case). All of us were crowded together with suspected drug dealers, people with no visas or passports at all, people whose flights had been delayed, and criminals arrested in the airport who were waiting to be extradited. I made a small desk out of my instrument cases, sat on the floor, and began writing music.

A young man in a navy blue uniform with gold epaulettes strode into the room. "Ladies and gentlemen," he intoned in a cultivated British accent. "My name is Lieutenant Raji Pandit. Whom among you would like a glass of water?"

(How gracious, I thought to myself, an example of Krishna-consciousness in action.)

"*Paracalo Kyrie. Theepsau*" ("Please sir. I am thirsty,"), cried an elderly Greek woman, raising her hand as she stood, much like the statue of Athena.

"That will be one dollar, U.S. currency only," said Lt. Pandit in curt tones. Every one of the involuntary citizens of No Man's Land groaned. A woman from Scandinavia put down her copy of *Rolling Stone Magazine* and came over to me.

"Do something," she said. "This is dreadful."

I took off the Guatemalan *ocarina* I still wear around my neck today, part of my traveling necklace with all the beads and trinkets acquired as gifts over the years from my concerts around the world. I began playing "Son de Palo Volador," an old folk song I learned when I was in Guatemala.

Lt. Pandit stopped haggling over the proposed dollar fee for the glass of water with the woman from Greece. He walked over to me, beaming.

"My heavens, that's splendid!" he exclaimed. "What a lovely tone you get from that tiny instrument. Let me fetch a *bonsri* (wooden flute) from the gift shop."

He scampered off and returned, clutching an armful of wooden flutes. He offered me a Krishna flute in C and we began improvising duets together. One of the stranded travelers took a small push-button accordion from her bag and joined in. A half-hour later, other airport employees, who were allowed access to No Man's Land, joined us, playing *tablas* and other instruments borrowed from the gift shop. The Scandinavian woman began to dance, and the rest of the temporary residents of No Man's Land joined in when I led them in polyphonic finger snapping, dividing the room up into four groups of finger poppers. At the conclusion of our World Premiere and final performance, Lt. Pandit came over and shook my hand.

"This was simply a marvelous time," he said. "I'm having the airline buy everyone dinner."

The captives in No Man's Land all applauded. The woman from Scandinavia came over to me.

"I've seen you Americans jam for years at all the jazz clubs in Stockholm," she said. "And I've seen Americans play jazz with other jazz musicians from all over Europe at our summer outdoor festivals. But I can honestly say that I have never witnessed an East/West one before. How did you do that?"

"I followed a universal principle," I said. "Many Native Americans have a motto: 'Respect, Love, and Sharing.' That's all you need to know to make music anywhere with anyone. You just put that into action."

"Yes, but how did you know what to do, when those people from India joined in with us and began to play those exotic melodies and rhythms?"

"Very simple," I said. "I listened very carefully to them. It's about sensing what to do and what not to do and following the ancient principle of how to make music with others when they are playing, which is simply, when in doubt ... leave it out!"

"But don't you ever feel awkward?" she said. "Aren't you somewhat uncomfortable when you, as a foreigner, are suddenly playing with people whose language you don't speak, in places where you have never been before?"

"No," I said. "I try to tune into wherever I am and whoever I am with at the moment. Back in the States, I play with the great Native American singer, Floyd Red Crow Westerman. He told me that every place he goes on the planet is just another part of his mother, the Earth. So wherever he is, that place then becomes his home. It's that simple. I feel the same way. I'm at home around the world, where ever I am."

This book is about the many paths on the journey of my life that have given me joy and the strength to continue as a full-time composer who is also an improviser, a conductor, a free-association scat singer, and an appreciator and sharer of all the many worlds of music I've been blessed to be part of.

In the opening lines of my opera, *Twelfth Night,* Orsino sings: "If music be the food of love, play on." I hope this book can share some of the recipes and dishes with which music nourishes our souls.

Music is and always will be about sharing that food of love with others. In our high-tech-cyberspace twenty-first century, people around the world can now share whatever they do in their lives with anybody and everybody, just as musicians have always done. And it doesn't require any sophisticated state-of-the-art technology or a battery of lawyers, accountants, career counselors, or marketing research experts to be able to sing your own song or tell your own story,

Music is just one of the many ways of doing this. It is simply soul-to-soul communication. That's why true music built to last has never come out of a can, an attorney's office, a machine, or the cement brain from the statue of a dead composer. It has always been made by people for other people to share.

Music comes from the Mother Earth, the rhythm of the stars, skies, and sea. It resonates with the heartbeat we feel while still inside our mothers, and the song all children on Earth have in their hearts.

Music comes from our grandparents' memories, from sounds created in concert halls, prisons, dance palaces, jazz clubs, mountainsides, jungles, churches, mosques, synagogues, boat rides, cattle round-ups, sporting events, weddings . . . an infinite number of places.

I've participated in musical events that occurred in many of these places. These experiences in so many different environments have all enriched the palette of what I have to work with when I compose for symphony orchestras, chamber groups, ballet, theater, film, and the human voice. The memories of all the events, people and places which touched my heart remain there forever, as silent as the inside of the small shed behind our farmhouse where I write my music. But even if they remain invisible and inaudible to the rest of the world, I still see and hear them every day.

And when I'm on the road, at the airport lounge, on a plane, in a motel room, on a train, bus, or in a car, even when thousands of miles away from our farm, every place becomes my studio and my home away from home. The music is always there to make me feel at home, and there is always someone knocking on the door to show me something new.

As I approach my late seventies in this new millennium, I see that all the experiences I have been lucky enough to be part of are one great journey, still unfolding. In a sense, the one hundred twelve formal compositions of mine are a journal of my life, expressed through music. I hope you can share some of the experiences that made these compositions possible by joining me and becoming part of the band as you read these accounts of some of my favorite adventures, places, and people.

Since *Vibrations* was published in 1968 and *Offbeat: Collaborating with Kerouac* was published in 2002, I've continued to discover new places in the world that I can now call home.

I've never planned anything in my life except to try to be the best that I could be every day, follow my heart, and utilize the tools my father and mother gave me as a little boy in Feasterville, Pennsylvania, growing up on a farm in the late 1930s. Even then, I always had a dream that someday, somehow, I might be able to be part of music in some way.

Seventy years later, I still hear the voice of my father when we would have heart-to heart talks, which usually took place when we were working together on our farm.

"Work hard every day at everything you do, David. Spend your time with people who know more than you do, and never be afraid to ask them anything that you want to know more about. Always show them respect, and then share what you've learned with others. That's what I learned from farmers when I was a young man."

This was what my father said to me almost every day of my childhood. I still try to put into practice his advice each day in the way I create my music and live my life.

Even today, I have people in gas stations, schools, parking lots, sporting events, and after countless concerts come up and say to me, "I wish I could go along with you to all these places, and be with all the people in and out of music you spend time with. Do you need a roadie? Could I get strapped in the baggage compartment? Do you need a harmonica player who can tap dance and do word processing?"

I hope this book can make you feel that you are there on the road with me and show you what it's like to be there. I hope you can get an idea of what it's like to write a symphony, make up a song, or play at jam sessions around the world where you don't speak the verbal language but can intuit the musical one.

I hope you feel that you are there too as I play with Dizzy Gillespie in Cuba, Masai tribesmen in Kenya, country musicians in Texas, in a bell tower in Holland, and at a workshop in New Orleans for 300 flutists with Sir James Galway two hours before he performed the world premiere of the flute concerto I had written for him.

I hope you'll understand what it's like to conduct music you have composed for a symphony orchestra, an opera, or a ballet. What it's like to work on a Tony Award-winning play on Broadway and what it's like to work on a colossal flop. And how you can have a family and try to have a life that fulfills their needs as well.

And perhaps most important, how to deal with the struggling and rejection that we all face in life between our occasional triumphs, without letting your own flame ever be extinguished, no matter how much it flickers.

I hope these adventures will inspire all the young people who read this book to dare to dream, find your own way to pursue your dreams, and never give up.

Almost every person I mention in this book gave much more than they received, did more than was expected, and added positive energy to the world. They all showed me that every person in the world has songs and stories to share. These are some of mine.

♪

Chapter 1

Merrymaking and Mayhem in the Mountains: Hunter S. Thompson's Final Blastoff

It all began when Doug Brinkley called me in June to let me know that Hunter's memorial event was scheduled to take place August 20, 2005, in Woody Creek, Colorado, and that I should try to save the date. Doug Brinkley, in addition to being Hunter's literary executor and editor of his three books of letters, is also the author of several other best-selling books, one of America's premiere historians, a galvanizing speaker, full-time professor at Rice University, father of three young children, organizer of George McGovern's seventy-fifth birthday celebration in Washington, to which he had invited Hunter and me as part of the program, and a loyal friend for the past twenty-three years.

Back on December 12, 1996, both Hunter and Johnny Depp were honored by the city of Louisville and made Kentucky Colonels. Poet Ron Whitehead and Doug Brinkley had invited me down to create some special music for that occasion, and the late Warren Zevon joined me on piano, along with Johnny Depp playing guitar, for a memorable evening of poetry, music, speechmaking, and post-ceremonial mayhem.

Doug and I have been at scores of events together since 1982 when we first met in Boulder, Colorado, at a weeklong event celebrating the twenty-fifth anniversary of the publication of *On the Road.* I knew that if Doug were there in Woody Creek to celebrate Hunter's legacy, and if Johnny Depp were involved as well, everything would end up coming off in good taste and presented in a joyous fashion.

Both Doug and Johnny are excellent at what they do, and they were both extremely close to Hunter and had great respect for him as an artist and a person. Hunter's son, Juan, and Hunter's wife, Anita, had the same high regard for Doug and Johnny as well. Doug and I kept calling one another over the next two months as the event was taking shape, so that I could figure out how I could best serve the program by contributing something that would be appropriate.

"Don't worry, David. Things are fluid, but just be there and be prepared to do whatever feels right at the moment," said Doug. "Both Johnny Depp and the family want to make it a memorial service as well as a celebration, and don't want it to be a media circus or another Woodstock. There will be other public events in the future where big crowds can come to celebrate Hunter. I wish we could invite all the friends we share in common who knew and loved Hunter and his work, but we have to respect his family's wishes. I am getting e-mails and phone calls from around the world. There is huge interest in this. Hunter wanted this kind of a final sendoff, and Johnny and Hunter's family are determined to see that it happens the way he said he wanted it to happen."

When I called Doug Brinkley on Wednesday morning, August 17, three days before the event was to take place the following Saturday night, and told him I was coming the next day to Aspen, he said that he hoped to also be arriving later that same Thursday night as well, and hopefully we could meet up that night if possible.

"Bring all your instruments and be prepared to jam with everyone. You'll find a way to make your "Theme and Variations on My Old Kentucky Home" come off, as you did when we were in Louisville. The final plans for the musical portion of the evening are still not set in stone, because we are still not sure who will actually show up, so just be ready for anything. I know you will make it happen, as you always do. Get some rest, and I'll see you in Aspen."

Since all I had planned for certain was to bring as many of my instruments as I could carry on the plane, pack a new suit in my bag to wear for the ceremony, and create several plans of different ways I could perform my "Theme and Variations on My Old Kentucky Home," regardless of who ended up playing with me, I decided to just think about all the good times I had with Hunter over the years and trust the fates to guide me when it was time to do the piece.

Improvising words and music on the spot and doing what feels right at the moment is what I have done since my days in the army in 1952, and what I have continued to do when the occasion calls for it in my non-symphonic performances around the world. My job in Woody Creek was to make the finale seem effortless and enjoyable for others and try to bring good feelings to Hunter's family, which is certainly what Hunter would have expected of me.

I spent the whole night packing and sketching out last-minute musical ideas, trying to figure out which instruments to bring with me, exactly what I should do to get a band of some sort together after I got there, and how I could possibly do it.

I was really excited to be returning to Aspen again, and spent the whole flight to Denver planning ten different ways to do my "Theme and Variations on My Old Kentucky Home" so that if I ended up having a large ensemble, it wouldn't be too long, but so that all the musicians would have a moment of their own to shine, no matter how many or how few ended up playing with me. I learned this from seeing Duke Ellington in 1941 in Philadelphia, where during his stage show, each player had a chance to shine.

After arriving in Denver, I ran down the seemingly endless corridors of the Denver airport, panting due to the five-thousand-foot elevation of the Mile High City, and just made the commuter flight to Aspen.

As the plane taxied onto the Aspen runway, just forty-eight hours before the event was to take place, I suddenly felt a blast of energy. When I got off the plane and smelled that Colorado late summer fresh air and looked around at the mountains, I knew that everything would turn out the way it was meant to be. Even though I hadn't slept in twenty-four hours, I felt rested and ready to go. I could feel Hunter's spirit and crazed energy in the air and hear that staccato voice barking at me: "Make it look easy. Keep it simple, Amram. There are too many windbags and lying lizards. Be honest, clear, and to the point." This was the advice that Hunter gave me, a young classical composer when we met in 1959, when he was a young reporter for the Middletown Record and lived in a tiny cabin on Route 209 a few minutes from where I used to have an equally tiny place, in the same foothills of the Shawanagunk Mountains in Cuddebackville, eight miles outside of Port Jervis in upstate New York.

Now, forty-six years later, here in the Rocky Mountains of Colorado, I knew that however chaotic this ambitious event might be, somehow everyone who came to contribute to Hunter's memory would all work together and we would all be able to pull it off. And that we would all be, in Hunter's words, honest, clear, and to the point.

After wandering around the small airport in Aspen for twenty minutes, hoping to find someone with a sign saying that they were looking for me, I was met by Emma Juniper, a young, energetic twenty-year-old college student who had been an intern for Hunter just a few months before he died. She was now working with Anita, Hunter's wife of the last two years, and her cell phone was ringing nonstop, with people calling from all over trying to get their names put on the list of invitees, as well as members of the production staff, journalists wanting interviews, and guests and participants in the event like myself who had been invited, who also needed to know where to go, when to be there, exactly what to do, and when to do it.

"The final schedule is still in formation," she said bravely, when I asked her the same questions. "It will be fantastic, but all these issues are still being decided, and I know it will all be fine in the end. We are all so happy that all of you can be here for Hunter."

Emma told me the names of all the people who had not arrived yet, which ones might come for sure and which ones were tentative, and how some of the crew had been here for a month, putting the finishing touches on what was the equivalent of a space shuttle launching at Cape Canaveral.

As we drove from the airport, she outlined for me the nearly impossible task of coordinating a whole evening with 487 officially invited guests attending a huge event in the outlying town of Woody Creek, while meeting the deadline of finishing the construction of the 153-foot tall tower from which Hunter's ashes would be fired into space from a cannon, coordinated with a lighting display, Japanese ceremonial drum group, and fireworks, as well as preparing and serving dinner, drinks, and a musical program for all the guests.

My mind reeled as she reviewed the other details involved in planning the whole program for the evening, which included arranging the transportation of all the guests, performers, staff, and crew to and from the field behind Hunter's house in a series of shuttle buses.

As Emma outlined the logistics, I realized that pulling the entire event off successfully would require a team effort akin to the Allies' cooperative triumphant moment in World War II when they completed the invasion of Normandy on D-Day.

"I hope you understand why no one could answer your phone calls and e-mails or contact you for the past two weeks, David." said Emma. "Everyone is so excited that you can be here to play, and I wish I could answer your questions now, but it is impossible for me to do anything to help you to figure out how to put together what you are going to do, except to go with the flow, and conscript some kind of ensemble with whomever you run across that you feel can perform your "Theme and Variations on My Old Kentucky Home," during the next two days, and be ready to play whenever we finalize the program, which may be just an hour or two before the event takes place at 7:00 p.m. Saturday night. We know you can do it."

"I'll try," I said. "Worst-case scenario, I'll play my "Theme and Variations on My Old Kentucky Home" on my Irish double-D whistle all by myself as an unaccompanied piece, and switch to the piano and lead the audience singing, although I'd rather have some other musicians play it with me, as I did in December of 1996 in Louisville for Hunter, when Hunter and Johnny Depp were both made Kentucky Colonels. That night in Louisville, I rehearsed with Warren Zevon playing piano early in the afternoon, with singer Suzy Woods and her bluegrass band in the basement of the theater, since they arrived two hours later, and with Johnny Depp a few minutes before we actually played, when someone went back to his hotel room and got him his National slide guitar.

"I had planned the whole structure of the piece the night before, when Ron Whitehead called me from Louisville and told me who he thought would actually show up, even though I had never met any of them before. After I got together with each of them separately, I revamped everything I had previously planned, and when we performed it, I gave everyone signals when to come in, and it was terrific."

"I'm sure you will have no problem this time," said Emma, who was able to listen to my ramblings while answering her endless calls and calming down those whose voices I could hear shouting out their problems through her speakerphone.

"Do you think Johnny Depp will play guitar with you again?" she asked.

"I'd love it," I said. "I didn't want to bother him, since he has such an insurmountable task trying to oversee all that is happening, but I wish he could. It was terrific having him play with me in Louisville. I'll ask him when I see him tonight."

"He's not here yet," said Emma. "I think he's arriving the day of the event. He had work he had to do in Los Angeles."

"Well, whatever happens and whoever shows up or whoever I run into, I have already planned so many different ways to do it here in Woody Creek, it won't take long to rehearse, since I have the whole structure in my head, and can rehearse it with each musician individually, and then cue each person at the performance for when they should play."

"It sounds like you have another perfect plan," said Emma. "Let me drive you to where you are staying so you can drop all those instruments off, and then we'll get something to eat. You look hungry."

As we drove from the airport to my lodgings, Emma demonstrated her linguistic ability in five languages, telling me about all the crazy events that had occurred in putting this spectacular together. Staring out the window of Emma's car, I was blown away by the unearthly feeling of this special part of the world again.

No matter where you looked, everything was peaceful and beautiful, all bathed in a Colorado summer late-afternoon gentle light that made everything appear to be perfectly fit together, like the old paintings I used to see in the illustrated book of Bible stories *Jacob's Coat of Many Colors,* which I used to read as a boy on our farm in Feasterville, Pennsylvania. As I read and reread the stories in the late 1930s, looking at the illustrations of shepherds tending their flocks in endless fields of rolling mountains, I always wondered if there was actually any place on earth that could be as idyllic as these paintings.

I realized as we drove toward Aspen that there was such a place, as I watched the countryside roll on by, reminding me of a Cinemascope movie, through the front windshield and side windows of Emma's car. I saw that like much of northern New Mexico's remaining unspoiled small mountain communities, Colorado's Aspen and nearby Woody Creek were both still a paradise in 2005.

The surrounding countryside is as breathtaking as any place in the world, and as we pulled into the Inn at Aspen, a small and comfortable mini-hotel on the outskirts of town, I could see that the rolling land a few miles outside of the town of Aspen still retains a remarkably pristine flavor. All the new structures are simple and seem to fit into the mountains, rather than competing with them.

As we drove into town, after dropping off my bags, I saw that many of the old hotels and weather-beaten winter houses downtown are still like the Aspen of the fifties and that its surrounding communities still have much of the same unspoiled spirit that I remember from when I first came to Colorado as a teenager in the early forties to visit, sixty years ago.

While I was waiting before meeting Emma at the baggage claim area, I saw that you can still see that same unspoiled quality today in the faces and hear it in the voices of people from Aspen when they greet you and when they talk to one another. The natural beauty and spirit of the people who have been there for generations transforms everyone who comes to Aspen and Woody Creek and the surrounding small communities and brings out the best in them. There is a great group of year-round residents who keep alive the traditions of the Western style of greeting and dealing with other people in an open way, which is vanishing from most places in our society.

Every summer, there are still series of world-class music festivals, including the fifty years of Aspen's world-renowned classical music festival, which had James Conlin conducting Mahler's Ninth Symphony the same night that Hunter's event was taking place.

Emma, who had attended high school in Aspen, told me that in spite of the current astronomical property values, there is a lot of old-time flavor, which remains precious to the local population, and that most of the residents, including those who come each year to vacation, want to keep it that way.

"Thank heavens for that," I said. "Hunter used to tell me how he and other activists would go to meetings and terrify the developers, and somehow manage to stop them, or at least slow them down from ruining one of the loveliest parts of the country that is still left. He used to tell me that he didn't want to see Aspen and Woody Creek become faceless towns with endless strip malls and fast-food emporiums, all in the name of progress. Thanks to Hunter and all the people he worked with over the years, they haven't paved over the mountains yet."

"Let's hope that doesn't happen," said Emma. "Every time I come back here, there is more building going on."

Emma took me to get a sandwich at Johnny McGuire's, the deli where many of her old high school chums gathered to hang out.

"Here we are," she said cheerily. "I'll treat you to the best sandwich in Colorado."

As we parked by the side of Johnny McGuire's, I could tell from the aroma that wafted through the pure air of downtown Aspen that I was in for a true treat. On the United Airlines flight from NYC to Denver, I had attempted to eat a few greenish nitrate-filled salami slices on stale crackers that disintegrated when peeled from the cellophane wrapper, accompanied by other varieties of equally carcinogenic junk food, for which I paid five dollars.

While racing to catch the connecting flight to Aspen, I stopped during my long airport dash to buy and chew on part of a foul-tasting veggie burger while on the run, packing the rest of it in my bag of flutes and attempting to chew at least part of it on the plane, but gave up after two bites. I was ready to finally have something healthy to eat and could hear my stomach growling at full volume as Emma described the treats I would have in store as we got out of the car and were ready to enter Aspen's premiere funky hole-in-the-wall takeout deli, Johnny McGuire's.

I realized after a day of airline food poisoning that I was approaching the Valhalla of small town American eating delights while on the road, in one of the places that looked like it still retained the spirit of mid-twentieth century small-town life. Johnny McGuire's is located in a wind-burned old building that looks like an old feed store, with a battered old red sedan parked in front of the entrance.

Emma told me that the old clunker of a car was still used to deliver food to townsfolk. Standing outside the deli and sitting on the steps was a cheerful group of apple-cheeked young high school-age kids eating sandwiches, telling jokes, laughing, and talking. Two of them, who Emma told me had just started college, greeted Emma warmly and told me that they were musicians with their own bands, had heard that I was coming to town to play a special piece for Hunter's event, hoped that I would jam with them if I had any spare time, and suggested which sandwich was the most delicious.

"How do you like this?" said one young man, pointing to the battered red sedan that was blocking the entrance to the deli. "I'll bet they don't have anything like this in New York."

The old red sedan looked like a fast food shrine because of the hand painted sign, "We Dill-Iver," inscribed on the side door, with a huge plastic five-foot faded green replica of a giant dill pickle mounted on the top of the roof, like the fin of a whale. There were also several bumper stickers on the back of the sedan, saying "Health Food Sucks."

I decided that I had to get some of these bumper stickers to share with my fellow part-time health food addicts who also occasionally fall off the vegetarian wagon and succumb to the delights of eating chicken and fish whenever possible. So after chomping on a delicious fajita wrap that Emma had bought for me, I walked inside the deli and struck up a conversation with the chef-manager-weather-forecaster-philosopher-storyteller in Spanish about how nice it was to be back in Aspen again, and how delicious the fajita wrap was.

Then when I finally got to the point and told him that I wanted to buy some of these great "Health Food Sucks" bumper stickers to give to my friends back East, he spoke to me in English.

"Peel one off the wall, my brother," he said, as he dumped slices of chicken into an enormous vat of black boiling grease, whose heavenly scent made me forget about my desire to eat only tofu burgers, watercress salads, and granola snacks. I ordered another fajita wrap, some gigantic dill pickles, a plate of coleslaw, a twelve-ounce container of chai tea, and some sweet buns.

"*Oye hermano,* you got a good appetite for an old dude. You look like you *hungry!* Everybody come in, same as you, to ask me for them stickers. We don't got no more right now ... *no tenemos.*"

"Gracias," I said, trying to hide my disappointment. "I'll be back."

I left the heavenly oasis of Johnny McGuire's and went with Emma to visit Bob Braudis, the sheriff of Pitkin County, whom I first met on December 12, 1996, when he accompanied Hunter for the ceremony in Louisville.

I always remembered how Hunter introduced me to the sheriff backstage that night, after Hunter had finished spraying one of Louisville's most prominent benefactors of the arts with a fog machine used to put out fires, in the middle of a flowery tribute being given to him. Scampering offstage, with a fiendish smile, Hunter put down the fog machine on the floor backstage, motioned me over, and introduced me to a huge six-foot-six man, who had been standing offstage watching the crazy ceremony.

"You'll now be safe whenever you come to Woody Creek, David," said Hunter. "This is our Sheriff, Bob Braudis. I could never get elected to office when I ran for Sheriff in 1970, so Bob did it for me."

"How did you ever get to be the sheriff of Pitkin County?" I asked Bob.

"It was easy," said Bob. "I came to Aspen as a ski bum. Becoming sheriff was a natural progression."

Now nine years later, I was walking into Bob's office in Woody Creek for a reunion, to join him again in an event honoring Hunter, but this time, both Hunter and Warren Zevon were no longer with us.

We talked about the good times we had during the no-sleep marathon in Louisville and how we all spent the night after the tribute concert celebrating with Hunter, Johnny Depp, Doug Brinkley, Ron Whitehead, and filmmaker Mark Reese, who manfully tried to interview the crazy cast of characters for an NPR radio special about Hunter, while working on his documentary film *Boys of Winter* about his dad and Louisville hero, Pee Wee Reese. Hunter kept all of us up all night, laughing and partying until the sun rose, and Sheriff Bob Braudis was a perfect example of the old New Orleans saying that you should always be the first to leave the battlefield and the last to leave the party.

Bob told me how we had to try to celebrate Hunter's life for the upcoming memorial ceremony, in the same way we all celebrated together for his tribute in Louisville.

"Johnny, Doug Brinkley, you, and I were all together in Louisville for Hunter. Now we're all here for him in Woody Creek. I was there the day he died. I'll never forget him," said Bob. "But no tears. Hunter wrote that when he died, there should be a party with all his old friends and he wanted to hear the tinkling of ice in glasses filled with some fine brew, after his ashes had been fired out of a cannon."

Bob gave me one Pitkin County Sheriff's Department mini-badge for myself and one for my son, to wear on our lapels to remember Hunter and Woody Creek, the place that Hunter loved so much and made his home for the last thirty-eight years of his life. Then he gave me a black and gold lapel pin with a tiny replica of the badge, with the logo "call us before your next party" engraved in tiny gold letters.

"We are going to respect his wishes and we'll have the best party ever. We'll give him a sendoff no one will ever forget," said Bob.

After we left Bob's office, Emma told me that she just had a call from Jon Equis, the events coordinator for the memorial, whose headquarters were in a house he had rented in Woody Creek next door to Hunter's house. He was having a jam session and party for the gang of volunteers who had been working non-stop for a month to get everything ready for the event.

Emma said that members of the crew all played music in addition to the technical work they did and that they all wanted me to come and tell them stories about Hunter, as well as play music with them.

"I still have some of my instruments with me," I said, pointing to my small black bag stuffed with various wind instruments, including my *dumbek,* the small Middle Eastern drum that I always bring with me. "*Sempre Peratis.* That means always be ready. I learned that in the Boy Scouts."

As Emma drove me up those winding mountain roads from Aspen to nearby Woody Creek where Hunter lived a few miles outside of town, I remembered how he described it to me in detail in one of his many New York visits, shortly after he bought his place in 1968, when we would sit in the back room of the Lion's Head Bar in Greenwich Village.

He told me how Woody Creek was still one of the last vestiges of the old Wild West, and that I should go there to visit him, and write a symphony using the sounds of the wind rushing through the night air of the Rockies.

Hunter loved music, and sometimes used to accompany us with hambone rhythms, slapping his thighs like a crazed bongo player while keeping excellent time, as the other musicians and I would play Irish reels, or folk musicians like Jerry Jeff Walker and Hunter's old friend Rosalie Sorrels would sing and play their guitars in the back room of the Lion's Head Bar at 2:00 a.m.

As we drove up toward Woody Creek at dusk, you could feel a sense of calm and imagine that the ghosts of Indians whose spirits still fill the mountains and valleys were welcoming you to a special timeless place where you felt peaceful and at home.

The winding roads have small valleys below, where houses are nestled into the hills, often with horses grazing, and even wild elk, all living harmoniously as if they were family members with the inhabitants of the tiny ranches, all surrounded by spectacular scenery and air that is so clean at 7,500 feet above sea level, you feel like you are in the Tibetan Himalayas, if not in heaven itself. I understood again why Hunter loved this place more than any other.

As we approached the house where Jon Equis and the crew were having their party/jam session, next door to Hunter's, I heard as well as saw, through the open windows, some amazingly good players all sitting in a circle and playing up a storm.

These musicians were part of the extraordinary crew of young people who worked with Jon Equis, the dynamic events coordinator. I was amazed that Jon was such a young man, exuding energy and enthusiasm and warmth, totally unlike what I imagined an events coordinator from Los Angeles would be like, especially for a project of such immense importance. Jon greeted me at the door.

"Please come in. Make yourself at home, have something to eat and drink and please feel free to join in the jam session. All my people have worked so hard, I want to give them a night where they can unwind and just enjoy one another. Many of them are also fine musicians, as you can see. Whenever the spirit moves you, just join them in the living room and play as long as you want to."

I ate some delicious fresh peaches and went into the other room to jam with them. They were each taking a turn, passing the guitar, playing old favorites as well as music of their own. I was amazed that even after working all day in the heat, they found the strength to play with so much zest and gusto. They exuded so much passion and youthful energy as they sang and played that they made me feel like a retired person.

I accompanied each song with one of my instruments, and when it was my turn to play something of my own, I borrowed a guitar and made up a twelve-bar blues spontaneous scat-rap with rhymes, as I have been doing for more than fifty years. I improvised a scat-rap about the time I first met Hunter in upstate NY in 1959 and all the good times we had shared over the years. After recounting some adventures, I ended the rambling account with a sing-along, singing the letters H-U-N-T-E-R, and getting everyone there to sing the letters back to me in swing time cadences. Then I added other phrases to complement the singing of his name with a series of layered riffs, just the way Count Basie got the brass section in his band to play rhythmic snippets and then counterpoint them with the reeds and the piano. Whether you do this with a band, a symphony, or a chorus of voices (or all three at the same time), it always produces a warm feeling like being at a sanctified Sunday morning church revival.

"How could you remember all those lyrics?" asked Foster Timms, a young songwriter and singer whose own songs were brilliantly crafted without a wasted word.

"Foster, I'm not a real song writer, with a sense of economy and haiku-like precision, like the way your songs are constructed or the way Hunter could nail any situation in one brilliant sentence. I'm more the James Joyce goes to Birdland and lets it all fly non-literary type. I just made all that stuff up on the spot. That way, I don't have to worry about having to have it judged, because it was all improvised just to enhance the moment, and therefore it had its first and last performance. That's not how I write my symphonies or books. Sometimes I'll take a whole day to get five seconds right."

"Wow," said Josy Amann, a fine young singer who had a family band in San Francisco with her husband, and whose brother was also part of the crew. The songs she sang at the jam session were constructed with complex rhythmic structures like music from India.

"You and Hunter must have had a lot of fun. I can't believe that you are seven years older than him. You must have been like an older brother to him when you met in 1959."

"Not really," I said. "After the first few hours I spent with him, he became a mentor to me. He was so brilliant, I kept quiet and listened a lot."

"We don't want to keep you up too late," said Jon Equis, after we had played for three hours.

"I don't want to keep *you* guys up too late," I said. "This is really fun. Let's play a few more."

Right on cue, a distinguished-looking man who said he was a publisher from Tucson ran out to his car and brought back a flamenco guitar and asked me to accompany him in the kitchen during the break. He told me that he had issued some of Hunter's writings years ago and had come to listen to and now felt like playing some music with us. He had on a white hat, white suit, and cowboy boots with raised monogram initials, and looked like a flamenco cowboy version of the author Tom Wolfe.

After playing with him for forty-five minutes, the jam session resumed in the living room, and I finally stopped playing at 2:30 a.m., after everyone else except Foster Timms, Josy Amann, and the imperturbable Jon Equis were ready to call it a night. After Foster played his last song, I packed up my instruments and asked Jon Equis about the program for Saturday night.

"It is still in formation," he said. "We'll let you know when we are sure who is actually going to show up. We are still completing the final details of the construction of the cannon, the fireworks, the lighting, transportation of the 487 invited guests, the guest list itself, and how to deal with the thousands of people who want to come to the event and are already here in Woody Creek but can't get in. We want to find a way that they can feel that they are somehow part of it, and show respect for the press people who have come from all over the world to cover the event, but cannot be allowed to attend the event itself. We have to find a way, as well as a time and place, for them to have interviews. So I have my hands full, but I know it will all work out. Everyone involved with this is here for Hunter.

"I know that for the second half of the program, after Hunter's ashes have been fired, preceded by the Japanese ceremonial drum group, we will have Lyle Lovett play a special song or two, have Jimmy Ibbotson of the Nitty Gritty Dirt Band play "Will the Circle Be Unbroken," then maybe have some other surprise guests, and then Amram, you will close the show with your "Theme and Variations on My Old Kentucky Home," with the audience joining in, and whoever you decide you want to play with you. Then I want to have you create a jam session like the one we had here tonight, but don't plan anything just yet. All this is subject to change. No problem. You look like you need some sleep."

"Definitely," I said.

"Find a way to get back here tomorrow and we can see what to do to make further plans for the music for the second half of the evening. I should know more by then. Some musicians are rehearsing here tomorrow afternoon, and it would be great if you could join them for their part of the show. During the jam session after the three planned pieces by Lyle Lovett, Jimmy Ibbotson, and you have been played, it would be wonderful if you could join these young musicians and bring that spontaneous spirit into the wee hours and add your support to these young players. They are great and they would like to have you play with them."

"I'll be here at your place tomorrow, if I can find a way to get here," I said.

"Someone else may pick you up tomorrow," said Emma, as she drove me back to the Inn at Aspen, through the full-moon starry night, which now looked like Van Gogh's famous painting of the same name, with the moonlight literally pouring over the mountains.

"I have seven other people to take care of who are arriving, in addition to helping Anita Thompson, who is swamped with people requesting interviews and requests for being added to the guest list, but call me if you get stuck."

"Do you know anything yet, in addition to what Jon Equis just told me, about the program order, and who will actually be playing?" I asked.

"We're still getting that together," she said. "Don't worry. We know Lyle Lovett will be flying into Aspen just before the event, and Johnny Depp will be arriving here a few hours before it begins. And John Oates might play a song or two. We just don't know anything for sure yet."

Emma dropped me off at the Inn at Aspen, and as soon as I got to my room, I crashed out, collapsing on my bed with my clothes still on, and slept for a few hours.

I woke up on Friday morning, took a shower for about twenty minutes, ate some of the wonderful fresh fruit grown at nearby farms at the breakfast special in the lobby, and was ready to go to wherever I was supposed to go.

I tried to call Emma, Doug Brinkley, Anita, and Jon Equis. All the cell phones at Jon Equis's command post were busy, and I couldn't get calls through to any of the other numbers, since my cell phone service didn't work well outside of the Aspen city limits.

I read the two local newspapers, ate some more peaches, and got a call from Emma, who told me that she didn't have one second free all day but that eventually someone named Rick would pick me up and take me to the Woody Street Tavern, close to Jon Equis's command headquarters. Emma said that this was where Doug Brinkley was expected to meet me for some interviews with reporters who wanted to rendezvous with us there, to capture some of the local color. After those interviews were completed, Doug could then take me back downtown to speak with reporters from several other papers, and then answer questions on camera for a new documentary film that was being made about Hunter by Alex Gibney.

After being interviewed for the film, I was supposed to go back to the Woody Street Tavern for another series of interviews, and after that return to Jon Equis's command post to rehearse with bassist Michael Jude and drummer John Michel of John Oates's band, who were playing with Foster Timms at the jam session the night before.

"We just added something new to the program," said Emma over the phone, which kept cutting in and out. "Everyone liked the way you played with them last night, and Jon Equis wanted you to play six songs with other musicians during the course of the evening, although we have no idea when that will be, if you don't mind playing that much."

"I am happy to," I said. "That's why I am here. How can I get back and forth to all these places with no car of my own? Who can take me so that I am sure to always be on time?"

"Don't worry," said Emma cheerfully. "I am sure it will all work out. After Rick drops you off, Doug Brinkley can take you to some of the places and it will happen. Right now, there are journalists getting local color at the Woody Street Tavern who would like to talk to you. After Rick picks you up and takes you there, you can go from there to downtown Aspen with Doug and then back to the Woody Creek Tavern for more interviews with somebody and then come here to Jon Equis's place again and rehearse with Foster Timms and the other musicians. Just do whatever happens. I hope this isn't too crazy a schedule. When you eventually finish rehearsing at Jon's before whatever we have to do this evening, do you need to take a nap?"

"That's very gracious of you, Emma, to be so considerate," I said. "But I think I'll stay awake until everything is over, so I don't miss anything. I took a nap in 1958. And it gave me a headache."

"That's hilarious," she said. "I will be sure to ..." I could hear a familiar sound of garbles and clicks as her cell phone cut out, which happened with many calls made to and from Woody Creek, whose topography was not designed by the Great Creator to accommodate cell phone addicts.

After Emma's call, I sat in the lobby for an hour, hoping somebody named Rick would come by to get me to the Woody Street Tavern, on the first leg of my day's journey.

A friendly young man walked into the lobby and said his name was Rick, and that he was taking me to the Woody Creek Tavern.

"Thanks for coming, Rick," I said. "My prayers have been answered. I was about to hitchhike, like I did in 1943, the first time I visited Colorado."

"Things are getting pretty stirred up around here of late," said Rick. "But we'll get it all together. We all love Hunter. He was one of us, so we'll all pitch in and give him the sendoff he deserves."

I squeezed in the back of Rick's van, and in a few minutes we drove past a bunch of mobile homes adjacent to what looked like a trailer camp and pulled up to the Woody Creek Tavern, one of Hunter's favorite hangouts.

The trailer camp was next door to the Tavern, an old fashioned bar and restaurant, with people sitting at tables outside, standing on the road, standing inside the bar, drinking, eating, telling jokes, yelling, laughing, and celebrating as if it were New Year's Eve, even though it was a hot sunny day at noon in August of 2005.

When I walked inside, I saw that the Tavern had gone slightly upscale since I was last there, with a new shiny tin ceiling, a new carpet, and a modern bathroom with shiny spigots on the sink, but in spite of these high tech improvements, it still retained the feeling of a wonderful raunchy Western saloon from the late nineteenth century. Some of the local folks looked like grizzled old hard-drinking, fun-loving cowhands, hard-living cow gals, or retired banditos, just like those wonderful old actors in the 1930s Western movies made in black and white by Republic Films that I used to see on weekends, when, as a ten-year-old boy, I would sneak in to see double features with my friends at a nearby theater in Frankfurt, a few miles from our family farm in Feasterville, Pennsylvania.

Standing at the bar and watching and listening to everybody, I flashed back to 1956, three years before I met Hunter, when Kerouac told me how, while growing up in the mill town of Lowell, Massachusetts, and seeing the old western films, he dreamed of going out West someday. And how much he loved Colorado when his dream came true in his many visits there in the late forties.

As a boy growing up in the South, Hunter saw the same films Jack and I did, and like so many of us, he had the same dreams of someday leaving home and seeing the mythological West, and maybe even living there. But unlike most of us, that's what Hunter eventually did. Hunter not only visited Colorado. It became his home from 1968 until he left us in 2005.

My reminiscing to myself was suddenly interrupted when a huge mustachioed man, who was toasting the blasting of Hunter's ashes with a series of chugalugs and whoops, spilled part of his drink on me by accident. I walked out of the bar and looked around the tables, filled with noontime merrymakers sitting outside the tavern in the blazing sun. Hoping the heat would dry the booze off the sleeve of my navy blue blazer if I could find an empty seat at one of the tables that was not in the shade, I suddenly saw a familiar face, which I had seen for a moment in the airport when I landed in Aspen.

It was the legendary reporter's reporter and *New York Post* columnist Steve Dunleavy, sitting on the outside porch having a late morning brew, as if he were the mayor of Woody Creek. Steve charmed everyone with great stories about the Mafia people he has known, interviewed, and become friends with, through his outstanding articles about how the government actually framed members of organized crime when they were unable to outwit the Mafiosi and had to resort to criminal tactics themselves, in order to indict them.

Steve was holding court and buying drinks for a group of rapt admirers, like an off-duty cowboy who had just completed a successful cattle drive and was now celebrating his stunning achievement.

I joined him and listened to his stories. Sitting with Steve in this rural setting on a bright, sunny, clear, blue-sky, white-cloud day made me remember nights in the back room of the Lion's Head Bar in the early 70s in Greenwich Village when off-duty reporters would sit together from 1:00 a.m. until closing time with Steve, Dennis Duggan, Pete Hamill, and others, drinking, talking, playing and singing Irish music—where Hunter loved to go when he was in New York.

Hunter would tell us about the paradise where he now had his own home in Woody Creek, and how the Woody Creek Tavern was a *real* bar.

Now Steve Dunleavy, along with hundreds of others from all over the world, was here for an event celebrating Hunter's life in the place Hunter so often spoke about with such affection when he was in the cement caverns of New York City, describing the characters who hung 'til all hours, in an old-time Western bar in the mountains, a few minutes from his home.

"Well David, I see your coat sleeve has already had a drink this morning. Why don't you have one too?" said Steve.

"Thanks, Steve. I'd better get a ginger ale."

"Fair enough," said Steve. "I'll get you that and have a real drink for you which I'll down myself, in addition to my own. Anyone else?"

Steve left and came back with a tray of drinks for the table, and regaled us with great stories, occasionally asking a question, which I knew he would be able to incorporate into another of his classic articles. Over the years, he never missed a trick.

As we sat outside, listening to Steve, old friends and strangers would come by our table, all of whom already seemed to be celebrating the memorial a day in advance. I think not only Steve and I, but everyone else there, kept expecting Hunter to walk out from the bar inside and join us.

Sitting at our table was the novelist Michael Swindle, whom I hadn't seen since 1972 when we were in Birmingham, Alabama, together. He was covering the event for the *Village Voice,* and we rapped about the South, about New Orleans where he now lived and all the friends we had, who like Hunter had Southern roots. The other journalists, who were also supposed to interview Doug and me, sat down with us and, after asking a few questions, joined in the party and occasionally would take notes when someone gave a great one-liner.

"Where's Doug Brinkley?" they asked me.

"That's what I'd like to know," I said. "I was supposed to meet him here so that we could both be interviewed by all of you and then go downtown. His cell phone has been busy all day. I know he'll be here. He has an enormous amount of things to take care of."

"Well, while we're waiting for old Brinkley to get here, let's cool it. We're not in New York," said Michael Swindle. "So let's all enjoy this beautiful day and relax and have another drink."

"Coming up," said Steve, getting up and returning with yet another tray of drinks. An hour and several trays of drinks later, Steve left to go back to Aspen to interview more people, and I was interviewed by an underground filmmaker, as well as by some young journalists and college students who wandered over to our table.

"It says on my map that the Woody Street Tavern is exactly 7,500 feet above sea level," said one of the kids, wearing a Gonzo T-shirt and carrying a knapsack full of his own supply of alcoholic beverages.

We welcomed him to sit down and join us at Steve's empty seat, and he told us he had driven all the way from a remote region in the state of Washington, near Olympia, to come to pay homage to Hunter.

"Drink plenty of water in addition to all that ginger ale," he said. "You shouldn't get dehydrated."

"I agree," said Michael Swindle. "I have been avoiding being dehydrated all afternoon, but not by swilling ginger ale like Amram. I prefer something a little more intoxicating."

As Michael ordered another round of drinks and we all toasted Hunter, everyone at the table told stories of how they had gotten here and what Hunter's work meant to them.

As the kid in the Gonzo T-shirt was slurping some Wild Turkey, which he had surreptitiously transferred from his knapsack and poured into an empty glass, and was telling us how he had first read Hunter's books while working as a logger during his summer vacation before completing his senior year in high school, someone drove by, stopped the car and said they were told that if they ran into me, I should accompany them to Jon Equis's house.

"I'm waiting here for Doug Brinkley," I said.

"So am I," said Michael Swindle. "I want to buy him a drink."

"He still can't leave Aspen yet. He's been swamped with work all day," I was told. "Come with me to Jon Equis's house."

I said goodbye to Michel Swindle, got in the car and was driven to the house. Jon greeted me at the door, and in spite of the incredible pressure to complete all the last minute details, he was as calm and gracious as if he were at home with a day off.

"Doug Brinkley couldn't get to the Woody Street Tavern," he said. "He will try to come here, and later on, while he is here working with me, I'd like you to rehearse with some musicians for an idea I am adding to the program. In the meantime, just sit tight. We didn't want you to collapse from heat exhaustion waiting for Doug at the Tavern."

Since there was a room full of people all asking Jon what he needed them to do, I tried to stay out of the way and spent time with the other event assistants, who still didn't know exactly what the program was going to be, but told me to just hang in there and be flexible.

"You're the least of our problems," said Josy Amann. "We have to print up the final list and it is now, according to Emma, exactly 487 people. This is three times as big as originally planned, and there are calls every minute from people who want to come. Doug Brinkley will be coming here to Jon Equis's house eventually to take you down to Aspen to be interviewed for the documentary film and to join him to see other media people. We know the music will be fine."

"O.K.," I said. "I'll sketch out some more alternate plans of how to do my piece, so whether we have twenty musicians or just me, it will end the program on a joyous note."

I sat at the edge of the living room, which was also jammed with people working, and wrote out several sketches. It was now 2:00 p.m., twenty-nine hours before the event was to begin. You could feel the high level of everyone's concentration in the room and hear whispered questions and instructions and phones ringing constantly. Still, there was an eerie sense of calm, like being in the eye of a hurricane, before the big blast.

Jon Equis's house looked and felt like the scenes on TV filmed from the Houston Space Center, just before a manned spacecraft is about to be repaired in outer space. There was total concentration and tension in the air, with everyone talking in measured tones through the headphone speakers attached to their cell phones while typing away on their computers. All the blue flickering light from the open desktop computers was a contrast to the much more inviting, spectacular, sun-filled views of the turquoise sky, silky white clouds, and the bright Colorado summer sun reflecting off the snowy mountaintops which you could see out the windows of Jon's house.

Somehow, this all resembled what it was like to look through the windows of a Jeep at the snow-peaked mountains and see the steady stream of tribesmen wandering through the trails of the Khyber Pass, where Pakistan and Afghanistan meet. But instead of men on donkeys loaded with smuggled goods, there was a steady flow of technicians from various crews who were carrying their equipment loaded on the backs of their four-wheel-drives, as they continued to put the finishing touches on the tower.

They walked back and forth, constantly milling in and out of the house, tiptoeing their way through the jammed living room, which had become Command Central, and stopping to whisper information or questions with the staff.

I could imagine Hunter all alone, typing away, in earlier days when he got up in the morning to write, and how he must have felt every time he looked out the window and saw this indescribably beautiful countryside, when the only thing you could see for miles were horses grazing.

In the midst of all the hyperactivity on this special late afternoon, two women were calmly making sandwiches, sometimes fifty at a time, for all the technicians, crew members, designers, fireworks experts, lighting engineers, volunteers, and staff members who, like me, were eating on the run.

As I crept over to eat another turkey and cheese sandwich on fresh baked bread, John Michel and Michael Jude from John Oates's band walked in with singer Foster Timms and asked me if I could rehearse with them upstairs for their part of the program.

"Jon Equis just told us that he would like to add us onto the program after Lyle Lovett, Jimmy Ibbotson, and you have finished playing," said Foster. "We'll probably just join the party members and turn the late late part of the evening into a jam session like we had last night here at the house, so that everyone under the tent will go home feeling even better. Can you rehearse six of my songs with me now?"

"Sure," I said. "I'll be happy to. I'm just waiting for Doug Brinkley to get up here to take me back to Aspen. I thought that we were supposed to rehearse later on."

"We were," said Foster Timms, "but it looks like later on is right now."

I rehearsed with the three of them for an hour. I asked the drummer John Michel if he knew the final order of the program for the event, precisely when each of us were supposed to play, and if he knew exactly who was going to be there during the course of the evening to play with me.

"We'll play whenever they say to," he said smiling. "I don't think they have the second half of the program set yet, but we'll be ready tomorrow night for anything and everything."

As I finished packing up my instruments, I was told by one of Jon Equis's staff members that Doug Brinkley had gotten stuck with even more endless details in Aspen to take care of, which was why he couldn't come to Woody Creek at noon to meet me.

The staff member explained to me that Doug had to turn his cell phone off the last two hours to remain incommunicado, because a huge number of people were calling him at the last minute from all over the country, asking if they could come to the event. As a result of trying to answer the barrage of non-stop calls, he couldn't get any work done.

Now, I was told that Doug was supposed to have a late afternoon meeting at the Woody Creek Tavern before coming to Jon's, and Jon's assistant suggested that I go back to the Tavern again to meet him, rather than waiting at the house. The art director for the event was driving that way and offered to give me a lift, and I was squashed into his Jeep with two other people, wedged between piles of art equipment. Now I would finally have my reunion with Doug.

When I arrived back at the Woody Creek Tavern, many of the same journalists, townsfolk, and fans of Hunter whom I had seen four hours ago were still sitting there outside the bar, drinking, talking, smoking, and partying.

Michael Swindle was still sitting in the same seat, interviewing local folks for his article for the *Village Voice*. I sat down next to Michael.

"Where's Brinkley?" asked Michael.

"He's supposed to be on his way," I said. "I came back here to meet him."

As we spoke, I heard a familiar voice singing a song with a perfect guitar accompaniment and knew it must be Jimmy Ibbotson. No one else could ever sound like him. I turned around, and standing there across the street from the Tavern was Jimmy Ibbotson himself, giving an impromptu one-man recital, singing some of his classic songs for a group of tourists, locals, news people, and passersby.

Jimmy has been revered for the past forty years as a dynamic singer-songwriter, guitar virtuoso, flutist, one-man orchestra, raconteur, and one of the original members of the Nitty Gritty Dirt Band. In Colorado, he is beloved as the fun-loving ambassador of Woody Creek, who always can make even the most terminally sour and jaded people smile and feel good about being alive when he sings his songs or tells his stories.

"Come over here, David, and play 'Mr. Bojangles' with me," said Jimmy, yelling into the microphone from across the street to be sure that I would hear him.

"I see you have your pennywhistles and *dumbek* with you, as always. Where's your French horn? Ladies and gentlemen, do you know who this is?"

Jimmy proceeded to give a ten minute infomercial of just about everything I had ever composed or conducted, and all the people I have been blessed to play with, until I felt that I was being eulogized at my *own* outdoor memorial service by a crazed but supremely charming leprechaun-musicologist-agent-tour-guide.

We played several pieces together. Jimmy is one of the rare performers who makes you play better and do things that you never have done before, and who inspires you to be creative.

Hunter loved Jimmy's spontaneous spirit as much as he admired Jimmy's outstanding music.

Someone from Jon Equis's crew signaled me as I was playing with Jimmy and, after we played a few more songs, came up to where we were playing.

"Brinkley just called and has finally extricated himself and is in his car on the way up to Woody Creek but wants to meet you at Jon's house, and then take you out to supper."

I said goodbye to Jimmy, and all the gang at the Woody Creek Tavern who were still going full blast, making more toasts to Hunter and one another, even though the sun hadn't started to go down behind the mountains.

"Like that young lumberjack-type cat from Olympia, Washington, said earlier this afternoon, you have to be careful in this high altitude that you don't get dehydrated. To your health," said Michael, raising his glass and downing another drink as I said goodbye again.

I was driven back to Jon Equis's house to finally meet up with Doug.

After waiting at Jon's house for a while, I started playing with some other musicians, and a half hour later the indefatigable Doug arrived, looking as dapper and unruffled as ever, in spite of having the busiest schedule of anyone I have ever known, and sleeping even less than I do.

"I'm so sorry, David," he said. "I haven't had one second since 7:00 a.m. this morning, but we'll go out to have a good meal and catch up. I'm so glad we are both here. It is going to be a marvelous event. I have exciting news to tell you. Let me have a few minutes to talk with Jon Equis and go over last-minute logistics."

Doug and Jon went over some new last-minute plans while I was playing music upstairs. Doug and I went out to dinner with some of his friends. As he drove me to Aspen, he told me of the last two months of his nonstop activities and of the enormous task of helping to organize this tribute to Hunter.

He said he felt that as exciting as this event was, it was just the first of many occasions to honor Hunter and his work, and in the future, he was sure that there would be many other celebrations that would be open to the public, where anyone and everyone could come to share their appreciation of Hunter's work.

Doug also showed me pictures of his two little children and told me about all the exciting work he was doing.

We had a delicious meal, and even though these were the first calm moments I experienced since getting off the plane, I could feel the electricity in the air, as if Hunter was hovering over us to make sure that the big blastoff would occur on time, with all the details executed correctly.

After we finished our dinner, Doug drove me back to the Inn at Aspen a little after midnight.

"I can't believe we are packing it in so early, like real adults," I said. "I can't see any dawn's early light."

"We have a busy day tomorrow," said Doug. "Johnny and everyone else will be coming in. Tomorrow is the day. At the moment, we have plans to meet at the

Woody Creek Tavern at noon, with all the domestic and foreign press, to give them their stories and explain one more time why they cannot be invited, because neither Johnny nor Hunter's family want it to become a paparazzi event and disrupt the memorial service leading into the music and then the party. I'll call you up tomorrow morning if there are any changes. I'm going back to the hotel, have a nightcap, and get some sleep. You should do the same. Tomorrow is the big day."

At 1:00 a.m. I called my three kids, Alana, Adira, and Adam, and gave them a summary of what had happened during the action-packed twenty-eight hours I had spent so far since arriving in Colorado.

I told them how I kept running into people who kept taking me to various places where I would end up playing music, until it seemed that I would not only perform my special version of "My Old Kentucky Home" as a theme and variations, as I had done for Hunter in 1996 in Louisville, but that I now had also become the unofficial sideman for almost all the other people who were playing for the entire second half of the evening, since almost every time I was taken to the event coordinator's house in Woody Creek, someone would be rehearsing, and I would be invited to join them.

"I wish I could be there," said Adira. "I remember what a good time we had when we went with Doug to the opening of the film *Fear and Loathing in Las Vegas* in New York, and the great party afterwards, and how funny Hunter was when he was hiding out in the basement watching a basketball game with us and the security guards while everyone wondered where he was, and how nice Johnny Depp was to me, and how after I went back home, you and Johnny waited until 5:00 a.m. to hang out with Hunter, who never showed up at his hotel and left you guys waiting all night. Please send my best to Hunter's family and to Johnny and Doug and to all the people there. Adam and Alana wish they could be there too, and we all send our love."

"We'll all go together for the next one and play a song together for Hunter," I said.

As I lay in bed, I thought of how proud I was to have three such great children and how lucky I was that they cared about other people. Since they were babies, I always brought my three kids to every event, whenever possible, and thought about how happy I was that they were able to meet so many wonderful people at an early age. Now all in their early twenties, they had their own lives but we still enjoyed hanging out, as well as playing music together. And they all read Hunter's books, and their friends did too.

I felt really comforted as I lay in bed, knowing that at sunset tomorrow, we would all take part in an event that would honor Hunter as a true artist, and that Gonzo would eventually join "Breakfast with Bonzo" and Maynard G. Krebs, the quintessential beatnik on the Dobie Gillis show, as part of the bulging landfill of American Kitsch, and that Hunter's books, like Kerouac's, would remain relevant and contemporary forever. Now neither Hunter nor Jack needed a label to justify the value of their work. Their books spoke for themselves.

I left an early wake-up call and crashed out.

As Doug had said earlier, tomorrow was to be the big day.

I woke up Saturday morning feeling like I was about to play in the final game of the World Series. Today now *was* the big day.

Before getting dressed, I took the silver flute that Jimmy Ibbotson had given me the day before and played it for about twenty minutes. I felt ready to perform my piece, whatever happened, even though I still didn't know when I would do it or who I would play it with or exactly when and where the other musicians who asked me to play with them would be performing.

I called all the numbers I had acquired in the last two days, in order to get a ride to the Woody Creek Tavern for the press conference at noon, where Doug had told me we were supposed to meet. Every single phone number I dialed was either busy, didn't answer at all, was inaccessible, or had a message saying to leave a message. I was accustomed to this by now, so I got dressed and played the flute some more, practicing different variations based on the melody and harmonies of "My Old Kentucky Home."

Just as I was ready to go down to the lobby and try to hitch-hike a ride to the Woody Creek Tavern, Doug Brinkley called me and told me to join him at the Jerome Hotel in Aspen.

"Another change of plans," said Doug. "Instead of the Woody Creek Tavern, we're going to have the press conference as part of a reunion of Hunter's old friends who have already arrived. There are now so many press people here, the Woody Creek Tavern is no longer feasible as a venue. The private room in the Jerome Hotel can be a much friendlier environment to let the journalists who have come from around the world all get a firsthand report of what the event is really all about."

"We'll also be signing some original art work by Ralph Steadman, to be sold at a later date to raise money for a foundation in Hunter's name. The hotel has a beautiful baby grand piano which you can play to mellow everyone out, the way you did at George Plimpton's reception for Hunter in New York a few years ago."

I ran downstairs and caught a ride from the van at the Inn, which was going into town and arrived at the Jerome Hotel at ten minutes before noon.

I saw people I hadn't seen for years, like Hunter's old friends from San Antonio, Gerry Goldstein and his lovely wife Chris.

"Are you going to make up one of your spontaneous rap-scat numbers at the piano, the way you did with Gary P. Nunn at our house in San Antonio all those years ago?" asked Gerry.

"No, Gerry," I said. "I kept you and Chris awake all night back then but today I'm going to restrain myself. I might do it at 4:00 a.m. in the wee hours, after the service is over and the party is in high gear, but this event right now is for the press to get 100 percent information about why the family and Johnny are doing this, and it's all about Hunter as a serious artist, so I am going to cool it."

"Well, please play us at least one of the tunes now on the piano that Hunter liked."

"OK," I said.

I played "Georgia," which I had done many times for Hunter when we burned the midnight oil anyplace where there was a piano, with neighbors who didn't mind late-night music.

At 12:10 the press conference began, but rather than being a series of prepared speeches, it was more Hunteresque, like a rap session.

All the reporters circled the room, talking to all of us, taking pictures and realizing that we all appreciated them being there to write about Hunter. It was more like a party than an uptight business meeting.

Hunter's son Juan was unfailingly gracious to everyone who interviewed him, answering the same questions he has been asked for most of his life, in his own sincere and thoughtful way. I stopped playing the piano, because people were trying to interview me while I was playing some of the other songs in addition to "Georgia" that Hunter liked, and I couldn't concentrate on playing and answering questions at the same time.

The reporter from Associated Press had seen the obituary that I had written for Hunter, which was printed in the *Aspen Daily Times* in its entirety that day, accompanying a fine article by Troy Hooper.

"I enjoyed your memorial tribute that you wrote for Hunter," said the reporter. "Is there anything you didn't mention in the obituary that you would like to add?"

I began telling him stories of fun-filled times spent with Hunter, meandering into descriptions of my own traveling over the years. I described what it was like living in the South from 1942 to 1952, and how jazz artists helped the doors to open up among all people before integration became mandatory, and the differences between Kentucky and its neighboring states. I rattled off a list of the great Southern writers whom Hunter was moved by and those he didn't particularly care for. After a fifteen-minute stream-of-consciousness rap, I saw the A.P. reporter's eyes beginning to glaze over

Suddenly, like the voice of a simultaneous translator speaking to me as I was rapping away, I could hear Hunter's voice, telling me what he told me nine years ago during that unforgettable evening of December 12, 1996, in Louisville, when one of the speakers on stage droned on, praising him.

"I wish he'd shut up. This isn't the Academy Awards or a Presidential Inauguration," he whispered to me backstage. "I'm simply a writer. These windbags have to learn to cut it short and get to the point."

Still, I felt there were some important anecdotes to share with the reporter, and as I finally started to come into the home stretch of my unsolicited monologue, I imagined I heard Hunter bark at me, "For God's sake, Amram, get off the soapbox, answer the man's questions, and go back and play the piano."

I ground to a halt, realizing that my encyclopedic ramblings were not what the AP reporter needed at this particular time.

"I'm sorry," I said. "I guess I wasn't really answering your question. I got carried away."

"That's all right," he said. "It's great stuff, but ... could you give me a *brief* statement of why this event is important?"

"Yes," I said. "Hunter Thompson was one of our great authors, whose brilliance was equaled by his honesty and idealism during some trying times. He spoke for many of us. He was our historian and our reporter.

"By honoring him tonight, we also honor the creativity and idealism of a new generation of artists who admire Hunter's body of work. I am sure that Hunter would want us to encourage them to find their *own* voice, to be brave and always try to tell it like it is. This is what Hunter always did. That's why his work will always be meaningful. He had high standards and expected the best from others."

"Thanks, Mr. Amram. That's all I need," he said.

I went back and played the piano, and finally the press people all left. Even though all of the journalists were informed that the event itself could not be covered by the media, they were all remarkably gracious and understanding, knowing that they were honoring the life of one of their own: a writer's writer and journalist's journalist.

All of us who knew Hunter now had a final few quiet moments to see one another again. We all knew that in the evening, it would be an event that only Hunter himself could imagine the outcome of, and however it turned out, there would be little chance for quiet conversations and intimate reminiscing. As we said our fond farewells to one another before leaving the hotel, all of us could feel the excitement building, with seven hours remaining before our collective adventure into the unknown.

While I was eating lunch, I got a call from Johnny Depp's representative, saying that Johnny would like to see me in forty-five minutes at the Jerome Hotel and to wait there for him, so that we could spend some time together.

After joining my friend Jorge Zamcona and having my first normal sit-down meal since I had arrived in Aspen, I waited in the lobby until Johnny arrived at the Jerome Hotel and invited me to come up to his room, where we could speak to one another alone.

Considering all the pressure of being responsible for such an ambitious event, he looked remarkably calm, and when I congratulated him on having become a father with two kids since we had last seen one another, he agreed that having children and a family was the ultimate blessing.

"I brought my guitar with me," he said. "Do you think we could play "My Old Kentucky Home" together, the way we did in Louisville?"

"I guess the old ESP and mental telepathy must still be working," I said. "I have been thinking about that since Doug Brinkley called me two months ago, but knowing how busy you are, and all that you have had to deal with to make this night possible, I didn't want to bother you. I would love that. We can even rehearse it this time. I remember in Louisville, we had about forty-five seconds together before we played it. We can do it differently this time."

Johnny had his guitar delivered to the room, and we practiced the whole piece, so that he would know in advance where he should enter, after I had played an introduction, the melody and a series of variations, followed by a series of plaintive wails at the end to summon up the spirits.

We ran through the whole piece, with me indicating where the other musicians would enter, after we played our duet, and where I would lead the audience in singing and humming behind the solos. I also explained what would happen if no other musicians were there and we had to play it as a duet.

"I'm still not sure who else will actually be playing with me, but with you playing, I know it will come out right, just as it did in Louisville," I said.

Playing with Johnny in his hotel room felt as natural as it did when we played together nine years ago. Johnny had started out as a musician, and has always remained one. His warmth and innate musicality as he strummed the simple but eloquent harmonies which Stephen Foster used for this masterpiece of a song made me able to forget about everything except the music itself, and gave me goose bumps just like it did in 1996, when we did it together in Louisville.

Kentucky was also Johnny's birthplace, and now in Woody Creek, Hunter's adopted home, we could complete the circle, through music, from Woody Creek to Louisville in 1996, back to Woody Creek from Louisville in 2005.

Sitting in the room, doing a new version of this classic song with Johnny again after all these years, made me play on another level. I imagined that any second we would both see Hunter come charging into the room, turn on a sporting event on the huge TV set, preferably a basketball game, all the while listening intently and drumming some ham bone hot licks with his palms outstretched, slapping his thighs, and giving us staccato whoops of encouragement as we played, interspersed with yelling at the athletes on the TV screen, ordering them to do better than they were doing.

"Here's what I hope will happen tonight," I said to Johnny. "After you play one chorus with me, following the introduction, we'll get Lyle Lovett to sing the words and then I'll get the audience to sing the bridge and play an obligato over it. I've known Lyle since the Kerrville folk festival when he won the new songwriter's contest. He's just as great a guy as he is a musician. I just hope his flight gets here on time, and that I get to see him to ask him. I am not sure who else is playing, but now we have a perfect plan, subject to change. I hope to also play the piano part the way I had Warren Zevon do it in Louisville, but they are not sure if the piano will be hooked up."

"Next time I'll bring my National slide guitar, like I did in Louisville," said Johnny.

"I really thank you for what you are doing for Hunter," I said.

"This is what he wanted," said Johnny. "I'm happy I can help to respect his wishes."

"I think what is being done here for Hunter is a first step towards acknowledging him as a great writer, first and foremost," I said.

"That's why we are doing this," said Johnny.

We talked about the way Kerouac was finally being appreciated as a true artist, rather than being mired down in the Beat cliché.

Johnny's sister Christi then took us to another room, and Bill Murray, who had played Hunter in a 1970 movie, came into the room and went over a statement that Anita had written. Johnny suggested that two outstanding musicians could join us when we played.

"Wow," I said to myself. "I'll actually have a band!"

Johnny couldn't have recommended two better musicians to join at the last minute.

They were Denny Freeman, the master guitarist from Texas who was on tour with Bob Dylan, and Bill Carter, the bass player from Austin who, with his wife, was a renowned songwriter. Denny, Bill Carter, and his wife admired Hunter's work as much as we all did.

When Johnny left the room to change, I talked through the piece, and told them that I would give them signals of exactly when to play, since I was still not sure if Lyle Lovett could do it, since he had not arrived yet. I knew now that if these latest plans for the piece changed at the last minute, they would know what to do. Texas musicians always do.

When Johnny came back, we all were driven from the Jerome Hotel to the venue in Woody Creek, passing by several groups of people with signs, small campfires, and booths where people were selling coffee, homemade CDs, T-shirts, and holding up signs for all kinds of causes, like a mini–Grateful Dead reunion.

They had come from all over the country to pay their respects to Hunter, all in their own way.

There was a TV hookup to show the big blast-off at a bar in Aspen where a huge throng had already gathered, but many had come to Woody Creek to be as close to the event as possible and see the fireworks light up the sky.

Anita had told me on the phone that she wished that all of Hunter's fans could attend the event, but since there were already three times as many people as had originally been planned, she hoped that in the future, there would be many other events where everyone could come and be a part of a series of celebrations open to the public, honoring his life's work.

"If we did this memorial in the East, you would have to hold it at Yankee Stadium," I said to the man sitting next to me in the van. "Hunter has a lot of fans, and I'm sure he would love that too. Doug Brinkley told me that this event tonight is the biggest bash for a literary giant since Victor Hugo's funeral."

As we drove up the narrow road toward Woody Creek, we passed more and more encampments with people who had come to pay homage to Hunter. I wanted to open up the side door of the van, leap out, and invite everyone to join us, but knew that this was not the time for that. I think all of us who were lucky enough to be invited felt the same way. We wanted everyone to be part of it.

I was happy that in two weeks, there was going to be a festival in Long Island called Bradstock, open to the public and dedicated to Hunter. I had invited Anita and she said that she would like to attend, to come and read some of Hunter's work and speak about him, and mingle with all the people in the greater New York area who admired his work.

We arrived at the gate, which was guarded, and after we went through security, we climbed up the hill to the entrance of an enormous tent, decorated with pictures of Hunter's favorite writers, welcoming us all.

A staff of elegantly dressed, well scrubbed, friendly waiters and waitresses greeted us with trays of mint juleps. The men and women who were serving everyone had that healthy Western aura, and really seemed to enjoy being at the party themselves. It was a different feeling than I ever could have imagined, with people all mingling and so full of life that it seemed like a family reunion or giant picnic, even though everyone there had a relationship with Hunter and still missed him every day.

Both George McGovern and Senator John Kerry seemed to be having as much fun as the sheriff, Bob Braudis, and other local folks from Woody Creek, all of whom were beloved neighbors of Hunter.

Everybody was hanging out with everybody else. There were no stomach-wrenching feelings of snobbery or fawning, networking and groveling. There were no press people at the party except for Katherine Seelye from the *New*

York Times, and reporters from the local Aspen newspapers and from the *Rocky Mountain News.*

There were no photographers creating a sea of blinding flashbulbs or frantic paparazzi corralling groups of the guests and forcing them to pose for pictures, like the nightmare scenario so often created, where everyone feels like an extra in a bad movie, becoming part of a mob to serve the needs of a giant promotional event, even though it is called a party.

Hunter's son Juan welcomed us all, and the highlights of the first half of the evening were brilliantly described by Katherine Seelye in her article in the *New York Times.* I am sure that some day soon, all that was said that night will be transcribed and available in books, on the Internet, and in the documentary film which Hunter's family chose to have made to record this once-in-a-lifetime event.

I was especially moved by Anita Thompson's reading of Coleridge's "Kubla Khan," and Juan Thompson's heartfelt tribute to his father. They made all of us feel like we were part of their family.

George McGovern and Ralph Steadman talked not only about some of Hunter's outrageous exploits during the 70s, but how he was able to always to cut to the chase and see through all the smokescreens and find those nuggets of gold that are the hidden treasure sought by the finest journalists, poets, authors, and historians... the truthful essence and larger meaning of events, with no frills and no hyperbole.

Doug Brinkley, looking as fresh and debonair as when I first met him in 1982, gave a spellbinding speech with no notes about Hunter and his work. He also described how Hunter understood the relationship of imagery and mythology of American heroes of the past like Paul Bunyan and Billy the Kid, and how Hunter himself related his own legendary place in modern society to their roles in American history.

Newscaster Ed Bradley touched everyone with his eloquence and warmth, as he told stories about Hunter and their friendship through the years.

Jann Wenner, the publisher of *Rolling Stone Magazine,* described how over and over again Hunter would pull a magical rabbit out of the hat when he and Jann worked together and how what resulted from his last-minute frantic writing turned out to be of lasting value, surpassing his often wild behavior with some of the finest writing that our culture has ever produced.

Sheriff Bob Braudis told us tales of some of the most memorable escapades that he and Hunter shared, bringing much-needed smiles and laughter to all of us.

Colleen Auerbach told us how Hunter had helped her daughter Lisl to be released from prison because of his devotion to her case and his belief that our system of justice had treated her unfairly, and after tireless work, helped her to gain her freedom.

Johnny Depp spoke so sincerely and with such modesty and loyalty about why he had done this for Hunter, reminding all of us why we were there, to share what Hunter himself had said that he hoped would happen someday after he passed away.

For more than an hour, we all stood silently, listening to one speaker after the other sharing their own stories, all helping to weave a tapestry of a true American Crazy Quilt. All the speakers added their own spice and flavor, like a great gumbo, and each speaker did it in a warm and loving way, with no phony theatrics.

I think all of us now saw Hunter in an even broader light, and when Juan intoned the final words, there was a pause, the Japanese ceremonial drummers began to play, and the lights changed so that the 153-foot giant tower now became a Technicolor obelisk, looking as if it would soar into space any minute.

As the drums grew more intense, the sides of the tower looked as if they were disintegrating and large fabric of some kind fell off the sides, and for some reason that I will never understand, many of us were moved at that moment to tears, as the cloth fell to the sides.

The cannon fired, there were fireworks that lit the sky, and a recording of Bob Dylan singing "Mr. Tambourine Man" played as Hunter's ashes fell from the sky to the ground.

At that moment, everything changed into a celebration, with timing equaled only by Hunter's fellow Louisvillian Muhammad Ali throwing a right cross at blinding speed, or Michael Jordan making an impossible but seemingly effortless move.

The entire gathering was suddenly transformed into an Irish wake or a New Orleans–style second line explosion of joy after the funeral, when the spirit has been honored and sent off, and immediately everyone knows that it is time to get down and party hardy, celebrating the life and the spirit of the dearly departed with gusto and élan.

I knew at this moment that all of us who were going to play music were supposed to begin the second half, but in the sudden cathartic blasts of energy and merrymaking that filled the tent, there was a gridlock of 487 people whooping it up, as the bar opened and great food arrived.

It was pandemonium. I wiggled my way through what had suddenly become a celebration like the one at the end of World War II at Times Square, with a lot of good times hooting and hollering.

Four hundred eighty-seven people had decided that we were all now going to join together in celebrating Hunter's sense of fun.

As I tried to squeeze through the crowd in order to get to where I thought we were supposed to play, I noticed the wonderful juxtaposition of a blonde-haired woman in a black cowgirl outfit, with a white peasant blouse and Hopi jewelry offsetting her ebony Zorro-style Mexican hat, flirting and dancing with a man in an elegant tailored Italian suit. They were surrounded by other women in evening gowns, some of their escorts wearing tuxedos with Navaho bolo ties and cowboy boots, and young people in jeans and T-shirts. Somehow, it all fit perfectly together.

I was concentrating like mad on what I would eventually say to introduce my piece of music as I attempted to complete the final roundup of who I hoped I would end up playing with, as well as exactly where and when. In spite of this, I peeked out at the crowd of merry makers under the great tent and looked forward to joining them at the party as soon as we were done playing.

Since no one was at the little stage where we were supposed to play, and Lyle Lovett was not playing to start the second half of the program, I wiggled back in through the crowd, and joined the party.

After helping myself to the endless buffet of all kinds of hot steaming delicacies that seemed to magically appear, I had second and third helpings of even more goodies brought non-stop by the crew who were now serving raw oysters and all kinds of savory high-calorie appetizers, drinks, and desserts.

Even though I was still famished after eating enough for three people, I moved through the crowd, searching for someone to tell me what I should do and when I should do it. I finally squeezed through the subway rush-hour crush of people again to the grass outside the tent.

In back of the tent was the small stage where I had been told we would play music during the second half of the program, but still no one was there.

The party had taken over.

I thought maybe there would be an announcement, since there was no printed program. I saw one of the people who was working with Jon Equis and went over and asked him what was now going to happen.

"We just about have the musical part of the program finalized," he said. "But Jon told me to tell you that we couldn't get you your piano."

"That's O.K.," I said. "I'll figure out a way to do my piece without it. I'll explain to the musicians I met this afternoon about a new plan, and whoever else I see, if they can find their way backstage. I think I know who will want to do it with me, if we can find each other, since it is pitch-black back here. Could we get a flashlight or a lamp?"

"We're working on that. Do you need to rehearse with them?"

"No," I said. "It's a little late for that now but the old boxing adage applies to this event tonight. Whenever a boxer is training too hard for a fight and sparring too many rounds to practice what he will do when he faces his opponent, that's similar to a rehearsal for musicians. The boxing trainers often admonish an overzealous fighter by saying, 'Don't lose the fight in the gym.' I promise my piece won't be over-rehearsed."

"I figured that would be the case," he said.

Behind the stage, hovering like a giant Roman ruin, was the enormous 153-foot-tall structure which had contained the cannon from which Hunter's ashes were fired. Now it seemed to stand like a sentinel, as a lonely reminder that Hunter had left the earth. But rather than being a gloomy reminder, it seemed almost as if it were comforting us, watching over the throngs of people who were now all talking to one another, eating, drinking, and sharing stories about special times they had with Hunter, many of which I was privileged to hear about for the first time, as I wandered back and forth from behind the stage to the tent just below, trying to find the other musicians who were going to play with me.

I finally left my instrument bag in the backstage area and walked back down to the tent again, which by now was bursting with manic party-action, with the volume of celebrating so loud that I wondered if anyone would be able to hear the music at all.

Suddenly I heard a familiar voice singing, and looking up at the stage, which was now lit, saw that Lyle Lovett, my old friend from the Kerrville folk festival, was singing one of his priceless songs, in his unique laid-back style.

I could barely hear him through the din of the crowd.

A woman, splendidly dressed in what looked like a pioneer homesteader's ball gown, shouted to the crowd, "That's Lyle Lovett. That's Lyle Lovett singing up there! Hush up! That's Lyle Lovett!"

People all moved up to the stage and stood, listening to him sing two songs he had especially prepared for the event.

His gorgeous phrasing and guitar playing made it seem like we were standing right next to Lyle's back porch, watching and listening to him play for all of us at his home on a summer night in Texas.

As Lyle finished his second song, I saw Johnny Depp standing alone, listening to Lyle's tribute to Hunter.

I went over to Johnny and told him that since Lyle probably hadn't been asked if he would sing the words when we played my set of "Theme and Variations on My Old Kentucky Home," we should ask him.

Johnny and I went around behind the stage to try to find him after he had finished, but there was still no light, and when Johnny went one way to look for Lyle, I stumbled over some drum cases in the pitch black and there was Lyle.

We hadn't seen each other since we played Farm Aid with Willie Nelson a few years ago. Lyle looked and sounded better than ever.

I asked him if he could sing "My Old Kentucky Home."

"Love to do it, David," he said. "But I don't know all the words."

"I don't know them all either," I said.

Like most people, I only knew the first verse of the song, and all of us wanted to do the whole song to honor Hunter.

"I'll try to see if I can get them for you," said Shelly Wilcox, an old friend of Hunter's, who was standing backstage with George Tobia.

"I'll call my son on my cell phone, which works up here, even though I had to sneak it past security. I'll ask my son to look up the words on the Internet, and then dictate them to me over the phone. George Tobia can write them down when I repeat them and I'll bring them back to the bandstand, and Lyle can sing them holding the paper. I'll have George use a felt pen if I can borrow one so that they are clear."

"Do we still have enough time for them to do this?" I asked someone standing backstage next to me, who looked like he might be the stage manager.

"I don't know," he said. "John Oates was just invited to sing a song or two before Jimmy Ibbitson sings 'Will the Circle Be Unbroken.' I think you do your finale after that."

"Great," I said. "That will give Shelly and George Tobia a chance to get the lyrics for "My Old Kentucky Home" from her son, if he is at home and one of them can write it down in time."

Johnny came over with his two friends I had met a few hours ago, guitarist Denny Freeman and songwriter/bassist Bill Carter.

"I asked when we are going to do your piece," said Denny, "but no one seems to know for sure."

"Please don't go away," I said. "I think the moment is drawing near."

"Do you need some drums?" asked John Michel, after he had finished playing with John Oates. "Sure," I said. "Since there is no piano available for me to play, I'll change that part and have the rhythm enter on cue, and Denny can play a sixteen-bar solo when I give a signal."

Jimmy Ibbotson came up with his guitar.

"Are you really going to play tonight on the silver flute I just gave you?"

"Definitely," I said.

"I think I'm on next," he said. "Come and play with me, and then I'll introduce you for the finale."

"Great," I said. "After I play 'Will the Circle be Unbroken' with you, please stay and play with us."

I told Jimmy the revised version of the piece.

"No problem," he said. "Just give a wink when it's time for me to play."

Jimmy played "Will the Circle Be Unbroken" and I accompanied him.

Suddenly I saw the sheriff Bob Braudis leaning over the front of the stage, gesturing in perfect time to the music, like an opera conductor who had been kidnapped from La Scala, Milan, and had now become a modern-day mountain man.

I pointed to my lapel, where I had pinned my golden Pitkin County Sheriff's Department mini-badge that he had given me the day I arrived, which now seemed like weeks ago.

"Do it. Do the song, Amram. Do it," said Bob, leading the applause for Jimmy's performance.

I looked over at the soundman and asked him who was on next.

"I'm not sure," he said. "They keep changing it, and we never got a definite schedule. I know they planned on having Lyle Lovett, Jimmy Ibbotson from the Nitty Gritty Dirt Band, and Dave Abrams."

"Great," I said. "Then since Lyle has sung and I just played with Jimmy, I'll stay on and invite the other musicians to join me."

"Are you Dave Abrams?" he asked.

"Almost," I said. "I'm David Amram."

"Oh," he said. "I know who you are. You're the guy my kids hear mentioned in that song on the Raffi recording, when he sings the song about peanut butter sandwich, jelly with jam, one for me and one for David Amram. Are you the same fellah?"

"That's me," I said. "Please tell your kids I'll tell Raffi that he has fans in Woody Creek. I guess it's time for me to do the finale."

"Hit it, Amram," said Sheriff Bob, leaning over the stage, and with a swoop of his arm, he commanded me to play, like an umpire calling a third strike.

I figured that you can't disobey the law, so I thanked everyone who had helped to make this event possible, telling the audience the history of how we had done this extended version of "My Old Kentucky Home" in 1996 for Hunter in Louisville, and then introduced the musicians.

After introducing Johnny Depp, I looked over toward Lyle Lovett, who was standing by a microphone at the edge of the stage, and I saw him holding two sheets of paper with gigantic scrawled words that I assumed must be the lyrics to "My Old Kentucky Home."

"The cavalry has arrived! Saved by the bell!" I said sotto voce to Sheriff Bob, who was still leaning over the stage, ready to whisper final words of encouragement in my ear, as if he were a coach giving me final instructions before place kicking a game-winning field goal.

I began the melody alone, and played it out of tempo, ornamenting it the way Indian *ragas* are established, with the basic elements slowly being revealed to the listener. Somehow, the sound of the silver flute, which Jimmy Ibbotson had just given me a few hours ago, quieted down the whole crowd of revelers and they came up from the tent below, surrounding the small stage and listening attentively. When I finished the introduction and first series of variations of the song as a solo, I ended with instrumental cries that are used in so many cultures to summon up the spirits, as well as to bid them farewell.

Now it was so quiet that the silence seemed to blend into the black sky filled with luminescent stars and a moon that seemed to have come out just to shine for Hunter.

I signaled Johnny, as we had rehearsed it in his hotel room, and he played the sonorous simple chords that captured the essence of Stephen Foster's song. I watched him, totally absorbed in playing his guitar with selfless concentration.

Then I was able to close my eyes and play the melody in perfect harmony with him, and Jimmy's flute that he had given me was so easy to play that I was sure at that moment that all this had been planned to be this way all along, and that maybe Hunter himself had masterminded it, and was chuckling with fiendish glee.

I cued the rest of the players when it was time for them to join in, and improvised another set of variations that just seemed to come to me, even though I hadn't planned to do that.

Now it definitely felt as if we were all being channeled by Hunter's spirit, taken to some peaceful place of long ago, where there was kindness and graciousness and communal love. Playing with my eyes closed, I could see Hunter's face in my mind, as he seemed to float above us in a rare moment of repose, nodding his approval. And I could feel his presence as I continued playing.

I felt as if I were doing this old song for the first time in my life, and that it was much more than a song about the old South.

It now seemed as if it were a love song for all people standing there to share, just like the works of the great Southern writers Hunter admired and felt a kinship to. I felt as if I were basing the variations on a melody of Bach or Mozart.

After the variations were done, I turned to signal Lyle to sing the words to the song, and to my astonishment, standing next to him was Hunter's brother Davison, sharing the microphone and the papers with the words scrawled on them, ready to sing along with Lyle, as if Hunter himself had returned for the last time to join us in our tribute to him. Sheriff Bob suddenly give me a thumbs up, as he saw my look of surprise as well as pleasure at seeing Davison Thompson magically appearing, without any of us knowing that he would.

"Now I know Hunter is in charge of this," I thought. "Hunter must have had the whole thing planned this way."

Lyle sang the song so soulfully, it sounded as if he had written it himself. Hunter's brother Davison joined in when I had the audience sing the chorus, and after Lyle sang another verse, I had the audience hum the melody of the chorus as Denny Freeman played an exquisite guitar obligato over the voices.

Now the back field of Hunter's place in Woody Creek, where all this was taking place, seemed like a sanctified church way down South, with all of us singing a farewell hymn to Hunter. This communal feeling was what I hoped I could bring for everyone to share when Doug Brinkley had called me two months earlier, and invited me to come, at the request of Johnny and the family.

I wanted this piece to honor Hunter, as all 487 people also wanted to honor him. I felt now that all of us who played this piece had helped to do that in the best way that we knew how.

I thanked all the members of this once-in-a-lifetime band for being so creative and musical.

Rather than moving down into the tent for the jam session, it was decided at that moment to stay where we were and Jimmy invited me to stay and play "Mr. Bojangles" as a duet with him, as we had done outside the Woody Creek Tavern the day before, only this time we didn't do the half-hour version.

As soon as Jimmy played the simple descending lines of Jerry Jeff Walker's song, there was a murmur of approval as he sang the song with his special style that had made it a hit in the 1960s. All these years later, it still sounded as if he were playing it for the first time.

People began swaying back and forth, and Sheriff Bob and s few others began dancing a slow waltz with whoever was standing next to them.

Now what had been like a church service changed into a Western dance hall. As Jimmy played song after song for another forty-five minutes, it was like a western swing band on a late Saturday night in a saloon in Austin when jazz and bluegrass and country pickers would all jam out. Jimmy and I took familiar songs that Hunter liked and stretched them out while everyone was dancing, combining the Texas two-step with jitterbugging, while Sheriff Bob and his endless stream of dance partners did a kind of Rocky Mountain version of a post–Martha Graham free-form interpretive ballet.

Then Foster Timms played a torrid set of his songs for almost an hour, and asked me to play with him and his trio of Michael Jude on bass and John Michel on drums.

We had actually rehearsed most of the songs we did the day before, and the three of them played with as much intensity as the musicians I performed with in Havana, Cuba, with Dizzy Gillespie in 1977, which, like this special evening in Woody Creek, was another highlight in my life.

In spite of the 7500-foot elevation and frantic last minute chain of events, I was transported playing with all these fine musicians, and thrilled to see people dancing to the music.

When we were done, Foster Timms said, "I can't believe you are going to be seventy-five in three months."

"I can," I said. "I'm wiped out. I've been playing for more than two hours non-stop."

As I was packing up my instruments, Sheriff Bob came back to give me a hand.

"Amram, what would you like to drink?" he asked.

"A gallon of water, Bob," I said, "unless you have some Geritol."

I joined the party, and had another plate of oysters, among other delicacies, and kept drinking bottles of water as I walked through the tent, seeing old friends like filmmaker Bob Rafelson, whom I hadn't seen since he left Greenwich Village in the 50s.

He was now living in Aspen, and we talked about old friends and bygone days, and news about other people we knew in common.

"It's like Hunter is our host for the evening, bringing us all together one more time," said Ralph Steadman.

I spoke to many young people from Aspen and Woody Creek who knew Hunter. They told me that they would go to his house and be asked to read aloud to him what he had just written, so that he could hear it, after which he would do the final editing. They told me that Hunter said he wanted the reader to feel that they were hearing his voice when they read his words.

About 4:30 a.m., with the party still in full gear, I was able to sit down with Juan at a table and talk to him about his father. I told Jaun about the relationship which men of our era, which Hunter and I were brought up in, had with our own fathers. I shared with Juan how those of us brought up in the Depression to be strong and stoic had to learn to be loving and affectionate with our own sons as well as our daughters, and how often Hunter had told me how proud he was of Juan.

Hunter had every reason to be proud of his son.

Juan fits the description of what his dad and all of us used to call a straight arrow. This was a term derived from an old Indian expression that was used in the 50s when referring to someone whose strength of character we admired. Often Hunter would join us when visiting New York, as we made toasts to those special people while we drank in the wee hours in the back room of the Lion's Head Bar in New York.

"Let's drink to a real man, a straight arrow," we would say, raising our glasses.

"Here's to one of nature's noblemen."

Juan was and is a noble man, in every sense. Modest, generous, gracious, and caring to his own family and an excellent author in his own right. He spent most of the night consoling others who were still devastated by Hunter's untimely departure.

Having the chance to finally talk to him alone, and letting him know how much he was appreciated and how many of us would always respect him as well as his father, was the perfect completion of my journey to Woody Creek.

Now it was 5:15 a.m., and I knew it was time to pack up and try to remember the highlights of the last three days so that I could tell my three kids about an experience that I will never forget.

I finally left about 5:30 a.m. to catch a shuttle bus back to where I was staying.

"Party pooper," said Sheriff Bob. "Why are you leaving so early? We need more music now and more times in the future to honor Hunter."

"I'll be back, Bob," I said. "We're having a festival in Long Island called Bradstock in two weeks, and the whole event is dedicated to Hunter's memory. Anita hopes to come there to read Hunter's work with music, and I'll be playing for her and telling everyone about what happened here. This is just the first one of many. We have to be sure that we get people to continue to read Hunter's books."

I went back to my room, and really enjoyed the solitude, where I could try to replay the entire three days and nights I had been in Colorado.

It didn't take long to fall asleep.

The next day, in the airport, I met a group of young orchestral musicians who were returning to their homes from the Aspen Festival, where they had played the final concert, performing Mahler's Ninth Symphony.

"I wish I could have heard your performance of the Mahler," I said to a young violinist sitting across the aisle from me on the connecting flight from Aspen to Denver. "We had our memorial for Hunter S. Thompson the same night."

"I wish I could have heard you play," he said. "I studied your violin sonata and your violin concerto in music school. What did you play for the event? Was it a chamber orchestra composition, with you as a soloist?"

"Not exactly. It's kind of hard to describe," I said. "You would have had to have been there to hear it."

"What was this Hunter Thompson like?" he asked. "They talked about him a lot here in Aspen this summer. He must have been quite a character. Was he really as much of a wild man as they say he was?"

"He was much more than that," I said. "He was a real artist. Let me give this to you to read. It might give you an idea how a lot of us felt about him."

I reached in my shirt pocket and took out the little poem I had written for a 1997 album I had made in Nashville, called *Southern Stories*, a few months after Hunter, Johnny, Doug, Sheriff Bob, and I had been together in Louisville in December of 1996, when Hunter and Johnny Depp were both made Kentucky Colonels.

The little poem was one of the song/stories I wrote and sang for my CD *Southern Stories*. It was a description of Hunter over the years since we had first met in 1959, entitled "Kentucky Southern Gentleman." It was one of a series of musical vignettes of my experiences living in the South.

I recorded it in Nashville with harmonica wizard Mickey Raphael, with whom I had played many concerts with Willie Nelson and my old army buddy violinist Vassar Clements. They both loved Hunter's work, and he loved theirs as well.

Like the "Theme and Variations on My Old Kentucky Home" I had first done in Louisville with Hunter and Johnny Depp in 1996, the album came about in a totally spontaneous and unexpected way. It was done in two sessions during my off-hours when the Nashville Symphony had me come there to conduct the premiere of my symphony *Kokopelli* on January 17 of 1997.

A few months later, I returned to Nashville when Kenneth Schermerhorn recorded *Kokopelli* June 23 and 24, 1997. Between sessions with the orchestra, I ran over to Studio B in Nashville and completed recording the songs for *Southern Stories*. I included one I had dedicated to Hunter, called "Kentucky Southern Gentleman."

I never thought that my new symphony would make it possible for me to be in Nashville and be asked by producer and musician Fred Bogart to make an album of this nature, while I was there with the Nashville Symphony. Fred Bogart also appreciated Hunter's work. Like so many other things where Hunter was part of the picture, it just seemed to happen.

I had brought a copy of the lyrics and a recording of the song with me to show to Anita before the memorial, but never had time to do it.

I handed the young violinist the crumpled up paper with the lyrics of "Kentucky Southern Gentleman" for him to read.

"This might give you some idea about Hunter S. Thompson and what he was about," I said. "I know his books certainly will. I'll be happy to send you a list of all that he has published."

I hadn't read the lyrics for quite a while, so I leaned over the aisle and looked at the paper as the violinist read what I had written.

This is what I wrote.

"Kentucky Southern Gentleman"
For Hunter S. Thompson

In his old Kentucky home he's still a legend
from those wild days of his youth
crazy nights of raisin' hell and days in high school
always searching for the truth

Secret hours in the library
reading Shakespeare and the book of Ruth
always a southern gentleman
often unshaven but never uncouth

Went up North to be a writer
his friends knew his gifts were heaven sent
lived in a cabin in Huguenot, NY
small town paper hardly paid his rent

Southern roots made him too proud to say a word
when he was down to his last cent
rode his crazy road with dignity
part-time mad-man, full-time southern gent

He left the paper, saw his country suffer
seemed America was committing suicide
crooks and politicians all looked the same
smiling on TV while so many died

Seemed words had no more meaning
if all our leaders double-talked and lied
fear and loathing filled the air everywhere
seemed there was no hope on either side

The southern gentleman hit the highway
gave us stories we could share
wrote of crooked schemes and shattered dreams
of people everywhere

Wrote of whiskey screams in motel rooms
where no one seemed to care
wrote of deep dark secret places
made us feel that we were there

More than thirty years have passed
since he began to roam
from that library in Louisville
where he used to read alone

Now his books sit next to Shakespeare's

built to last forever, strong as stone
books that call us all to join him
in his old Kentucky home.

David Amram, June 1997

"That's nice," said the violinist, handing me back the paper. "He sounds like he was a fascinating person. I wish I could have known him."

"You can," I said. "Read his books. You'll really enjoy getting to know him that way. Just like you feel close to Mahler after you just played his symphony. Like Mahler, Hunter was unique. He had his own voice, and his work is for all time. Read his books, and you'll get to know him."

When I got home, I told my son Adam all that had happened and then called up my two daughters, Alana and Adira.

"It sounds like it was awesome," said Alana. "All my friends saw the fireworks on TV when they blasted off his ashes. I wish I had been there."

"I remember when we saw Hunter the night when the movie about him premiered in New York," said Adira. "He was so much fun and so nice to me that night. I wish I could have gone with you this time. Write it all down, Daddy, so you don't forget it."

"I'll try to," I said. "I want to share my good luck of being there with all the people who couldn't come, so that they will feel that they were part of it too."

"Write it all down now, Daddy, the way you just told us about it, before you forget it," said Alana.

"I'll do the best I can," I said. "That's what Hunter always did."

♪

Chapter 2

Kenya, Africa: The Mother of Us All

In 2007, when you look back into the rearview mirror of history, the 1970s were a time when the world was opening up for change throughout all of Africa. There are well-documented accounts of the struggles for liberation in Angola, Mozambique, South Africa and throughout the continent during this tumultuous era.

Liberation was the watchword. Just like the lyrics to the Bob Dylan song indicated, the times definitely were a-changin'.

All of us who lived in New York were excited by the daily reports of the decolonization of many new emerging nations throughout the world, and especially those in Africa.

But many of us had a myopic view of anything or any place that we hadn't personally visited, especially places as far away as the emerging new nations in Africa. Most of our information of what Africa was about still came from travelogues and bad movies. Reportage in the media of the details of the political changes taking place and the history of why these upheavals were occurring was often contradictory or confusing. And there was torpor in the air during much of the early 1970s, following the collapse of the activism of the sixties. This new ethos of full greed ahead seemed to move many into a state of lethargy and disinterest in what was happening around the world, in spite of all the social changes that were occurring.

Watergate had become a macabre TV reality show that filled the air with distrust of our elected public officials. Hunter S. Thompson wrote brilliant articles for *Rolling Stone Magazine* and two classic books about these bizarre times that remain definitive portraits of America's post-60s near–nervous breakdown.

Most people were led to feel that news had now become another form of home entertainment, and if it was in any way upsetting or displeasing, you could change the channel and it would go away.

As a result of this new consciousness, or lack of it, one of the news reports that appeared to be somewhat exciting, at least to a few of my friends, especially those who always searched for information that was off the radar, was the discovery that took place in Ethiopia in 1974. It wasn't very political, by any stretch of the imagination. It was announced that humanity's oldest bones had been discovered in November of 1974 in Africa. Since the story was not related in any way to geopolitics, this news item about an anthropological breakthrough didn't strain any of our minds.

According to reliable sources, the fossilized remains of a three-million-year-old skeleton were exhumed by a team of reputable scientists. They named the skeleton "Lucy," and while this event didn't make the network news, or the front page of the *New York Times, Rolling Stone Magazine,* or the *Village Voice,* our three papers of choice, it was big news at both the 55 Bar and its neighboring watering hole, The Lion's Head Bar, both located on Christopher Street in Greenwich Village.

Many of Greenwich Village's leading weekend aficionados of ancient history were thrilled to hear about this historic discovery of an ancient skeleton in Ethiopia, Africa. One night, shortly after the discovery, Lucy's remains became the *raison d'etre* for a heated monologue by one of the 55 Bar's favorite habitués, who was visiting the Lion's Head Bar next door when I walked in.

"Big news from Africa. They just found out Lucy's been hiding in Ethiopia for the last three million years. Dig this: they just dug her up. So later with the Beatle's 'Lucy in the Sky with Diamonds,'" said Johnny Welsh. "She needs a new song now. She's not in the sky. She's down in the earth with her momma Africa, surrounded by Ethiopian diamonds."

Johnny Welsh was an old friend of Terry Southern's and mine from our 1955 days together in Paris. Johnny was celebrating, buying drinks for everybody to commemorate this historic scientific breakthrough.

"We have our own Lucy rediscovered in Ethiopia. And she's been sleeping like a baby there for three million years. Here's to you, sweetheart. To Lady Lucy."

Johnny led another in a series of toasts to no one in particular by downing a vodka martini in one gulp and continued his public service announcement.

"John Lennon's song about Lucy was cool. 'The girl with the kaleidoscope eyes.' That's some hip lyrics. But he's talkin' about an Englishman's Lucy. Our Lady Lucy didn't need to be given an English name to tell her who she was or where she came from. She had her own damn name three million years ago and she's been sleeping where she came from ever since. She lived her life the way she wanted, long before any so-called Europeans arrived on the scene to do their caveman number two million years later. Our African sister Lucy didn't need any Beatles-loving grave robbers called anthropologists to dig her up and give her a new name, because she's been on the set where her people come from in the very same place where *all* the people on the planet earth come from.

"So our Lucy's not in the sky with diamonds. She's right where she belongs, with her mama, our mother Africa. And you know, Dave, Africa is the mother of *everybody*. Here's a toast to mama."

"I'll drink to that," I said.

"Hear, hear. I second the motion. Buy me another one, Johnny, and I'll sing you a song," said Malachy McCourt, clearing his throat and gesturing expansively like a Celtic Rudolpho in a production of *La Bohème* before bringing down the house with an aria to his beloved Mimi.

"I'll buy you a drink if you *don't* sing," said Mike Reardon, the bartender. "Johnny's making a serious point. Africa is opening up. Scientists should be over there to help build things up, not dig people's bones up. I hear it's fantastic there. I'd love to go over and see what's happening."

"You'd love it, Mike. It would change your life," said Johnny. "Someday, Dave, you've got to make the African scene. You know what a ball we had in Paris. But you can't imagine what it's like to walk down those streets in Accra, the capitol of Ghana, and hear that music.

"Let's have another toast to where Lucy has been sleeping all these years, all the way over in Ethiopia. And here's to freedom and liberation. We don't need colonials to tell us what to do any more. And we don't need anthropologists to give us their names or tell us who we are."

A series of high-pitched yelps of approval filled the bar at the Lion's Head, interspersed with shouts of "Brits out of Ireland," as toasts were made to the emerging African nations. After Malachy sang a few songs, we forgot all about Lucy and spent the rest of the night talking about Patrice Lumumba, the writings of Franz Fanon, and all the South African expatriates we knew who were living in New York and working for independence for everyone in their homeland. As often happened after midnight at the Lion's Head, the bar turned into one huge university debating team, consisting of all its patrons and staff all yelling to each other at the same time.

That night at the Lion's Head bar, Johnny had reminded all of us to remember that while the continent of Africa was an ancient place that had been under the domination of various colonial powers for such a long time, it was now coming into its own at a breakneck pace.

And this had been happening for the past ten years. When Jomo Kenyatta was elected the first prime minister of Kenya in 1963 and then became Kenya's first president in 1964, posters of him appeared all over New York, and many young people began to dress like him, in royal African garb, even carrying a walking stick similar to his.

"Africa is the mother of us all," Dizzy Gillespie said to me one night in the early 70s at the Village Gate when we were relaxing in his dressing room between sets.

"That's where some of the best music in the world comes from, David. You can hear it every day in all styles of music, even in the symphony music you love so much. From Beethoven on down to what Stravinsky and Gershwin and Ravel got from us. It's there. And you can take all the music from way back and go all the way up to what we're playing here tonight. No matter what type of music you have, there's always some African in it.

"Africa is where it all began. Medicine, science, astronomy, mathematics, the pyramids ... that's where it all came from. Check it out."

Actually, I had been trying to check it out since the very first time I met Dizzy, back in 1951 in Washington, D.C., when he and his quintet came over to my basement apartment on 16th Street to jam and finally crash out after their gig at the Spa in Baltimore.

While the other four musicians in his band were catching a few winks, with two of them lying on my bed and the other two sprawled out on the floor, Dizzy sat on my one easy chair and I sat on my piano bench while he talked to me, a twenty-year-old wide-eyed kid, about the concept of Pan African music until we could see the dawn seeping through the windowsill of my basement apartment.

Dizzy told me that night in 1951 about all the places in the world that African people had been, and how every place they went became influenced forever by the music that these Africans brought with them.

"You'll hear it all around the world," he said. "Everything from Flamenco music in Spain, which the Moors left behind, to the belly dance music of Egypt, the drums of the West Indies and Cuba and Brazil, the second line march music in New Orleans, and all the jazz and blues and gospel that we hear every day here at home. It all comes from our presence. Pan African music is our history of where we've been and who we are. Don't forget what I'm telling you."

I never did forget what Dizzy told me, and up until his death in January of 1993, every time I was with him we would talk about all the different kinds of music of seemingly endless varieties whose roots originated in Africa.

In 1955 when Dizzy played in Paris and Johnny Welsh and I stayed up with him until dawn after the concert, he talked about Pan African music, encouraging all the Parisian musicians who listened to him to learn about Algerian music and North African drumming styles.

In 1977, during our trip to Cuba, he spent hours before and after our various concerts that we gave on board on the way to Cuba, telling me about how, from 1947 until 1949, the great Cuban drummer and singer Chano Pozo and he would spend time on bus rides together on the way to concerts with Dizzy's big band. Dizzy said that Chano would sing him chants from Africa, which were still done in Cuba, and also show him some of the fundamentals from the encyclopedia of rhythmic patterns, which were the foundation of what was later named Afro-Cuban music.

When Dizzy returned from his 1989 tour of Africa, I went over to his house in New Jersey and he told me of all the treasures he found every day he was there with the music and the people.

"It took me a long time to finally go there," he said. "I took my band for my State Department tour back in 1956 to the Middle East and Turkey and we were so close to going to tour all of Africa, but it took me until now to finally get to visit the whole continent. It was worth waiting for. I know you went to Kenya years ago. You've got to go back and see the rest of the countries. East Africa is just a start."

As usual, Dizzy was right, and this is something that I still hope to do. I'm still waiting, in 2007, to have the chance to get back to Kenya again and stay long enough to tour the whole continent.

But during that night at the Lion's Head in 1974, when we were toasting Lucy being rediscovered in Ethiopia, I never dreamed I would ever go to Africa at all.

A year later, in November of 1975, through a series of crazy events, I had the chance to go to Kenya, East Africa, and it was an experience that I have never forgotten, one that continues to enrich my life every day, more than thirty years later.

Like so many of the other highlights of my life, this first trip to Africa happened as the result of a combination of good luck and the random twists and turns of chance happenings. I doubt that any career counselor, guru, or astrologer could have ever predicted that any or all these events could have possibly ever led to anything of value.

It all began in April of 1975 when I was invited to perform at Reverend John Gensel's weekly jazz vespers services at his small church in Manhattan. When I arrived at the church, Rev. Gensel told me that after I was done playing for the jazz vespers service, he would like me to speak to a group of people at the church about the influence of jazz in the music created by classical composers of the twentieth century. He also asked me to talk about how jazz was enabling the new generation of rock musicians to expand their musical vocabularies, and finally to talk about the influences of jazz in our language and dress. Then, following some questions and answers, he told me that he would like me to lead a jam session with everybody in the room participating.

I thought all this sounded like a great afternoon, and I told Rev. Gensel that I would be happy to do whatever he wanted and that I was glad to be there again with him and all the fine musicians who always dropped by to play.

Rev. John Gensel constantly had exciting events happening at the church. He was a champion of jazz and of those who created the music. He often paid musicians out of his own pocket in order to keep jazz before the public. During the 1960s, when the musical-industrial-complex declared that jazz was dead again, John Gensel created a haven for jazz players of every style, from the pioneers of the twenties to the latest innovations of contemporary players. All of us who were devoted to the music knew we had a place to play, create, and share each other's high energies and mutual love and respect.

I did what John Gensel requested me to do during the vespers service and had a fine time playing with different musicians who dropped by. Then I gave my little talk, fielded some questions, gave some answers, and ended up the afternoon leading a jam session. For the grand finale I made up a song with rhymes from topics suggested by the audience. I designated each of the four topics to four sections of the audience, as if they were now a four-part choir, and toward the end of the song, I had each of the four sections sing the topics back, one at a time, with simple melodic figures I gave them, all of which fit together, making them sound like a big band of the 1930s playing riffs together.

After the music ended, we all attacked the Oreo cookies, cupcakes, donuts, and Lipton Tea served in grab-your-own styrofoam cups. It was a typical jazz vespers post-concert swing and bebop reception. Musicians, ministers, jazz fans, and regular members of the congregation all milled about, rapping and having a good time.

As I was eating a stale cupcake and looking for a styrofoam cup to wash down the dried-out crumbs, a friendly looking man with a sandy-colored George Bernard Shaw-style beard and twinkling eyes came over to me and shook hands.

"David, I'm glad to see you here. I like this scene of Rev. Gensel's. He uses music as a way of getting everybody together. That's what it's all about. No explanations, no introductions. Just the happening of it and the release of the Holy Spirit within us all. My name is John Taylor. How'd you like to go to Africa at the end of '75 for the World Council of Churches and do the same kind of thing with thousands of people that you just did here this afternoon?"

"Wow. Thank you," I said. "I'm not even sure of exactly what I just did, but if you liked it and you want me to come to Africa, I'm ready to go. I've always wanted to get there."

"I'll contact you," he said. "I have a feeling you could do something unique."

He seemed sincere, but I wasn't sure if I would ever hear from him again.

I had received so many irresistible offers so many times of dream events that never happened that I didn't tell anybody about his offer because I thought it might never happen. But each day I thought about it and hoped that somehow he would call and make it happen.

A week later, to my surprise, he did call, and over the next few months I would hear from John Taylor and see him, and each time he seemed to be serious. He wasn't a clergyman, but I was told by Rev. Gensel that the World Council of Churches found John Taylor to be an indispensable source for finding new ways of bringing the performing arts and religion together. Rev. Gensel told me that John Taylor had worked with Diego Rivera and Orosco and was a highly accomplished muralist, painter, cartoonist, and photographer, who believed that his life in the arts meant more than just advancing himself and his career. He was committed to bringing art and religion into the lives of everyone.

In September, John Taylor called and met with me. He told me that he wanted the performances I would present in Kenya to include musicians conscripted by me from all the people in Nairobi who were attending the conference as delegates. He also requested that I search out local musicians from Kenya and invite them to participate with the delegates.

"You can have quite a show," he said. "There will be people from more than one hundred countries attending the conference, and your job will be to get them all to join in, along with all the Kenyan musicians, for one huge international ensemble. I want you to help everyone to feel free to touch that universal spirit that lives within us all. You can start the ball rolling the first day you get there by having a series of mini-concerts and jam sessions in the Delegates Lounge every night during the three weeks of the conference, all of which can build up your repertoire for the closing ceremonies. By making music together with everyone there, you can provide a harmonious and truly spiritual conclusion to the whole three-week conference. And of course, don't forget that I want you to include all the local musicians from Kenya to be a major part of everything you do. We are in their home as their guests."

"That sounds like a real challenge," I said. "But I'm definitely up for it. I hope I get a definite word from the office of the World Council of Churches soon."

"You will. God moves in slow and mysterious ways, and so does the organization, but in the end, everything always comes out right."

Another week went by with no confirmation, but John Taylor called and told me that I should expect to arrive in Nairobi at the end of November, that he now hoped that there would also be a symphony orchestra and chorus coming from Germany to participate, and that I should be prepared to conduct the Brahms *Requiem* and Beethoven's Ninth Symphony, in addition to organizing all the other musical events leading up to the final concert.

"We're still waiting to hear about their final funding, but it's 99 percent a sure thing that the symphony and the chorus will be there," he said.

"That's close enough for me," I said. "I'll be ready."

I bought new copies of both the Beethoven and Brahms scores and started studying them, marking them up like a road map so that I would be ready at the first rehearsal. I also called up my friend Johnny Welsh to tell him the good news of my going to Africa and he told me where to go in Greenwich Village to purchase a book of conversational Swahili.

Another week went by and I still had no contract of any kind from the World Council of Churches. While I wasn't sure if this still was really going to happen, I wanted to be prepared if it did, so I kept studying the scores and practicing a few sentences from my new book of conversational Swahili.

October 6, seven weeks before John Taylor told me that I was due to arrive in Nairobi, I went to a doctor in New York City for only the third time in twenty years. Even though I had been on a health kick all summer and running several miles a day, I was having strange pains in my stomach, losing my hearty appetite, and feeling weak and dizzy.

My doctor told me I had serum hepatitis.

"That's impossible," I said. "I'm never sick."

"You are now," he said. "Go home and lie down."

Lying in bed that first night, I called and cancelled a week at The Other End, a Carnegie Hall concert for the UN that I was scheduled to conduct, and all my other engagements for the next month.

My old army buddy, violist Midhat Serbagi, came over to visit me the first day I was in bed. Midhat was getting the musicians for the orchestra I was supposed to conduct at Carnegie Hall for the concert presented by the UN.

"Midhat," I said. "My doctor told me I could probably conduct the concert at Carnegie Hall if I had a chair to sit on so that I could rest up for a minute or two between each piece, but that I might die as a result. I thought about doing it anyway, but figured that if the doctor were right, it would definitely be a downer for the audience if I expired on the podium or during the reception afterwards. I think we have to get someone else to conduct it. I'm really wasted. I can't even roll over in bed without getting tired."

"Dammit, Dave," said Midhat. "It serves you right. You haven't slept since I've known you and you're always running all over the place and writing music all night and never taking care of yourself. You're going to be forty-five in a few weeks. You're not twenty-two anymore. You're not a kid in the army any more. Act your age. SLOW DOWN."

"I am slowed down, Midhat." I said. "I can't even move."

"Ah," said Midhat. "Don't expect me to feel sorry for you. I know you'll be up in a few weeks, and a few weeks after that you'll go back to your insane schedule like nothing ever happened. I know you. Get well, for God sakes. It's depressing sitting here seeing you looking like a corpse. You're turning yellow!"

"Well, thanks for cheering me up, Midhat," I said. "I'm feeling better already."

"You better," said Midhat. "I'm having a New Year's Eve party and I'm expecting you to come and play."

"I'll be there," I said. "I'm supposed to go to Africa at the end of November, after I solo with the Toronto symphony, and after Africa, I'll be back in New York before New Year's Eve. The doctor said he thought it was possible I could do both Toronto and then Africa if I stayed in bed for a month or so. He said he didn't like my schedule but he admired my upbeat attitude. I've got to get well. I can't miss the chance to go to Africa."

"Africa?" said Midhat. "Take me with you. I'll carry your bags if you're too weak. Man, are you lucky. Get well. Don't miss that."

"I won't," I said. "I've been waiting all my life."

Midhat gave me some Lebanese pastries he had brought in a brown paper bag, and a container of home made *umjedra,* a tasty traditional Lebanese dish he used to cook for us on his hot plate in the barracks when we were in the army.

"Get some sleep," said Midhat, as he was leaving. "Everyone else does."

As I lay in bed, I decided I was going to make it to Africa no matter what happened. Rev. John Gensel called and told me he was praying for me. Floyd Red Crow Westerman, the Sioux singer I played with whenever our paths crossed, was in town and came by and told me about some Native American remedies that would help me to become well. Then he burnt some sage, and the carbon-monoxide-tinged New York City air which filled my apartment when the windows were only half opened was now temporarily transformed, making my old apartment feel like we were at the outdoor powwow grounds of one of the many reservations where we played together.

"I feel better already," I told Floyd as he was leaving.

"That's why I came," he said.

A lot of other friends came by to cheer me up, and all of them seemed to understand how much I wanted to make the trip to Africa.

A few weeks later, I convinced myself that I had made a miraculous recovery, got out of bed, and was able to slowly walk a few blocks to visit my doctor, to see if he agreed with my self-diagnosis. He told me it was unusual to be up and about so soon, but that I seemed to be in good enough health to make the trip to Canada, play with the Toronto Symphony, and then go to Africa.

"Great, Doctor. I can't thank you enough. I really feel fine now," I said. "For the last few weeks I actually got to sleep every night."

"Most normal people do," he said. "Try to see if you can live like a normal person. Give it a try. You might like it."

I walked home and an hour later received a phone call from a woman at the World Council of Churches.

"Good afternoon, Mr. Amram. At long last, I am delighted to tell you that your round trip ticket to Nairobi and back has finally been confirmed and put in the mail and should be at your apartment by tomorrow. You are to fly to Toronto, do your matinee concert with the Toronto Symphony, fly to London that evening, and then change planes for Nairobi, arrive early the next morning and rehearse as soon as you get off the plane with the symphony and the chorus who are flying in from Europe. We are almost certain that they will obtain their own funding to be there on schedule, actually the day before you arrive, so that they can get acclimated.

"Mr. Taylor also said that you could start conscripting the international ensemble of everyone you can gather for the global community orchestra, as he calls it, that same evening, following the rehearsal with the orchestra and the chorus for the Brahms and Beethoven.

"I must say that this sounds a little hectic to do all in the same day. Especially after you have completed such a long trip. We've heard that you have been under the weather. Are you certain you can meet the requirements of this rigorous schedule?"

"Absolutely. Thank you. I'm thrilled. Please be sure that you sent me the ticket. I'll get my vaccinations tomorrow," I said. "I'm ready."

My ticket arrived in the mail the next day, and I got all my shots required to make the trip. Even though they made me feel worse than when I had hepatitis, and my left arm was swollen and aching, feeling like it might fall off, I didn't care. I knew I was on the way to Africa.

A few nights later, as I was packing up to go, Floyd Red Crow Westerman came by and gave me a silver and turquoise ring.

"Wear it," he said. "It will give you good power and help you to stay well while you are in Africa and help you to come back feeling even better."

I was elated. After dreaming of going to Africa ever since speaking to Dizzy Gillespie in 1951, now in November of 1975, as I had just turned forty-five, I was going to go to Africa for the first time. And I knew that I was definitely ready.

I clambered down the stairs from my apartment to the street with my suitcase stuffed with my symphony conductor's outfit—a set of tails and white tie, white vest, formal black shoes, and for the rest of the trip, a bathing suit, a pair of jeans, one summer suit with a shirt and tie that I hoped would match, all the instruments I could squeeze into the remaining space, four disposable razors, and my toothbrush. I also had my French horn, with the case taped up, covering many of the stickers I had from around the world, including my "Dizzy Gillespie for President" bumper sticker that Dizzy had given me during his 1964 campaign.

Before catching a cab to the airport, I went to the neighborhood news store to say goodbye to Morty, the local newspaper and magazine dealer, street philosopher, and self-appointed social arbiter of our block.

"Where to now?" said Morty, handing me a copy of the *New York Post.*

"Africa, Morty. I'm going to Nairobi, Kenya."

"Whatta ya going *there* for?" Morty asked me.

"Africa is the mother of us all," I answered.

"Well, don't forget to come back. I can't afford to lose a good customer," he said.

I arrived in Toronto November 28 for a rehearsal and matinee concert with the Toronto Symphony. I was invited there for a young people's concert as a soloist, playing different instruments from around the world and showing kids how these instruments developed over centuries, becoming the modern ones played in today's symphony orchestras. I played my African talking drum, my Syrian *dumbek,* wooden flutes and *ocarinas* from around the world, Irish pennywhistles, my Lakota courting flute, an Arabic *shanai,* a *shofar,* and my guitar, and got the kids to sing and clap poly-rhythms to fit into a song I made up about creating music together. I also told them about community music-making in Africa, which I had learned about in New York from musicians from Ghana, and that when I came back to

Toronto from Kenya, I hoped to have some new authentic East African music to share with them.

Estelle Klein of the Mariposa Folk Festival came back to my dressing room after the concert at Massey Hall, before I had to leave for the airport in Toronto to catch my evening flight to London. She gave me a going-away present.

"You'll need this on the plane," she said, smiling.

It was a paperback copy of *Anthology of Jewish-American Literature.* I started reading "Fate" by Isaac Singer as British Airways Jumbo Jet flight 600, a flying hotel, hummed across the waters of the mighty late November Atlantic toward jolly old England.

I finally dozed off and had a mini-nightmare that the pilot of the plane got lost and that instead of finally arriving in England and changing planes to take us to Africa, he went the wrong way. Instead of arriving at Heathrow Airport in London, the plane landed in Hollywood on a highway next to the mountain where the famous Hollywood sign is displayed.

"You are going to see what Africa is really like," bellowed the pilot over the intercom. All the passengers were herded off the plane by a group of fierce-looking soldiers wearing nineteenth-century uniforms with rifles, knapsacks, and white pith helmets.

"You are being escorted by members of the Dundee Diehards, the volunteers who fought the Zulus in the Battle of Islandlwana in 1879," said the pilot, who had now emerged from his cabin, dressed like a Bengal lancer from a Twentieth Century Fox production.

"Yeah, and the Zulus kicked Queen Victoria's British army's ass," shouted Johnny Welsh, who in the dream was suddenly now one of the passengers on the flight.

"Arrest that man," said the pilot, and Johnny was taken away in handcuffs.

I woke up in a panic, feeling really confused and depressed and decided not to dare to go back to sleep, in case this bad dream might really happen. Anything was possible in Hollywood. I had decided in 1962, after composing the score for *The Manchurian Candidate,* that while I loved Los Angeles and enjoyed seeing good films, my road in life as a composer was going to be the long hard one which my heart told me I must be on, and that Hollywood was just a rest stop, not the final destination.

This is why I was going to Africa, instead of actually living in Hollywood and writing a score to accompany films about Africa, which might be as silly as my nightmare. I realized how lucky I was to be able to still try and pursue my dreams.

As the other passengers were sleeping, comforted by the soft purr of the jet plane slowly floating in the sky over the black waters of the Atlantic Ocean below, I looked out the window of the plane into the starlit sky and began thinking about what Dizzy Gillespie had told me back in 1951 when he described how the African drum was the first drum of all mankind and that every group of people had their own ancestral drum, each of which represented all of the collective heartbeats of every person on earth. Remembering that cheered me right up, and I took out my book on conversational Swahili and started trying to learn a few more phrases.

As I thought about what it was going to be like to be in Africa, I got the feeling that I had already been there and was now actually returning, even though I realized that this was going to be the first time I had ever set foot on African soil. As I wondered why this feeling was so strong, I recalled what Johnny Welsh, pianist Randy Weston, and poet Ted Joans told me: that this timeless land and the spirit of its people were part of every human being's experience, imbedded in everyone's collective unconscious.

When Randy Weston returned from Nigeria in 1961 he told me that he knew before he got there that he was going home. Ted Joans told me he felt the same thing each time he went back to Africa. This feeling of returning to an old familiar place was really buzzing through my mind now, even though I knew that I had never been there, at least not in this lifetime.

Sitting in the silence of the dark plane just before dawn, I felt that I was going back to the original place on Earth where we all come from, and that therefore I was going home to the same distant place where the bones of Lucy had been rediscovered after three million years. And that as Johnny Welsh had said, Lucy's remains were the ancestral bones which were discovered in the place where all human beings came from millions of years ago. If scientists had now found the oldest location of our existence here on Earth, this place had to be everyone's original home. What else could Africa be? We must have all come from somewhere. And while some of us stayed there, others of us left and wandered to different parts of the globe. Now I was wandering back.

The sun rose over the ocean's horizon and as I looked out the window of the plane, I realized that the next sunrise in twenty-four hours would be the one I would be seeing in Nairobi, Kenya, when we were due to arrive in the early morning. We were given a small breakfast plate, and as I chewed on a cardboard-textured croissant that tasted like flavored sawdust, I flashed on Sutter's Bakery's magnificent hot buttery early morning croissants right around the corner from me in Greenwich Village. I longed to wolf down one of those Sutter's heavenly morning snacks, as I gnawed on the dried up remains of the one provided by the airline.

"Would you care for another croissant, Sir? I do hope you are enjoying your voyage with us."

Offering me another stale croissant was a charming male air host, in a white flannel jacket and black bow tie, elegantly tailored and smiling like Cary Grant, full of graciousness at 5:45 a.m., as the plane flew over the hills and lakes of Southern Ireland. His graciousness and good English manners made up for the indigestible croissant, overcooked rubbery omelet, and cold acidic coffee.

But I didn't care about the food. I was transfixed as I looked below, over the wing of the plane. I had never seen Ireland before, except in my dreams. As I stared down at the beautiful greens and blues, I could hear Tommy Makem, Dennis Duggan, Tony Hayes, Joanne O'Donnell, Sheila Moriarity, Nick Browne, Frank McCourt, and Jack Deacy all singing "Will Ya Go Lassie Go" in the back room of the Lion's Head Bar at 3:30 a.m. Greenwich Village time, or at Malachy McCourt's bar on 13th Street, The Bells of Hell.

I wished that there was some way that I could ask the pilot to make an emergency landing so that I could get out of the plane for an hour and visit Tom Clancy on his farm, which I knew was somewhere down below. Since British Airways provided no parachutes, I knew that leaping out of the plane was not a possibility either, so I waved out the window and figured Tom Clancy would get my message telepathically.

I knew I would get to Ireland and play there some day, and I finally did thirty years later in October of 2005 when I was invited to the Cork Festival. But in November of 1975, it was the time to go to Africa, and nothing now could stop this from happening. In twenty-four hours, I would be flying over Kenya, as the same sun rose over a different part of the same planet Earth.

However, life is full of surprises.

"Ladies and gentlemen," crooned the flight attendant of British Airways, in a maitre d' style New York free-Shakespeare-in-the-park seedy English actor voice, sounding like a worn-out Fortinbras.

"Heathrow Airport in London is fogged in at the moment. We are terribly sorry to report that we must now proceed to ..."

An enormous groan filled the Jumbo Jet, drowning out the flight attendant, who was just beginning to get into his oratorical form.

There was no more view out the windows of the plane anymore. It looked like we were encased in a vat of white cotton candy, in a cocoon of fog, until we finally came to a crunch-thud-bounce and shudder-grind tire-squeal landing at a mysterious airport somewhere deep in the English hinterlands.

I dragged the bags from the overhead rack of the plane and joined all the other passengers as we all waited nearly an hour to claim our baggage. While we were standing around, shivering in the unheated baggage claim area, I went to buy a newspaper, and noticed to my surprise that all the newspapers were Scottish. I asked the newspaper lady the name of this lovely English village. I couldn't understand what she said. Figuring it must be due to my ears being out of commission from the change of air pressure after a long flight, coupled with an addled-brain in-plane movie hangover (a blood and guts Charles Bronson feature), I went back to wait for my bags and asked the baggage man which part of England we were in.

"This is Perth, laddie. Perth, Scotland!"

Holy Hepatitis, I said to myself. Mother Africa is going to think I'm a no-show. I knew I had blown my connecting flight to Nairobi. We were supposed to change planes in London and here we were in Scotland.

We were told by the disembodied voice of another mellifluous-sounding British Airways official that we would have to wait to find out whether the fog would lift in London in the next few hours. If it did, we would re-board our plane and continue the flight. If not ... "other procedures will be explored."

We ended up taking a ride in an unheated train and arrived at London Station at 4:45 a.m.

As we got out of the train, there was a mad scramble for baggage, with all of us pushing the baggage carts ourselves through the station to a double-decker bus that took us to a British Airways ticket office downtown. We passed Hyde Park and Victoria Dry Cleaners, two landmarks of late London nightlife. The streets were as quiet as the inside of a Wall Street broom closet at five a.m.

"Africa, where are you?" I said to myself.

We unloaded all our baggage again (some already lost after being put in the wrong buses) and stood in line to reconfirm our plane tickets at the British Airways downtown location. In order not to fall asleep while standing up, I talked to a woman from Amarillo, Texas, who was going to South Africa. She was bubbling with energy and sported a gigantic beehive hairdo. She had a cactus-sagebrush-old western-desert-style way of talking, and told me she was on the way to J-town (Johannesburg) and that I should come on down and visit for a spell and go water skiing if the folks in Kenya would give me some time off.

I finally got to the ticket counter and got booked on a flight on East African Airlines, leaving at 4:45 that afternoon. All I had to do was get to the airport, check in, and go to a motel provided by the airlines, where I could eat, take a shower, and sleep lying down in a warm bed with sheets and blankets.

The van finally arrived to take me to the motel near the East African Airways section of the airport.

I had a real English breakfast, after which I took my longest bath in years. I was so wrecked I couldn't sleep, so I called up André Previn. Then I called up my cousin, Robert Amram; writers Fran and Jay Landesman; music journalist Mark Gardener; a Charlie Parker scholar and champion of jazz, French horn virtuoso Barry Tuckwell; and singers Annie Ross and Georgia Brown.

It was great to talk to them but since I still couldn't sleep, I decided to check out British TV. There was a terrific music show about Bartók, Bach, and how classical music is constructed. The narrator wasn't a dreary snobbish elitist, nor did he appear to be desperate to portray himself as a cutting-edge trendy over-simplifier of high art. He was just someone who obviously loved what he was doing and knew a lot about music.

I switched to the other two channels that were available in my room. Both channels had wonderful shows. I realized that in England, TV is used in the daytime to educate the public rather than spreading violence and infantile behavior into people's homes. And there were no mind-numbing commercials.

I figured that any country with such great daytime TV shows could be excused for having occasional bad luck with inclement weather for arriving passengers. I turned off the TV, laid back on some pillows, and thought that as a safety measure I should call up East African Airlines to confirm my 4:45 afternoon flight before crashing out for three hours of sleep.

"Oh, yes, Mr. Arnroons. That flight is cancelled."

Arg-h-h-h, I groaned, staring at the blank TV screen. Am I ever going to get to Africa?

Since it would take a month by sea, I decided to call British Airways, even though they had assigned me to the flight on East African Airlines, which had just been cancelled. To my delight, I found out that British Airways had actually booked me for this evening at 7:00 p.m. by mistake, exactly twenty-four hours later than I was supposed to be booked originally, which turned out to be perfect. As I talked to the ticket salesman on the phone, I could hear the shouting over the phone from the growing mob of people stuck in the airport. I found out that the fog had resulted in stranding more than a thousand people, who were now crashed out all over the airport, with only ten clerks available to attempt the impossible task of trying to take care of everybody. I was really grateful to be hiding out in the motel provided by East African Airlines even though I was no longer going to fly with them.

I decided I'd better not go to sleep or I'd never wake up, so I went down to the restaurant for another round of well-needed eats. I noticed many of the men in the restaurant were elegantly dressed in tailor-made suits, not a hair out of place, chewing without seeming to move any muscles in the head area. The same seemed to be true when they talked. Their wives and children looked equally elegant and were well behaved and quiet.

This was shockingly different from the New York City style of family dining out, with screaming, arguing, laughing, plate-licking, talking and laughing with your mouth full of food while yelling at the waitress, eating off each other's plates and at the same time pursuing toothpick-dental checkouts between courses, supplemented by cigar and cigarette smoking with occasional ashes falling into your neighbor's plates, accompanied by an occasional soft belch and many loud slurpings while drinking coffee.

The restraint and good manners of the English diners was a revelation. Also I noticed that all the men who were wearing neckties seemed to have them tied at strangle-tension at all times. I suddenly thought that this might be the source of the famed British stiff upper lip, because since the invention of the necktie, upper-middle-class British gentlemen often appeared to Americans to have been in a state of semi-asphyxiated strangulation. But the overall gentility was calming and appealing, compared to the frenzied pace of New York to which I had become accustomed.

I saw, while sitting in the airport restaurant, that this was a whole other world, different from New York's big town way of doing things, even though I found New York to be irresistible, with its freedom to let the old total madness hang out when getting a quick lunch or 4:00 a.m. final chow down. It was acceptable in many places I went to eat in the wee hours when the night owls emerged, to slop your mustard, mayonnaise, pickles, hot sauce, relish, ketchup, barbeque sauce, and greasy fried onions all over your hamburger on an English muffin, most of which would slide down to the slippery floor of any of the local filth-caked fast food temples of grease all over the city, as you yelled out great ideas with your mouth full, knowing that pausing to chew slowly might make you lose time while climbing the ladder of Success. And often doing this while standing up or walking down the sidewalk, gesticulating with your free hand while shoving food down the hatch with the other. I could see after a few minutes that the British were definitely different when it came time to nourish oneself in the company of others.

After eating, I returned to my room, packed up my instruments once more into my main suitcase, stuffed between my ever-growing pile of laundry, and checked out of the motel. I waited in the freezing drizzle and caught a bus back to the British Airways terminal. I was told by a charming young ticket salesperson that I would have to take the bus back and get East African Airlines to re-validate my ticket for the flight they had cancelled, in order to be allowed to go on the 7:00 p.m. British Airways flight I had just been promised. The reason for this was that East African Airlines had put a tiny sticker over my original British Airways flight, and according to regulations, only someone working for East African Airlines could pull this tiny piece of paper off, after which they had to sign a paper stating they had removed the sticker.

At East African Airlines, the salesperson refused to pull the sticker off and change my ticket back, even though the flight they had booked me on had been cancelled.

"Mr. Omrak, we have a 10:00 p.m. flight that is just as nice. Why do you want to fly British Airways?"

"Really, I don't," I said. "But I've already sent two telegrams to Nairobi, and I'm a day late." I then told him my whole story.

"You see, Mr. Omrak, this would never happen on East African Airlines," he said without cracking a smile.

I was wondering what magical powers his airlines had to make fog disappear, but with existential Zen chutzpah you only get if you live in New York, I patiently kept asking him to change the ticket, which he finally did. I went back to British Airways and got my new ticket, still not believing that I would ever get a flight to Africa. Now it seemed that I finally had.

Picking up my bags, I began to walk to gate nineteen and started to pass out. My cholera shot in my left arm was beginning to hit my neighboring smallpox vaccination shot like a sledgehammer, and I felt myself about to retire for a while on the floor of the terminal.

"Hey mate, ya need some help?" asked a cheery voice. A noiseless electronic cart came up behind me and I was saved. I was driven to gate nineteen, and after a twenty-minute wait on line, I entered the plane, got to my seat by a window, and fell out. I began to dream of a great bird, circling over the trees on a hill somewhere in Africa. Suddenly the bird began to drop and I saw it was enormous and saw it was going to land on top of me before I could ...

"Ach! Enschuligan Zic Mir Bitte!"

I woke up as a blonde-haired young man stared down at me apologetically, having dropped his brown leather briefcase on top of me. I nodded and fell out. Every five minutes he poked me awake, since I had answered him in German, to tell me about his romance with a young woman he was going to visit in New Delhi, further on down the line from Nairobi. I kept falling out, until the hostess almost broke my arm trying to wake me up to see if I wanted to buy a $2.00 earphone set for the in-flight movie. I realized sleep was no longer possible in the Western world, so I gave in, plugged in my earphones, and found out the whole sound system for our section of the plane was broken.

"Just two minutes, Sir, and we will attend to it," said the hostess, displaying the same exquisite manners followed by no action that I had experienced for the last twenty-four hours.

Twenty minutes passed and the hostess remained in her cubicle, smoking a cigarette. I timidly knocked on the door and asked her again if she could fix the sound. All the people in my section with earphones had nodded out with their earphones on, sleeping through the static.

"In just a minute, Sir, as I told you previously," she said, in a cross voice.

I walked back to the next section, found an empty seat, sat down, and watched *Return of the Pink Panther,* more calming than the Charles Bronson flick from the flight from New York to London. Then I went back to my seat, climbing over my seat partner, who was asleep, and fell out into my first real sleep in a few days.

I woke up, looked out the window, and there it was.

Africa. At last. The mother of us all.

I stared out the window for two hours and saw Mount Kenya in the distance just before we landed in Nairobi. Even in an airplane, you could feel those spirits talking to you and welcoming you. By the time I was through customs, I could feel the great vibrations of being in a new nation. You could sense immediately that people had some control over their own lives. Even though we were in a crowded modern airport, it was as exhilarating as breathing fresh air after leaving the Holland Tunnel during rush hour. The pollution of racism that constantly affects our daily lives in so many subtle ways in America was not part of the feeling in this airport.

All during my stay in Nairobi, I saw that while racism always exists on some levels everywhere in the world, it was amazingly less prevalent here. Color meant nothing except color. People from all over the world were there in the airport, but there were no paranoiac half-stares and tension. I grabbed my bags and moved toward the exit to the street. I looked up and saw the bearded figure of John Taylor bounding toward me. We stood, staring at each other, like a modern day version of Stanley and Livingstone greeting one another in the bush.

"I can't believe you made it," he said.

"Did you get any of my three telegrams?" I asked.

"No," he said. "I just figured you'd be on this plane."

This type of telepathic communication happened constantly during my time in Kenya. Like Brazil, Cuba, Central America, and many parts of the United States that are still Indian country, the psychic feeling is in the air. The sense of spirit fills everything in Africa. I never had one second where I felt lonely. The spirits of others, from the past as well as the present, always surrounded you.

As we drove toward the center of Nairobi, John told me that the arts program for the Council of Churches was submerged in a sea of political and organizational bickering. Also, the choir that was going to sing the Brahms *Requiem* and the last movement of Beethoven's Ninth symphony, as well as the symphony orchestra from Germany, had both failed to show up. Their last-minute funding never came through.

"I feel terrible telling you all of this," said John.

"That's okay, John," I said. "We'll do something else instead. I brought all my instruments. Don't worry."

John looked relieved.

"What do you have in mind to replace the symphony and the chorus?" he asked.

"I'll do what you wanted me to originally do in addition to the classical part of the program. I'll just hang out here and find people who want to play music, and encourage others to feel welcome to join in, and make it like Gustav Mahler's *Symphony of a Thousand*. By the end of the session a few weeks from now, we should have a three-hundred-voice choir accompanied by an orchestra of all the musicians I meet, which we can call the Nairobi Pickup-a-monic."

"I knew I could count on you to come up with something," said John, looking a little puzzled but very relieved.

"Well, whatever it turns out to be, it will be something joyous and celebratory," I said. "That's my job."

We arrived in downtown Nairobi, a gorgeous city full of tropical trees, modern buildings, and crazy shops selling everything from *Playboy* magazines to tribal shields. Traffic zoomed past, as people out on the streets from all parts of East Africa made the vibrant city sidewalks feel like a home for everybody. Panhandlers, pencil salesmen, safari tour guides, visitors from all the Western countries, jewelry salesmen, and policemen and policewomen dressed in English-style uniforms, were all part of Nairobi's afternoon panorama. It was like the picture I had in my mind in the third grade when I read about the ancient cities of Nineveh and Tyre. Being there now made me glad to be alive.

I went into a store, which, like many others, had a large picture of Jomo Kenyatta in the window. I bought a new book on how to speak Swahili and checked in at the hotel. I went to my room and paid the bellman.

"I see by the case that you have a French horn. Are you a musician from the United States, Sir?" he asked.

"Yes."

"I adore the work of Charlie Parker and Louis Armstrong, who I also believe is known as Satchmo. Two different styles, but the same passion. Satchmo was here in Kenya. He was a very beautiful man. Are you here with the World Council of Churches to play music for the church people?"

"I'm going to play with anybody for everybody," I said.

"Ah, that is good. Very good. I will come to hear you with my family. Good luck to you. *Kwahare*. That means goodbye. Say it with me one time. Kwahare."

"Kwahare," I said.

"Try again."

"Kwahare."

"Better," he said laughing. "You will learn. Swahili is like music. Very beautiful to hear. You just try and you will learn it easily. I went to the university in London and find English to be a challenge, but since I studied hotel management, I am learning two other languages as well in our university here in Nairobi. I am sure that you will enjoy your stay. I hope you have the opportunity to see some of our beautiful country."

We shook hands and as he was about to go downstairs, some other people who worked in the hotel came down the hall. We began to talk, they asked me to show them some of my instruments, and a half an hour later my room was full of people all playing music and singing.

This happened almost every day I was in Kenya. I realized, as I did when in Brazil, that I wasn't crazy or a compulsive obsessive when I played music with other people any place, any time, anywhere, whenever it felt appropriate to do so without disturbing others. Here, my first day in Kenya, making music together was as natural as breathing the air.

I knew from having this happen so often in my life that this was normal, but understood that modern society often clubbed people into submission spiritually to the extent that many people's natural spontaneity and creativity often became atrophied and ended up withering on the vine. This certainly didn't happen for one second during my trip to Kenya.

I also found this first day that the extreme politeness and respect that Kenyans have for visitors was in no way part of a servant-master relationship. This was the way they were with one another, and as a result, with strangers.

Naturally, some tourists who were paying a small fortune to come to a strange land expected to have people who served them grovel in order to receive a good tip. This happened a thousand times a day in New York City and all over the world.

I saw it happen only occasionally in Nairobi, usually by the visiting safari-freaks, dressed up in tailor-made uniforms, often with matching outfits for their wives and children (like junior Ernest Hemingways). In addition to barking crisp commands to every African who was there to do a service for them, like the chase scenes from the 1930s production of *King Kong,* when the hero was screaming at the natives, the safari fanatics all became commanders-in-chief in every situation possible. When there were no Kenyans to shout at, they appeared ready to shoot all the wildlife on the African continent, looking as if they expected to blow away a stray elephant or giraffe or lion at any moment, as they paced the hotel lobby and the streets of Nairobi in their jodhpurs and pith helmets, waiting for a stray animal to stroll by. They were often imperious and rude, but most of all to each other.

Still, I understood they had probably saved money for years to come to Kenya and become *bwana,* the old image of Mighty Whitey, or, for the visiting women, Jane in the *Tarzan* movies, the Great White Goddess of the Jungle, before going back to their jobs at home and being yelled at and abused by their own bosses.

No one seemed upset by this, and many Kenyans told me they found it amusing. This kind of behavior was a marked contrast to what I saw most of the time in the hotel, on the street and in people's homes I was lucky enough to be invited to. The politeness, respect, love, and true consideration African people have toward one another made most loud, aggressive, disrespectful visitors cool out after a week or so in Kenya. From these earliest moments when I arrived until I left three weeks later, it certainly made me feel cooled out every second that I was there.

Later that afternoon, John Taylor came to see me and introduced me to John Garrett. He was quiet and unassuming, and spoke in a low voice, but you could see when you looked into his eyes that John Garrett was a true man of faith. You felt his humanity and awareness immediately, and his eyes told you that he had come through a lot of scenes and struggles without giving up.

He told me that he lived in the Fiji Islands, having left his home in Australia to work with a congregation he had helped to create as a missionary. When he spoke about the people of Fiji, he didn't have that anthropologist style of referring to human beings like different parts of an old automobile you were trying to replace by shopping at different junkyards. You could see that he saw people in a spiritual way and he was converted as much by his congregation as they were converted by him. He talked about the beauty of life in Fiji, and how art and religion were all part of everyone's way of life in the Islands.

He stated simply that it was the natural order of things for people to have their own theater, dance, instrumental music, and poetry read aloud, that this occurred in places where everyone in the community was welcome, and that you didn't need to construct an Alcatraz for the Performing Arts when you were in Fiji.

He told me that he felt that an empty field, a hut, or the sand by the open water was as fine as a concert hall to present an evening of music and dance. He also felt art and religion were the same thing. I could hardly wait to meet some of the other people whom John Garrett knew who were attending the conference.

We walked to the Kenyatta Conference Center, part of a twenty-eight-story modern building with a revolving restaurant on the top floor. We went inside. The downstairs was an African bazaar with crafts, beautifully patterned cloth dresses and *dashikis,* religious articles, records of African music, and people from all over the globe mingling with each other, smiling, talking, laughing—and so comfortable in spite of the intense energy level that I suddenly realized no one was worried about being ripped off, and, with the entire planet Earth represented, there was no weird *staring*! Everybody was hanging out with everybody else.

Priests from the USSR, Greek Orthodox churchmen, Tanzanian preachers, New Jersey ministers, Norwegian reverends, bishops from Japan and Korea, and a lot of nondenominational sinners were all communing harmoniously at a worldwide get-together.

I eased over toward the Assembly Hall. It was like a junior UN, with earphones at each desk to translate in most of the world's languages whatever was being discussed. The speaker of the moment was droning away in a voice remarkably similar to the low-pitched murmurs of my college economics professor, known to George Washington University's class of 1952 as the Sandman. Feeling myself about to join some of the others in soft snoring, I was reinvigorated by the hearty handshake of a Brazilian fundamentalist preacher who extended his hand from the tapered sleeve of his super-dap four-button pimpmobile-style jacket. I was about to take his hand in mine for some international brotherhood and a chance to wail away in the Portuguese I had learned when I was in Brazil in 1969, when he beat me to the punch by handing me an autographed color photo of himself and turning with perfect timing to hand out some more of the same to everybody he could hit on among the thousands of delegates.

Some of the delegates who were less lucky had no chance to avoid being overstimulated by his great hustler energy unless they were sleeping. The speaker ground on, sounding like the famous Lenny Bruce routine "Religions Incorporated."

A man in a homemade clerical outfit with frayed cuffs approached me.

"*Jambo* (How are you?)," he said.

"*Vizuri, Sanna* (Very well, thank you)," I answered.

"I am Bishop Jimmy LaNanna. Welcome to Kenya. You are a musician, I see," he said, looking at my bag of flutes, drums, my guitar, and French horn case. "I also play music, but now I am a fundamentalist minister. Before I was saved, I was a hooligan. I drank and was always fighting. Now I teach judo and karate to young city boys, but only for self-defense. And the discipline of the body makes the mind and spirit more alive. I am Masai. We are still warriors at home."

He pulled out a wooden club from behind his frock, which looked like an Irish *shillelagh,* called an *orinka.* He showed me in pantomime how you could whip it toward an animal end-over-end and kill any creature within seventy-five feet. Some of the delegates who hadn't fallen asleep looked a little frightened. Jimmy put his *orinka* back into the folds of his cassock.

"I have translated many prayers and tales of the Bible into Swahili and Maa, the language of the Masai people. The teachings of Jesus are simple enough for any man or woman on Earth to understand on some level. They need no explanation or interpretation. They are honest and true. This poor man speaking is trying to find his faith, not to share it. Let's go for a walk. He is saying nothing."

Jimmy and I spent the afternoon and night walking around the streets of Nairobi. Every few feet he would stop and talk with different people, telling them about what I was doing there at the conference, what he had been up to lately, and then giving me a fast history of each person ever since he had known them, where they came from, how many were in their family, and all the experiences they had shared. It took almost six hours to walk about a mile and a half.

It reminded me of the night I spent with Odetta in the summer of 1971 celebrating the end of my recording session when I conducted three of my compositions for symphony orchestra. We spent the entire seven hours on five blocks around MacDougal Street and Bleeker Street in Greenwich Village hanging out with different people we knew or met while walking slowly to visit some of our favorite places.

The street life in Nairobi had that same feeling of being one large home for everybody who was there. We passed by a Moslem mosque, a Buddhist temple, a synagogue, and down into the area where musicians all hung out. The African Moslems had restaurants where you could eat the most fantastic food while the Middle Eastern and African music took you on the magic carpet to previous lives and other times.

Jimmy talked about reincarnation.

"I'll come back again as a tiger. I was one before," said Jimmy as we ate our third helping of meat stew and fresh green vegetables that made you feel their life with each swallow.

"I'm coming back the time after next as an eggplant," I said. "That's why I try to be a vegetarian. Except when I eat meat."

We had a little jam session with some of the musicians and passersby after we ate and started walking back toward the Kenyatta Center. Jimmy said he would come back with some friends to play with me the following night when I was supposed to meet with Peter Janson and his Song Orchestra. Peter was from Germany and had brought a band with him of young players from his home town who were performing modern liturgical music that included jazz, rock, and folk music. I could already see the beginnings of an international orchestra that would include enthusiasts from his group as well as some of the Africans I had met on the street with Jimmy LaNanna.

Back at the Kenyatta Center, I ran into John Garrett at the door. He took me to the pressroom to meet some of the reporters who wanted to interview me. There were hundreds of reporters and TV men and women, typing up endless documents, drinking coffee, smoking cigarettes, sneaking drinks from flasks, sipping tea, telling jokes, reading old newspapers, interviewing people, and waiting for the Big Story to occur. The head of the pressroom told me he now lived in Switzerland but was from New Jersey. On his door was a homemade sign saying, "CIA not welcome here."

I was interviewed by journalists in French, German, Italian, Spanish, and Portuguese. Then I spoke to newsmen from Scandinavian countries, England, Ireland,

and many of the African nations, as well as the AP, Canadian papers, and the *New York Times*. After five hours of this, I was ready to fall out.

To restore my equilibrium, I sat at the desk of the *Voice of Kenya* reporter and radio commentator Sampson Lipuka to practice some elementary Swahili. After he was kind enough to teach me some more phrases, he asked if we could play some music together. He played my guitar and I played the horn, and in a few minutes we had a little international jam session, with reporters, cleaning men, and delegates joining in.

A young man with a drum came up after we completed an improvised scat-rap sing-along I made up about my tumultuous trip from New York to Perth to London to Nairobi and introduced himself.

"Jambo, my man. I'm Steele Buta. I played African drums with Satchmo when he was here in Nairobi. I hope you can sit in with my group. We're called the Funky (spelled Fanki) JuJu Band (JuJu means magic). We're playing on the twenty-seventh floor of the building each night, and we'd like to play with you, man, and have you play with us."

"What time do you start?" I asked.

"In about an hour. Around 9:00, 9:30."

"Great. I'll be there."

I ran down to my room in the hotel, changed, drank a pot of chai tea and went back to the conference center on the twenty-seventh floor, to the revolving restaurant. The Fanki Juju Band was playing some great music as people ate, drank, and danced. You could see the lights of all of Nairobi at night through the large bay windows that moved slowly as the whole restaurant revolved. At one point in the 360-degree slow turning, you could see, beyond the last twinkling lights over the mountains, the outline of the dark flat countryside. I was told that this was Masai land, which still belonged to the tribal people whose ways had not changed since way before the Gospel was preached.

And here we were, in a restaurant constructed inside of a huge slowly revolving tower, with a band using electronic instruments, playing rock, Calypso music, and later in the night, Swahili songs, using the music and rhythms that went back in time to the beginning. The dance floor was crowded with a worldwide group of people; Hindi-speaking Indians in turbans who were born in Kenya and church delegates from around the world doing the Boogaloo and the Twist to get some true religion in their aching bones after a day of hearing speeches. People from The Fellowship of Reconciliation (with whom I had gone to jail in 1971, protesting the war), Japanese couples, and Africans from every part of the continent, all having a good time.

During the break, while Steele Buta and his band had a drink, I gave the owner's brother, who was in charge of the bar, my guitar and he played me a traditional Kenyan folk song. Some of the waiters joined in, singing and playing percussion using spoons, knives, forks, and anything available. Within minutes we had a new band, wailing away, and we were joined by the people who were working in the kitchen. Then Steele's band played another two-hour set and invited me to play with them.

I saw I wasn't going to sleep much in Kenya, but as my composition teacher at Manhattan School of Music, the late Vittorio Giannini, used to tell me when we complained about arriving at 8:00 a.m. for our early morning theory classes, "Sleep's a waste of time!"

After Steele was done playing and the band packed up, the musicians, waiters, and local cognoscenti all got together and talked about music and religion.

"Many Christian missionaries tried to stop us from being Africans," said Steele Buta. "But we refused. We have to move and sing in our own way, even when we pray. What is natural for the British is not natural for us, even if we believe in the same God. We have our freedom now. We in Kenya can now be ourselves."

As all of us talked through the night, it became apparent that Christianity and democracy were something that many Kenyans felt close to, because both Christianity and democracy were already close to the ways of many tribal customs and religious practices that had existed before recorded time.

As everyone talked, I realized that many Kenyans felt that if they were to live in a Christian world, what Christ preached should be practiced. They also made it clear that they felt that the blessings of democracy should apply to every man, woman, and child in Kenya, not just for one economic class.

"If you say you are a Christian, and you steal my land after you have saved my soul, then I must resist. And the harder you push, the harder I am forced to push back. We want schools and knowledge of technology, but we want to keep our own humanity. We do not put our old people in homes. We have respect for our old people. We have respect for our women, and we love and care about our children in this country. And we teach our children to love and respect each other and themselves."

This was straight talk from Steele Buta at 3:30 a.m., and it was something that I heard many times in Kenya. When I went out into the countryside and saw the huts and shacks people lived in, with their small gardens and animals in back, with women carrying loads on their backs and often balanced on their heads, working with the men, I also saw that there was still a sense of respect and love that people had for one another, and a sense of community that the Western world seemed to be losing more of each and every day.

People I met that night at the Tower Restaurant and people I was with on the streets and in the countryside would always talk to you, as well as any Africans they met, about their family, telling you about their mother and father, how many brothers and sisters they had, and ask you about your family.

It was the complete opposite of the ego-oriented, family-hating, old-age dreading, self-centered, consumer-mad, pseudo-hip narcissistic nouveau-degenerate life style being jammed down the throats of all of us in America and much of the Western world by the endless avalanche of swill dumped upon us by TV, radio, most films, and tabloids.

The one thing that all the delegates who hung out with the people in Kenya (rather than just looking for lions to photograph) found out was this shared sense of humanity. This seemed to apply to anybody and everybody, as long as you acted in some kind of human fashion.

"Are you going to safari, David?" asked Gabby Wamala, one of the great drummers with Steele Buta's Fanki Ju-Ju band.

"No," I said. "I understand that it is good for business to have people pay and look at animals. I love nature, being brought up on a farm. I hear that the lion is courageous, the tiger is strong and fierce, and the elephant is wise, but I'd rather be with people for this trip. If I want to see an elephant, I can take the subway when I get back to New York and go to the zoo. But I doubt that the elephant would want to see me. He would rather come home and be here, and I am sure that he has seen enough tourists taking his picture in New York and in Kenya. I think animals should be free just to hang out with one another, unless they invite you to join them."

Everyone who could understand my rapid-fire New York-Feasterville-Pennsylvania-Washington DC accent roared with laughter, and Steele Buta translated it into both Swahili and proper slowly spoken well-articulated King's English.

"They want you to put that into a song at your concert, when you make up all the words," said Steele.

Someone said something to Steele in Swahili, which he translated for me.

"Most visitors here go to see the animals, go to their hotel, buy some souvenirs and leave Nairobi, and know nothing of African peoples. We are friendly and like to exchange ideas with people. We are exchanging music with you, and we learn from each other. Man, it's nearly 4:00 o'clock in the morning. Let's go and eat some breakfast."

We all went out to an all-night Arabic restaurant, like Mamoun's Falafel cubby hole on McDougal Street in Greenwich Village, and after a late-night/early-morning feast, with more conversation about religion, animals, music, women, and boxers from Nigeria like the great Dick Tiger, I went back and fell asleep about 6:30 a.m., tired but inspired.

I felt at home.

It was decided that the two formal concerts I would give would include the Fanki Ju-Ju Band and anyone else who wanted to come and play with us, and that in all the pieces we played we would concentrate on showing the African roots in music from the West Indies, Brazil, Cuba, Puerto Rico, jazz and blues from the United States, and many of the Middle Eastern countries that incorporated African rhythms into their music. We decided to end each concert with a long jam session featuring everybody.

Steele Buta also asked me to make up songs on the spot, using suggestions from the audience, which is something that is often done in African music.

We had a two-hour rehearsal with Steele's band and knew we were ready for our first concert. The rehearsal itself was like a concert, except that the audience was just all of us who were playing.

At the concert, the musicians all played so well together, with such a strong communal spirit, it reminded me of the times I played with Oscar Pettiford in his great all-star big band at Birdland back in the 1950s, or when I would walk a few blocks from my old Greenwich Village apartment to go and sit in with Thad Jones/Mel Lewis's peerless big band on Monday nights at the Village Vanguard in the 1970s, or when I would play with Dizzy Gillespie and Mingus and jam with Thelonious Monk and feel transported by the collective spirit of their groups.. It was like the feeling in 1971 when I soloed with the America Symphony Orchestra at Lincoln Center in the premiere of my *Triple Concerto for Woodwind, Brass and Jazz Quintets,* and the whole orchestra seemed to lift right off the stage as if we were all suddenly airborne through the music.

Everybody became an extension of Steele's band, with everybody listening to everybody else, and surrendering themselves to the music, and it was cooking!

That first night we played in an amphitheater, with all the delegates and others looking down at us, perched in their chairs and squinting past the microphones on their tables, as if they were judging us like the Nuremberg trials.

But any sour or surprised expressions soon changed, and by the fourth piece, they were smiling, clapping, and singing along, and some got up and started dancing in the aisles.

After the concert, we invited everyone in the audience to join us and had a huge jam session. The editor of a North Carolina newspaper sat in with us, playing drums, and some Peace Corps volunteers bonded with a group of Kenyan-born Indians, all scat singing in Hindi when I played "Blue Monk" on the old out-of-tune upright piano, accompanied by all kinds of East African drums and percussion instruments and a concertina player named Joachim from Austria, who had brought his squeeze box with him to the conference.

The delegates and Kenyans in the audience all started snake dancing and everyone was having a great time. Finally, we all went up to the twenty-seventh floor to the restaurant and had a big party and another jam session with the band who had replaced the Fanki Ju-Ju Band for the night.

"Man, you really surprised us," said Steele.

"When you said you were going to give a concert, we thought you were going to conduct hymns all night, or bring in arrangements like Tom Jones or other big international acts."

"That's right," said Gabby Wamala. "It's best just to play together what the moment makes you feel. Then it always will be beautiful, and always come out right."

"That's right," said Steele. "To-*gether*."

I had Sunday afternoon off, so I thought I should see something of the countryside. I had been all around Nairobi, walking with musicians to the university, when I was interviewed on the *Voice of Kenya* TV and radio.

I mentioned to Sampson Lipuka, as we walked on the quiet Sunday morning, how beautiful the foliage, flowers, trees, and even the sky were in the city.

"You must go to the countryside," said Sampson. "Even a few kilometers out of the city. Try to see the Bomas dancers on this one day off. You will see dancing and hear music you will never forget."

I walked over to the travel agency and asked the salesman for a ticket to go and see the Bomas dancers.

"I am sorry, but they are not dancing today. Instead, we have a tour to the Masai dancing. Please go to the Kenyatta Conference Hall to be transported there."

I thought this meant that the Masai would be dancing at the theater where the Bomas dances were to have taken place, so I bought a ticket and went to the front entrance of the Kenyatta Conference Hall.

I was told to enter a large Volkswagen van, with four German tourists, an Italian minister from the Merovingian sect, the daughter of a missionary from Albany, NY, and her friend from the Philippines now living in Philadelphia, who told me that her sister sang with the Gregg Smith singers in New York. We began to talk as the van roared out of town like the chase scene in the movie *The French Connection*.

Even with the driver's zigzagging to avoid hitting other cars, bicycles, people walking, and stray dogs and cats, it was peaceful and relaxing, as the bus driver told stories of his whole family and carried on conversations between monologues with anyone in the van who wanted to talk to him, blissfully honking his horn at the last second to avoid near catastrophes, without ever interrupting his train of thought.

It was like the crazy day I spent driving through the streets of San Francisco in another Volkswagen van in 1965 with Neal Cassady at the wheel, except that we never left the city. That day in San Francisco, the volume level inside the van, with Allen Ginsberg and Gregory Corso shouting at one another as well as at the passersby, was much more hysterical than the million-year-old sense of calm and groundedness that all of us in the van in Nairobi felt, as we drove past the outskirts of the sprawling city of Nairobi.

The countryside was amazing, with reddish soil giving birth to gigantic plants of all kinds—trees, flowers, vines, and foliage so lush that you could almost feel and see everything growing as you watched through the windows of the speeding van. Most of the dwellings outside of Nairobi were just shacks, but there were gardens, chickens, and other kinds of livestock, and the people looked healthy and many, young and old, waved to the van as we passed them by.

We slowed down as we entered a village where a wedding was in progress and the van driver stopped and had a fifteen-minute rap in Swahili and Kikuyu with some of the attendees, later telling us that the bridegroom was a fellow athlete and amateur cricket player. His friend ran off and came back with a basket of all kinds of home-cooked food from the wedding, gesturing to us in sign language to eat, and then touching his heart with his fist.

"Thass-a nice man," said the Merovingian minister to me. "Big-a heart. Like Italian. Share what-a you got."

We drove off and passed more villages. Some consisted of homemade shacks and some consisted of pre-fab mini-housing developments, like the ones in Long Island or the stretch between Dallas and Mesquite, Texas, but always with some space between them, often with a scattering of mud huts interspersed. But there were always gardens and animals, and when the van driver stopped again to socialize and was given more fruit and vegetables, they were the best I had ever eaten in my life.

We had now been in the van for almost two hours when we started ascending a huge hill for about fifteen minutes. The driver turned his head back toward us while still driving, and interrupting his stream-of-consciousness monologues, began to speak in stentorian tones, like an airline pilot over the intercom, or an announcer at a championship boxing match, or a general addressing the troops.

"Now, ladies and gentlemen. *Now*... you see before you ... the most majestic, world-renowned ... GREAT ... RIFT ... VALLEY! Feast your eyes upon it."

The driver's Shakespearean oratorical style and his spellbinding delivery of his homemade infomercials were a work of art in themselves. He told us that he had gone to college in England to study engineering but really wanted to be an actor, and had hung out with students from the Old Vic Theater during his off hours in London. While each of his raps were brilliantly articulated, the stunning beauty of what surrounded us simply couldn't be described in words, so he abruptly ended his talk, and joined us in absorbing the beauty all around us. Each of us sat in our own silence, as we slowly tried to absorb every detail of the enormous expanse, which lay below where the van was parked at the top of the huge hill.

"This makes the Grand Canyon look like an irrigation ditch," said the woman from Philadelphia.

As far as you could see, there was what seemed to be an endless series of enormous rolling valleys, with mountains in the distance reaching up to the clouds, and between the mountains you could see more valleys and more mountains. It was like looking at the endless expanse of the ocean when you are out at sea. Even the driver seemed overwhelmed and joined us in silence for about ten minutes. We all sat quietly, becoming part of what we all felt was a state of pure timelessness.

The driver started up the van and for the first time was silent as all of us slowly moved back into the present.

"Now, ladies and gentlemen, to continue," he said, returning to his normal manic state, and, mashing down on the accelerator, jolting us all back into a tourist state of consciousness. "Here you can see out the window to your left two signs of progress."

We all craned our necks and saw a huge radar station in the distance and by the roadside a gigantic billboard with a Colonel Sanders chicken logo, with the beloved Colonel dressed in his customary white suit, but now transformed into an African-American, looking like Al Jolson in *The Jazz Singer*.

"Your American corporations will do anything to sell us your goods," said the van driver to me. "And we all know that good taste is always superseded by the desire to make money. We know Colonel Sanders is a white man everywhere else, so we are not concerned that he has converted to trying to look like us. We don't care what color he is, as long as the chicken is not overcooked. But we pride ourselves in our own cooking. I don't think they will stay in business much longer here in Kenya. Instead of painting his face, his corporation should take some lessons from us in how to roast a chicken properly. We are excellent cooks, and we know the difference."

The radar station and the Colonel Sanders billboard were emblematic of much of what I saw that day on the trip; the oldest and the newest in an unplanned partnership. It seemed that somehow the sense of oldness could accommodate anything new, as if nature itself remains patient, knowing that all that was created before we began littering the world would still survive when trash technology slowly rusted away and disappeared.

I realized at that moment that all you could hope for was that Kenya could keep its remaining unspoiled land and retain its soul, as it continued as a free nation to raise its living standards for all its people, without destroying itself in the process.

"Now we are about to enter Masai Land," said the driver.

"Is that all Masai Land that we just saw?" asked the missionary's daughter.

"No, not yet," said the driver. "What we are about to see is what was given to the Masai people. Six thousand acres. They raise humped Boran cattle. It is too dry to raise many crops. Not enough rain. There are also wild animals. See how peaceful it is?"

"Achtung!! Sehst du das?" screamed one of the German tourists, whipping out his Nikon camera and almost knocking out the window of the bus as he swung around and started snapping away at a giraffe that had ambled by, seeming to look at all of us squashed in the van as if we were animals in a cage whom the giraffe was visiting at a zoo on wheels.

"Don't get excited. There are many giraffes here," said the driver calmly, stopping the bus so that the German tourist could continue, as everyone else with a camera began to load up and fire away. "There are also leopards, buffalo, zebra, and lions. Even baboons."

The driver winked at me as he watched other passengers now all beginning to shove each other at the windows so that they could each get their pictures, even though the giraffe stood gazing at us, appearing bored by our presence, as he slowly chewed his cud.

Then the giraffe, with ultimate cool, turned its head ever so slightly away, as if to say "no more pictures today, please" and slowly ambled off in a dignified trot into the distance.

We drove a little farther and entered into what looked like a series of dog kennels, lined up by the side of the road.

"What are those?" I asked the bus driver.

"The last remnants of colonialism," he answered.

I saw people moving in and out of them, dressed in rags, and realized without having to ask that they were not tending to their dogs. This is where they lived. This was the only time in Kenya where I saw people who looked so servile and depressed.

We drove another two hundred yards and made a sharp turn, and suddenly saw a huge manicured hedge, surrounding a large Victorian-style house.

"Here we are. Everyone out, please," said the driver.

We all got out of the van. It felt good to stretch our legs, breathe the perfect air, and look at a locale that was just like the movie set for the 1944 cinematic classic *Jane Eyre*. I expected Orson Welles and Joan Fontaine, the stars of the film, to come out of the main door of the house, leaving their dressing rooms during a break in the shooting, and invite us in for tea. Instead, a young blonde woman in a riding outfit with polished high boots greeted us.

"This is the main house of the Mayer's Ranch," she said crisply. "You are now invited to come inside. The Masai begin their ceremonies at exactly 3:00 p.m. Then you may return for high tea and scones at 4:00 p.m."

We entered the house, surrounded by immaculately mown grass, hedges, and small flower gardens, all constructed to provide a view of the neighboring mountains. There was also a croquet court and a neatly trimmed Scotch terrier. Inside the house were some disgruntled young Englishmen and women, who were employees of the ranch, and native Kenyan servants, in outfits like the ones in *Gone with the Wind*.

The woman in charge and her English staff ordered all the Kenyan servants around, usually accompanying their crisp military-style commands with finger snaps. Still, it was obvious that compared to the dog kennel–type hovels outside where the servants all lived after a hard day's work, being a house servant was a better job than mowing the lawn, trimming the hedges, and hand-tilling all the gardens, all of which was done by the Kipisgis people, who came from Lake Victoria and spoke their own Kipsigis language.

I went outside to talk to the bus driver. The little brochure handed to us said that the Masai people lived nearby "by special arrangement with the Mayer's family, who owned the ranch." I asked the driver if the Masai who were there worked for the ranch when they weren't performing for the tourists.

"Of course," said the bus driver. "They have to survive."

We began to talk, and he told me that his whole family lived together about fifty kilometers from where we were.

"Sometime you should come back to Kenya and really see how so many of our people still live. Even today in most of the villages, the people will take you in, feed you, clothe you and look after you, as long as they don't feel you are going to steal their cattle. They don't care if you are a Mzungu (white man). They only care how you behave. They judge you by your character, not your skin. The Masai are still a very proud people. They were strong warriors. They and the Kikuyu used to fight one another, but now we are eliminating tribalism in Kenya. You should go see the dancing. It will give you a better understanding of the people. And the singing is very interesting. Especially so for you, since you work in music."

I thanked the driver for sharing all this with me, left the bus, and walked over toward where he told me the dancing would begin. Some of the junior warriors, called Ikillani, came up to me. They had long hair dyed red and their skin also had red dye, made from lamb's fat and red earth. They held their spears and spoke to one another in Maa. Then, smiling, they pointed to my two shiny pennywhistles and indicated they wanted me to play them.

They all began laughing, and in sign language told me that they would like to try to play them. I handed them over, and they began tootling away, taking turns and encouraging each other. Then I took one back, and began playing a duet, fitting in my part to the squeals produced by one of the young men who kept laughing uncontrollably after each squeaky note that he produced.

An older man from the group of senior warriors, called *Ilingeetiani,* walked over and said something. The young man I was jamming with handed me my pennywhistle back, and the older man gestured for me to follow him. I walked with him past a group of other young men with spears and sat down on a log next to him, which I realized was like a front row box seat, perfectly located to watch the dancing. We were early, so since there was no performance, we began talking in sign language, and he pointed to my English/Swahili mini-dictionary. I gave it to him and he quickly hid it under his robe. I got the feeling immediately that even while we were told that the dancers and craftspeople could keep whatever little they earned from the tourists, they had to give most of it to the Mayer's Ranch.

We continued our conversation in sign language and by ESP, the non-verbal telepathic way of communicating that birds and so many animals use. ESP is how musicians, actors, high wire artists, and basketball players often communicate. It felt comfortable to sit next to him, as if I were sitting on someone's back porch.

We watched the young men warming up for the exhibition they were to give. They were jumping, stretching, singing, laughing, and having a good time with one another. They all looked extremely healthy and proud as they continued their warmups, like major leaguers doing their pre-game exercising as the tourists began to file in, arriving from other vans and mini-buses.

The Masai women began to appear, carefully spreading out their beadwork, jewelry, and a great variety of handicrafts. Everything they displayed dazzled you with fantastic colors, intricate but always symmetrical designs, and, like all African music and art, radiating spirit and energy.

The tourists all sat on logs as the young dancers continued to do their warmups, now accompanying themselves with rhythmic humming, all the while glancing at the tourists, who by now had whipped out all kinds of equipment: still cameras, video cameras, motion picture cameras, tape recorders, instamatics, and Polaroids that set off flashes, all like some kind of surreal press conference in the middle of the Masai reserve.

"What do you think the young men are saying to one another?" asked the missionary's daughter.

"Probably, they are saying, what a bunch of schlemiels we have with us today," I said.

"What's a schlemiel, David?" she asked.

"It's hard to translate," I said.

"Is that a word the Masai use to denote someone who is intrusive?" she asked.

"No," I said. "But in this situation, that's essentially what it denotes. I think we all have to learn to be a little more respectful of one another. I'm working on that every day myself and know that I have a long way to go. Music helps you to try to be that way, but then you have to apply that good conduct and those good intentions to everything else you do in life."

There was a moment of silence, a transition from the warming up to the beginning of the performance. The young men started humming a repetitive rhythmic pattern which was identical to the syncopated structure of the Charleston, which we hear every day in our music in the United States.

After the pattern was sung several times, one of the men began to sing his own music in counterpoint to the pattern being chanted by the others. I was told later by the bus driver, when I asked him, that the pattern was a chant describing what was happening that day.

The singing then stopped and the men divided into two groups and began what looked like target practice, as they threw pieces of green fibrous stalks at one another with incredible speed and accuracy, which you could hear crashing against the zebra-skinned shields of their opponents who stood at a fifty-foot distance.

Then they began brandishing their wooden clubs called *orinkas,* the same kind that the preacher Jimmy LaNanna showed me at the Kenyatta Center, which he had later hidden in his cassock.

Then there was more singing, accompanied by giant leaps in the air by the young men, all synchronized to the chanting. As you sat there, it was like being in a time machine that brought you back tens of thousands of years, and then, like having a round trip ticket, returned you from those ancient times right back up to the Now.

It defined the concept of Timelessness.

Sitting there on the logs, all of us from different countries around the world were now united through the magical and inexplicable power of the music, singing, and dancing. We were surrounded by the bursting panoply of colors: beads, headdresses, dyed hair and skins, the shields made from animals, and the brilliant blue sky with mountains stretching out in all directions under the low-lying clouds in the distance.

Suddenly everything seemed to freeze for a moment in time and we all felt that we were now transported into a new world. We were all put in a spell so strong that I was sure that all of us would remember this moment for all of our lives. I'm not sure we ever would have snapped out of it if the Englishwoman in charge hadn't suddenly barked directions at all of us.

"You may go now to buy the beadwork and photograph the remaining dances. Come now, if you please. Let's get to it as quickly as possible."

The tourists, many of whom we hadn't seen before, clambered down, taking their cameras and pointing them right into the faces of the dancers, while others began haggling with the women who were selling their exquisitely crafted necklaces and jewelry.

Meanwhile, the dancers resumed what was like a reprise in a Broadway show during a curtain call, smiling and laughing, seemingly oblivious of the tourists, indicating that they knew that we would soon return to our vans and leave, and leave some of our money with the women, while the dancing and singing, which had been here forever, would continue to go on forever.

"Five minutes until tea time," intoned the British woman, like a headmistress, in her icy but well-modulated voice. "Let's not be late."

As most of the tourists and members of our small group followed her obediently, a middle-aged American couple standing next to me moved down to one of the dancers and the man took out what looked like a beat-up Boy Scout knife. He gestured, indicating he'd like to trade it for the dancer's headdress. The dancer stood motionless and did not respond.

"Come on, Keemosabe," said the man, using the fake Indian name invented for the Lone Ranger TV show. "This good trade, Keemosabe. Knife sharp. Made in America. Genuine Boy Scout."

The young dancer gave the tourist a quiet bone-chilling stare, like the baleful glare that Sonny Liston, the former heavyweight champion, would give to his opponents as the referee would give the boxers their final instructions before the fight began.

"Come on now," said the American man, unfazed. "This good deal, my friend. *Authentic American Boy Scout Knife.*"

Another dancer, who had been watching this Kabuki-esque theater of the absurd, took out a foot-long knife and in pantomime pretended to cut off his own nose, and simulated committing hari-kari, indicating that he already had all the knives he would ever need, and that if the tourist wanted to buy a headdress, he could pay for it.

Meanwhile, the woman the American man was with approached one of the other dancers and began snapping her fingers and doing a bump and grind, while the dancer stood motionless, staring in disbelief as the other dancers began laughing as she continued her disco-inspired gyrations.

"Put that damn Boy Scout knife away and get a picture of this with the movie camera," she yelled at her partner.

The dancers all watched her twitching and grinding away and then began talking among themselves as if she wasn't there and this had never happened. Then they turned their backs until the couple went away.

I shook hands with the older man I had been sitting with. During this bizarre interlude, he sat quietly, with a dignified expression and a slight smile as if all of this was just another footnote in the endless journey of the Masai. You could feel a sense of history in his presence, but unlike seeing a statue or a painting, you felt in him the feelings of his ancestors, all of which emanated from him even as he sat in silence.

We walked together up to the main house and he handed me a beautiful beaded necklace, and when I thanked him in the Maa language, by saying "*ashi naling,*" which the bus driver taught me, I added a second thank you in Swahili, "*assante sann.*"

We shook hands again and looked in each other's eyes. This was something that I saw African people from all parts of the continent do all the time with one another. Touch and look right into each other's eyes, and into the other person, just as Dostoyevsky wrote when describing how the eyes are the vessels of the soul.

We parted and after he had walked away, I turned and entered the main house. The missionary's daughter looked distressed and came over to me.

"I was really hurt by the behavior of some of the people here who are visiting this very special place. Their lack of respect was really shameful. We are here to represent the progress and enlightenment of the Western world. Considering the fact that so-called Third World people are supposed to be backward and therefore should look to us to provide a better life for themselves, we could all certainly use a crash course in good manners and basic decent behavior toward our fellow human beings. My father's work as a missionary was to try to bring the teachings of Jesus to people in the world who were suffering and uplift them in their daily lives, as well as giving them hope, teaching them the principles of compassion and universal love. He told me after he had been in Africa and had seen the rudeness exhibited by many visitors that perhaps we needed our missionaries to flood the United States and Europe to remind people of how to act in a civilized fashion toward one another."

"We have the most wonderful country, and I love it," I said. "But sometimes I guess we forget to practice the basics. The American Indian Community House in New York City has a bumper sticker they sell that says, 'Respect, Love and Sharing: The Indian Way.' My relatives from Savannah all tell their children, and practice themselves, the first principle of civilized behavior: 'Always mind your manners.'"

"Amen, David. I wish they'd been here today to suggest that to some of these bozos."

We went into the room with all the other visitors and drank tea, ate tasty scones and tiny watercress sandwiches on white bread with the crust removed, and then were told that it was time to go.

"You should have been here in the old days," said an elderly English woman, as we all walked across the large room toward the front door.

"It was so much more pleasant before all this Kenyatta business. Our whole family left and moved back to our home in London. This country has become a dreadful place. I returned to show my grandchildren the scenery. I look forward to leaving as soon as possible."

I talked to the bus driver about the woman's conversation as we drove back to Nairobi. I told him how much Kenyatta was admired in the United States, and how exciting many people in our country felt about the whole decolonization taking place throughout Africa.

"We are on the move, but we certainly have a long way to go," he said. "Twelve years of freedom is a short time. Our leader, Kenyatta, is not perfect. We all know he takes a little from the pot for himself. Some outsiders say that now an African elite has replaced the English elite. You see Africans educated at Oxford University driving Mercedes, and you saw the huts and shacks that people live in. You have probably met the rich European and American farmers, ranchers, and business entrepreneurs who are making money here.

"But we are a thousand times better off than before. We are Kenyans. We love our country. We are proud to be free, and proud to be learning and practicing respect and love for each other, in a real democracy. We still have old tribal customs, and a history of conflicts, but we are now all Kenyans. I hear many of your people and people from other countries complaining and criticizing yourselves, your cities and your countries. That is a good thing, I am sure. But we Kenyans love it here. We are ashamed of nothing. This is our land. Many of the missionaries brought us a Bible and told us that Jesus was white, that the black man who believed in the old ways was now a devil, with horns and a long tail."

"That's not in the Bible, as far as I know," I said.

"Obviously not," said the bus driver. "But that's how they made us feel. We no longer accept that. Those of us who now believe in Christ are trying to follow his teachings. We are forming our own African Church in order to follow what Jesus preached. We teach our children to memorize the Sermon on the Mount, so that they will know that true Christians all over the world live with love in their hearts for all people."

"Amen," said the Italian minister.

"Amen," said all the rest of us in the van.

We rode back to Nairobi in silence, watching the endless vista of the Great Rift Valley and reveling in the beauty of what we had seen in the morning and observing all that we had missed.

"I am happy to have been with all of you today," said the bus driver, when we pulled up in front of the Kenyatta Center. "I hope that all of you remember everything that you saw and learned today and share it with the other people at the conference, and with your friends and family when you return home. As we say in Kenya, 'Kwahare.'"

The next few days before my big final concert, I spent hours tracking down everyone I had been playing with at our nightly international jam sessions at the Delegates Lounge, at the restaurant on the twenty-seventh floor of the Kenyatta

Center where Steele Buta's band played, and various venues throughout the city where I had met so many gifted musicians who lived in Nairobi. I invited them all to come again and play, sing, or participate in some way for the final program, and then kept re-arranging the program so that it would appear to be planned for years in advance.

One evening, after one of the endless mini-jam sessions I had in the Delegates Lounge, where I was now acting like a Marine recruiting sergeant, with a sign-up list on a table by my side, I met Claire Acca, of the Shoshone-Paiute people. She was invited to the conference as the representative of all the Native American people who practiced Christianity throughout the United States. She told me that in addition to fulfilling the request of what she had been invited to do, she also hoped to make people at the conference aware of the presence and importance of all Native Americans of every religious belief, including traditionalists, who still maintained the ways of their elders from thousands of years ago.

Claire told me she was a senior at Arizona State College, where she was to receive a degree in education. She was planning on teaching on a reservation when she graduated. She also told me, at one of the little pre-concert raps I gave before I played some traditional Lakota and Cheyenne social songs, that all the Native American people I mentioned who had guided me in how to learn this music were people that she knew of and respected.

"The songs you played and sang that you learned from Floyd Westerman, Vine Deloria, and Gus Greymountain are very important, as a way of sharing the history of our many Indian nations," she said. "They call us all Indians at home, but we are many people, with our own special ways. Every Indian nation has something special to share with the world. I'd be happy to perform with you at all the remaining concerts that you do."

We took the elevator to the twenty-seventh floor, where I sat in with Steele Buta's Fanki JuJu Band, feasting on the energy and joy that they brought to the music every second that they played for an hour and a half. I went back to the table and sat down with Claire again, and talked about the writing of Laguna poetess and old friend Leslie Silko and poet Simon Ortiz. Kulwat Mayer, a native-born Kenyan whose parents had immigrated to Kenya, came over and joined us.

"I see you and David have finally met. He seems to know many of your fine artists."

"That's true," said Claire. "I hope we can let everyone at the conference know about Floyd Westerman's great song, "Custer Died for your Sins." We all know it at home, at least all Indians do. And all Vine Deloria's books are important to show the whole world about the best that America has to offer. I wish every one of our hundreds of Indian nations could be here to represent us all, from Alaska to the tip of South America. The whole continent is a gift from the Great Creator to all people, and we were there first and for fifty thousand years have respected this gift. This is something all true Christians and people of every faith should know about. I saw the Masai dancers when I first got here, before I met David. They were so proud. They reminded me of my people."

"You are what we call a real *red* Indian," said Kulwat. "We feel you are close to our people. Not just by name. We know Columbus was lost and thought he had landed in India. No matter. We feel a kinship spiritually with all cultures like yours that have retained their knowledge of self, in spite of all oppression. Do the red Indians leap up and down like the Masai when they dance?"

"No," said Claire. "It's different. We dance very gently. When our moccasins touch the ground, we do that as if we were caressing it, to show our reverence for our Mother Earth. The soil and the mountains and the streams and rivers and our Father Sky are sacred to us. That's why it hurts to see the land being polluted and torn apart. The Indian way is to live in harmony with nature. And our land is *still* being stolen, bit-by-bit; treaties are *still* being broken, and FBI agents are hunting down and harassing our leaders and medicine men if they speak out.

"I'm here to try to tell the people of the world about Indian people in the United States. We are trying to get a fund for a law center in Washington to train lawyers to help out our cause. It's been very hard to get to speak here at the conference. I didn't come here just to look like someone from a book about Indians. I have something to say.

"The American delegates condemn apartheid in South Africa, which is the right thing to do, but they won't let me speak about repression in the United States against our people. The women's liberation group from the United States came down very hard on me when I told them that the repression of my people was my first concern. How can I be concerned about their anger that they earn only $45,000 a year while their husbands earn $65,000 a year, while young boys commit suicide on our reservations, and women have to walk miles to buy food that is overpriced? They want me to sign a protest form complaining that they don't have enough say in how the conference is run. I tell them I can't sign that if they won't let me speak.

"All of what they call Third World women have come to me to tell me to stay strong and not give up. But it hurts so much to have these women from big cities with a whole lot of money criticize me as if they never hear what I am saying. I understand their hurt feelings and I respect their pride. Why can't they hear what I am saying for my people? Why can't they ever stop talking and listen?

"I tell them that we think of motherhood as something sacred. We respect and love our men. We don't think that looking after our children is a burden. We have our old people and children all live together. Still we have our privacy, even though many of us live in the same place.

"I wish they could listen and open their hearts to understand what I'm trying to say. We don't tell them how to live or who they should be, or tell them they have to be like us. We respect them, and admire these smart women who want to advance themselves and get an even bigger slice of the pie. They should respect our people who welcomed their ancestors to America enough to let me speak on my own.

"I want to be able to tell everyone here that when they leave the conference and go back home, American Indians want them to tell the world that we no longer accept being referred to as the vanishing Americans.

"We are still here, and call ourselves Native Americans, and our men, women, and children will no longer remain quiet. If the World Council of Churches thought they got me as their Thanksgiving decoration, they picked the wrong turkey."

"I thought all that you speak about stopped one hundred years ago," said Kulwat. "We don't know anything about all you have told us over here in Kenya. All we know is what we see in American movies. We know there must be more than that. We know all about Tarzan movies, which show us the big white man with the monkey who swings on a rope and is supposed to be scaring the alligators and hundreds of savages in the jungle when he lets out those horrid screams. We all laugh at that. We see *Gunga Din* and see the British shooting everyone who looks like an Indian except for the poor chap playing the bugle, until he gets it in the end. And in the cowboy movies, we see the white man on the horse kill all the red Indians and the ones who stay alive only say U-N-N-NGH! But we didn't know that all the politics weren't straightened out by now. I certainly hope they let you speak."

"Most people at home don't know what's going on," said Claire. "That's because we don't have a lot of money or political power, but we are on the move. We have our ways, our different Indian religions, and our many cultures. Young Indians from all the nations are no longer ashamed or afraid of being Indians. Many of the boys are wearing their hair long again. And like the Kenyans, all of the tribes are finding a way to join together."

"It's an interesting phenomenon here in Kenya, being of Indian extraction," said Kulwat. "I used to suffer from racialism myself. I used to look down on black Africans. They would say to me, 'Why do you keep apart from us and not mix with us?' I would answer, 'Why do the Masai and Kikuyu fight among one another?' Now I see it is changing. Many people still may not like us. But I am Kenyan. And I now fight racialism every day. First in myself and then in others. Since the liberation, all of us do.

"This message is in the song "Harumbee" that we played at your concert, David. At the end of the song, when we sing '*Kila-rangi tuna penda,*' that means literally, 'every color, we love.' I would say those are quite unusual words for a national song. We are a minority in Kenya. Similar to you as a Jew in America, David. We speak Hindi among ourselves, but we also speak Swahili, and I was born here and our family will stay here. We love this country and the people so much; many of us have never left it, even to visit other parts of Africa. I have never been to India."

"Maybe this conference will show all the tribes of the World to love themselves and one another," said Claire.

"That's what Christianity is supposed to be about," said Kulwat.

"A lot of our prayers are about that too," I said. "*V'uh ah-hofta l'reyecha kamocha* in Hebrew means 'Love thy neighbor as thyself,' which first appeared in Leviticus, way before Jesus was reported to have said it in Matthew 51. And Psalm 133 from the song of ascents of King David. *Henay ma tov oomah hayeem shevet achim gamya chad.* Which means, 'Behold, how good and how pleasant it is for brethren to dwell together in harmony.' My father taught me all that as a little boy."

"Amen, brother," said Kulwat. "Now that we've been saved, let's go eat."

The next day, Kulwat, Claire and I were invited to the Asian Youth Conference Tea Ceremony, where Aoki, an illustrator and photographer from Japan, led the ceremony. After the first part was over, Aoki came to where we were standing and offered to show the three of us how to meditate.

I couldn't believe it. Aoki wasn't asking us to pay him, or have us sign up for a three-month course, or join a group. He just graciously offered to show us how to begin using the basic techniques.

In the 1960s, twenty years before the explosion of New Age shysters of the 80s misrepresenting ancient forms of spirituality, accompanied by Bible-thumping TV evangelists, I had already seen a growing army of the swinging 60s con men passing themselves off as holy men; we nicknamed them Gurus with Limos. They preyed on the built-in low self-esteem that many of us were brought up having, and like most psychiatrists, made sure that the first principle you learned about how to save yourself was where and when to make your payments promptly.

I was told in New York by many people from India and Japan that any spiritual hucksters calling themselves gurus who charged exorbitant fees while misrepresenting sacred traditions would be stoned to death for impersonating a holy man if they behaved this way at home.

Today, in 2007, the BurgerKingization of almost every religion is merchandised through the media. There are many attractive spokesmen and spokeswomen, preferably movie stars, all representing how to achieve bliss, as well as how to become prosperous and irresistible by paying a huge fee to achieve the instant enlightenment of your choice.

The 1960s and 1970s versions of bogus faith healers, phony psychics, and shyster shamans would be ignored today, and those second-rate hustlers of thirty years ago would have to resort to the Internet to try and nab some customers. In 1975, these kinds of misguided con men wouldn't have dared to appear at the conference in Nairobi. No one would have paid any attention to them. Everyone here was for real.

I was surprised and grateful to be shown by Aoki how to meditate and was given a mantra. His openness and generosity in showing Claire, Kulwat, and me these basic techniques out of the goodness of his heart reinforced the idea held by many at the conference that Jesus, Moses, Buddha, Mohammed, and other great spiritual leaders were not about making their followers dependent personalities, financial life-time slaves, or addicts. Or ever making religion a business.

"I can't believe you showed me this," I said to Aoki. "In New York, I was told I would have to pay more than a thousand dollars for a two-week course to start to learn how to meditate, and seven hundred and fifty dollars for my own mantra."

"Yes," said Aoki. "From what I hear from my friends who live in New York, these types of disreputable people are probably failed entrepreneurs without the skills or imagination to compete in the highly competitive world of legitimate business, so they turn to the easier route of fake spiritualism. We have our share of criminals and disreputable characters in Japan, but the merchandizing of Buddhism is off limits to them. Even though the tea ceremony you saw today is adapted from pre-Christian times to enhance our own form of Christianity, we would never charge money for any information we share.

"Jesus, to the best of my knowledge, had no admission charge when he delivered his Sermon on the Mount. Nor did Moses when he delivered the Ten Commandments. Buddha never indicated he wanted his teachings to become part of a corporate entity.

"Anyone who charges you money for enlightenment is an uninformed or confused person whose guidance is worthless. All who have learned from the masters always give it away. Just because the knowledge that the masters have shared with the world has always been given to us for free, this information is not worthless. It is priceless."

"*Arrigato mas,* Aoki," I said. "I'll remember that."

"So will I," said Mohammed Akbar, from Pakistan, who had joined us in our conversation. "I am a convert to Christianity from a predominantly Muslim country, but in Pakistan, many of us share each other's ways of expressing our devotion to a higher power."

The tea ceremony was concluded and Mohammed Akbar and Aoki led some chanting and prayers as a special thank you for all in attendance. I was asked to play my little Krishna flute to contribute something made up on the spot, as part of this ecumenical ceremony. At the end of the ceremony, we all went to the front of the room and were asked to sign a large book which Aoki had brought, and to write a word or two in our native language, with an expression of our own way of celebrating the higher power, regardless of our religion.

I wrote, "Thank you for sharing your knowledge with all of us. Shalom. David Amram, United States."

As I walked away from the table and greeted the room full of delegates from around the world who had all come to this ceremony to learn something new, a woman put her hand out, grabbed mine, and gave me a hug and a kiss on the cheek.

"*Habibi. Ana mobsud chollis* (My dear, I feel great)," she said to me, in the vernacular Arabic spoken in Lebanon. "This world is *fishmook* (crazy). We are the same people. I was brought up in Jerusalem. I speak Hebrew too. I now live in Lebanon, and I have converted to Christianity. We Arabs and Jews are the same people. It is politics that divide us. It is European, Russian, and American politicians that make us kill one another.

"I am closer to you, Amram, than almost anyone here. If you ever come to Lebanon, you can stay with my family, and I will make you the best hummis ba tahini you ever ate in your life, and we will have Beirut's best musicians come to the house, and have a music party to celebrate our meeting in Africa. There is a reason for all of us being here. This is 1975. The world is changing. We can change it for the better."

Later that day, Claire Acca and I went to the small one-room studio of the national TV station for their show, *Voice of Kenya.* I had been invited to play music from the United States as well as all the other countries I had been to in my life.

"Please come on the show with me, Claire," I said. "Since the conference is not giving you a chance to speak and deliver your message because the U.S. women's ad hoc group is freezing you out because you won't sign their petition, we can have an end run.

"You can be part of my band, playing the Lakota frame drum and Oneida rattle I brought with me, and then when I introduce you as an American musician with a lot to say, you can speak. At least a lot of people in Kenya will know why you are here, and whom you are speaking for. Hopefully the people running the conference will see and hear you, and if they do, I know they will want you to speak and share your views with everyone who is here at the conference, and throughout Kenya, regardless of whether the U.S. women's group wants you to or not."

"Okay," said Claire. "You know, traditional people don't have women play the drum, but I think the Great Creator will understand that this is a way to allow me to have the opportunity to speak."

After I had my introductory remarks completed, in my newly acquired Swahili, which got chuckles from the host and the cameraman, I began introducing Steele Buta and three members of the Fanki JuJu band, whom I had invited to come be on the show with me. I told the story of how we had all met. Then I introduced, as a special guest, our drummer and rattle player, Claire Acca.

"Can you tell us more about your friend?" asked the host.

"Yes. Claire Acca is a Native American of the Shoshone-Paiute people. Her people have been living in the American continent for fifty thousand years. My family has been there for only one hundred years. So she has more to say than I do about the history of our beautiful continent. I am grateful for the chance our wonderful country has given my family to pursue a better life. The Amrams and almost all my fellow immigrants of the past two hundred years live in a great country.

"Claire's people all made us welcome when we arrived, and now many young people are beginning to see what we can all do to correct centuries of injustice toward the Indian people. And learn about the many cultures and ways of worship of the hundreds of nations of Native Peoples, which are a gift to all of us in the United States and around the world. She can tell you what she knows, and what she and her contemporaries are doing."

"Welcome to Kenya, Claire Acca," said the host. "Please tell us all about yourself and why you are here at this World Council of Churches International Congress."

Claire spoke for about ten minutes and gave an incredible talk. It was a lesson for us, listening to her as she recounted the thousands of years of Indian history preserved through the oral tradition, the story of the first settlers arriving on boats, the slaves who were imported from Africa and how they struggled for their freedom, the waves of immigrants who came and moved west, and the ability of the Indian people to survive to this very day and the need for all people to live in that great circle of life together in harmony.

She was spellbinding, and in her soft-spoken way, could have given this as a presidential inaugural address to everyone in America and throughout the world. Always dignified and articulate, she was the best representative of the best that America has to offer the world. There was a moment of silence after she had finished.

"Claire Acca, you have told us all what it is to be a real American," said the host. "Now, David, I would like you and Steele and Claire and the three members of the Fanki Ju-Ju Band and your three other friends who dropped by the studio to all play a finale for our audience. I see you have invited Maria, our South African sister and vocalist with Steele Buta's band, and your friend Reverend Jimmy LaNanna, who I see is unpacking your French horn from its case. I didn't know you played the French horn, Jimmy.

"We would love it, David, if you could make up one of those songs as you have been doing every night at the Delegate's Lounge get-togethers. Our audience would find that most unusual. And please include any phrases in Swahili, Kikuyu, and Maa that you have learned while you have been here. Our TV audience will surely find this to be amusing."

We set up a rhythmic pattern with a few chords, and then Rev. Jimmy LaNanna let out some ear-splitting bleats and honks on my French horn, which sounded like elephants trumpeting a call to arms during one of their stampedes (since, as he told me later, this was the first time he had ever attempted to play a French horn). The cacophonous noisemaking served as a unique introduction to the song I made up, making it appear as if Rev. Jimmy's crazed noisemaking was supposed to have happened that way. When he paused to take a few breaths, while Steele Buta and the others tried to control their laughter, I began a song about hearing the distant calls of the elephants I had heard when on a tourist bus, going to visit the Masai with a group of safari camera hogs on their vacation photo op.

The twenty-five minute improvised lyrics were considerably less than a masterpiece, but they set up the improvised instrumental and vocal solos that followed, and provided some well-needed chuckles. While the story of the song was beyond silly, it ended up having a basic structure when I had the whole group sing along, spelling out *asante sana* (thank you very much) one letter at a time, using old-time jazz rhythms and old-fashioned talking blues harmonies. The host, cameraman, and the people in the studio room, which was now packed with curiosity seekers who had seen Claire on TV and wanted to come to see what was happening, all joined in, singing and clapping.

After we completed the song, there was thunderous applause as everyone congratulated each other for their fine performances.

"I think that will now become the theme song for our show," said the host.

The show concluded and the cameraman came up to me and gave me a power handshake.

"That was beautiful, what you just did, and what your friend Claire just said. Don't worry. You can say what you think here on our *Voice of Kenya Television*. We believe in free speech."

By the time the final concert began to close the ceremonies I had a whole variety show of people representing forty-three countries participating, with names of the pieces from the different countries, the names of all who were playing, and short notes about each piece of music we were doing, with the lyrics to "Kwahare" written phonetically for everyone to sing together as the last song.

All the delegates and Kenyans whom I had met knew that they would also take part as members of the audience, if not on stage. Many of the leaders of the conference had seen Claire on television, and she was now being interviewed by all the media attending the event and asked to participate as a speaker, as well as doing a signing during the worship service where she signed in pantomime as the Lord's Prayer was recited by a young woman from the West Indies.

For the musical portion of the program, our two-and-a-half hour show, with no intermission, seemed to go by in a few minutes and we ended with the Kenyan farewell song "Kwahare."

"Don't ever forget us, David," said Steele when we all went out to celebrate after the concert. "Remember the song says that we shall see each other again, if God be willing."

"I'll never forget you or the song," I said. "I'll do it in jazz, folk, and symphony concerts, and teach it to others. I'll always remember you and Kenya."

The next day I went to the airport and entered the plane packed with delegates who were going to London to change planes for further destinations. We all started singing "Kwahare" as the plane took off. As the plane rose over the mountains, I knew that down below the Masai and all the others still were there as they had always been, living their lives, guided by the roots that they honored, which went back to when men and women first lived on Earth. They were there before jet planes flew over them, and are still here. They weren't incarcerated in a museum. They were living proof of the durability of humankind and showed us all the ability of survival when you have a way of life you treasure and a history and language you maintain. And they were still here as our plane was flying six hundred miles an hour over their villages. I said a silent prayer of thanks for the blessing of being there. Once again, music was my passport to the world.

At the London airport, while waiting for my connecting flight to New York, I ran into Margaret Mead. I knew one of her relatives, Jeremy Steig, the innovative young flutist with whom I had played in Greenwich Village, and had promised him I would send his love when I saw her.

"Tell Jeremy he is sounding better than ever," she said. "I loved his last record. I wish he had been here to play with you. With both of you performing, the closing concert would still be going on. Did you see how all of what they call the Third World nations now are becoming so modernized? Electronic communication has changed everyone's lives around the world. I only hope that what the peer culture calls progress doesn't destroy the values of the world's oldest remaining cultures. Did you know that there is now a young fellow from Samoa who just entered Harvard Law School? I knew his grandmother in the 20s when I lived there. At that time, they all lived their tribal life. No radio, no TV.

"Now even the handful of remaining traditional people have access to the outside world. In another thirty years, it won't be the slightest bit unusual to see many Samoans going to Harvard and Yale. And coming back to their homes with all the knowledge to modernize their societies. That's how fast the world is moving. Tell Jeremy to send me his next recording, and to call me in New York. We'll teach him 'Kwahare' to play with his band. It's a delightful little song. I can even sing it myself now."

Finally I got on the plane to New York. There was no fog, and as the plane took off for the last leg of my journey, I sat back in my seat but couldn't sleep. I kept thinking about Kenya and trying to plan some way to get back and see the rest of Africa as well. I was only forty-five years old and knew there was still plenty of time. And I realized that I wanted to see the rest of the world too, like my uncle David, my father's brother after whom I was named and who had been a merchant seaman. I had always been fascinated by the stories of his travels that he told to my sister and me.

Still, I was looking forward to getting back to Greenwich Village to my old one-and-a-half room apartment at 461 6th Avenue, and then leaving and traveling around the United States. Now I had two new songs I could play and sing in Swahili, to share with others what so many Kenyans had shared with me. And I realized how lucky I was to have started playing jazz in 1943 in Washington, DC, after we moved there from our farm in Feasterville, Pennsylvania, a year earlier, and to be exposed to musical and spiritual concepts that were African in origin.

So many of the finest things in our lives as Americans come from these precious roots, and so few of us know about it. Seeing the enthusiasm of so many Kenyans and the pride they had in their young nation reminded me that two hundred years ago, we had freed ourselves as a colony, to search for a society where liberty, justice, equality, brotherhood, and sisterhood were a dream that could now be realized. And I saw from the people from around the world who were at the conference that many were on a march for freedom today. And I realized that this march is never over, and that we were all welcome to join in that march, by opening up our minds and hearts and working together toward establishing the values of caring and sharing among our own families, our neighbors, and all the people of the world.

As I got out a pile of blank laundry slips to write all this down on the way home, I said to my seat partner on the plane, who had attended the conference, "We may have a long way to go, but at least now, we know *which* way to go."

"Amen, David," said my seat partner. "I see you are filling out one hundred laundry slips, or writing another version of the Encyclopedia Britannica. I'm going to sleep. Write on, write on."

"Celestial snoozing to you," I said. "I'm going to jot down a few thoughts about the trip."

"Do that," he said. "Wake me up when we get to New York. I'm going to dream about the journey to Africa. Good night, David. See if you can get at least an hour's sleep."

I continued writing nonstop until the plane landed in New York, just as I was about to run out of empty laundry slips to write on. Miraculously, more than thirty years later, in spite of all the twists and turns of my life's never-ending journeys, I was able to find the old yellow laundry slips in an unmarked shoe box in my shed behind the house at our farm where I write my music.

Now, I can finally share what I experienced in Kenya with you and everyone else who reads this book.

For more than thirty years since my trip, I have performed "Kwahare" all over the world. It is amazing how a short piece of music can tell so much, paint a picture of a far-away place, and make listeners feel that they are in that very place when they hear that song or sing it. The music brings you there every time.

Now, with the Internet and World Wide Web, anyone with access to a computer can see pictures and films of the people I wrote about, from the Masai to the modern urban Kenyans. You can watch ancient ceremonial dancing, accompanied by the timeless drumming and singing, or see the interior of a state-of-the-art discotheque in downtown Nairobi, where tourists and natives dance together to the DJ playing Afro-Pop.

But anyone who is fortunate enough to have the chance to go there will never need to go online to remember what Kenya looks like or feels like. Once you've been there, Kenya, its people, its music, and its indefinable spirit stays in your memory and your heart forever.

Kwahare, Kenya.

♪

Chapter 3

Natural Ambassadors

On a sunny morning in the streets of Havana, Cuba, May 17, 1977, I clambered down the gangplank of the M.T.S. Daphne cruise ship, carrying all my instruments. Dizzy Gillespie was already on shore, the first one of us to leave the ship, surrounded by adoring fans and acting as a one-man State Department representative of the best that America has to offer the world.

"David, come on over."

I followed Dizzy Gillespie, as I always have since first spending time with him in 1951, and I walked past the Havana policemen to the crowd of Cubans waiting on the other side of the street by the dock, where our cruise ship had just landed.

The policemen saw my flutes sticking out of the bag I had slung over my shoulder and smiled as I walked past them to the crowd to join Dizzy, who had already started spreading his special cheer to the informal welcoming committee of passersby and curiosity seekers. Dizzy was in top form, doing his incredible antics, performing pantomimes of crazy characters, demonstrating his puffed-out cheeks to children and their parents, telling jokes and signing autographs, and he now signaled for me to play.

To set the stage for me to give an impromptu street performance, he imitated a whacked-out Pan playing his pipes with his fingers in the air while simultaneously singing the drum parts of the Cuban *guaguanco*.

I took three flutes out of the bag and started clapping a clave rhythm. Everybody on the street joined in immediately, and I began playing the flutes. Ray Mantilla, the renowned Latin percussionist from New York, joined me, playing the *cabasa*, and the crowd got even more enthusiastic as Dizzy cheered them on.

Earl Hines and members of his band came across from the dock and joined us, in what had now become a dockside party in downtown Havana. As I played, Dizzy gave me a nod of encouragement as he did in 1951 when we first met in my basement apartment on 16th Street in Washington, D.C. Just a glance of approval from Dizzy was all any musician ever needed, to know what to do and whether it was being done correctly. Now Dizzy and I were together again, as we had been so many times since those early days of the 50s, on a sunny morning in the streets of Havana.

It was also a special treat to be back in the company of Stan Getz and Earl "Fatha" Hines. All of us crossed paths through the years in different parts of the world, but now the four of us were all together in Cuba, all part of the first New York/Havana block party since 1961, and it seemed as if it were all planned that way.

Dizzy, Stan, and Earl didn't even need to play their instruments during those first moments when we mingled with the crowd. Their presence was like music. While Earl and Stan watched calmly, Dizzy, Ray Mantilla, and I didn't want to waste a minute. This was the first time in our lives we had ever been to Cuba and we knew we only had thirty-six hours in Havana before the M.T.S. Daphne, which had sailed from New Orleans, was due to depart for Nassau. As Ray and I played and the crowd cheered, sang, and danced on the sidewalk, all of us realized that while we had landed only thirty minutes ago, we were now at home in Havana.

After playing on the street for just a half an hour, the universal magic of music had taken us out of all the politics that had divided our two countries and brought us into the soul part of Cuba that neither capitalism nor communism could ever destroy, the part of Cuba that was eternal—the spirit and music of a unique culture that has influenced the music of the United States in many ways that most of us were not even aware of in 1977.

Afro-Cuban music comes from the ceremonies of many ancient West African religions, including the Yoruba tradition, which in its present form has different rhythms for each of the Saints' holidays. Many of these rhythms remain sacred to this day, only played for religious ceremonies. Certain secular rhythms derived from folkloric West African music were brought by the Cuban drummer Chano Pozo in 1947 to New York, where Chano and Dizzy collaborated in creating some historic compositions, presented in concerts and recordings that turned American music around forever, despite Chano's untimely death in 1949.

The concert in Havana that we were scheduled to play in thirty hours was dedicated to the memory of Chano Pozo. In spite of the embargo, the Carter administration had given permission for the first time since 1961 to allow American tourists, led by American musicians, to all sail together on a jazz cruise from New Orleans to Havana and give a goodwill concert, as a first step towards finding a rapprochement between the two countries. Ray and I, with our impromptu performance at dockside, were serving as the opening act for things to come, with Dizzy as ringmaster.

Just before the M.T.S. Daphne landed in Havana, one of the passengers on the ship asked Dizzy what finally coming to Cuba for the first time meant to him, after his years of championing Afro-Cuban music throughout the world.

"I'm here to collect!" he answered.

After playing the flute and French horn with Ray for what was now a whole block of onlookers, I began talking in Spanish and English to people in the crowd, and watched Dizzy continue his collecting.

What he was collecting was not the usual royalties most musicians receive over the years from sales of recordings. He was collecting the love from the throng of Cubans on the street that afternoon, just as he has from so many people from around the world who have heard Dizzy as a performer and innovator, or have known Dizzy as a person.

The crowd was having a great time, like a neighborhood block party in New York in the heady days following World War II, where the streets of big cities were full of energy and a place to commune.

Dizzy continued as our cheerleader and ambassador, dancing with women who were standing in the front of the crowd, picking up children and whirling them around, always in time to the music, as Ray and I continued playing, until we were instructed by an announcement in English and Spanish through a bullhorn to all gather to be escorted by the Cuba Tour officials for a trip through the city.

The well-dressed passengers of the M.T.S. Daphne began coming ashore and getting in their cruise buses to go on a guided tour of a housing project, the home of Ernest Hemingway, and for a swim on the beach. There was a special bus for the musicians, but Dizzy, Ray, and I felt that we wanted to go out on our own.

"The musicians must come right away, or their bus is leaving. This bus is leaving. I repeat, the musicians must come *now*..." We heard the voice, sounding a little more frantic, coming over the bullhorn as concerned-looking officials waved for Dizzy and all of us to board the bus.

"Gracias, y-all. Thank you but no thank you. Hasta luego," said Dizzy, waving to the tour directors as the crowd laughed. He resumed one of his pantomimes, imitating a passenger on a ship seeing a whale in the distance and diving overboard and then trying to swim back to the ship. Following screams of laughter and more hugging of children and showing them how to puff out their cheeks, he turned to me.

"This is so fine, David. Dig these people. Aren't these kids beautiful? Later with the bus ride, Man, we can go anywhere any time we want because we're natural ambassadors. We don't need some jive tour guide to tell us what's happening. It's already happening. We're here."

Dizzy mischievously gestured towards the old buildings with their peeling paint. Then, like Marc Anthony delivering his speech to the Romans in Shakespeare's *Julius Caesar*, he stretched out his arms as if he were embracing the crowd, and in a basso profundo stentorian tone, like a network news announcer, addressed the crowd and the nervous-looking Cuban tour guides and officials.

"Guess what, y'all. Guess *what*!"

The crowd quieted down and strained to see and hear as Dizzy paused and held up his right hand as if he were taking an oath of office.

"Señors and señoritas, I got an announcement of international significance for y'all.

"I'm seeking political asylum!"

Ray Mantilla translated what Dizzy said and the crowd and police cracked up laughing. The Cuban bureaucrats, the Cuba Tour director, and the drivers and guides looked even more confused and nervous.

"Maybe we should get on the musician's bus now; the Cuban officials look panicked," I said to Dizzy.

"We don't need to get on the bus," he said. "We can take a cab or walk. We're free people. Let's just hang out until we find some musicians from here. Nixon sent the ping-pong players to China to score points for us over there. President Carter allowed us to be the first to come here since Castro took over, to come and play our concert tomorrow night. We don't have to give out or take in any propaganda. Let's just hang out. We'll be cool wherever we go. We're natural ambassadors. Let the bus go without us. Play some more."

The Cuban officials looked perplexed as Dizzy continued to ignore their request to get on the Cuba Tour bus and instead resumed trading jokes with people in the crowd and dancing with more young ladies, as Ray and I played and got the audience to join us for more singing and clapping.

"*Que pasa, amigos?*" Dizzy shouted to everyone in the crowd, as he whirled his dance partner in a series of spontaneous arabesques, and a sea of smiles and shouts were returned, like a call and response in a church down south. Even the grim-looking police, as well as the government officials who were trying to round up the anarchistic musicians, were now all smiling. Dizzy's free spirit and *joi de vivre* was irresistible.

After another half hour of merriment, we stopped playing for a few minutes and Ray Mantilla began smoking a huge Cuban cigar and rapping in fluent Spanish to everybody, explaining that his family came from Puerto Rico and Peru. Earl Hines stood smoking his pipe like a perfect Buddha as some of his fans told him in English and Spanish how they had heard him in different parts of the world over the past forty-odd years. Stan Getz looked on quietly, as if he were seeing a movie, chuckling at each of Dizzy's new series of wild theatrics.

Ray and I explained to some of the people on the street that we were going to play a concert at the Teatro de Mella the next night with Earl, Dizzy, Stan, and my band, and that we hoped Cuban musicians would play with us. People in the crowd told us that they knew about the concert through a radio station in Miami, and that you needed an invitation to come.

Finally, the police dispersed the crowd and the other musicians finally got on the Cuba Tour bus, while Dizzy, Ray, and I began walking the streets of Havana, running into all kinds of people who guided us to where there was live music.

From the time we landed in Havana until we left, our musical pilgrimage turned out the way all of us had hoped it might. At various jam sessions, at people's homes, in bars, and at two informal get-togethers that the Cuban cultural minister had planned, Stan Getz, Dizzy, Ray Mantilla, and I continued to encounter and jam with extraordinary musicians and invite them to play with us at our concert the next night.

Some of them said they would try to come, some said they were not invited to attend the concert, and some were hesitant to commit themselves to a crazy band of North American enthusiasts. But as each hour went by, we found more closeness and less concern about who or what we were supposed to be. None of us mentioned anything to do with politics. We knew from all the musicians and other refugees who had escaped from Cuba that there was a government that was so strict that no one dared speak their mind for fear of being put in prison. In spite of this, we noticed when we walked the streets on our own that there were no prostitutes, pimps, junkies, young people who looked hungry or had bad teeth, or fear in any person's face as we wandered around Havana.

We found out that even though it was a dictatorship, free national health and dental care were part of the Cuban system, as well as Sunday clean-up day, where the whole town spent four hours straightening up each block. There was a spirit and pride that energized us all. Even if our politics were different, we all felt at home as visitors in Havana. I saw again, as I have seen my whole life, everywhere I have been in the world, that music transcends politics. As musicians, we were able to go beyond all that and just be fellow human beings.

A few hours later, Stan Getz, Earl Hines, Dizzy, Ray, and I, along with all their band mates, met at the Havana Libre for an evening of music at the outdoor gardens. We entered upstairs and were told to go down a flight of stairs where tables had been set up for us to meet with the Minister of Culture.

"Listen to these cats," said Dizzy, pointing to a room where some incredible music was floating our way. We followed the sounds and entered a dark hall full of Cubans of all ages, dancing up a storm. The band was playing a combination of disco, rock, jazz, salsa, and traditional Cuban music that stopped us in our tracks. We sat down and saw some of the musicians we had run into earlier in the afternoon playing in the band.

They invited us to join them, and a few minutes later we were all playing together. The group was called Irakere. Arturo Sandoval, the brilliant trumpeter, and Paquito D'Rivera, the gifted saxophonist and composer, ended up playing with me in my part of the concert the following night. As we jammed together at the Havana Libre, we were having a rehearsal for the concert to follow and didn't even know it.

Forty minutes later, we were told the Minister of Culture was still waiting for us, but since we were all upstairs jamming, it would be appreciated if we would come downstairs and join him. We went downstairs to the garden and met the minister, as well as Leo Brouwer, a symphonic composer, conductor and jazz artist, whose work I had heard of, but whom I had never met before.

Leo told me about traditional Afro-Cuban music and its influence on his symphonic works. Brouwer led a Latin-jazz group of his own, as well as writing symphonies. When I told him about my first job in New York, playing with Charlie Mingus in 1955, he told me about a piece for jazz group and symphony dedicated to Mingus he had composed, and told me that he would send me the orchestral score. I gave him a record of my own *Triple Concerto for Woodwind, Brass and Jazz Quintets* and he told me how I could find his other music to conduct someday in New York.

Leo Brouwer had a genuine love and respect for the old Cuban folk music as well as jazz and contemporary symphonic music, and we spent an hour trading rhythms. I wrote down the Arabic, Armenian, Yemenite, American Indian, and Appalachian clogging rhythms I had learned in recent years, and he showed me some of the complicated Afro-Cuban rhythms.

Different groups played through the night, and Elio Revé and his Charanga band blew us all away with some old-time music that made us all feel we were dancing together.

We returned to the dock and boarded the Daphne at dawn for three or four hours of sleep, and when we dragged ourselves out of our bunks on the ship, took a shower, and gulped down some strong black Cuban coffee, we were ready for the next jam session at a nearby hotel that was reserved for U.S. musicians and their guests. Fortunately, Richard Severo, the distinguished journalist from the *New York Times*, came along and wrote a perceptive article about what, for us, was the jam session of all jam sessions. Also, Leonard Feather, composer, pianist, and the dean of jazz journalism, Ira Sabin, editor of *Radio Free Jazz*, and *Downbeat*'s roving reporter and conga player, Arnold Smith, were present, and documented it.

They all agreed that Irakere, who all showed up to play with us at the jam session, was a remarkable group of musicians. They played with such intensity and fire that at one point Dizzy Gillespie, after Arturo Sandoval finished a sweep of triple-tongued notes ending on a crystal-clear double high C, whipped a white tablecloth from an empty table and waved it as a flag of surrender for all of us. Still, in spite of the incredible energy level and fierce concentration by the musicians of Irakaere, the music that filled the room was joined with laughter and cheers. Dizzy made sure of that, reminding us all that even the most serious art is always about bringing joy to the world.

Stan, Dizzy, Earle, and members of our bands were invited up to play, and we all had to outdo ourselves to keep up the energy level. Mickey Roker, Dizzy's great drummer, laid down some rhythms to introduce us before we joined in that had the Cubans cheering before we started playing.

It was now six hours until concert time, and we were ready. Rather than being exhausted, we were all energized by one another.

At nine o'clock that night, Earl Hines opened the show, and backstage you could feel the warmth coming from the audience. The house was packed and thousands of people waited outside. A Cuban official came over to me and spoke in English.

"Amram, the Assistant Minister of Culture has a message for you. He needs to speak to you immediately, before you and your quartet do your solo portion of the concert. Please meet him in the dressing room."

I ran back to the dressing room and saw Paquito D'Rivera, Arturo Sandoval, the four drummers from Los Papines, and Oscar Valdes, the nephew of Vincentico Valdes, a popular singer of Latin music in New York.

"We have musicians to play with you and your quartet, Amram," he said quietly. How many of them would you like to use?"

I looked around the room. My piece, which I had written for the concert while on the boat ride from New Orleans to Cuba, was called "In Memory of Chano Pozo." I had written a part in the middle where I hoped that Cuban musicians might possibly be able to join in, and after their solos, all continue to take the melody out, followed by a coda where we would have a thunderous final section, honoring the old and the new in Afro-Cuban jazz. Now, I saw that this could happen.

"*Es possible a tocar con todos?*" (Is it possible to play with everybody?) I asked, gesturing to all the musicians in the room.

There was a thirty-second silence.

"Oh, Lord," I thought to myself, "over-enthusiasm has blown it."

All the musicians remained quiet as the sounds of Earl Hines playing a soft ballad onstage floated all around us.

The Assistant Minister of Culture stared at the floor and then his face brightened. *"Este gringo es totalmente loco* (This American is completely crazy). Sure, why not?" he said, and everyone's faces brightened. He waved to all the musicians he had assembled in the dressing room to join me for a strategy session, like football players having a final conference before a game.

For the next few minutes, I sang everybody their parts, arranged a group of signals, wrote out some chords and instructions, and trusted in the power of music itself to pull us through.

The female announcer introduced us and said that as a surprise we were having eight guests play with my group, the first time American and Cuban musicians had played together in a public concert since 1961.

Everyone in Havana knew the four members of Los Papines, as well as Oscar Valdes Jr., Arturo Sandoval, and Paquito D'Rivera, and there was an intense silence and air of expectation as we entered the stage that always brings out the best in musicians.

I announced in Spanish that we were playing a new composition, *En Memoria de Chano Pozo,* which I had written in memory of Chano Pozo, and started out playing the piano alone. After the somber introduction, our quartet of American musicians joined in, and just before the section where the Cubans were to make their first entrance, I looked over at Los Papines' lead drummer Papine.

Like the master drummers I played with in Kenya and other great musicians around the world, it was like we were reading each other's minds and knew what we were going to do before it happened. I could feel the whole hall fill up with a spirit as Papine stared at me.

Somehow, while still playing the music, I could feel some indefinable force leading me into playing something I had never played before, as if Papine were guiding me into a new world, and someone else was now using me to play, as if I myself had now become an instrument. I could see and hear what I was going to play before I played it.

I had a similar experience twenty-five years later when I played at Victor Venegas' house for his wife Ida's twelfth anniversary of her initiation into the Yoruba religion. It was the same feeling of surrendering yourself to a higher power that I experienced when I played with Los Papines that night in Havana and felt that strong spiritual guidance emanating from Papine, the leader of the group of four brothers.

This is what happened years later when I was invited by Victor and his wife Ida for the first time in my life to participate in a ceremony, I was signaled to play a rhythm on an African beaded gourd called a *shekere* while the message of thanks to the spirits was sung in a prayer to placate Elegua, the *Orisha* (spirit presence) who guards the crossroads of life, and can send you down the wrong one if you are disrespectful. He can put a kind of psychic roadblock in your way without you knowing it. As I played the part assigned to me to accompany the drums and bell patterns and the singing of the prayer at Victor's apartment, surrounded by offerings at the homemade altar, I could feel the presence of Elegua's spirit in that room. Everyone else could too. I never would have played the *shekere* or been to a ceremony of this nature that night if I hadn't been invited, and I told Victor that I was reminded of the moment in Havana in 1977 when Papine seemed to summon up these same spirits at our concert.

"It's deep stuff," said Victor. "Los Papines were brought up with that. It's sacred. Ida felt you should be here. We don't have to talk about it. You felt it. She knew you would."

I never would have even written what I am writing now without speaking first to Victor's wife Ida and her brother to see if what I had written is permissible to write about. She told me it was.

In the concert in Havana, when I realized that I was now entering into a place I had never been to before, Papine's right hand went up, and when I nodded to cue the entrance of the eight Cuban musicians, it felt like we were all being led by an invisible conductor. Papine signaled his three brothers, the band, and the audience, using only his eyes, and as his hand came down on his congas, Arturo Sandoval, Paquito, and Oscar Valdes came roaring in together like a well-rehearsed symphony.

The whole audience burst into cheers, and the entrance of the eight musicians joining my quartet was so exciting I almost fell off my piano stool. Everyone took solos and we all ended the piece as if we'd been playing together for years. Fortunately, someone on the ship recorded it, and the subsequent album *Havana/New York* includes this first musical interchange with Cubans and Americans collaborating in harmony, exactly as it happened during the debut of the piece on this historic night. That performance became the basis for a formal symphonic composition, *En Memoria de Chano Pozo* which is now played all over the world.

In the second half of the concert, Stan Getz played a scintillating set and Dizzy came out with his band for the grand finale.

After playing some of the compositions that he wrote with Chano Pozo in the forties, which combined Afro-Cuban music with jazz, Dizzy called all of us onstage and it became a jazz party, or what the Cubans call a *descarga*. At one point while I was playing a French horn solo, I looked over and saw Dizzy dancing onstage with Stan Getz. We would have played all night, but we were receiving frantic signals that the Daphne had to pull out of port and it was time to pack up.

Dizzy bid everyone farewell over the microphone, like a great sports announcer, calling us back onstage for a final curtain call.

"Let's bring out one more time—Stan Getz ... Earl Hines ... David Amram ... Los Papines ... Paquito and Arturo ... Charlie Parker ... and ... Mao Tse-Tung!"

It took us another hour to say our goodbyes to everyone backstage and rush back to the ship.

"You guys did a great job," said a doctor from California as we boarded the Daphne. "You did the United States proud."

All of us felt proud to be representing our country with the music that refuses to die and that transcends all boundaries, the music that we spend our lives learning and sharing. The down-to-earth, mysterious, unpredictable, ever-changing world of jazz and all the music of the world that the art of jazz embraces, like the one-time-only music we created in Cuba that night.

Dizzy and I went to his room and started talking. I told him about the five countries in Central America I was going to visit the following October for the State Department, to conduct symphony concerts and have workshops in jazz and folk music.

"I hope I can get the same spirit in Central America as we did tonight in Havana, Dizzy."

Dizzy looked over the top of his horn rimmed glasses with his all-knowing glance. "No problem. Just let the music tell you what to do. Like I said yesterday, you know tonight's concert had to be the way it was going to be. It had to be warm and full of love. That's why God put us here. He put us here to play music for everybody and with everybody. Just remember why you're put here and you'll do fine."

Three months later, in the summer of 1977, I conducted a free outdoor concert with the Brooklyn Philharmonic in a park in Brooklyn. The program included the first version of what became my 1978 completed orchestral work, *En Memoria de Chano Pozo,* based on what I had played in May of 1977 in Havana. It was just a sketch for the orchestra of what became a thoroughly composed piece.

A young man approached me just before the concert began and said, "Mr. Amram, I'm Luis Chaluisan. I saw you on TV with Dizzy, Stan Getz, Earl Hines, and all the great Cubans and want to know if I can dance with my friend Rosie during the middle of your Chano Pozo piece, when the "Montuno" section occurs.

"That would be great," I said. "When you hear the *son clave* change to a rhumba *clave,* then you can both start. Ray Mantilla and Nicky Morrero are sitting in with the percussion section of the orchestra, so they'll help to keep it all together."

When the orchestra reached the middle part of the piece, where the rhumba *clave* is used, Luis and Rosie came from the side of the stage and began to dance on the grass, in between the orchestra and the audience. In the still summer nighttime air, it all seemed so natural that the park was transformed into an outdoor flashback of the great days of the Paladium dance hall of the 1940s, when Latin music exploded and was heard around the world and Tito Puente was discovered, at the same time that Dizzy Gillespie and Charlie Parker collaborated with Machito and Mario Bauza in what became known as Afro-Cuban jazz.

The audience in the park went wild, and when we played Mozart later on in the concert, you could hear a pin drop. The inclusion of traditional Afro-Cuban musical roots with dancers in a symphonic setting seemed to clear the air for the musicians as well as for the audience, and the Mozart symphony sounded so pure and clear that you could imagine the whole audience was now back in Mozart's time, sipping white wine and wearing white powdered wigs as the boy genius Mozart sat in the audience enjoying his own exquisite work. The new sounds inspired by Cuban music made the old music inspired by European roots sound fresher.

After the concert, Luis and his partner Rosie came back to see all the musicians. Ray Mantilla, who had played this piece with me in Cuba two months ago when it was just a sketch, came with Nicky Morrero, the brilliant timbale soloist, to congratulate Luis and Rosie for their dancing,

"You guys tore it up," said Nicky.

"We got it all together tonight," said Ray Mantilla. "Mozart, the rhumba and the *gauguanco.* They can't shut us out no more. *La musica Latina* just invaded the symphony and look how the people dug it. It's here to stay."

"*Fabuloso,* Luis," I said. "*Que chevere. Gracias para tu trabajo.*"

"*No hay problema*," said Luis. "The boys in the band were smokin'! I never heard a symphony sound like that. Those cats sounded like real *salzeros*. When's the next gig? I'm ready to dance some more."

"How did you know about the concert?" I asked.

"I'm the dance critic for *Latin New York Magazine*," he said. "As soon as I got a press release about the concert, I said to Rosie, no way I'm missing this, I told her, whatever, we gotta make this one."

"Well, Luis," I said. "If there's a critic that dances like you, there's still hope for New York to remain *numero uno* in the world of the performing arts. We've got to do more stuff together."

Over the years, we did, and in June of 2005, we went to Germany together to perform at the Bonn International Theater Festival.

Knowing of the collaborations of Luis and myself over the twenty-eight years since our first encounter in Brooklyn in 1977, a journalist from WEPA interviewed me after I returned from Germany in a wide-ranging series of questions about my involvement in Latin music, as well as my specific work with musicians from the Afro-Cuban tradition, and also questions about music in general.

By this time, in the summer of 2005, the doors of many of the treasures of Latin music were opened up to the world. Paquito D'Rivera and Arturo Sandoval had moved to the United States and become worldwide musical icons, Latin music of many genres was being taught in schools, the Lincoln Center had its own Afro-Cuban jazz orchestra in residence, and I had met hundreds of musicians and people from all walks of life who had left Cuba and moved to the United States, including my own distant cousins, Jose Amram and his extended family. When Jose was driving by our farm in Putnam Valley, N.Y., while on his vacation from Florida, and saw the name Amram on the mailbox, he came by our farm house to buy some eggs and ask if I were related to the David Amram who was adapting traditional Cuban musical roots to his own compositions for symphony orchestras and other musical ensembles.

I told him that was me and he said we were distant cousins.

He told me that even for those like himself who left the country for a better life in the United States, the timeless music of Cuba, like all great music, transcended politics and remained a precious gift to the world, touching the hearts of everyone who got the chance to hear it.

Here is the interview with WEPA from June 17, 2005.

1. What genre do you classify your work?

Music from the heart, built to last. In all the idioms I work in, this is the common thread.

2. What is the main premise of your work?

I always try to tell a story and paint a picture, either in sound and/or in words or both together. I believe, whether written down for a symphony or jamming at a *descarga*, that there should always be a beginning, a middle, and an end, and it should always feel spontaneous.

I always try to achieve this feeling, whether I am backing up the words of Jack Kerouac, accompanying Willie Nelson at Farm Aid, having my music played by the New York Philharmonic, conducting one of my operas or symphonies, or playing with inmates at Attica prison.

I always try to do what is appropriate when I am performing or conducting. I follow the Zen proverb "less is more." When I played with the National Symphony in 1951 in Washington, D.C., my French horn teacher Abe Kniaz said, "When in doubt, leave it out."

The same principle applies to the way I write my compositions. I try not to waste a note and make every note count.

3. How did you start off?

When I was six years old, my father bought me a bugle, and I started blasting away. I started playing trumpet a year later, and then I started pounding away on the piano.

My uncle David, after whom I was named, was a merchant seaman. He got me interested in traveling the world and emphasized the importance of always paying attention to everything and everybody and trying to learn the languages, music, and history of every place you are in life. As a kid growing up in rural Pennsylvania during the Depression, I was taken by my uncle David to hear the Philadelphia Orchestra and Duke Ellington's band in Philadelphia. He showed me that both jazz and European classical were great kinds of music and that both were worth a lifetime of study. ·

4. Who inspired you musically?

Mozart, Duke Ellington, Bela Bartók, Los Papines, cantor Yossele Rosenblatt, Mario Bauza, Charlie Parker, Um Kalsum, Ali Akbar Kahn, Candido, Thelonious Monk, Hector Berlioz, George Gershwin, Dizzy Gillespie, Dimitri Mitropoulos, Tito Puente, Bach, Celia Cruz, Enrico Caruso, Aragon, Bix Beiderbecke, Gustav Mahler, Johannes Brahms, Willie Nelson, James Galway, and Paquito D'Rivera, and there are thousands more.

5. Do you think Latinos/women have to work harder than any other race in the entertainment industry?

I think all of us who come from a cultural perspective and celebrate our ancestral history and roots have to work harder. The primary prejudices in society are way beyond the various forms of racism and sexism that we all encounter in society in general every day, and in the entertainment industry as well.

The biggest struggle against prejudice is finding a way to deal with the people who make decisions who are themselves so far removed from their *own* culture, and so far removed from the reality of what 99 percent of the world is dealing with every day to survive. As a result of being ignorant, most of those in charge in all the areas of the entertainment industry are frightened by anything that is pure and soulful and truthful. And they usually have lost the ability to hang out with other people and pay attention, which is the only way to find out what is happening. And most people who think that English is the only language worth learning are petrified by anyone who speaks another language.

So rather than rejoicing in the gifts that are brought to the United States from all the countries of South America, most entertainment industry honchos don't see that Latinos represent a vast array of cultural treasures that should be utilized and promoted. Instead of celebrating this, and finding a constructive way to use all this talent and sense of tradition, they find this strong identity threatening because they don't have a sense of love of their *own* roots. And therefore they assume that the entire population of the United States must feel the same way.

A de-culturated person is always frightened and therefore hostile to *any* person of culture. Because those in charge are usually unaware of, or afraid of, what is pure and soulful and truthful, they feel a necessity to revert to stereotyping, therefore limiting the potential use of the talents of *everybody*.

In the case of Spanish-speaking people, it seems that those in charge always want to either ignore or put Latinos in degrading roles, in the same way that Hollywood has traditionally stereotyped all men of Italian descent as being gangsters, African-Americans as being mostly pimps, whores or buffoons, Caucasian southerners as toothless mental defectives, cowboys as homicidal maniacs, Indians as savages, and Asian Americans as unintelligible clowns or kung fu experts. And women, regardless of their culture, have traditionally been used primarily as sex symbols who are generally considered to be washed-up over-the-hill senior citizens by the time they reach thirty.

While this is slowly changing thanks to independent film makers, the challenge for Latinos to rise above the stereotypes of the Juan Valdez coffee commercial or Carmen Miranda with her fruit basket hat is further compounded by zero understanding and respect for the gift of ALL the Latin American cultures that continue to enrich the United States and the rest of the world every day, even while these contributions are not yet fully acknowledged by the establishment.

People love Latin music, whenever they can hear it, and when I was in Germany in the summer of 2004, creating the music for Luis Chaluisan and Maria Hernandez's show, the Bonn International Theater Festival, our program was the hit of the Festival. The Germans appreciated every second of Luis's life stories about the Nuyorican experience. No Germans asked for a refund because Luis was also speaking in Spanish as well as English. They loved it! They were captivated by Maria Hernandez, just as I know that mainstream America would also be.

Because our peer culture is unwittingly victimized by a colonialized attitude that anyone who speaks English is genetically incapable of learning another language (even if their own families didn't speak English before coming here), Latinos are automatically stigmatized as being "ethnic" (a sociological code word used to describe everyone in our population who has a language and culture that they treasure and proudly maintain) and are therefore considered to be "foreign," which even includes Puerto Ricans, even though they serve in the U.S. Army, vote, and pay taxes.

But this is all changing, and the decades of struggle of both male and female Latino artists has enabled a new generation to be able to create new work that will overcome all obstacles and be a shining light for everyone in America and the world to cherish and appreciate, as the globalized entertainment industry continues to gradually lose control and finally totters off into the sunset, eclipsed by the magnificent energy of Latino and other cultures from around the world which have been deemed as having no mass appeal.

The Internet and the World Wide Web make it possible for new voices to be heard and new pictures and faces to be seen. And this is just beginning to happen. And nothing can stop it, so we must all be brave and continue to pursue excellence.

6. How do you want other Latinos/women to perceive your music?

I just hope they can find the time and a place to listen to it. If they do, I am sure that they will know what is happening. I hope it makes them feel good, makes them want to dance, sing, and be loving to their loved ones, and most of all inspires them to create their *own* works of art. I believe our job as artists is to inspire one another.

In 1492, my Sephardic ancestors were exiled from Spain and Portugal, but I still carry memories of that in my heart, as my own family brought me up to think about it, and my times spent in Latin America as well as Spain and Portugal have influenced my music.

I always felt at home in Spain, Portugal, and Latin America. Ever since I moved to New York in 1955 I have played with and for Latinos and Latinas for the last half century. I feel more at home today with the treasures of Latino music, dance, theater, and literature than I ever have. I may look like a *gringo loco* but I don't sound or act that way. I am perceived through my music and my actions toward others by the way I am, and that makes me feel very fortunate, because as a result, I don't ever need to say all this to an audience or group of people of any culture.

That's because it is naturally in my music and my genes.

7. In your opinion, what is setting music back? If nothing, what is bringing music forward?

True music, i.e., music created with purity of intent and an exquisite choice of notes, will always move things forward. And in the case of Latin music, celebration and knowledge of roots, from the *bomba* and the *plena,* to the *guaguanco,* the *rhumba,* and the *samba,* can now all be studied and seen, along with the dances, on the Internet. Japanese, Chinese, Middle Eastern, and traditional Irish music, jazz, blues, cajun and bluegrass music ... all of these, which are also a priceless gift to the world, can now be accessed through the Web, whether or not the music industry can deal with it or not. Then you can turn off your computer and go out into the world and know what to look for.

There is an army of young musicians of every genre whom I hear and play with all around the world, so music is way ahead of the *business* of music.

8. Would you rather be in front of a camera acting or behind the scenes composing music for a film?

When I am being filmed for TV and movies, I am performing music, speaking about it, and conducting and narrating. It is always a joy, but I am being myself, not acting.

My only acting role was in the 1959 documentary silent film, with Jack Kerouac narrating, *Pull My Daisy,* for which I also composed the music and the title song forty-six years ago. In the film, I was Mezz McGillicuddy, the deranged French hornist. I wasn't acting. I was just being me. I have too much respect for actors to ever call myself one.

I loved composing and conducting the scores for the films *The Manchurian Candidate* (1962), *Splendor in the Grass* (1960), *The Arrangement* (1969), and *The Young Savages* (1960), shot in NYC. I used Latin music, which was unheard of then in HollyWeird for feature films forty-five years ago.

I wrote, orchestrated, and conducted every note of all the scores, as well as playing with the jazz and Latin musicians I hired, and I didn't use any ghostwriters, orchestrators, or synthesizers.

Today, this would be next to impossible to do for most major Hollywood feature films. When I composed the scores for *Splendor in the Grass, The Manchurian Candidate, The Young Savages,* and *The Arrangment,* I was left alone to write the very best music I could write. Today they usually have a music supervisor and the composer is used like a sheet rock installer, putting musical plaster and putty in the cracks. And most composers hire ghost writers to grind out most of the score.

This is changing, however. Today, independent and documentary filmmakers are the new outlets for film music of real value and the thousands of young filmmakers will straighten things out. Film music is an art, when it is created artistically.

9. Do you have any big events coming up?

Charles Mingus told me in 1955, when I played in his band—my first gig in NYC—that "every night with me is Carnegie Hall." I always remembered this, so to me everything and everywhere is a big event.

My seventy-fifth birthday tribute, November 19 at The Tarrytown Music Hall with an all-star group of jazz, classical, and Latin musicians, as well as actors and authors I have worked with all my life, is going to be incredible, and will be filmed.

I am also playing the Guinness Jazz Festival in Cork, Ireland, in October and conducting, narrating, and playing in a symphony concert in Patchogue, Long Island, August 6 and 7, celebrating the Beatles' use of music that can make people appreciate the symphony, as well as their use of music from India and the influence of poetry inspired by the writings of Kerouac, with whom I collaborated in NYC's first-ever jazz-poetry readings in 1957.

I am also composing *Symphonic Variations on a Song by Woody Guthrie,* commissioned by the Guthrie Foundation at the request of Woody's daughter Nora. Each variation will include a different region of America that Woody lived in during his years of travel. One of the variations will include his years of living in Brooklyn and will be constructed as a musical description of Latino, Chinese, African-American, Jewish, Greek, and Irish music that Woody heard and loved and wrote about, as he went on the subway to Coney Island from Manhattan and heard all the different languages and music in all the neighborhoods as people got on and off the train. I met Woody on the Lower East Side in 1956, so it will be a special thrill to hear this symphonic piece played when it is finished.

10. Have you accomplished your dreams? If not yet, where else do your dreams take you—a few years from now?

I always tell my three kids that I am just getting started and will never finish all I have to do. My new book, *Upbeat: Nine Lives of a Musical Cat,* is almost completed, as the third in a trilogy, joining my other two books already in print, *Vibrations* and *Offbeat: Collaborating with Kerouac.* I will finish the third book this year. I am also working on a piece for chorus, narrator, and orchestra, *Missa Manhattan,* with a text by author Frank McCourt, which uses the traditional text of the Mass with a history of immigration to New York, starting with the Indian people who were here, and ending with today's new Americans from all over the world who come here for a better life.

Within a few years, I hope to see the day come when all the things I have touched upon in this interview, all the sincere forms of music, the beauty of languages, the treasures of Latino culture, the genius of jazz and its creators, the great works of the European masters, the brilliance of Asian and Middle Eastern art and philosophy, the spirituality of Native American music and history can all be included in our classrooms, on the radio, and seen on TV and in our films, so that young people can have what they deserve to have, which simply is the chance to know about all these great things which can enrich your life.

All of us who have kids want to see that they, as well as everyone else's kids, have access to what is life affirming, soulful, joyous, healthful, artistic, sophisticated, down home, sincere, and for real.

We are finally concerned in our society about pollution and cleaning up the environment so we don't all choke to death or die of poison from the food we eat or the water we drink. Now we must become concerned about the pollution of our cultural environment, and the poisonous garbage that we jam down the throats of our children. Our artists, poets, playwrights, composers, dancers, actors, singers, filmmakers, public school teachers, athletes, and just about everybody can all find a way to do a little something to upgrade the environment and show that heritage, family, and respect for one another are the most important things in life. We must teach our kids that throughout our lives, just because the gifts of heritage, family, and respect for one another are free and have no price tag, that doesn't mean that they are worthless. They are *priceless!*

11. What is one mistake that you do not want anyone to recreate?

In the case of Latin music, never to play out of *clave*. Fortunately, I have played with enough masters to either be *en clave,* or to be capable of knowing how to humbly ask someone who knows more which form of *clave* is correct for the specific piece being played. And when in doubt to *leave it out.*

12. Do you have any words of inspiration for artists that want to follow in your footsteps?

In the arts, or whatever you want to devote your life to, when people tell you that you can't do that, you are not qualified, you are not the type of person for that and that you should grow up and give up trying, respect their opinion and understand that while they may have already been hurt by their own disappointments in life, and that they may be brilliant people and even love you or be related to you, have respect for what they are saying to you, but ... *hang out with somebody else!*

The cast of *Pull My Daisy,* 1959, (left to right) Gregory Corso (back to camera), artist Larry Rivers, author Jack Kerouac, David Amram, and poet Allen Ginsberg. Courtesy of David Amram.

Jack Kerouac, artist Dody Muller, and David Amram at a party in New York City, 1959. Photo by John Cohen. Used with permission.

David Amram with Leonard Bernstein. Photo by Henry Grossman. Used with permission.

Playing at the grand finale of the historic first U.S.-Cuban musical exchange in Havana, May 18, 1977, at the Teatro de Mella are (foreground, left to right) Paquito D'Rivera, Stan Getz, Dizzy Gillespie, Arturo Sandoval (on trumpet, face obscured), and David Amram on French horn. A member of Los Patines is in the background. Courtesy of David Amram.

David Amram (in white, top right) with Claire Acca (bottom left) and the Reverend Jimmy LaNanna (bottom with guitar) and members of the Fanki Ju-Ju Band in 1978 at the World Council of Churches Congress in Nairobi, Kenya. Courtesy of David Amram.

Entertainers who performed in the 1978 concert following "The Longest Walk," a six-month march across the United States in support of improved human rights for American Indians. (Left to right) Mohammed Ali, Buffy St. Marie, Floyd Red Crow Westerman, boxing promoter Harold Smith, Stevie Wonder, Marlon Brando, Max Gail, Dick Gregory, unidentified man, Richie Haven, and David Amram.

Bob Dylan with David Amram in 1980 when Dylan was inducted into the Songwriter's Hall of Fame. Courtesy of David Amram.

David Amram, Percy Heath, and Dizzy Gillespie at the Thelonius Monk Tribute in Constitution Hall, Washington, DC, 1986, hosted by Bill Cosby. Photo by Michael Wilderman. Used with permission.

David Amram playing "Pull My Daisy" on the carillon in Goes, The Netherlands, 1997. Photo by Christopher Felver. Used with permission.

David Amram playing with Willie Nelson and members of the Dennis Alley Indian dancers at a Farm Aid concert. Photo © Ebet Roberts. Used with permission.

Amram's *Trail of Beauty* was performed by the Philadelphia Orchestra on tour at the Kennedy Center, Washington, DC, March 7, 1977.

Author Carolyn Cassady, David Amram, and George Whitman, founder of the Shakespeare and Company Bookstore in Paris, celebrating the 50th anniversary of the store in 2003. Courtesy of David Amram.

David Amram and Ray Barretto, New York City, 2004. Photo by Christopher Felver. Used with permission.

David Amram, Floyd Red Crow Westerman, and Dennis Banks at the Red Onion, North Beach, San Francisco, celebrating Amram's 75th birthday. Courtesy of David Amram.

David Amram's daughters, Adira Amram (left) and Alana Amram (right, with guitar), perform with the Amram Family Band at the Woody Guthrie Folk Festival, July 2006, Okemah, Oklahoma. Photo by Jim Dirden. Used with permission.

Adam Amram, drummer, plays with his father, David Amram, during the "Lowell Celebrates Kerouac" 20th Anniversary Concert in Kerouac's hometown, Lowell, Massachusetts, July 7, 2007. Courtesy of David Amram.

♪

Chapter 4

Kokopelli: Walking the Native American Trail of Beauty

On a sunny day in 1983, I was playing a free street concert in downtown Brooklyn with my jazz and world music quartet at a street fair. Our special guest was Floyd Red Crow Westerman, singing his songs, speaking and doing some traditional music with me as his backup player.

In 1983, when this daytime out-of-doors Brooklyn street concert took place, it was six years after Floyd's first-ever appearance on national television, in a documentary about my music for PBS *Soundstage,* an hour show that won an award as the best original musical documentary film of the year. In addition to Floyd, the show included guests Dizzy Gillespie; Steve Goodman; Pepper Adams; Latin greats Nicky Marrero, Alfredo de la Fé, and David Perez; Mantwilla Nyomo from Zaire; vocalist Bonnie Koloc; mandolinist Jethro Burns; and members of the Chicago Symphony performing the last movement of my *Triple Concerto for Woodwind, Brass, and Jazz Quintet and Orchestra.*

There was a special moment in the show when Floyd and I played "Mastinchele Wachipi Olowan," a Rabbit Dance melody used as a social song and often played at round dances by the Lakota people. Many viewers wrote their local PBS stations for months afterward, commenting on how incredible he was. Floyd was such a galvanizing presence that anybody who saw him or met him always remembered him the rest of their lives. When he sang and played his powerful songs from his now classic *Custer Died for Your Sins* album, people were spellbound. Floyd never had to put on an act. He was himself at all times, and that was all he needed to be. When he became an actor, it was a natural extension of who he was.

Now, during this afternoon concert in Brooklyn with Floyd, I was representing the Brooklyn Philharmonic as their director and conductor of free school time, family, and parks concerts, a position I held for twenty-nine years, from 1970 until their funds ran out in 1999. Since the street fair couldn't afford to hire the symphony, I was there as their goodwill ambassador with my quartet and Floyd. Even the most conservative classical music lovers, who had wandered by in hopes of hearing Handel's *Water Music* or Bartók's *Rumanian Dances,* two of the most requested pieces for our outdoor symphony concerts, were not shocked by my change of roles from being the orchestra's conductor/composer/narrator to being a multi-instrumentalist street performer.

Today in 2007, many orchestras are reassessing how to reach new audiences, and many of the young conductors, soloists, and orchestra members are finding innovative ways to reach out to their community at large. And in addition to programming quality music of serious composers who work in many cultural genres not included in the tunnel vision of the Austro-Hungarian Empire Achtung approach of many orchestra managements, I was allowed to do anything that would help create awareness of the outstanding musicians of the Brooklyn Philharmonic and the great varieties of music that they themselves were devoted to.

By appearing at events like the street fair as a musician who played jazz, Latin, Native American, and world music, my role as a conductor and composer was never menacing or condescending to the large audiences we reached.

As a result of many joyous grassroots concerts of this nature, many people came to hear the orchestra play the treasures of European classical music that we performed in more traditional concerts. They felt, after seeing me at street concerts, parks concerts, and in public schools, that they would enjoy coming to the Brooklyn Academy of Music or anyplace else I conducted, feeling that they were *welcome,* and knowing that they would have a good time once they were there.

In 1983, I was fortunate enough to be able to do what was then still a rarity at best, and I was the only conductor associated with any orchestra in New York encouraged to be doing cross-cultural programs where I could broaden my role to being someone who was presenting all genres of music built to last, with each piece of music being done in the correct way, whether it was music by Bach, Charlie Parker, or a new piece never played before.

In our regular symphony programs, we pioneered combining music of the European masters with composers and soloists who embraced the music of Latin America, Canada, Asia, Africa, the Middle East, and all the sounds of New York City, jazz, Afro-Cuban, and traditional Irish and West Indian pieces that were interspersed with short works by Beethoven, Berlioz, Bach, Brahms, and Bartók.

In 1970 when I started the series with the Brooklyn Philharmonic at the Brooklyn Academy of Music, no one was doing anything like this. I was not being politically correct or multicultural. Those terms didn't exist in 1970. Other orchestras began to use our programs as models for how to bring quality music to young people and to communities where symphonic music was something that was considered to be a form of expression where most people of all ages felt that they were not welcome.

Our soloists for my concerts included Wynton Marsalis when he was still at Juilliard, Nina Simone, Eubie Blake, Lionel Hampton, Odetta, Ron Carter, Candido, Dave Valentin, classical piano virtuoso Ursula Oppens, Paquito D'Rivera, Randy Weston, and scores of violinists, cellists, pianists, and opera singers from the greater New York area who wanted to perform in programs that reached large audiences in the parks and schools of New York City.

We also included traditional music of Native America; I would play one short social song with drummers on almost every program. We also presented the New York premiere and gave many performances of a wonderful piece by the American Indian composer Louis Ballard, *Scenes for Indian Life,* which audiences loved. And we did two separate evenings featuring the music of Jim Pepper. One of the concerts included the premiere of his *Witchi Tai To,* with Jim performing with his own band, accompanied by the orchestra.

As I look back today in 2007 and plan for the future, I see that all I have ever wanted to do is to present the best music possible in the most honest, accessible way, and make each program a special experience for the audience. This makes me no different from the majority of dedicated musicians around the world who love what they do and want other people to share in the joy of music.

I have always felt that the way to achieve this goal, when you are in the role of being a conductor, is to have every musician in the orchestra feel special and appreciated, with the hope that a positive, upbeat group feeling will be transmitted to the audience and create the environment for magical things to happen.

By the time Floyd Red Crow Westerman came to Brooklyn to play with my quartet in 1983, I had mentioned his name so many times at so many concerts that every musician who played with the Brooklyn Philharmonic and the thousands of people in the audiences of our variety of free concerts were aware of his name and the music he had shared with me. He was not yet a movie star. His critically acclaimed 2007 Johnny Cash tribute was still just a dream. All of that came later. But Floyd never needed fame to be able to capture an audience or any person he crossed paths with. He had a presence and a way of speaking that galvanized everybody he was with, and he also had a phenomenal sense of humor which enabled him, after almost bringing an audience to tears, to suddenly reduce them to gales of laughter. I was so happy that we were now able to be playing together in New York again, and that Floyd was so appreciated by the large crowd that had come to hear us.

After our first set, we were taking a break when a young man approached the bandstand. He was dressed up like a classic Twentieth Century Fox Hollywood caricature of a cigar store Indian, with dyed black hair and blond roots protruding from his headband. As he made a beeline toward Floyd, he looked like he was going to a masquerade party or auditioning for the role of Tonto in a dinner theater production of *The Lone Ranger.* Floyd braced himself for the oncoming onslaught.

"How, Chief," he said to Floyd, with a raspy Brooklyn accent. "I come to share powerful vision with you. I have sacred wampum and will trade you for your silver bracelet. I give you magic stones, two tomahawks, and dream catcher you hang on wall. You give me bracelet. Also have classes I give in sacred ways and sweat lodge ceremonies every Wednesday night in Canarsie. You come I give you guest speaker fee of $25. You think about it, Chief."

The man tried to hand Floyd some small stones, a plastic baggie of junk jewelry, two miniature tomahawks, and the dream catcher for him to look at. As Floyd stared at him quietly, the man ogled Floyd's shiny silver Navaho bracelet.

"How 'bout it, Chief? I give extra $10 and one more tomahawk."

"Thanks, but no thanks," said Floyd, pointing to the dream catcher wall ornament. "Please tell my Asian brothers in Hong Kong who made that piece of junk that they have the feathers on their version of our dream catcher hanging in the wrong place and that the Lakota people didn't use plastic handles for their tomahawks. And since I assume you are speaking to me so that I can make a sound decision of whether or not to accept your business proposition, you can speak to me in complete sentences. I went to college, and was planning on entering law school, so I am capable of completing a sentence or articulating any thought that comes into my mind. I'm sure that you can do the same when you are addressing me. I would also suggest that you don't try to merchandize sweat lodge ceremonies or anything to do with our spiritual ways. The Great Creator might forgive you, but the Better Business Bureau might not."

"Here's my card and a flyer in case you change your mind, Chief," said the man sheepishly.

"Me no change mind," said Floyd, in a basso profundo voice. "*Shechamina weechasa* (What a jerk). Get lost. I have spoken."

The man slunk off and the members of my quartet cracked up laughing.

"Business as usual, fellahs," said Floyd to the band, smiling sardonically. "It makes us laugh too, Dave. The White Man, in his desperation to find his own identity, is embracing self-appointed shamans with felony raps to teach enlightenment they themselves know nothing about. And charging big bucks to present seminars about our sacred ways, taught by people whose bloodlines came from England and Poland, who have adopted themselves into nonexistent tribes, using old Indian names, and misrepresenting themselves as Native American medicine men and women. We say to them to remember their old European motto 'Physician, heal thyself.'

"They've stolen all our land, lakes, rivers, and all our underground natural resources. Now they are trying to steal our culture, spirituality, and traditions. But they can't steal our music, at least not yet! It's too sophisticated and complex. It takes us a lifetime to learn a song. That's why involvement with our traditional music, and the way you honor it in your compositions, means something to me. You're constantly trying to learn to sing it and play it right, before you put it on paper. You always honor the names of those who taught you the music, and where it comes from. The copyright law says our traditional music is public domain, but the law of common sense and elementary decency tells us the Great Creator gave us those songs. They are there, and we find them in the air, the Mother Earth, the sounds of our brother the eagle, the crow, the horse, the buffalo, and the stars and great waters. That's why we give you our social songs. You can honor them in your own way, and tell young people around the world about us, through our music. It is a good thing when you perform it as you learned it on the *shee-ho*, our Lakota courting flute, and use our drum and singing style in the way many of us have shown you. Either way, you can speak for us in places where we are not present. That's why I'm glad to be playing with you again today, here in the asphalt jungle of Brooklyn with your band at this street festival. When we play together, we paint a picture. Me, the Lakota guitar-picker, and you, the Sioux Jew."

After the break we continued playing, and after our quartet had done a song from Egypt and Thelonious Monk's *Blue Monk,* there was a special moment in the show when Floyd and I played *Mastinchele Wachipi Olowan,* the old Lakota round dance melody. Floyd was brilliant as ever. Then the crowd stood in silence as Floyd sang his song about missionaries coming to the reservation to convert the Indians and coax them to abandon their traditional spiritual ways while simultaneously taking their land. The people on the street nodded their heads, smiled and shouted encouragement when he sang his song "Here Come the Anthros," about anthropologists with foundation grants robbing graves, photographing sacred sites, and stealing bones and works of art in the name of institutionalized preservation. And they roared with laughter when he explained that the Lakota people were going to create their own Anglo-Saxon museum, which would contain padded brassieres, the lawn mower, running sneakers, Frisbees, outdoor barbeque grills, and the hula hoop as authentic artifacts of the white man's culture.

We completed our two-hour set, and as we were packing up, Floyd turned to me and said, "We've conquered New York again, Dave. We had several hundred people this afternoon here in Brooklyn. Remember when we played for the Longest Walk in Manhattan in 1978 and only got thirty people? We're slowly building an awareness. It's only been four hundred winters since the white man made his intrusion on this continent. At the rate our audience has been growing since we started playing together in 1971, by the most conservative estimate, using the principle of geometric progression, four hundred winters from now, in the year 2383, we'll be able to fill Yankee Stadium."

"And four hundred years from now, if we're still around, we'll be mature enough to handle the success," I added, as I packed up all my instruments.

"We're already successful, Dave. It's just that hardly anybody knows it yet," said Floyd, laughing.

"Floyd, we've already played benefit concerts at the Aurelia Reserve in Ontario, Canada; Akwasasne Reservation in upstate New York; for the Longest Walk in places all over the country; folk festivals in the United States and Canada; in Washington, D.C.; at the Armory with Muhammed Ali, Marlon Brando, Richie Havens, Dick Gregory, Buffy Sainte-Marie; and even the concert we did in front of the Washington Monument with Joanne Shenandoah when only nine people showed up. These were all great, but this is the first time we ever played in such auspicious surroundings."

I turned around and pointed behind the bandstand, where you could see the huge building that bore the emblem "The Ex-Lax Building." It was the central offices of the corporation that manufactures anti-constipation remedies.

"Well, Dave," said Floyd, in his deep resonant voice. "All I can say about playing for the first time in my career in front of the Ex-Lax building is ... it's been a very *moving* experience."

We finished packing up, and as always, Floyd and our band spent another hour hanging out, talking to each other and members of the audience. Guitarist Vic Juris, bassist Victor Venegas, and drummer Ignacio Berroa all loved and respected Floyd and enjoyed being with him. Finally, we ate our last Brooklyn street fair gourmet specials: calzones, souvlakis, Jamaican meat patties, enchiladas, knishes, and egg rolls, and gathered up my kids to return to Manhattan. We said goodbye one last time to all the people we knew or had met at the street fair. Everyone loved what Floyd did and the spirit with which the band played. We hated to leave. Floyd got into our Chevy van, loaded down with our instruments and the kids, and we drove toward Manhattan.

"Back into the belly of the beast," said Floyd, laughing.

We took the Brooklyn-Queens Expressway toward the Midtown Tunnel and passed the huge cemetery where you could see thousands of gravestones for a mile or more.

"That's what Indian people call Marlboro Country," said Floyd, gesturing toward the vast expanse of tombstones.

"Here's an old song we can sing. It's the one you used for the last movement of your symphony *Trail of Beauty* that you learned from us. Alana ... Adira ... listen to Uncle Floyd."

My two daughters stopped wrestling in the back seat of the van and quieted down.

"This is the old Plains song we adopted for the American Indian Movement, and it has become our theme song. We call it the A.I.M. song. Dave, I want your two girls to learn this one. Someday, when they learn to sing it, I'll hear them, wherever I am."

"I sing real good already, Uncle Floyd," piped up Alana, in her four-year-old voice.

"I know you do," said Floyd.

"Me, too," said Adira. "I sing better than Alana. She squeak too much, when she sing."

"No, no," said Floyd. "You're both sisters. You are each the best. You sing this song with me and you'll be even stronger."

Floyd sang the first phrase, and then Alana, Adira, and I joined in. I had shown the kids how you follow the lead singer by always being a fraction of a second behind, so that while the chorus is in perfect synchronization with one another, they are all a tiny bit behind the same music being sung by the lead singer. It was the same principle as the Count Basie band playing together in perfect unison, but always a hair after the beat. As we were all singing, while driving to re-enter Manhattan, I remembered how I learned this particular Native American style of group singing at the Taos Pueblo in 1982, when I did some concerts for *Beyond Treaty* with Floyd and Richard Archuleta, the most gifted young traditional singer in Taos at that time. Benny Concha, a great hoop dancer and musician, was also featured in the program.

"Richard," I said. "How is it possible for everybody to sing such complicated music, and put it together perfectly, when the lead singer is always a little ahead? I never heard music anyplace in the world that is done that way."

Benny paused to reflect. Then he spoke. "We call that *'Tumkwahey.'*"

"Oh," I said. "What does that mean?"

"Well," said Richard, smiling. "There's really no English word for that."

"So much of what we have in our language can't be put into English. You have to live it to understand it as a concept," said Benny Concha. "It's like our dancing. You can't explain it or teach it. You have to be around it all the time and feel it. And then the Creator helps you to do it."

"The best way I could explain *tumkwahey,* Dave, is to put it this way," said Richard. "It means being in the shadow of the lead singer, always pressing onwards."

"Thank you, Richard. Benny, thank you. I better write that down so I don't forget it."

I took out my notebook of music paper, where I was sketching my cello concerto *Honor Song for Sitting Bull,* and wrote down what Richard said.

"Now I see the concept behind what I've been hearing. I know it sounds crazy, but that's what Mantovani, the old English conductor, used to do. He would have the first chair violinists, violists, and cellists play all together and all the rest of the string players of the orchestra play the same thing a fraction of a beat behind them, and it made the orchestra sound huge, like it was playing in an echo chamber. He created his own unique sound and toured the world. But he hardly ever played any deep music. It was mostly pop-elevator style."

"We don't do any pop-elevator style music, but our music is definitely deep!" said Benny Concha..

"And it's beautiful," said Richard. "Now when you sing with Floyd, or when you write a piece for symphony and honor one of our old Taos songs, you'll know what to do. This is America's oldest classical music. Our pueblo's been here more than two thousand years. And we've been here on this continent fifty thousand years."

The memory of our conversation in Taos ended as I pulled up my van to the corner of 6th Avenue and 11th Street. I turned to Floyd. "While we were singing the A.I.M. song with you and the kids, I was thinking about Richard Archuletta and Benny Concha in Taos a year ago, when they explained to me what *tumkwahey* was all about."

Floyd laughed and said, "I know you were thinking about them. So was I. I could see us all there together, as we were singing on the way here. That time in Taos gave you a clear message about the intricacies of our music. You're getting closer all the time. And the girls ... Alana, Adira, you're really singing better every time I hear you. Listen to your Daddy when I'm not here. He'll teach you what I taught him, as I was taught. And then you can share it with others. Now you tell your Daddy and Uncle Floyd what's written on that bumper sticker from the American Indian Community House that I gave you to put on the back of your van."

"The Indian Way. Respect, Love and Sharing," piped the girls in unison.

"Good. Always remember that," said Floyd.

"And remember the drum. In our music, the drum represents the first sound we ever hear and feel. It is the sound of our mother's heartbeat when we are inside of her. When we are born and come from her into the world, the drum becomes the heartbeat of all living things ... humans and our relatives, the birds, animal and plant life, the whole universe.

"Your culture refers to them as animals, birds, insects, varmints, wildlife, vegetation, flora, and fauna. But we don't have those words in our language. They are all part of our extended family. My college education was to prepare me for law school. My true education, in the old ways of my people, taught me that we have no such word for animal or plant. All living things are our relatives. We are called a two-legged. A horse or a dog is called a four-legged. A bird is called a winged. Now see that dog over there?"

Floyd pointed to a dachshund next to our van. As the girls looked out the window, the dachshund lifted his hind leg, relieving itself.

"I know, Uncle Floyd. That's a three-legged!" said Alana, excitedly.

"Very good, Alana," said Floyd. "Now that you know about all your relations and who you are, you can learn about where you are. Just remember, when you hear our music, you will understand a lot of things about this place we call America. Many people live their whole lives here and never know where they are. When you hear our music, and when you sing our social songs or dance the Round Dance, you are in tune with the Great Spirit. This place we call America is part of our mother, the earth. No one owns it. It was a gift from the Great Creator.

"Our traditions and ways are so simple; most people don't pay attention to them. Most people who came here uninvited years ago, think we, the oldest people on the continent, are extinct. They don't realize *they* are a temporary historical intrusion on fifty thousand years of continuity. We are still here and still hope that we can get someone to listen to our voices. Both of you have a good start. You are both free spirits and no one can ever own you. When you hear our drum as we sing, look in the sky, and see if you can see a face you know in the clouds. Even in this prison called New York City, always remember you're in Indian Country."

We got out of the van and went up to my apartment. Floyd always stayed with us when he came to New York. Even though we had just one and a half rooms, it didn't matter. Lora Lee and the children always looked forward to being with him, and, like me, Floyd prided himself on being able to be anywhere with anybody and having it be a harmonious experience.

We had a great home-cooked meal of pasta, eggplant parmigian, broccoli *raab* and other delicacies Lora Lee made from the secret recipes that her grandmother created for her family's restaurant, and we all played some music together afterwards, with Lora Lee singing some of her own songs and Floyd singing Johnny Cash and Kris Kristofferson songs while the girls played percussion and I backed up everyone on pennywhistles, French horn, and piano.

Finally, after Lora Lee and the kids fell asleep in the loft bed upstairs and the couches downstairs, Floyd and I sat up till dawn, talking about the old Native American social songs we had heard throughout the United States and Canada in our travels, and how important it was for Native American music to enter into the mainstream, without losing any of its beauty and spirit.

"We don't want our music to become watered down to make it more palatable, or, even worse, institutionalized and put in a bottle of formaldehyde, like a skull of our ancestors stolen from a burial site. Our music is so varied; it speaks about our presence on the entire American continent. It can stand on its own," said Floyd, as we gobbled up some canolis left over from our feast.

"From Alaska to Brazil, there are thousands of varieties of Indian music, language, and dance. Whenever our music is presented in public, it has to be done in the right spirit. Otherwise, it will end up suffocating to death in prison like most of the penitentiary-type mausoleums where they squeeze all the juice and joy out of the priceless music of Mozart, Bach, Beethoven, and all the other European masters you always talk about. If we're not here to do our music in the real way, they'll institutionalize it and bury the soul of the music and its creators in those cement tombs they call museums, concert halls, and conservatories, and strangle our music to death, in the name of art.

"Juilliard should have the Porcupine Singers from South Dakota come to their school and teach all the students about our music. They should have Richard Archuleta and Benny Concha come from Taos and show how our music and dance all come from the same place. They should bring the Winnebego fancy dancers to teach what rhythm is about. The way you did with the Toronto Symphony in 1979 when you invited Winston Wuttunee to sing and play the drum with the orchestra in the concert you conducted at Massey Hall. Why can't other conductors and composers present indigenous American music in America? They should teach our music in all the elementary schools.

"Our music, and all that goes with it, could be the civilizing force we need to keep this country from falling apart. Our music teaches everyone how to live together in a circle, as a family. Some day, Dave, this will happen. That's why we were brought together. We were meant to find new ways to share our music with the world. That's why we're here."

Floyd had to leave the next day and we said goodbye.

"We'll be together again soon," said Floyd. "Be proud of your children and stay close to them. *Tumkashika kteychee yaung telo* (Great Spirit be with you). *Doksha kola* (Later my friend)."

"*Washte kola* (Good my friend)," I said. "Love to your family, and as they say in Texas, shalom y'all."

As I watched Floyd walking down 6th Avenue toward the subway, with his guitar on his back, going to catch a train on his never-ending touring of the country, I started thinking about how we had first met in New York. And remembered all the experiences and adventures since then, playing together over the years, reinforcing one another's music. Somehow, it seemed as if it had all been planned—and if it was planned, how lucky I was to be a part of that plan.

I remembered how I told Floyd, when we first played together in a concert in 1971 for DRUM (Determined Red Man's Unity Movement), that my interest in American Indian music came naturally. I told him how, in the 1930s on our farm in Feasterville, Pennsylvania, my two uncles visited us all the time. They both had an interest in and knowledge of Native American music as well as all the people from the various Indian nations of Canada, the United States, and Latin America who created it so long ago and kept adding to it up until the present time.

I shared these memories with Alana and Adira the same afternoon that Floyd left when they asked me when Uncle Floyd was going to come back to see us. Then they asked me to tell them some of the stories that my uncle David used to tell me when I was about their age in 1937 and he would come to visit us on our farm. Those stories he told my sister Marianna and me were all about the years he spent with the Indians in South America.

I told the girls that afternoon, as I had many times before, how my uncle David had farmed with my father for four years in the 20s. After tireless work and with no money, he left our 160-acre farm in Feasterville, Pennsylvania, to see the world, shipping out to sea as a teletypist for the Grace Lines. Before cargo ships replaced people, merchant seamen like my uncle David could get off at any port until their money ran out and always catch another ship to work on. Most of his fellow merchant seamen would leave ship and squander their money drinking or gambling.

Uncle David didn't drink or gamble, so when his ship first landed in a South American port, he left whatever ship he was working on for six months with all his savings and traveled through remote mountain areas of South America. He made lifelong friends with many Indians in several countries and kept returning for many years, every time his ship landed in a port where there were Indian people he could visit. Even after he got married, he returned whenever he could to visit with Indian friends.

During his years of on-shore wanderings, he even was credited with discovering a new species of grasshopper that the Indians had shown him, which he named *Lethus Amrami*. He donated it to the Academy of Natural Sciences in Philadelphia. He used to laugh about it when he tried to get us to pronounce the Latin name.

He even worked briefly for the National Geographic Society as a self-trained cartographer, preparing maps of the Chiapas jungles of Mexico and others in Guatemala. He was offered jobs to become a traveling etymologist and cartographer but was too free a spirit.

"David and Mariana," he would say to my sister and me, holding up the book with the Latin name and photograph of the grasshopper named after him. "The Indian people discovered this grasshopper thousands of years before Rome or the Latin language existed. And they never had to put it in a bottle to prove it existed. It was part of their family. And they could talk to it. I heard them talk to all animals and sing songs for them. If the Indian people I was with in South America lived here on the farm with you and your father, they would have a song for each cow, pony, chicken, duck, deer, bird, and everything you see here every day. They can ride horses with no bridle or saddle, just by communicating without words. And they can play homemade flutes and *ocharinas* and make you cry. I wish I could play you some of their music. I wish I could sing you one of their songs the way they do."

Uncle David loved all kinds of music as much as he loved life, but the only piece he ever played for us was *Old Man River* in E-flat on the piano. But his stories of the times he spent with Indian people, and his love of their music, made me grow up thinking about it. He would take my sister and me into the woods, have us close our eyes and spin us around, and then ask us where our farm was.

"The Indian people I knew never had a compass. And they could walk for days and always know where to go, even if it was three days' walking distance in a place they had never been to before. They told me they could ask a bird for direction, or look at the sky, and always know where to go."

That sounded pretty far out to my sister and me, but we knew Uncle David was honest. "Listen to the birds," he would tell us. "That's who the Indians always told me are the best musicians."

My other uncle, Milton Nahm, came from Las Vegas, New Mexico. He was born at the beginning of the century and brought up with Indian people. His family had a junkyard, and because of his outstanding academic abilities, he became one of New Mexico's first Rhodes Scholars. As a result of this award, he was given a four-year scholarship to Oxford University in England. He graduated at the top of his class and was given a job in the philosophy department at Bryn Mawr College. He married my father's sister, Elinor, who worked at the college bookstore for forty years.

He would come to visit our farm to hunt in the woods and help us out with farm work. When he taught at Bryn Mawr, students told me years later he affected a kind of a British accent that he had learned at Oxford. But when he saw us at the farm, he always lapsed into his gruff New Mexico cowboy style of speaking, the way he had been brought up in Las Vegas. With his shotgun and old jeans, with a flask of whiskey bulging out of the back pocket, waist-high brown rubber boots, and a canvas duck-hunting jacket, you would never think he had been a Rhodes Scholar and was now a philosophy professor at a prestigious East Coast college for women.

"Boy, David," he growled, as he sipped a shot of whiskey from his back pocket flask. "These goddamn Eastern college people think they know it all. They don't know anything. Take away their money, put them out in the mountains with a knife and a knapsack and they'd die in a few days. They're all a bunch of goddamn snobs! They should spend some time with the Indians and learn how to become civilized. They would learn to treat every person with respect and never snub anyone. You and your sister have to come out with me some summer and go hunting and ride horses with the Indians and come to some powwows and learn some of the dances and hear the singers. It's a whole world of its own. I can hardly wait to get back."

As brilliant a scholar as he was, he always felt like an outsider. Underneath his gruff exterior, he was a kind and compassionate man, but he was always uncomfortable with most people. He was so homesick for New Mexico, he went back every summer until he died, from the day school was done, until the day he had to return to teach. He loved his hometown of Las Vegas, New Mexico, and nearby Taos, where he first arrived on horseback in 1916 from Las Vegas as a teenager.

"I may be the son of a junk dealer, and I know some of these spoiled brats call me the Jewish cowboy professor, but I learned more from the Indians I grew up with in New Mexico about life than any of these so-called intellectuals will ever know. I studied philosophy, and I was a damn good student. The top of my class. But my own life's philosophy came from being brought up with Indians. They know what human existence is all about. And they are true artists in every sense. If you want to be a musician, David, you better learn about the first American music. The Indian people have the most beautiful variety.

"And just the way they can survive and adapt and still remain Indians, no matter what they have to do to stay alive and feed their families, they keep their music alive and keep most of it to themselves. At the same time, they have been able to learn everyone else's music. Did you know that two of the greatest jazz trombonists were Indians? Jack Teagarden and Big Chief Russell Moore. Remember their names."

I always have.

Over the ensuing years, Uncle Milton gave me recordings, books, stories, and endless encouragement for my hopes of being able to honor American Indian music in some of my classical compositions. In 1977, forty years after he and my uncle

David first began telling my sister and me about the Indians and their music, the Philadelphia Orchestra premiered my composition *Trail of Beauty,* for solo oboe, mezzo-soprano, and orchestra, based on poems, prayers, and traditional melodies of different Native American peoples. My uncle David and uncle Milton attended.

My uncle David, then in his seventies, still had his same old wild spirit and zest for life. He no longer shipped out to sea, or wandered through the hills of South America until his money ran out. He had gotten married, had three terrific children, and had become a used-book salesman, traveling throughout the East Coast with piles of old books in the back of his car until they were all sold. He had so much charm and spirit that people would often buy some of his books just to be sure he would return on his next trip to tell them some of his long stories about Indians in South America, Central America, Mexico, and other tales of all the places he had traveled.

On the opening night of the Philadelphia Orchestra concert, Uncle David arrived at the backstage entrance of the Philadelphia Academy of Music three hours before the world premiere of *Trail of Beauty* was scheduled to take place. I was told by the security guard and several friends in the orchestra that as members of the orchestra arrived to unpack their instruments and warm up, Uncle David extended his hand and greeted them.

"Hi. I'm the *real* David Amram. My nephew David wrote this piece you are playing. I steered him in this direction in the 1930s when he was a little shaver. I took him to hear Duke Ellington at the Earle Theater in 1941. I took him to hear the Philadelphia Orchestra as a little boy. I always told him about American Indian music. Thank you for playing his piece. He's a good boy. He's my nephew, named after me!"

When the Philadelphia Orchestra took *Trail of Beauty* on tour, violinist Bob dePasquale asked me, "Are you bringing your Uncle David on tour with us? We need him. After all, as he says, he's the *real* David Amram."

My uncle Milton was less flamboyant at the premiere. After the concert, I went over to talk to him.

"Thank you, Uncle Milton. You started me off a long time ago thinking about this music."

"I'm proud of you, boy," said Uncle Milton. "I wish all the Indians I grew up with in New Mexico could have been here to hear this tonight. When I closed my eyes, I could see their faces and see them singing while the orchestra was playing."

Two years later, in the summer of 1979, I conducted *Trail of Beauty* in New Mexico at the Taos Summer Music Festival with their symphony. The auditorium was sold out, and when more than a hundred people from the Pueblo came, many of them sat outside, wrapped in blankets. The doors of the building were opened and the music filled the night air along with the sounds of crickets and birds. In the last movement, I could hear many of the Taos Indians hum along with the orchestra during the passages that included some of the traditional melodies that they knew.

I called up Uncle Milton in Philadelphia after the concert and told him about it and thanked him for all he had done to open up the door for me to follow the path that had led me, through the music, from our farm in Feasterville to New Mexico where he was from.

A few years later, when Uncle Milton's wife, my aunt Elinor, passed away, there was a memorial service at Bryn Mawr, where she had worked for forty years at the college book store. Inside the old ivy-covered building where the service took place, my uncle David played my Six Nations frame drum, and I played the Lakota courting flute. We played an old Taos social song, honoring Elinor's memory and Uncle Milton's love for her.

Her ashes were later scattered in the San Cristobal Mountains, close to where my uncle Milton had been born. She had grown to love New Mexico and the Indian spirit as much as her husband Milton did. Whenever I pass through Taos or Las Vegas, New Mexico, I think of them and play one of the old songs I learned there.

When I returned to Taos and visited people in the Pueblo the following year, Lorenzo Suazo and others shared some of their timeless songs with me, explaining how they had been lovingly preserved for hundreds of years, many from Indian nations who had traveled for years to trade goods with one another at the Taos Pueblo. These traders would also exchange songs, which became known as song swaps.

In every case, these various songs and chants, like all great music, make you feel part of the past and at the very same time bring the past into the present.

Both of my uncles are gone now, but today, whenever I play some of the old songs with my son Adam playing the drum and my two daughters playing the rattles, I feel Uncle David and Uncle Milton looking down on us as a family, knowing that we are playing for them. And when I close my eyes and play the music and sing the songs in different places around the world, I am transported back to the places where I first learned them. I feel the night air of Taos, see the bright stars shining above the Indian temple atop Mount Tepozteco in Tepoztlán, Mexico, and hear the birds singing in Inchillum, Washington, where Floyd Westerman and I went to a sweat lodge and sang songs after the Indian activist Yvonne Wanrow won her historic court case.

And I remember playing music at an Indian arts festival around the fires with David Redbird and traditional flute maker Louis Webster at the Menomonee Reservation in Green Bay, Wisconsin. I smile at the memories of scores of concerts all over the country when Geoff Carpentier, Lakota painter, architect, poet, and drummer, and I would play together, often at jazz and spoken word festivals honoring Jack Kerouac and his writing.

And I think of the Lakota hoop dancer and flutist Kevin Locke, when we played duets on courting flutes at the all-Indian Arts Festival at the Mikasuki Reservation with Native American performers Buffy Sainte-Marie, actor Will Sampson, Floyd Westerman, and comedian Charlie Hill. And the honoring song for Sitting Bull that Kevin Locke taught me that weekend became, a few years later, the theme for my cello concerto *Honor Song for Sitting Bull,* composed in 1983.

And I often hear in quiet moments the keening sound of Roland Moussa, Apache singer-songwriter, as we played for a field full of beer-drinking kids following Melanie, Arlo Guthrie, and Sha Na Na at Richie Havens's free Woodstock thirtieth anniversary commemoration concert in Bethel, N.Y., and how when Roland sang his "Indian Prayer," twenty thousand kids became so quiet you could hear the crickets.

And always, wherever I am and whoever I am with, I can hear the sound of the drum, the indigenous heartbeat of our continent, guiding me wherever I play around the world, with and for Indian people or any sincere musicians in Brazil, Central America, the United States, Canada, Alaska, Asia, and throughout Europe.

"We are all drum people," I was told once in Vancouver, by Winston Wuttunee, the Cree singer I worked with many times. "Europeans, Africans, Asians. We all have our ancestral way of expressing our collective heartbeats. The English settlers forbade us to use our drums. We did anyway. They forbade every place they conquered the right of the people to use their own drum. Then they tried to forbid the language, the religion, and the teaching of history. But it always started by imposing a death sentence on the drum. Because as long as that drum is alive, we survive. The drum is the essence of our experience. The drum is our heartbeat. It is our connection to the Great Creator and to each other."

One night at my apartment on 6th Avenue in Greenwich Village in the winter of 1976, a few months after I had returned from Africa, I was working on the orchestration of *Trail of Beauty*. I received a phone call from Vine Deloria Jr., author of several classic books, including *Custer Died for Your Sins*, which Floyd Red Crow Westerman had made into the title song of his album of the same name.

Vine had helped me choose the traditional Native American texts to set for the solo singer in *Trail of Beauty* and would call me once a month to see how I was coming along with the piece.

As I was orchestrating the second movement and in a kind of trance, hearing the actual sounds of Lakota singers and drummers in my head, and trying to match those sounds with symphonic instruments, my phone rang.

"David, this is Vine. I'm around the corner at the Lion's Head Bar. I don't care what you're doing. Drop it and come over right now. I'm sitting here with a man you have to meet. His name is Bobby Bridger. He is a country songwriter who is setting a part of John G. Neihardt's *Twilight of the Sioux* into a forty-minute piece of music that is really impressive. You've got to come over here right now and talk to him. He is doing the same thing in his type of music as you are in the piece you are writing for the Philadelphia Orchestra. He's not an Indian, but he's like my own brother. I'd die for him.

"He is a descendant of the famous mountain man Jim Bridger. Drop whatever you are doing and get right over here. I'm sitting at a table with David Markson and Pete Hamill and a bunch of crazy Irishmen singing, as you can hear, since they are drowning me out. Get right over here. *now!*"

Vine never sounded this excited before, so I jogged for three blocks from my apartment on 6th Avenue and 11th Street to Christopher Street and Sheridan Square and went down the stairs and entered the Lion's Head Bar.

"God love ya, Amram. You're here just in time to play with the boys. Where's your French horn and pennywhistles?" asked Malachy McCourt, who was standing at the bar, greeting strangers, telling stories, and singing along with the choir of intoxicated revelers whose music was pouring out of the back room.

"Actually Malachy, I just came to see Vine Deloria, who just called."

"Well he's back there with the boys in the other room. You'll have no trouble finding him. He's with some kind of cowboy fella with a big hat and a guitar with a feather attached to it. You missed some great singing tonight. The lads are in great form. Can I buy ya a drink?"

"Thanks, Malachy. Can you get me a ginger ale?"

"A *what?*" said Malachy. "I asked ya if ya wanted a drink. This isn't a soda fountain."

"I know, Malachy," I said. "But I'm in training, I'm working on my symphony and I just took a break to come over here to meet Vine's friend."

Malachy bought me a ginger ale and I went into the back room just as the singers were coming into the home stretch of the old song "Will Ya Go Lassie Go." They finished, hoisted their glasses in a toast to one another and after a round of applause and whoops of appreciation for themselves, took a break to fuel up.

"This is the pause that refreshes, Amram," said Dennis Duggan, the journalist who never passed up the opportunity to sing a song anywhere at any time for any occasion. "While we're on our five-minute sabbatical to refill our engines, you can run home and get some of your instruments. I see you've come here empty-handed tonight. Where's your horn and whistles? Did someone rob you? Have you forgotten the commercial message, 'Don't leave home without them?' Where's that horn? Someone buy Amram a drink. He looks anemic."

"I'll buy Amram another ginger ale, Dennis. He's in training, writing a symphony that I gave him the text for," said Vine Deloria. "Here I am, David, over in the corner."

I looked over my shoulder and there was Vine, sitting with David Markson and Pete Hamill and a slim young man with a guitar, wearing an enormous gray felt Stetson ten-gallon hat, who looked like a combination of a cowboy and a well-dressed mountain man. I went over and shook his hand.

"Good to meet you, David," said Bobby Bridger, in a soft musical Louisiana accent that was music to my ears. "Vine's told me a lot about you, and what you are doing with American Indian music. I hope I didn't interrupt your evening of working."

"Bobby, it's my treat to meet you," I said.

"David, Bobby, you are now brothers," said Vine. "You two had to meet. Now I have to go and talk to some publishers to see about the release date for my latest book. New Yorkers keep terrible hours. How are you coming along with *Trail of Beauty?* Are you done yet?"

"No, Vine," I said. "But I'm getting there."

"Good," said Vine. "Floyd and I are counting on you. Indians we know all over the country have heard about it, and they're waiting to hear it. When the Philadelphia Orchestra broadcasts the piece, they will copy it off the air and share it. Since Floyd and I are mentioned in the program notes you sent me a draft of, you'd better get it finished. I called you because Bobby is doing the same thing in a whole different way. He is honoring our traditions in a country music style that I don't think has ever been done before. He's not using authentic music the way you do, but he captures the spirit of Neihardt's *Twilight of the Sioux.* You both have to get together. I know something good will come of it. I have to go now. I'll tell Floyd that I got you and Bobby together."

Vine left, and after five minutes of talking to Bobby, I felt as if I had known him my whole life. He told me of how he was writing a long epic forty-minute piece about the glory days of the Sioux Indians, which he called *A Ballad of the West*, and how he was inspired by many of the same American Indian musicians whom I also had played with.

As the drinks flowed around us, the cigarette smoke filled the air, and the conversations and general merriment increased in intensity, the second round of singing started. I apologized to everyone in the bar for not rushing home and getting my instruments so that I could play with all the singers until 4:00 a.m., as I so often did. The Lion's Head Bar, along with The Bells of Hell Bar, were my conservatories for learning traditional Irish music, as well as great places to hang out after a day and night's work was completed. I invited Bobby to come visit me at my apartment.

"Ya must be gettin' old, Amram," said Malachy, as Bobby and I were leaving. "It's only midnight. Where's that storied stamina and energy yer known for?"

"I have to get home and talk to Bobby," I said. "He's doing the same thing I am doing with the new symphony I'm writing. He's also doing a piece with Vine's help, working on an extended composition based on American Indian texts, but in a different genre of music."

"Well, tonight the Lion's Head can say that in addition to the superb vocal performances being rendered by our lads in the back room, we just had our first cowboy and Indian cultural conference," said Malachy. "God love ya both. Get that symphony finished, Amram, so you can have a real drink again. Drinkin' that ginger ale will kill ya."

Bobby and I walked over to 6th Avenue and went to my apartment. He took out his guitar and played me a superbly structured forty-minute piece he had composed, singing with a pure voice that took you back to another time of an unspoiled America, with lyrics and melodies that made me forget I was in New York.

"How was it?" asked Bobby, as I sat in silence after he had finished.

"It was so beautiful, Bobby, that I didn't even want to say anything. I could hear a whole orchestra playing when you were singing, but with you and your guitar, you are a whole orchestra. If there is anything I can do to contribute, let me know."

"I sure will," he said. "I'd like to hear what your piece for the Philadelphia Orchestra is like."

"I wish I could play it for you," I said. "It's for full symphony orchestra, with a solo oboe and mezzo-soprano, so I can just peck away at the piano and play some of the themes on my Lakota courting flute."

"Well, let's hear whatever you can play from it," he said.

I played him tiny excerpts from the piece, as I had done for Floyd Westerman and other Native American musicians who had shown me different kinds of music. Then Bobby and I played some old classic cowboy songs together.

As the sun was coming up, Bobby packed up his guitar and as he was leaving he said, "This all happened for a reason. There's a tiny festival that takes place every May in a teeny town in Texas called Kerrville. They don't pay anything except your expenses, but since I'm on the board of directors, I'm allowed to invite a guest every year. Because this May is during the bicentennial year, I'd like to invite you to come and perform. I think they'll like you there, and I think you'd really like the festival. It's all Texas musicians, and I know they would enjoy hearing all the different kinds of music you play from around the world, and also would love to hear some American Indian and Central American Indian music performed on authentic instruments. I'm trying to see if we can get Floyd Red Crow Westerman to come too. A lot of your old friends, like Townes Van Zandt, Carolyn Hester, and Gary P. Nunn, will want you to come, and you can sit in with Gary's band."

"If you're there, Bobby, and they ask me, I'll be there too,' I said.

I always knew that meeting Bobby was a special night in my life, but never dreamed that it would be the beginning of a whole new series of events which would eventually lead to my writing the symphony *Kokopelli* twenty-one years later.

I went to the Kerrville Festival in May of 1976, and like everyone else who has ever been there in the thirty-one years since then, I was completely blown away by the non-stop warmth, familial down-home Texas openness, and collective healing power of hundreds of people from every walk of life all celebrating music together. The onstage performances we gave were just a prelude to the campfire picking sessions where families with just their sleeping bags, pup tents, homemade campers on the backs of pickup trucks, vans, or just hammocks, all came to celebrate being alive and staying as long as possible.

Almost everyone played some kind of instrument and sang, and the talent around the campfires was phenomenal. I heard more good songs the first weekend I was there than I had ever heard in my life. And the performers hired to play were all outstanding, original, and gracious to one another. It was Zero Music Biz Heaven, and I played with Bobby Bridger, Carolyn Hester, Gary P. Nunn, and many other folk singers and songwriters I had performed with over the years in New York, whenever I was asked to come and sit in with different bands.

Now I had the chance to be with them in the West, playing for an audience to whom the music was an integral part of their everyday lives. And everywhere I went, all around the campgrounds and in the town of Kerrville and the surrounding countryside of the Texas hill country, you could feel the influence of Indian culture, which had become a part of traditional old-time Texas music and poetry, as well as Texas arts and crafts.

During my concert, when I played *Mastinchele Wachipi Olowan* on my Lakota courting flute and sang the song in the traditional way, I thought I could feel the spirits of Indians long gone who had played in that same part of Texas, centuries before any of us boat people were lucky enough to get here to this beautiful part of the world. I invited Gayle Ross, a Cherokee story teller, to play the song with me, and we have done it together for over thirty years since then, whenever and wherever we are in the same place.

When I played the song "Kwahare," which I had learned in Kenya, I saw hundreds of people of all ages in cowboy hats singing along in Swahili after I taught them the words from on stage. I knew Bobby Bridger was right when he said that I would feel at home in Kerrville. Texas songwriter John Reed described my performance in a song he wrote called "Kerrville as per Usual" with the lines "African flutes and cowboy boots." For my encore, I sang "Pull My Daisy," with lyrics by Kerouac, Allen Ginsberg, and Neal Cassady, and did my scat singing. Then I made up a whole scat-rap-song-story in rhymes that I sang about meeting Bobby Bridger in New York with Vine Deloria and the pieces we were both writing, honoring the music and history of Native American peoples.

To my delight, everyone seemed to be able to tune in to my improvised rhyming scat-rap, even though every songwriter there and most of the audience were masters of brevity and understatement, all coming from the Texas tradition of saying it all in a few words. I realized that Kerrville was the kind of place where you could do just about anything, as long as it was for real, and it would be appreciated for what it was. This was exactly the same feeling I always had when Floyd Red Crow Westerman and I played for Indians on reservations, at Indian musical festivals, and at Indian benefits.

"We don't care about categories," Floyd used to say to me. "We don't care what something is called. We care about what it is."

By the end of the Kerrville festival, I knew I would come back whenever possible, and I have for the past thirty-one years since then.

On the last day of the festival, Gary P. Nunn invited Bobby Bridger and me to join him for a farewell final all-day music and storytelling get-together at a tiny town called Luckenbach, population seven, whose motto is "Everybody's Somebody in Luckenbach."

"You've got to meet Hondo Crouch," said Bobby. "Aside from being one of the funniest and most loving people on earth, he knows more stories about the Apaches and the history of other Indian nations in Texas than anyone you'll ever meet."

After driving from Kerrville through Fredricksburg, we turned off the main highway and went down a series of narrow dusty dirt roads, and just when it seemed that we were lost, saw a sign that said, "Welcome to Luckenbach (pop 7). Everybody's Somebody in Luckenbach."

When we arrived at where a lot of cars were parked, there were several familiar faces of people from the festival mingling with local farmers and tourists. Most of the people who had made the long journey had come to meet Hondo Crouch. They knew about Hondo after hearing Waylon Jennings's song about Luckenbach. Hondo was its legendary mayor and founder, as well as the head of all the institutions in the hundred-foot-long row of connecting shacks that made up the imaginary town. Hondo was the head honcho of the Luckenbach Airforce, town jail, post office and general store. The whole place was like a huge doll's house, and a refuge for grownups to come to an imaginary frontier ghost town.

Meeting Hondo was a joy. Warm, sophisticated, and brilliant, his down-home style allowed you to enter into his world. With his charismatic smile, impeccable cowboy attire, and flowing white hair, he took you on his own time machine back to the mythological past of cowboys and Indians and then returned into the present, with jokes, songs, and stories that made you love being in the homemade mythological town of his imagination, in spite of knowing that eventually you would have to leave Luckenbach and reenter into the technological and increasingly dehumanized society known as the adult world. But after spending some time with Hondo, you now knew that you would be able to handle it, realizing that you could create your own refuge.

We talked, swapped tales, jokes, philosophy, and farming stories, and played and sang the whole morning and afternoon. Other people floated in and out, joining us in songs, anecdotes, and sips of ice-cold Dos Equis beer.

Although all of us wanted to move in and stay in the fantasy land of Luckenbach for the rest of our lives, we knew that we had to get back to Kerrville for one more farewell dinner and then go our separate ways until next year.

"Come back and visit soon," said Hondo. "And tell your friend Ramblin' Jack Elliott to come back and pick some more in Luckenbach. Drive friendly."

Hondo handed me his card. It said "Hondo Crouch—Imagineer."

As I drove back to Kerrville in Gary's truck, through the countryside on tiny dirt roads leading to the highway to Fredericksburg toward Kerrville, I thought of how much Hondo reminded me of Ramblin' Jack Elliott. Hondo's elegance, humor, and love of a time long gone was something that all America hungered for ... the simpler, purer way of life when people were more important than machines and tender loving kindness was more important to pursue than only chasing money.

In my head, I could hear how we had played "Red River Valley," with Hondo making up verses as he went along.

Later that night, I played "Red River Valley" with Gary P. Nunn, Bobby Bridgers, Steve Fromholz, Carolyn Hester, and Allen Dameron, making a spontaneous set of variations of my own on my Irish double D whistle. I remember thinking of what a wonderful piece could be written based on this classic melody.

On July 4, 1976, I finished the final measure of *Trail of Beauty*. Two and a half months later, on September 27, Gary P. Nunn called and told me Hondo died. I had his card in my pocket. I stared at it, and read the inscription. "Hondo Crouch—Imagineer." I could still feel Hondo's spirit, and knew I always would.

After the Philadelphia Orchestra played *Trail of Beauty*, I wrote several other orchestral and chamber works that were inspired by the vast variety of music of Native Americans that I continued to learn over the years and included works by the American Indian composer Louis Ballard in many symphony concerts I conducted around the world. And every year at the conclusion of the Kerrville Festival, I would make my annual pilgrimage with Bobby Bridger and Gary P. Nunn to Luckenbach to play music, drink beer, listen to stories and songs, and end up playing "Red River Valley" in memory of Hondo. Every year I went back to the Kerrville Festival to play, and even conducted a series of Baroque music festivals with a chamber orchestra held on the ranch.

In 1991, the Kerrville Music Festival was celebrating its twentieth anniversary. The festival's founder, Rod Kennedy, asked me to write a concert piece for the occasion. Since the stage could only hold a small number of musicians from the Austin Symphony and San Antonio Symphony and just have enough room for the gifted solo flutist Megan Meisenbach to perform standing in front of the orchestra, I decided to compose a theme and variations on the melody "Red River Valley" for flute and strings. I dedicated it to my wife, Lora Lee, and to the memory of Hondo Crouch.

The folk festival was transformed into a classical music festival for one night, and my new piece went beautifully on a program that included Samuel Barber's "Adagio for Strings" and songs orchestrated and performed by some of the festival's favorite singer-songwriters, all of whom were playing their music with an orchestra for the first time.

Composer Dick Goodwin came up to me after the concert. We had met in Austin in 1971 when he played bass in my *Triple Concerto for Woodwind, Brass and Jazz Quintets and Orchestra* with the Austin Symphony. Dick was now the chairman of the music department at the University of South Carolina and wrote symphonic music, as well as being an outstanding multi-instrumentalist, conductor, and singer.

"You did it, David. I think you are going to get a lot of mileage out of this piece."

Hondo's daughter, Becky, and her mother, Shatzie, were in the audience, and said that they loved the piece. That was all I needed to hear.

Shortly afterward, Julius Baker, world-renowned flutist with the New York Philharmonic, recorded "Theme and Variations on Red River Valley" and it began to be broadcast all over the country. Three radio stations in New York all played "Theme and Variations on Red River Valley" the same day. Several people called our house, fearing that I had died. That's because contemporary classical works aren't played that much, except for at the composers' one hundredth birthdays or at their demise.

On my sixty-fifth birthday, November 17, 1995, National Public Radio broadcast a tribute to me and included the recorded performance of "Theme and Variations on Red River Valley" in the early morning. Shortly afterward, around 9:00 a.m., I received a phone call.

"David, this is Myrna Panitz. I am the wife and now the widow of Murray Panitz. I heard your piece on the radio played by Murray's old friend Julius Baker and I would like to have you to write a piece in memory of Murray. But I don't want a flute concerto. No one could play the flute like Murray. I want a piece for orchestra."

I was struck silent. My mind raced back to 1957, when Dan Cowan and Seymour Wakschal took me to the Little Orchestra Society in New York to hear the concert that they were playing so that I could hear a special musician in the orchestra.

"You've got to hear the flute player, Murray Panitz," said Dan Cowan.

"He's the greatest," said Seymour Wakschal. "He'll make you cry."

At the concert, I heard Murray's unique way of playing. It spoke to you. He made the music his own. After the concert, I met him.

"I like what you are trying to do in what I've heard," said Murray. "You're not fashionable, you're musical. Don't forget the flute when you compose, and write us something nice to play. A lot of modern composers forget we can still play melodies. You can do it."

We became friends and he always encouraged me to continue putting different kinds of music together. When he became solo flute with the Philadelphia Orchestra, he performed my woodwind quintet with the Philadelphia Orchestra's first-chair players. During subsequent concerts, Murray always cheered me on and gave me words of encouragement as well as good musical suggestions whenever the Philadelphia Orchestra performed my music.

When I sent him a wedding invitation in 1979, he wrote back, "I'm sorry I can't come. I used to eat at Ralph Ecobelli's restaurant every summer when our orchestra was in residence at Saratoga. Congratulations on marrying Ralph's daughter, Lora Lee. You'll be one composer in America who is guaranteed never to go hungry. Mazel tov! Murray."

"David, are you still there? I'm calling long distance. This is Myrna Panitz. Did we get disconnected?"

"Excuse me, Myrna, I got spaced out," I said. "I started remembering a lot of stuff about Murray. I'd love to do it. My only concern is that the Philadelphia Orchestra schedules their program three years in advance."

"I'm not thinking about the Philadelphia Orchestra yet," said Myrna. "They can play it later. I'm thinking about the Nashville Symphony. I moved to Nashville, and they have a wonderful orchestra. Do you know about them? Their conductor, Kenneth Schermerhorn, has done miracles."

"Of course," I said. "Ken and I were in the Seventh Army Symphony together in 1953. We've been friends ever since."

"Listen to me, David. If I commission you to write the piece, can you write a symphony that includes all the kinds of music you know about, but with at least one main Indian theme? That theme could lead into many other kinds of music, and at the end, you could have the Indian theme return.

"Like César Franck did in the last movement of his famous Symphony in D Minor with its cyclic form. Or like Wagner did in his operas. Is that possible? I'm not a composer, but when I heard your "Theme and Variations on Red River Valley" for flute and strings with Julius Baker playing the solo part over the radio, I started thinking about Murray and how nice it would be to have a piece written just for him that he would like.

"You know I went to Eastman School of Music with Murray, but I studied piano, not composition. Even though I'm not a composer, I thought of the idea of a piece for him with an Indian motif because Murray loved playing your piece *Trail of Beauty* that you wrote for the Philadelphia Orchestra. He felt that you were on to something new. And you know Murray was very critical. If he thought something was junk, he would say so. He lived for his music.

"When the Philadelphia Orchestra had the first rehearsal of your piece, he came home and told me about it. He even brought home the flute part you wrote to play for me before it was played at the opening concert at the Academy of Music, so that I could hear some of the melodies of the piece. He usually didn't do that. He wanted me to hear it.

"He said he thought the whole piece really captured the feeling of being with the American Indians, He loved that kind of music that they do just as much as he loved the classics.

"If you could capture the feeling of the cowboy's way of life with your flute piece with strings, "Theme and Variations on Red River Valley," and make it a real piece of music, not just schmaltz crap, I think you could do the same thing composing a piece in memory of Murray, and have at least one movement inspired by the music of the Indians. You already did a whole symphony like that with *Trail of Beauty*, but for this piece, I'd like to see you do it with other kinds of music as well. I'm not trying to tell you what to do, but I think this is what Murray would have liked. And if the music's good enough, and if musicians really like it, it will get played a lot, and he'll always be remembered every time the piece is played.

"Now I don't want you to think I'm telling you what to do, but I guess I am in a way. I definitely *don't* want a flute concerto. Nobody could ever play the flute like Murray, I mean *nobody*.

"I want the piece to be like a concerto for orchestra, where everybody has something good to play and a moment to shine at least once during the piece. And after the premiere, I am going to pay for the reception and invite all the members of the Nashville Symphony and their wives or husbands to come and eat and drink. This will be on me.

"Murray was an orchestral musician, and he loved his colleagues and always felt they weren't given the respect that they deserved. That's something that used to bother Murray. He felt that the musicians in the Philadelphia Orchestra never got thanked enough, even though they got paid so well. I want this piece to be a thank-you to all musicians who play in orchestras. If you can write a piece that will do this, I'll provide the thank-you meal for all of the musicians afterwards. Maybe everybody thinks I'm crazy, but I'm not. I know what I want. Think about it."

"I am," I said. "You already gave me some great ideas when you were talking. Maybe we could base the piece on the legends and stories about Kokopelli. He was the mythical Indian bearer of fertility and life and he was also a flute player like Murray. He sowed the seeds and created magic with his music. And he traveled all over among the Pueblo people throughout the Southwest as well as Mexico.

"I could write the first movement based on the special feeling of the music of the Pueblo Indians. Their music is completely different from the Plains people's music. I based *Trail of Beauty* mostly on Lakota and Cheyenne social songs, except for one movement that used an old Pueblo song as an accompanying figure in counterpoint to my own melody. I could write my own theme in that style."

"Okay," said Myrna. "But how about including other styles of music later on in the piece? Can you fit them into the piece, and make it sound like they should all be together?"

"That's my job, to figure out how to do it so that it is a really good piece of music, where the audience doesn't need to read eight pages of program notes or hear a lecture or consult an anthropologist or astrophysicist to understand what it is about. Let me start planning and I am sure that I can do it. This is the first time that I have been asked to use these elements in a piece. For most of my life, I have had to beg to persuade orchestras and soloists to let me do it. Musicians and audiences have always loved to hear these elements used in a classical way, but people who run the scene are usually petrified. That's all changing now, thank God. I have a feeling that this can really be something I can do with all my heart. Murray was always great to me, way back when we first met, and I was just starting out in New York in the 50s, and he always encouraged me to follow what it was I felt I wanted to do. And he was a real purist.

"As you remember, *The Trail of Beauty* was written to honor the memory of Marcel Tabuteau, the great oboe player I used to hear as a boy when my uncle David took me to hear the Philadelphia Orchestra."

"I remember your Uncle David," said Myrna. "Who could forget him? What a *meshugenah*. Now he was *really* crazy. He was backstage every night when they played your piece, schmoozing with all the players. What a character. I think he drove Murray and the other players in the orchestra cuckoo, coming two hours before the concert and telling them all stories, but he was a lot of fun."

"Well, my uncle David's the one that got me to first hear classical music, as well as jazz. He also came to hear Murray when they played my woodwind quintet in Philadelphia. This new symphony could also be a piece for me to thank the Philadelphia Orchestra for the inspiration they have been in my life. And my father-in-law, Ralph Ecobelli, will want to hear the piece too. He remembers what Murray used to like to eat when he came to Ecobelli's Restaurant in Ballston Spa after the orchestra had finished playing their concert at the Saratoga Performing Arts Center. And you know Ralph's daughter, my wife Lora Lee, used to see Murray at the restaurant when she worked there as a kid, every summer that the orchestra came up to Saratoga in August."

"It sounds like it will be a family affair when we do the symphony," said Myrna.

"Most important, Myrna, you and Ken Schermerhorn and the musicians and I all want the piece to be the very best that I can possibly compose and have a life of its own after I'm long gone, and that's all any composer can ask for.

"We won't have anyone panting down the back of our necks telling us how to do it. Everything you said you would like me to do already has given me ideas, even if those first thoughts lead me to something completely different from what you thought of. I don't really know what I will end up doing, but I know I want to do it.

"You know I am a stickler for construction and clarity when I compose, so it won't be a 'James Joyce gets stoned and goes slumming to Bird Land' mishmash, rambling on and on through different idioms, interspersed with ten pages of avant-garde instructions for the musicians to see how many hideous sound effects they can produce before they empty out the hall.

"I'm going to try to write a piece that honors Murray and his pure and enduring musicianship and relate his devotion and high standards to the musicality of the Pueblo people and all the other cultures I have learned about from my life experiences. I'll use those idioms that have become part of me, and go from there. It will be another adventure into the unknown. That's why it is exciting to do it.

"I think each movement could start with the flute introducing the thematic material and then feature different instruments throughout the symphony to make it a kind of a concerto for orchestra, as you suggested, where the spirit and life force of Kokopelli invigorates each section of the orchestra to shine."

"Whew!" said Myrna. "I'm not sure I know what you're talking about, but I think we are on to something. You keep thinking and I'll call you back in a few days. Maybe you could even write a sketch of a theme and play it for me over the phone on that Lakota Indian flute of yours. Murray loved that flute of yours that looks like a duck that you carried around to all the rehearsals. He always remembered when you played it for everyone in the orchestra at the first rehearsal of *Trail of Beauty*. The orchestra still remembers the look of astonishment on Ormandy's face when you played that duck flute and sang some of the authentic Indian melodies for the whole orchestra. They thought he would fall off the podium. But in the end Ormandy ended up actually liking the piece. Especially after it got such good reviews. You go to work. We don't have a lot of time. I hope you can get it done on time.

"Well, I don't want to sound like I'm haranguing you, but get started right now if you can. And give those adorable kids a hug. They must be getting big. I'll call you in a few days. Get to work."

I was excited. Rather than feeling that Myrna was imposing herself on me, her enthusiasm was invigorating. I took out my Lakota duck flute, called a *sheeho*. It was the same traditional courting flute that I had played for Murray and the members of the Philadelphia Orchestra at the first rehearsal of *The Trail of Beauty* in 1977, almost ten years earlier.

I first began playing the sheeho with Floyd Red Crow Westerman in 1970 and have played it ever since, to this very day, for and with other Native Americans throughout the United States and Canada and in all kinds of folk, jazz, and classical concerts and festivals in all the countries in which I perform around the world. I used it on my tours for the State Department. I played it in China in 2005, and in Latvia in 2006. Now I was playing it at home, searching for what I thought would paint a picture of what Kokopelli was really all about, playing my flute as if I were serenading him.

Suddenly, as I was playing with my eyes closed, a melody just came to me, as if someone were sending me a message over the phone or on a postcard, or a musical e-mail. I wrote it down and played it back. I realized that while it was not a traditional Pueblo flute song, it felt like it was. I went to the shed behind my house and started to use the piano and write sketches, harmonizing it, adding counterpoint, and making it into the beginnings of an orchestral piece. I realized that I was already beginning to write a symphony and decided at that moment that I would find the time to complete the whole piece, even if Myrna changed her mind and decided not to have it done or chose someone else to do it.

I came out of the shed and it was morning. My three children, Alana, Adira, and Adam, were up, eating breakfast and ready to go to school.

"What were you doing in there all night, Daddy? Writing more music?" asked Adira.

"I was beginning to write a new symphony," I said.

"Why you stay there all night?" piped up Adam.

"Once he starts, you can't get him to stop," said Alana.

"That's the truth," said Lora Lee. "He gets in that zone and he doesn't stop."

The kids went off to school, and I got some sleep. After I woke up a few hours later, I called the Laguna poet and novelist Leslie Silko on the phone and told her about the whole idea for the symphony. I said that I wanted to be sure that if I used the name of Kokopelli in any way, I was doing it in the right way and not vulgarizing or misrepresenting an important figure from a culture into which I was not born.

"Just do what's in your heart," said Leslie. "We all see Kokopelli in our own way, and if you are trying to honor him and the music that relates to his specific culture, I'm sure it will be like your other pieces where you honored other styles of our music. When you accompanied me in Taos when I read my poetry and Simon Ortiz's poetry, and when you played for me in New York, and when you scored my film about the Laguna Pueblo, it all felt right.

"We knew you were trying to do your best, and that you were not just another rip-off artist. No one can ever fool a bunch of Indians for very long. We know who's real. After four hundred years of dealing with liars, we can tell the difference. I'll give you a quote for what I feel Kokopelli means to us. And the title of the first movement, "Lene Tawi," is the right one for a flute song from the old Hopi people. We have the same kind of songs, too. I think that honoring the spirit of Kokopelli this way is a good idea.

"I hope you can send me a tape of the piece when it is done. I have the tapes you sent me of your cello concerto, *Honor Song for Sitting Bull, Trail of Beauty,* and the concert you did with Jim Pepper with the symphony where they played his music and Louis Ballard's music. Why don't more American Indian composers like Jim Pepper and Louis Ballard get their music played? You have done it, why don't others?"

"Most classical conductors don't know that there are any," I said. "But that's all going to change. Just like you and Vine Deloria are making people aware that there are American Indian authors and novelists. Every time you and Vine come to New York and give a reading from your books, the whole city gets nicer for a moment."

"I always enjoyed it," said Leslie. "I remember every time I came to New York to do a reading and you would drive me and a bunch of friends from the American Indian Community House, all piled into that old Chevy van of yours, and cruise all around town, with your kids all howling in the back seat. Please send them my love. Mine are all big now. I am writing so much I don't get away to see people. Can you believe that Floyd Westerman is now a movie star? *Dances with Wolves* was a good start toward waking people up to know that we are still here. It was a wake-up call for America after four hundred years of her slumbering."

"Well, I hope this new symphony will get people interested in some way as well," I said. "I'm going to use my own themes, rather than using traditional ones, but still I want to be sure that I am honoring the essence of Kokopelli in the right way, so that I am not desecrating his name. You know the road to hell is paved with good intentions."

"I sure do," said Leslie. "I'll send you a note telling you what I feel about Kokopelli. Of course what I will write you are just my own personal feelings. Everybody has their own way of seeing him. Write me what you feel, and I'll tell you what I feel about what you've said."

I sat down and on the bottom page of the first sketch of the opening theme, I wrote, "Kokopelli, the magical spirit widely known among the Pueblo peoples, is always depicted as a flutist, carrying a sack of seeds on his back. Leslie Silko, the award-winning Laguna poet, told me her people feel that Kokopelli's symbolic planting of the seeds represents the spreading of the life force, giving joy, hope, and energy to everyone when he plays his flute.

"The entire first movement, 'Lene Tawi' ('Flute Song' in the Hopi language) is based on an original melody of mine. The movement begins with an introductory motif on the tympani. The rhythm of this motif, followed by the main theme introduced by the flute, is the basis for the entire symphony, recurring in various forms throughout all three movements. The flute melody, now having sown the musical seeds for all to hear, is played by the strings and various choirs of the orchestra and is restated and developed. Hints of the second movement are planted in the listener's ear as well, and then the flute returns with the initial theme. The final fragments of this melody conclude the movement with soft, mysterious sounds evoking the quiet nightfall in the Indian pueblos of New Mexico and Arizona."

I called Leslie back the next morning and read her the note, explaining that it was an outline of the first movement, as if I had written program notes for someone else's piece after it had been completed.

"That sounds good," she said. "Do what comes naturally. Just follow your heart. That's what I do. All the music is out there. Just think about Kokopelli and he'll play a song for you. Send me a tape after it gets played. I doubt that I can come to Nashville. I'm trying to meet my own deadline for a big new book. Someday you have to bring all your family and come and visit here.

"I'll get back to New York for a reading there after my new book gets published, and when I do, we'll take a ride in that old van again. When you see Floyd Red Crow Westerman, send him my love."

"I will," I said. "And I thank you for helping me to get started."

"It sounds like you've almost finished the first movement," she said.

"No," I said. "What I read to you is what I hope the piece will be, from what I hear in my head, but writing down the right notes will take a long time. But now I have a plan, which is really a map leading me to a musical destination, and now I have to start going slowly down that road to reach it."

"I know you'll get there," she said.

"I'd better," I said. "The woman who wants me to write it already has a date she wants it to be performed. I'll do it. I'm going to write it even if she changes her mind. I can see the whole piece, in my mind, way off in the distance."

"Good luck," said Leslie.

I stayed up until 3:00 a.m. hiding in the shed, composing. The next morning at 6:30 a.m., I heard the phone ring. At first I thought I was dreaming, but it kept on ringing and I fumbled as I almost dropped the receiver on the floor.

"Who is calling you at this hour?" asked Lora Lee. "Is it Gregory Corso, still up after a night of partying? You and your crazy friends. Why can't they grow up?"

"I dunno," I mumbled.

Clearing my throat so I wouldn't sound like a zombie, I croaked sleepily into the phone.

"Good morning. Hello."

"David, are you up? This is Myrna. Am I calling too early? I have already spoken to the Nashville Symphony and they like the idea. We are on for a concert at the beginning of January 1997, with a Mozart piano concerto and Strauss's *Rosenkavalier Suite*. Mozart, Strauss, and Amram. How does that sound? Are you up for it? Can you do it? Kenneth Schermerhorn loves the idea. He says he would like you to conduct the premiere. Can you get it written in time?"

"I guess I'll have to," I said.

"Well, good. Then let's go to work," said Myrna. "I'll call you every day and see how you are coming along, if you like."

"That's okay," I said. "It might be better to just call once in a while. I don't want to run up your phone bill."

"Ha, ha. Don't be funny," she said. "I can't help it if I am enthusiastic. Everyone thinks I'm crazy, but I'm not. I miss Murray every day and this will be a way to be with him."

"I spoke to Leslie Silko," I said. "She likes the idea and she helped me to feel how to approach the first movement and the whole piece, and how to think about Kokopelli."

"I have a Kokopelli silver pendant I got when Murray and I were in New Mexico years ago," said Myrna. "I'm going to mail it to you for you to wear. It's yours now. Murray would want you to have it, since you're writing this piece for him."

"Thank you, Myrna," I said. "I'll put it on my necklace with all the other gifts that are there. Let me read you what I have planned for the first movement."

I read Myrna the notes.

"I'm not the one that's crazy, you are," she said. "I love it. I won't bother you, but do you mind if I call you sometimes to see how the piece is coming along? I'll promise not to call so early. I know you have to get your sleep."

"Call any time, Myrna," I said. "My composition teacher, Vittorio Giannini, used to tell us when we yawned in class, 'Wake up! Sleep's a waste of time.'"

"It's not a waste of time for me," whispered Lora Lee. "She has such a loud voice. Tell her to get off the phone."

"Myrna, thank you for calling," I said.

"I'll call back in a few days and we'll figure out how to pay you," she said. "You'd better get to work. There is a date for the premiere. I'm so excited."

"Me too," I said.

I dragged myself out of bed, made a pot of chai tea, went into the shed, and composed uninterrupted for hours.

Three days later, a small package arrived from Nashville in the mail with a silver Kokopelli wrapped in tissue paper inside another envelope with a note attached with scotch tape:

"This is for you David
from Murray and me
Get the piece finished on time
Love
Myrna"

Two days later Myrna called back, and I thanked her for the silver Kokopelli. I told her how I had planned the rest of the piece and read her rough notes I had already written for the entire piece, which would now serve as a map for how I would construct the entire symphony.

Since I had already told Myrna that the first movement was planned as a journey by Kokpelli's side to all the places he traveled, I read her the notes I had written for the last two movements.

"Here's what I have outlined, Myrna," I said. "The second movement, 'Mizmor Kaddum' ('Song of Antiquity' in Hebrew) will honor the songs and travels of the Central European cantors who kept the prayers alive through song and gave renewed life, hope, and pride to all the congregations they visited in their travels. The music would reflect their journeys and the ghettoized life in the *shtetls* of Central Europe, often similar to the lives of Indians in the United States who were confined to reservations, but whose music enabled their souls to soar and be as free as the spirit of Kokopelli."

"Good," said Myrna. "I like it. How 'bout the last movement? How is it going to end? We don't want the audience to fall asleep."

I told her that it was going to be a fiery finale called "Danza del Mundo" (Dance of the World) and that this movement would honor the Mexican, Central American, and Caribbean presence of Kokopelli's spirit. In addition, it would include not only elements from the Indians from these countries, but also the sounds of Afro-Cuban music and the American blues, both of which, like Kokopelli, traveled across borders and existed side by side with the many forms of traditional music of the millions of Indian people throughout South America.

I also said that toward the end of this last movement, the opening flute song, "Lene Tawi," would return triumphantly, with all the other themes of the symphony joining in harmoniously.

"I like it very much," said Myrna. "It sounds like you've already written it. Even Mozart wasn't that fast. What's up? Are you that fast?"

"No, Myrna," I said. "No way. I think fast on my feet, and I can improvise music and words on the spot, but I compose very slowly. Sometimes it takes hours just to get one measure perfect. But I try as hard as I can to always make it sound natural and effortless. This will be a huge challenge. But I really want to do it."

"If you really want to do it, then you will, David. Let me know what it will cost and you've got yourself a deal. Are you sure you can have the piece ready for the first rehearsal on January 15, 1997? The concert will be January 17, and you are supposed to conduct your piece. They are holding the date for another week. Otherwise they'll program a symphony by Charles Ives instead of your piece. Are you sure you'll have it ready?"

"Yes," I said without hesitating. "I'll have it done. I've never missed a deadline."

"Well, don't miss this one," she said.

For the next week, I continued sketching out more ideas, plans, notes, and themes.

Over the next months I worked constantly, wherever I was. Endless hours in my shed behind the farmhouse, on planes, in airports, in motel rooms, anywhere on the road where there was a piano free, and wherever I could sit down with score paper and compose.

I decided to call the whole symphony *Kokopelli,* and wrote the following dedication in the score:

"In memory of Murray W. Panitz and his family, this symphony is a way of saying thank you for the blessing of his life and artistry, which continues to enrich us every day.

"To my dear friend Kenneth Schermerhorn, the gifted men and women of the Nashville Symphony, and Myrna Panitz, who commissioned the composition. And to Kokopelli, who continues to bring us music every day."

Myrna called back a few days later. "David, I don't want to push you, but are you *positive* you can have the symphony written on time to play in January of 1997?"

"Yes," I said.

On December 31, 1996, I received the final proofed and re-edited score, which I went over for the thousandth time and added final tiny corrections to put in the parts for the first rehearsal on January 15, 1997, sixteen days later. I spent hours each day studying the score, as if a stranger had written it. Since Ken had asked me to conduct the premiere, I wanted to know the piece as well as if I were conducting Stravinsky's *Rites of Spring,* even though my piece was much simpler to put together.

"I think it would be fun for the orchestra and the audience to have you conduct it," said Ken. "I'll sit at rehearsals and be your extra pair of ears."

As the conductor, I had to become totally objective about my own piece. I could no longer think of it played lovingly in slow motion, so that I could savor every note I had written. I had to think of it in terms of bringing it to life, by observing the correct tempos and phrasing that I had written in the score, adjust shadings, and help the musicians to eventually take it off the paper and make it their own so that I could almost disappear, except for the crucial places where they needed me.

It was finally time to rehearse *Kokopelli*. Due to karmatic blessings, Ken Schermerhorn had decided to schedule the 10:00–12:30 rehearsal for *RosenKavalier Suite* by Richard Strauss and the Overture to *The Barber of Seville* by Rossini for the first two and a half hours, and let me rehearse my piece for an hour and a half from 2:30 to 4:00 p.m.

I sat on the side of the stage and watched Kenny conduct the orchestra. He had been music director for twelve years and had become a beloved and revered figure in the city of Nashville. He had told me this last year had been the best of his life. The latest CD recording he made with the Nashville Symphony had been compared with the Berlin Philharmonic. After all the years of conducting all over the world, he was being acknowledged as a major musical figure of our time.

"We're lucky to have him here," said a member of the orchestra before the rehearsal began. "He should be conducting the New York Philharmonic."

As I watched him rehearsing, I flashed back to 1954 when I was playing horn in the Seventh Army Symphony and Ken had moved from playing trumpet to becoming our conductor. It was his first conducting job for Uncle Sam. We all felt a wave of good energy as soon as he stepped on the podium and led us in the Overture to Beethoven's opera *Fidelio*. As I watched him conducting here in Nashville on the morning of January 15, 1997, forty-three years later, that wave of energy had become distilled into a steady fire of concentration and mastery of the music that communicated to the orchestra. They were playing up a storm, even though it was just the first rehearsal.

I could hardly wait to start conducting my piece. I knew this orchestra was *hot!*

I still had two and a half hours to put tiny corrections in the parts and study the score while Ken was conducting the two other pieces. At the lunch break, Ken and I ate sandwiches in the basement and talked about all our old friends who were members of the Seventh Army Symphony from nearly half a century ago.

Jim Cook, who had played horn with us way back then, came by during the break and showed us photos from 1953 of Ken and me in Tyrolean hats and lederhosen, the leather shorts that Bavarian mountain climbers wore, playing with the oompah band that we had formed to get free beer in the various beer halls we visited in our tours with the Seventh Army Symphony throughout Germany.

Two musicians from the Nashville Symphony came by and saw the photos of two young musicians dressed up like rejects from the cast of *The Sound of Music*," in ill-fitting lederhosen playing for a group of bombed-out German barflies.

"You guys must have had fun," said a violist.

"We still do," said Ken.

It was time to rehearse again. Ken introduced me to the entire orchestra and we began to play the symphony. It was a complicated piece to read through the first time. I had prepared every cue, each entrance, and all the dynamics and tempo changes until I had the piece memorized. This way, I could make mental notes of where to make all the changes and adjust tempos and balances as we were reading through it, without making the musicians stop each time. If a conductor stops every few seconds during the first reading to make small corrections, this disrupts the flow of the musicians' discovery of seeing the whole shape of the piece, by overwhelming them with details before they have an idea of what the piece is all about.

Rehearsing is a process of adding corrections and filing them in your mind as if you were chalking them up on a huge blackboard in your imagination. After entering every correction to the score that you have already memorized and that is written on that blackboard, you continue until you stop at the end of a movement. Each correction is added in a different colored chalk than the one you see on your memorized score on that imaginary blackboard.

At the end of the movement, or if you have to stop before then, while the musicians are taking a breath, you go the blackboard stored in your imagination and review these corrections chronologically with the orchestra. It's just like replaying a video of a road race on a TV monitor and showing the musicians where they made a wrong turn and how they can do it better the next time. But during the rehearsal, you strive to have a maximum of playing and a minimum of talking. By rehearsing in this fashion, you know the musicians' concentration won't be short-circuited by stopping every few seconds and correcting something. You make those corrections later. The great conductor William Steinberg showed me this in 1969 when he conducted the premiere of my Horn Concerto with the Pittsburgh Symphony. He didn't stop once, and at the end of the piece he went back and calmly told the orchestra every tiny detail of what needed to be done. He indicated to me that you save your repartee, anecdotes, salutations, personal messages, philosophic insights, jokes, gossip, and sharing of spiritual revelations and opinions about geopolitics until the fifteen-minute break when the musicians put down their instruments and collect their thoughts, have a cup of coffee, make a call on their cell phones, or read a paper.

And Steinberg also showed me that it was occasionally a good idea to put into practice what our great system of jurisprudence provides each and every one of us as citizens, namely that both the conductor and the musicians have the right to remain silent and let the music do the talking. During this first rehearsal of *Kokopelli*, the musicians of the Nashville Symphony were outstanding, and I could hear that the piece would eventually become so itself in time. After each movement, I made some suggestions, went over a few spots, and ran through each of them again. The musicians were now beginning to hear what they should do, and also hearing what everyone else was playing as well. As the orchestra played and brought the piece to life, I thought about how I had called Leslie Silko months earlier, asked her about the significance of Kokopelli and what it meant to her, and how I had told her that I didn't want to disrespect the beautiful tradition I was not born into.

"You're on the right path, David," she told me. "Go with your heart. You'll find the right direction."

As the orchestra finished playing the first movement, I thought I could feel her smiling. I could hardly wait to send her a tape of the upcoming radio broadcast.

The spirit of Kokopelli had guided me to write a strong and truthful opening movement. It was all I had hoped it could be.

The second movement, "Mizmor Kaddum" ("Song of Antiquity" in Hebrew), was a kind of Kaddish or prayer for departed souls that I wrote in memory of Murray Panitz. Two primary themes in a melancholy mode, the final played by the flutes and the second by the cellos, sounded great the final time we read through it. We had read and rehearsed two movements of the piece in an hour. I knew I had done what I had set out to do, and that by performance time, we would have these two movements cooking!

A member of the orchestra, Vivian Bartles, daughter of Joseph Bartles, a fine jazz musician and composer I had jammed with in Washington in 1952, came up to me. "Thanks for writing such a nice cello part for us," she said. "I wish my dad were here for this. He used to tell me about your jam sessions in your old basement apartment with the jazz and folk and symphony players all getting together and playing. He told me that Charlie Parker and Dizzy Gillespie both came there when they were in town."

Ken came over. He was beaming. "Bravo, Private Amram. These two movements are gorgeous."

"Thank you, Sergeant," I said.

Ken had been made sergeant when he began conducting the Seventh Army Symphony to give him a bigger salary and more military panache.

"I hope they can play the last movement," I said. "It's got a lot of good notes."

"This orchestra can play anything," said Ken. "That's why I love being here. They come to play."

The third movement, "Danza del Mundo" ("Dance of the World" in Spanish), used the five individual rhythms of the *guaguanco*, a complex Afro-Cuban musical form that is part of the rhumba family and accompanies singing and dancing. I started to really get serious about understanding it after playing the concert in Cuba in 1977 with Los Papines, the acknowledged masters of the modern form of this sophisticated traditional music.

I remembered when Dizzy Gillespie, Stan Getz, Earl Hines, and I jammed with them and Los Papines showed us all the parts and how to put the *guaguanco* together the way it was done traditionally.

"Oo-weee!" exclaimed Dizzy, after we had received our crash course in the rhythmic construction of how to play all the parts at the same time. "That *guaguanco* is mean! Get close to that, David, and put it in a symphony."

And here I was twenty years later in Nashville, and I finally had. My earlier symphonic piece *En Memoria de Chano Pozo,* written in 1977, had a *guaguanco* flavor, but didn't use all the rhythms that I used in the last movement of *Kokopelli.* This last movement, "Danza del Mundo," came a lot closer. The rhythms led into a lively theme evoking late-night revels in an imaginary Latin dance hall. The *guaguanco* pattern then changed to a *seis para ocho* (six-eight time) African rhythm that introduced a twelve-bar blues theme played by different sections of the orchestra.

As the orchestra was tearing through this music with enthusiasm, I imagined I could see Murray and hundreds of musicians who had passed on to the other world. They were all sitting in white tie and tails or white shirts and black skirts, in a great circle, playing along with the members of the Nashville Symphony from their stage in the great concert hall in the sky, but since they couldn't ever get fired now that they were in heaven, they were rocking in their chairs back and forth, swaying as they played, tapping their toes while all the other departed spirits were standing around them, snapping their fingers, bobbing their heads, smiling, and shouting whoops of encouragement, urging the orchestra to move and groove.

I realized that I had better stop daydreaming and come back to earth and do my job and help out the orchestra when needed. But it was a good thought and it stays in my mind every time I watch an orchestra on TV and see the conductor looking like an executioner about to pull the switch and the musicians all looking like they are about to receive last rites.

Leonard Bernstein, Dimitri Mitropolous, William Steinberg, and many of the other master conductors I worked with showed me a long time ago that abusiveness toward others is only an expression of serious mental problems, not the key to leadership, and has no place in music, and that the more the musicians feel respected and nurtured, the more confident they will be and the more beautiful the music will sound. And that they also appreciate it if they feel that the conductor is listening to them and tuned in to the moment every second.

As the Nashville symphony began to feel what the music was about, they began to swing. They took the notes off the paper and made it sound live. As the piece developed to a huge climax, the Kokopelli theme from the first movement returned, and all the other themes of the first two movements and fragments of themes from the last movement were superimposed over the opening melody.

César Franck had done this in his D Minor Symphony, which Myrna had alluded to when she first called me to write the piece. Benjamin Britten did the same thing in his *Young People's Guide to the Orchestra.*

But no one had done it combining Native American–flavored music with the *guaguanco,* jazz, and music inspired by Middle Eastern music and Central European cantorial chants. Even though the musicians were struggling with all the notes and rhythms, I could hear what it would become.

At the end of the rehearsal, I said, "Ladies and Gentlemen. Thank you; you are incredible. No composer could dream of more than what you are doing. Tomorrow, we'll get the balances, tempos, and phrasing. By concert time, it will be ... *fantissimo*! In the words of the great Muhammad Ali, before his first fight with Sonny Liston, 'We'll shock the world.'"

"I'm glad you appreciate us and have so much fun working with us," said Vivian Bartles. She had played my cello concerto, *Honor Song for Sitting Bull,* nine months earlier, and knew what my music sounded like when it was fully rehearsed.

"This is a really fine piece," she said. "The orchestra likes it. They're going to *really* play it, and the audience will love it too."

Ken came up and added, "You're going to knock their socks off. Let's go out and chow down, soldier."

Ken and I went out and spent the night talking about all we had been through since the army. Music, children, dreams, pain and joy, and most of all, the importance of enduring friendship.

"After forty-three years of trolling, we finally hooked the big one!" said Ken.

I reminded Ken that his name was in the score. "Three hundred years from now, musicologists will freak out when they study all this, and wonder what it was all about," I said.

"That will be very helpful to both of us," said Ken wryly.

"Mostly the music will still be here," I said. "And we'll be cheering all the young cats to continue to wail down on Earth from our condo in the great ballpark in the sky."

At the final rehearsal the afternoon of the world premiere on January 17, 1997, the orchestra played the whole piece. They owned it now. It had become theirs.

"You did a good job, Dave," said Ken. "They can play it, and enjoy doing it."

"It's a beautiful piece, David," said Peter Serkin, who was there to play Mozart's Piano Concerto no. 21 with the orchestra to close the program. I had known Peter since 1960, when he was just about to turn thirteen years old. We met at the Marlboro Festival, where his father, pianist Rudolph Serkin, invited me to be composer-in-residence the following summer. Peter had become a giant in classical music, and a pioneer of performing new composers' music as well. I stayed and listened to him, accompanied by the symphony conducted by Ken. I knew the concert would be an unforgettable experience.

It was. The audience cheered the whole evening. The whole concert got terrific reviews, and the next night, my piece got a standing ovation from the audience. Lora Lee flew down to share the music with me. Without her patience and support, I never could have written it, with all the days and nights I spent in my back shed.

Mickey Raphael, the harmonica virtuoso from Willie Nelson's band, came to the opening night of the series. Mickey was a total musician who appreciated all forms of music. As a performer, he could create a perfect composition every time he played. We had played Farm Aid together several different times since Willie invited me to join him in Lincoln, Nebraska, for Farm Aid. Willie had asked me to make up a song about farming and then to join him and play it with his band. Sandy Bull, a fine musician from New York, came along.

My old friend, singer/songwriter John Prine, came with his wife. We had played together with Steve Goodman at folk festivals and concerts all over the United States and Canada.

"Dave," said John Prine, "I've never seen you dressed up before."

"Same for you and Sandy and Mickey," I said. "All you guys are wearing ties. I've never seen any of you dressed up either,"

I realized that despite all the years I'd known them, they had never heard any of my music that I actually wrote down. They had only heard me when I was improvising words and music.

"You've got to write a piece for Willie's band to play with the symphony," said Mickey.

"Write a piece for *oud, sarod,* and orchestra, and I'll play it," said Sandy.

John Prine and his wife both laughed. We stood there, introducing each other to everyone backstage. It was like a huge birthday party, rather than a stiff reception with angry-looking people glancing hungrily about to see who was the most important person in the room to network. The room was filled with real Nashville southern graciousness, warmth, and gentility.

Symphony musicians, patrons of the orchestra, Myrna Panitz, songwriters, stagehands, and anyone who came back all seemed happy to be there and appreciative of the fine playing that took place.

Finally, the house manager told us we had to leave the building. We all went out to a local beer hall/eating place to celebrate.

"We did it, Private Amram, we did it!" said Ken exuberantly.

"I think Murray would have loved it," said Myrna. "After Nashville records it, we'll let the Philadelphia Orchestra play it. Everyone remembers the twenty-eight years Murray played there. No one played the flute like Murray. Tomorrow night, after the performance, we'll have my party for the whole orchestra and their wives and have a toast to Murray."

As we celebrated the moment, I thought about the long trail leading to *Kokopelli*. All the seemingly unrelated events and twists and turns that led up to my composing this piece and how I composed it somehow made sense. I saw that, just like a chef or a painter or a playwright, my job as a composer was to put things together in a way that had an organic structure that seemed natural and pre-planned and that had some nutritional value, providing vitamins for the soul.

As everyone ate and drank, I thought about Murray and Hondo Crouch. I thought about what Hondo had done twenty-one years earlier on that sunny afternoon on the back porch of his general store in Luckenbach, Texas, to inspire me to write "Theme and Variations on Red River Valley," and how Myrna Panitz hearing it played on the radio twenty years later made it possible for me to write *Kokopelli*.

The memory of the experiences that led me to composing *Kokopelli* remain with me today during every waking moment. And I think about how Kokopelli himself continues to plant seeds each day, wherever he is, to nourish, to inspire, and to share beauty and life force with others.

And I always think of how my father and my uncle David and uncle Milton taught me to have respect and pay attention to everything and everybody and look for the essence, rather than being distracted by labels or stereotypes. And how they opened up the doors for me as a child to see that we live in a special place in the world with the original Americans, the native people we call Indians, who have been here for many millennia and who have so much that we can learn from, including their unique forms of musical expression.

And I think every day about Floyd Red Crow Westerman and Vine Deloria Jr., and all the Native Americans I have played for and with during much of my lifetime, and all that they have taught me, as well as what they have taught my own children

By trying to honor their many cultures through my music, I hope that my work can be a small thank you for the privilege of living in this beautiful Indian land we call the continent of the Americas.

♪

Chapter 5

Bouquets and Bombs on Broadway: Agony and Ecstasy on The Great White Way

The first music I ever composed for the theater was in 1945. It was an organ grinder's waltz for a high school production of *A Man with a Flower in His Mouth,* by Pirandello. I scored it for all the woodwind players I could round up who were willing to sit backstage until their brief moments of glory occurred when the theme and variations were played on cue. I'll never forget the rush of hearing the music as the lights went down and the set appeared when the curtain opened. It made the music feel completely different than it did when played in an empty room. The music made the set look and feel different when it was added to the production. I've been in love with the theater ever since.

The first Broadway show for which I composed music was *J.B.,* written by poet Archibald MacLeish in 1958. Elia Kazan directed it, and Christopher Plummer, Pat Hingle, Raymond Massey, and Nan Martin starred. It won the Pulitzer Prize and ran for a year, and it is still performed all over the world.

I wrote music for many off-Broadway and Broadway plays and composed scores for more than thirty Shakespearean productions, including Joe Papp's Shakespeare in the Park in New York, the Stratford Shakespeare Festival in Connecticut, the

Phoenix Theater, and the Repertory Theater of Lincoln Center, as well as for television dramas and films. But I always knew my calling was for more than writing music cues.

I enjoyed writing music for the theater but felt that composing symphonies, concertos, operas, ballet scores, chamber music, choral music, and pieces for wind ensembles and jazz, Latin, Middle Eastern, and world music ensembles was what I was meant to do.

I also loved performing and conducting live concerts, so after Leonard Bernstein chose me as the New York Philharmonic's first composer-in-residence in 1966, I curtailed a lot of my theater writing and concentrated every minute on pursuing what most people considered an impossible dream.

Now in 2007 and beyond, as I write this, I'm still pursuing the same dream, creating music that stands on its own.

Music that can be played from what is written down on paper and that can take the musicians and the listeners to all the places I have been.

Music that is strong enough to survive without my having to be there to explain it, conduct it, or perform it when it is played.

This is what playwrights, painters, sculptors, authors, poets, and architects have always told me they have tried to achieve in their life's work. While they love collaborating with others, they want to also create work that can stand on its own and doesn't require them to have to always be there once it has been completed. By having their work now belong to the world, they are free to start all over again each day and create something new for others to work with in the future.

Gifted musicians, dancers, and singers stimulate and challenge us as composers to come up with something better each time we compose music for the concert hall.

The actors I have worked with over the years in the theater have also always been a source of inspiration for new ways of approaching creative challenges. Almost all of them, once they saw that you respected them as they painstakingly struggled to create the character they were to become, would willingly share their special courage, devotion, idealism, and love of their craft with everyone they worked with, including any composer who wished to hear their input and reactions to the music we had created to enhance the atmosphere of the entire production.

The actor's constant desire to give a truthful performance to honor the playwright's intentions, combined with their skill to somehow transform themselves into becoming another person by creating that very person within themselves, was always magical to behold. And their ability to withdraw from the person that they had created and become a different person, as they were required to adjust to the new situations which the other actors were creating, and replace the person they had previously created with a new one, was always thrilling to see.

Sometimes, these adjustments continued for weeks, with each actor changing what they had just arrived at, until the whole play became unified. Watching the actors go through this selfless process was always a lesson in dedication, humility, and artistry. It showed all of us who were there how to be part of the whole.

Great actors, like great athletes and great musicians, are always studying everybody and everything, as a way of understanding all the aspects of what makes a character ring true. By observing the physical and the spiritual aspects of everyday people, the small things that often went unnoticed by others, actors constantly add to the toolbox of their craft each time they build a new character.

Observing actors as they observed others, on stage or in the streets, was always a lesson in itself.

I saw how actors studied the grace and clumsiness of other people's body language. I watched them as they listened intently to the unique sounds and inflections and regional accents when people spoke on subways or on park benches, and saw how the actors paid attention to the pace and timing of the way these people spoke.

I felt them directing all their attention to observing little things expressed by strangers: the subtle glance, the smirk, the furrowed brow. And I tried to tune in to the way they studied the unspoken psychic interaction between people they observed off stage and how they transferred this knowledge to what they did on stage.

I realized that the dedicated actors all maintained a constant awareness of how vital it was to be in touch with the feelings generated by their fellow actors and the audience.

Most important, I learned from working with actors that true acting or true creation of any kind isn't about mimicking, posturing, or pretending. It is about becoming and being.

Every night when a show was being done, the timing and ESP reaction of each actor to the other actors on stage and how they played off the vibration of the audience cast a spell on all the members of the audience, as well as on the backstage workers like myself. All of us working on a show, whether appearing on stage or working behind the scenes, heard the roar of the crowd, smelled the grease paint, and felt the glorious rush of energy when it was showtime.

Once you have experienced it, the theater, like music, becomes a part of your life.

In almost every production I ever worked on, I would hang out whenever I could with the actors, the playwright, the director, the stage hands, and the lighting and set designers. All of them had lessons to teach me about becoming a better composer and better performer. In exchange, I would contribute spontaneous extra-curricular activities after a hard day of rehearsals or following an intense evening performance and entertain everyone who attended our endless informal cast parties with little jam sessions, improvised poetry raps, and spontaneous happenings, inviting everyone who felt like it to participate.

Since I wasn't an actor (proven by my one and only non-performance with my fellow cast of other non-actors in Kerouac's film *Pull My Daisy*), I would always instigate some kind of post-theater carryings-on to celebrate everyone involved in the production by playing, rapping, and always requesting real actors to join in, without any inhibition. Regardless of how much I would carry on at these good time happenings, all members of the cast of whatever play I was working with always knew I was an appreciative and respectful fan of *real* actors, rather than being an exhibitionist ham pretending to be an actor.

In 1980, I hadn't written music for a Broadway play in more than ten years. I still maintained my lifelong friendship with actors Jerry Stiller and Anne Meara, with whom I had first worked in the summer of 1957 when they starred in Joe Papp's first season of free Shakespeare in Central Park.

I played many benefits with Ossie Davis Jr., Ruby Dee, Keir Dullea, Colleen Dewhurst, Ed Sherin, Earle Hyman, Dustin Hoffman, Julie Harris, Tony Randall, Jerry Orbach, E.G. Marshall, Maureen Stapleton, Jane Alexander, Zero Mostel, Jason Robards Jr., Bill Cosby, Jerry Stiller, Anne Meara, and hundreds of other gifted performers I was privileged to work with over the years.

I was also influenced by many of the directors for whom I composed music. I saw how they brought the plays to life, from the first draft of a script to the opening night performance. I watched them as they guided the whole process of staging the play, to enhance the flow of the story itself.

I marveled at how they could coordinate all the elements of lighting, sound, costuming, pacing, and editing of the script, and motivate the actors to go places within themselves that they had never visited before. The theater directors did this in the same way that the most masterful old-time symphony conductors helped to create a great performance.

The true maestros of the symphony orchestra world would always oversee every detail of what the composer had written down on his or her score paper, and then help when needed to inspire the way the musicians were interpreting it, all to create a memorable experience for the audience.

This is what the symphony orchestra conductors like Dimitri Mitropoulos, Leonard Bernstein, and George Szell did, when they motivated musicians to do the impossible and make it appear effortless.

Like these legendary maestros of the concert hall, theater directors Elia Kazan and Sidney Lumet, for whom I composed music, made everyone involved in a production excel and dig deep, while reminding us that each of us were part of the whole and must always be willing to adjust and change our work to fit into the larger picture of what the whole production was all about.

Giants of the American theater with whom I was lucky enough to work, like Arthur Miller, Paddy Chayefsky, Harold Clurman, Elia Kazan, and Joe Papp, continued to encourage me to dare to pursue the seemingly near-impossible dream of being a composer of all the kinds of music I have learned to play and then incorporate these many idioms into my classical work. They showed me, by example, that you never have to give up or lower your standards, no matter how difficult it might appear to pursue your dream. We all maintained friendships long after collaborating in the theater.

In 1980, when I received a phone call from Bobby Lewis to compose music for a Broadway production of *Harold and Maude,* I was hard at work in my cramped apartment on 6th Avenue in Greenwich Village. I had a wife and baby for the first time in my life, and in between feedings and diaper changes, I was composing the first draft of the opening movement of *Ode to Lord Buckley,* a concerto for alto saxophone and orchestra.

"David," said Bobby in his mellifluous and irresistibly charming and warm way, "that little voice I hear over the phone is going to need more than sonatas and concertos dedicated to her. If this play *Harold and Maude* equals the success of the film, your daughter will be able to go to college and even medical school. It's a marvelous play, by the same author who wrote the screenplay. I want songs, distant string quartets, waltzes, and some real chamber music compositions. I want a real composer. That's why I'm calling you."

Bobby Lewis, one of the pioneers of the Group Theatre and The Actors Studio, was a hero in the American theater, and I couldn't say no. I knew just being with him would be an experience I would cherish all my life, whatever the results of the play's commercial success. I had seen the movie and enjoyed its outrageous and original story.

"I'll have to warn you, David," said Bobby. "The Broadway theater is changing drastically. The serious plays are becoming a thing of the past. The old reputable producers with taste and knowledge are becoming dinosaurs. The eighties are making Philistinism chic. Vulgarity is becoming the norm. But we'll have a marvelous time trying to pull off a miracle. Let me send you a script and see what you think."

Three hours later, a script arrived by messenger. I read it late into the night, as my wife Lora Lee and baby Alana slept peacefully in our loft bed built over the piano. The script was wild. Reading it was like hanging out at an all-night get-together at a coffeehouse in the Greenwich Village of pre–World War II, which I had been told about by old timers in the early 1950s, when I first arrived in New York. They would tell me about all the old-time bohemians of the Edna St. Vincent Millay era of the 1920s who rapped incessantly, with jokes, philosophy, and great rambling discourses that wandered and returned, punctuated with guffaws and more coffee.

Harold and Maude reminded me of descriptions I had heard about these fabled days of bohemian life in post–World War I Greenwich Village. The adaptation from the film was written for the stage in a delightful rambling style. I had never read a play like it and thought it was amazing that it was being done on Broadway. It was funny, touching, and original. And there was music throughout, all kinds of music. I called Bobby back the next day.

"What do you think, David?" said Bobby. "Does it inspire you to come north of 14th Street?"

"I love it, Bobby," I said.

"I hear some reservation in your voice," said Bobby. No one in the world could fool him about anything.

"It's great, Bobby. I know I could write all kinds of music for it, but to be perfectly honest ... it's a little long."

"Of course," said Bobby. "It's more than four hours, but we can trim it to Broadway length without violating the story or the characters. And we'll have a decent budget to pay the musicians. The producer was a student of mine!"

I decided I had to do it.

Since I had met my wife Lora Lee in 1975, she had never seen any theatrical work I had done. Now, after I completed a score for this new play, I realized that we could go together and sit in the audience at a Broadway show.

"Lora Lee, I'm going to write music for a new play on Broadway. You've got to get a new dress. We'll have fun," I said. "You can come to opening night, and we'll trip the bright lights of the Great White Way, see the show, go to the cast party at some great place, and wait for the *New York Times* rave review."

"Are you sure?" she said.

"Well I know we'll have fun seeing the show," I said. "And I know Bobby Lewis will be able to get two seats for us and one for your father and your brother. We'll have to get a babysitter for one night."

A few days later I went to the first reading.

All the actors sat around a table with scripts, were introduced to each other, and then read the play. In addition to brilliant young actors like Keith McDermott playing the role of Harold, there was Denny Dillon, who went on to star in a hit TV show.

The surprise addition to the excellent cast was Janet Gaynor, now in her seventies, playing the role of Maude. Janet Gaynor was making her Broadway debut. She had won the Oscar in *A Star Is Born* in 1936, the first year the Oscars were given publicly. She had retired from films, and thought so much of the script that she decided to come to New York to star in the play. She had a purity and innocence that put a spell on all of us as she read her part. She was as thrilled as the young actors to be in a Broadway show.

There was an enormous amount of music to write because the play was more than four hours long, and had music throughout.

"Just write gorgeous music, David," said Bobby. "We'll cut most of it out as we make changes, but I know it will be distinguished enough to rise from the cutting room floor, and be of use to you later on for one of your compositions. I want you to write the best score you are capable of. No one will arrive a week before opening night and demand that you change your style and rewrite the entire score. We're going to give the Broadway audience our very best work. And I expect the very best from you."

Every day I went to rehearsals, and every night I went home and wrote music long after Lora Lee and our baby Alana were sleeping in the loft bed of our one-and-a-half room apartment. I would stagger into rehearsals the next morning and play what I had written for the actors and Bobby Lewis.

"Marvelous," said Bobby. "Let's have more music."

I was barely able to keep up with all the music Bobby wanted. I worked pretty much around the clock. Two weeks later, Bobby greeted me with a smile.

"David," he said, "we're going to bill the production as a play with music, not a drama with incidental music. This could become an opera some day."

I made a piano recording of the score, and Janet Gaynor and I rehearsed the songs I had written for her. She sounded lovely and had an unspoiled quality that made everything she did fresh, honest, and touching. Since I was also required to write music for the transitions between scenes, I began to time them, and out of curiosity, timed the whole play, scene by scene.

"How's it coming along, David?" said Lora Lee. "The music is nice. How are rehearsals going?"

"It's terrific," I said. "But I think they've got to start doing some serious cutting."

"Why?" she asked me.

"Because it's now nearly five hours long," I said. "And that's not counting intermission or scene changes. But the playwright is coming from California and he'll tell us what to do."

"Did you see the papers?" said Lora Lee. "He's been chosen to direct *Nine to Five* with Dolly Parton and a fantastic cast of actors. Do you think he'll have time to come to New York and spend a few weeks with a play?"

"Of course," I said. "His film *Harold and Maude* is a cult classic. He'll want the play to be just as concise and flowing. He'll see it's perfect."

A few days later, the playwright, Colin Higgins, arrived. I sat at the piano and played the overture, fantasizing at the same time of the future of the same music being played as the overture to an opera of *Harold and Maude* after its successful record-breaking five-year run on Broadway and several world tours. And of course, setting up college builder funds from the royalties so Alana and the other children Lora Lee and I hoped to have could all go to universities and start their own families some day. And a month after the triumphant opening, take Lora Lee and our baby Alana on a trip to some place in the world where I wouldn't know anyone, wouldn't have to make even one phone call, and could spend six weeks celebrating the good life, as the money was pouring in. And then come back from our first-ever vacation and start writing the opera *Harold and Maude,* commissioned by a major opera house.

As all these daydream fantasies of sugar plum fairies bombarding me with imaginary trappings of international acclaim were attacking my mind, I snuck a look at the playwright. He was smiling and nodding his head in approval.

By now, the play was so long that it took most of the day to read through.

"Cast," said Bobby, "you were all a director's dream. This evening, we'll re-write and make major revisions and cuts and it will end up being a two-hour drama. See you tomorrow."

I went home. I knew much of the music would disappear as the play would be shortened to half of its present length, but that was part of my job—to do what had to be done to contribute to the overall success of a unified creative effort. With Bobby as the captain of the ship of state, it would surely sail into the harbor as a winner.

The next day I got to rehearsal early. There was a strange hush in the rehearsal hall as the actors came in. The buzz of excitement, the smiles, and twinkling eye contact had disappeared. My ESP told me something was not happening that was supposed to happen. Bobby Lewis entered the room. He always exuded so much optimism and energy and good feelings that I knew whatever seemed wrong would be fixed. He could make a group of people standing around in a subway station an exciting dramatic experience.

"Good morning, David, you're here early. Has your muse temporarily withered? I thought you'd be at home with your lovely wife, tending to that adorable child, or writing a new symphony."

"No, Bobby," I said, suddenly relieved. His cheer and wit brightened up the whole room. Still, the actors looked worried as they took out their scripts. "I just came to get the cuts so I could start fixing all the music that needs to be changed. You know the motto in Afro-Cuban music—*'Estar siempre un pas adelante'* ('Always be a step ahead')."

"Absolutamente, Señor David," said Bobby.

"What did the playwright decide to cut?" I asked.

"Nothing," said Bobby. "Colin Higgins told me that he enjoyed it all and left this morning. He didn't discuss it."

"When is he coming back?" I asked.

"I don't think he is," said Bobby. "He's directing *Nine to Five,* which is sure to be a mega hit film, and I think he forgot about his colleagues toiling in the vineyards of the theater. But we shall prevail. Be prepared for some storms at sea. But like *Mutiny on the Bounty,* where Fletcher Christian took the wheel of the Bounty and sailed to Pitcairn Island after Captain Bligh was forced to abandon ship and row the stormy seas to distant lands, our ship of state *Harold and Maude* will survive our playwright leaping overboard to go to the Elysian Fields of Hollywood, and we'll sail into port a winner with a two-hour-and-forty-minute show."

"Well said, Bobby," said Janet Gaynor.

"Block that metaphor," whispered Denny Dillon.

The cast assembled and Bobby began a fantastic forty-five minute monologue, recounting his favorite catastrophes in the theater, including one story where, during an out-of-town tryout of a serious drama the entire set collapsed, blowing out all the lights in the theater and setting off a fire alarm, creating total panic. As the audience rushed towards the exit, the costume designer leaped over the rubble of the stage and screamed at the lead actor, who was climbing out of the wreckage, "The ruffles on your tights were sewn on four inches too high!"

"You see," said Bobby, "overspecialization is a curse in the theater. We must always remember we are collaborators. We all work together, for and with each other, for the greater glory of the whole. We have some serious cutting and editing to do. Since our playwright Colin Higgins has gone back to greener pastures, we will proceed as if we were cutting Moliere or Strindberg, who alas, have gone on to the playwrights' ultimate theater in the sky. If we succeed, Colin Higgins will have a hit in Hollywood with *Nine to Five* and a simultaneous hit on Broadway with *Harold and Maude.*"

Bobby probably could have inspired confidence in the passengers on the Titanic, so we all felt relieved. During the entire day, great portions of the play were cut. I realized I'd have to write new music—a lot of what I'd done no longer fit, because the whole play was being revamped.

I went home and spent three days writing and rewriting, and then spent almost an entire sleepless twenty-four-hour stint with the music copyist getting the parts copied for the recording of the music, which was to be synchronized offstage, and played on cue.

Two of New York's most accomplished French hornists, Peter Gordon and Robert Rouch, were part of the ensemble for the recording of the score.

"Dave, this is some fine music," said Robert Rouch. "This sounds like chamber music. I can't believe they'll use something like this on Broadway."

"That's because of the director, Bobby Lewis," I said. "He loves Brahms, Bartók, Gershwin, and Charlie Parker. That's why he hired me."

"Good luck," said Peter Gordon. "I want to get some tickets and see this."

"After a few months, I can get some freebies," I said. At the very moment I said that, my life-long ESP reality-radar truth gyroscope alert system sent a neurological spasm through me.

"It might not be a few months. It might be a bomb," said the voice that has always guided me. The same voice that told me to take the long hard road for greater glory was telling me my dreams of a stash of cash were misplaced.

"What's the matter, Dave?" said Bob Rouch. "You look like you're freaking out."

"No," I said. "Everything's cool. You all sound great. But maybe I should get you and Peter and all the musicians passes for the previews."

We finished recording the music and played it all for the cast the next morning. They all enjoyed it, and Denny Dillon did an improvised dance while the overture was played back a second time.

"Bravo, David," said Bobby. "It's real music. Not Broadway trash!"

"I like the instrumental accompaniment to my sunflower song," said Janet Gaynor. "It reminds me of Schubert Lieder. I was afraid they were expecting me to be a Broadway belter. Thank heavens you wrote something lyrical and sensitive."

"That music is groovy, my man," said one of the stagehands I knew from the Brooklyn Academy of Music where I conducted the Brooklyn Philharmonic every year. Like me, he was now working for the theater in Manhattan. "Those are some hip sounds. I hope they don't cut it all out."

"What do you mean?" I said, sensing disaster creeping up around the corner.

"Listen, brother. In Brooklyn, you do those concerts for the kids with the symphony, and those programs in the parks with jazz and Latin guest artists soloing with the symphony and nobody messes with you. They cut you some slack and you wail. I've been checking you out for ten years in Brooklyn. This ain't Brooklyn, baby. This is Broadway. The producer's been sneaking around, and he's trying to take over the show. He's bringing in a demolition expert, special effects people, and new sets that are supposed to move on cables when you crank them—that are never going to work. He's going to blow the whole scene."

"But he was Bobby Lewis's student," I said feebly.

"Yeah. Well, he ain't in school now. He owns the school. He's got the bread, and he wants to kick some ass!"

"I hope you're wrong," I said.

"I wish I was," he said. "But I'm not. I'm back here doing my job, and checking out what's going down. Maybe a miracle will happen. The producer might get kidnapped until the show opens."

I suddenly felt dejected, but tried to hide it. All the actors appreciated my enthusiasm. It was genuine, because they were all so talented and devoted and all loved the theater.

"David, you're looking terribly pensive," said Bobby Lewis.

"Well," I said, "I hope everything is all right."

"Of course everything is all right," he said. "You've written some marvelous music. We have an exquisite play, although it still needs to be cut into half of its present length, and Janet Gaynor has all the purity and freshness of an ingénue. Have you been hearing rumors about producer anxiety?" he asked, suddenly fixing me with a stare that made it impossible to diplomatically sneak away from an honest answer.

"Well," I said. "A little bit."

"Of course you have," Bobby said airily. "The producer had a hissy fit and the whole crew heard him. He wants to bring in a whole crew of special effects people. The opera *Aida* needs elephants on stage when it's staged at the Roman Coliseum. *Harold and Maude* is fine done simply on Broadway. We have acting values and an intelligent audience. After he wastes all his money with explosive devices and scene changes that don't work, he'll change his mind and stop interfering. Remember, he was my student!"

I went home feeling much better. The next day I came back for the first technical rehearsal. This was a chance for the actors to see the demolition expert in action and learn how to walk around the stage when the new set devices were put into action, with all the stage hands turning cranks as the whole stage was supposed to change from scene to scene.

As I entered the stage door, I heard groaning and shrieking creaks that sounded like dinosaurs trying to scream for help as they attempted to extricate themselves from a primordial cranberry bog. I entered the backstage area and saw the stagehands cursing as they cranked various levers, none of which seemed to work. The groaning, grating sounds grew louder. Suddenly, an enormous explosion rocked the theater.

I flashed back to basic training at Fort Breckenridge, Kentucky, in September of 1952, when gunfire accompanied tanks running over our heads as we cowered in the fetal position with our heads two feet below ground level in barrels. The clanking of the treads from the tanks as they ground against the barrels, combined with the gunfire and gleeful screams of the instructors, gave all of us a lifelong revulsion to what heavy metal rockers call "white sound." This was supposed to prepare us to go to war, but somehow all this cacophony seemed inappropriate for a poetic comedy like *Harold and Maude*.

I eased towards the stage and saw Bobby Lewis looking somewhat perturbed.

"I think the special effects are a bit much," he said diplomatically to the demolition expert.

"Wait, Bobby," said the explosion specialist. "You haven't heard my Big Bertha Bomber effect. This will kill 'em!"

"That's what I'm afraid of," said Bobby tartly. "I can see a hundred pacemakers destroyed and several concussions in our audience. I think we must remember the Zen saying, 'Less is more.'"

The special effects man then unveiled his newly constructed gallows where Harold was supposed to entertain his family by pretending to hang himself.

"This is a fantastic effect, Bobby. When the lights come up, the audience will think Harold is actually hanging from a noose and has had his neck broken. The actor has to be careful to stay at the correct angle, so he doesn't get strangled, but that shouldn't be a problem."

"Our insurance doesn't cover suicides and public executions," said Bobby.

Keith McDermott, who always exuded confidence no matter what was demanded of him in playing the role of Harold, looked warily at the gallows.

"I feel like the victim in a new version of the old Gary Cooper movie, *The Hanging Tree*," he said.

For two days, we struggled with technical rehearsals, trying to get the scenery changes, explosions, and hanging sequences to work smoothly. They never could function the same way twice, and now the play took nearly four hours, even after all the cuts.

"David, you have to write some more marvelous music," said Bobby. "All the scene changes are taking forever. I'm only worried that the dreadful noise those machines make would drown out even the loudest *tutti* passages of Berlioz's Requiem. Perhaps you can write something so clever that it will distract the audience or play in counterpoint to this entire atrocious racket. It sounds like we're doing a 1930s Socialist treatise on the construction of the Holland Tunnel by sandhogs."

Another huge explosion interrupted our conversation.

"Please," said Bobby, "the rehearsal is over."

"I know," said the special effects man. "I thought you might like to hear this new series of explosions. They're devastating!"

"They certainly are," said Bobby. "But right now I can't hear anything. Please go home, before I have to consult an eye and ear specialist. I'm about to have photos taken of the production, assuming the theater doesn't collapse."

The special effects man began packing up.

"Just listen to this one, Bobby," he said, and before people could even cover their ears, an enormous explosion went off, filling the theater with acrid smoke as the photographer entered.

"Is this the *Harold and Maude* production?" he asked, as he took a handkerchief from his pocket and began coughing into it after wiping his eyes.

"Yes," said Bobby. "But it is beginning to have an uncanny resemblance to a staged version of *The Battle of the Bulge*."

The actors came out on the stage for a cast photo and individual shots and stills of the production.

"David, I'd like a shot of you playing the piano with Janet Gaynor and Keith McDermott both singing some of those lovely songs. If we become permanently hearing-impaired before the show opens, we can look back fondly on these delightful moments of the production. But please comb your hair first."

I sat at the piano and pictures were taken. I thought about Janet Gaynor winning the first Oscar ever given forty-three years before this production. She had the same sweetness, dignity, and vulnerability in 1980 that she did in 1937.

"David," she said to me, after the pictures were taken. "I know you've done a lot of work in the theater on Broadway for dramatic plays. This is my first time on Broadway. Is it always like this? Your music is fine. It's simple and it adds something without getting in the way. But those special effects and machines for changing the scenery and turning the set around every which way are so distracting I forget my lines, or even where I am. My ears are ringing. And nothing seems to work."

"I think Bobby is going to put his foot down," I said. "He's meeting with the producer tomorrow to see if everything can be simplified so he can get back to cutting the play and working with the actors," I said, hoping to make her feel more secure. She looked right into my brain with her large unwavering eyes. I could see she knew that I was trying to make her feel appreciated but still was aware that I was worried too. And I knew she could sense the first inkling we both suddenly felt of impending doom.

I felt like we were out at sea, having a friendly conversation in the elegant ballroom, just as the Titanic was about to hit the hidden iceberg.

"You're very considerate and reassuring, David. I'm glad you combed your hair for our photos. I'll see you tomorrow, and I look forward to the new music you'll bring us. Good night. Give your baby daughter and your wife my best wishes."

I was amazed at how gracious she was. I realized she knew we were about to hit the panic stage of the production, and yet she was trying to make the whole cast and all the backstage workers feel good.

I went home and tiptoed over to my desk to write more music. Lora Lee and Alana were asleep in the loft bed. About 4:00 a.m. Alana woke up. I got her bottle and, after feeding her, started writing some new music to fill in the dead space that was now added to the play during the scene changes where there was nothing that the actors could do while the parts of the set changed positions in slow motion. It was now the responsibility of the lighting designer and me to make this unfortunate series of interruptions into meaningful moments for the audience.

"David, are you writing more music?" said Lora Lee.

"Yes," I answered.

"It's going to end up being an opera?" she asked. "How can they use all that music you have written and keep on writing?"

"Most of what I have done so far won't be used at all," I said. "They'll end up cutting most of it from the show when the play gets cut again, but I'm trying to help out."

"Well, it sounds beautiful," she said. "You can always use it for a symphony or chamber piece some day, if it hits the cutting room floor."

"Don't worry, I will," I said.

I worked till 7:00 a.m. and then got four hours of sleep so I could go back to the theater at noon to play what I had written for Bobby and the cast.

I entered the theater and there was a deathly stillness in the air. It was like going to a wake in a funeral home where the open casket drew everybody's energy out of them and made the reality of our mortality seem so overpowering that no words were necessary. Silence and prayer were the only ways to deal with this feeling.

I went over to Denny Dillon. She was always a bundle of energy, with a scintillating sense of humor. Her small part was brilliantly done from the very first reading, and I knew she could not only cheer me up but would know what was happening. She was constantly aware and studying the whole production in order to have her part fit what came before and after her big scene.

"Denny, what's happening?" I asked.

"I think Bobby and the producer got into a serious argument. Bobby wants to eliminate most of the special effects and mechanical scene changes, simplify everything, and work on the play and the acting values. I don't think he feels the audience is coming to see a demolition derby."

At the end of the day's rehearsal, Bobby gathered us all together.

"I wanted to talk to all of you so you wouldn't be upset tomorrow when you see a closing notice posted on the backstage bulletin board. It's not customary to post one ten days before opening night, but we'll live with it, and still put on a great show. I'm proud of all of you, and I'll do everything I can to salvage your good work and the beauty of the play. This is the producer's first time on Broadway.

There's still hope. As you all know, he was once my student. Now I regret to say, I'm beginning to doubt his abilities as a scholar when he has to put the knowledge I bestowed upon him into action.

"I reminded him today in our latest meeting that Shakespeare, not me, wrote 'the play's the thing wherein we'll catch the conscience of the king.' People come to the theater to share the magic of the author's words brought to life by the actors, leaving enough space for the audience to be part of the whole experience. *Harold and Maude* is not a Marine training film, or a National Geographic tour of exploding volcanoes. It's a poetic love story, full of wit and charm."

I continued rehearsing the songs with the actors and during the next week watched them grow shorter and shorter and gradually disappear entirely. The constant scenery changes still never worked on time.

Finally, time had run out. We had to admit preview audiences and, while the critics from the media weren't coming for another few days, the toughest critics of all were going to fill the house. Preview audiences were usually people who wanted to get an inexpensive seat to a show and also have a chance to second-guess what the outcome would be by opening night. In New York, the preview audiences were notorious for their outspoken reactions, not only during intermission but often during the shows themselves, where they would yell encouragement or criticism of the actors' performances. If you could please these grassroots critics, you knew you had a chance.

In the preview performances, the set changes from scene to scene, with their complicated mechanical maneuverings, often wouldn't work at all, so that after the first breakdown, the stagehands could never catch up with the play. No matter how hard they cranked, once they got behind because of a mechanical breakdown, they could never get to the next scene on time. As a result, the actors were forced to improvise their way around the set, while the lighting designer tried to cover up the misplaced positions of the actors.

Because of all this confusion, the actors were now often in the dark, trying not to fall off the various ramps which were protruding in the wrong places, meant to be part of the scenes which had already taken place. And meanwhile, the World War II–style special effects cut loose, often in the wrong scenes because of the panic backstage where no one was sure what was happening.

This did not go unnoticed by the preview audiences. During intermission, they complained about the deafening explosions and the smoke from the special effects that left them adjusting their hearing aids while coughing and rubbing their eyes. *Harold and Maude* was in trouble, and everybody knew it.

"Why don't someone tell the producer to supply gas masks and ear plugs?" remarked one annoyed theatergoer, between hacking coughs, in front of the candy concession during intermission.

"Yeah, and tell them to be careful with them *meshuga* sets. I come all the way from Brooklyn to see Janet Gaynor. She's bee-oo-ti-ful, and she almost got crushed between them sets when they started movin' in on her when she was singin' that song there that you wrote, what-dya-call-it? Oh, yeah, the "Sunflower Song," am I right, or what? I thought they was gonna squash her dead. That's no way to treat a star! Who do they think they're kiddin'? "

"You're my kind of drama critic," I answered meekly, and returned to my seat to pray that the last act would go more smoothly.

After the show was over I heard several more complaints from the uninhibited members of the audience who loved to attend previews to keep alive the New York art of schmoozing and kibitzing. I then went backstage, and the stagehand I knew from the Brooklyn Academy of Music told me one of the producer's assistants instructed the crew backstage to change the sets while Miss Gaynor was singing, even though the squeaking and clanging upstaged her, to "give brisker pacing to the scene."

Keith McDermott, the gifted young actor playing Harold, had been saintly through the entire ordeal. He had been considerate and supportive of Janet Gaynor, and he risked his life every night as new ways were devised to hang him from a scaffold, explode him, and then have to go home and memorize new lines as the producer had the play re-written each day. Somehow, he was able through all of this to learn to play the banjo, performing some simple music I had written for him, after the company agreed to purchase a banjo.

"Assuming a miracle doesn't occur, please take the banjo when the show closes," he said. "We're not going to have a long enough run for me to ever learn how to play it beyond the simple things you showed me."

Finally opening night came. Lora Lee wore a beautiful dress, her father Ralph and brother Tommy came from upstate New York, and with a babysitter watching Alana, all four of us got to the theater early.

Outside the theater, to my horror, I saw all the rehearsal photos posted under glass, where you usually see the final production pictures. All of the actors had on street clothes, and there were even pictures of me at the piano in a funky tweed coat with holes in the sleeves, rehearsing with the actors.

Bobby Lewis was in the lobby, greeting friends from all over the world who admired his lifetime of achievement in the theater. I introduced him to my father-in-law and brother-in-law.

"I hope you enjoy the show. I know you'll enjoy David's music, what little remains after our trials and tribulations. I'm happy we could work together, David, and we shall again in more sane circumstances. I only wish we could all celebrate at Sardi's later tonight, but the producer not only put up the closing notice ten days ago, he also canceled the opening night party. You might say he has prematurely thrown in the towel, as they say in boxing. My only regret is that Janet Gaynor and the actors deserve much better treatment, and so does the playwright. But the film remains a classic, and some day the play will be staged simply and tastefully, the way we all envisioned it."

Bobby moved on, greeting other people, and the four of us sat down.

The lights went down, and the overture began. The lights came up, and the first scene was wonderful. Then it was time for the first scene change, and the grinding of gears and scraping of the sets grew louder and louder, until the whole set started swaying as if there was an earthquake. There was a loud murmur in the audience because for a moment it seemed the entire multilevel tiers of sets were going to collapse on top of the actors.

Suddenly there was a huge squeal, followed by a clank and something sounding like a gunshot. The sets shuddered to a complete halt, midway in the first of fourteen scene changes, and remained there for the rest of the evening. The cable that moved all the various parts of the set had snapped, and the actors had to improvise, climbing around the scenery, platforms, and props.

When the first series of explosions took place, it was obvious the special effects man had saved Big Bertha for opening night. Or perhaps the producer was trying to get revenge by asserting his final creative addition to his vision of an exciting evening in the theater, by literally blowing it up. The deafening roar and sonic boom was followed by a collective scream of terror from the audience. A cloud of noxious smoke wafted its way through the audience, and almost like a carefully orchestrated choral composition, you could hear layers of wheezing, coughing, and gasping make a wave of sound from the front row to the back row of the theater and then through the balcony, following the smoke. Several members of the audience got up and left, rubbing their eyes as they tried to breathe. The actors continued, but for ten minutes, they were drowned out by the audience's respiratory problems.

"This sounds like Bellevue Hospital Emergency Room on Saturday night, for Chris-sakes," said a man in front of me, as he wiped his eyes with his white silk scarf, before blowing his nose and coughing up some phlegm into it. "I'm paying forty-five dollars to get asphyxiated."

At intermission the lobby resembled the dockside Parking Violations Bureau Garage. This is where hundreds of people go at night to stand in line, waiting to reclaim their cars that have been towed away. The theater lobby had this same mixture of gloom, anger, and a sense that people were being victimized.

The audience continually shrank in size during the evening, and every special effects shocker sent new people heading for the exits. It was like being in a major league ballpark for a Sunday game and having the home team losing 25-1. The theater was filled with an eerie silence, with only the true believers remaining. In a way, it was very beautiful, because everyone sensed they were seeing something that wouldn't be around much longer, and therefore could savor the experience, like an anthropologist seeing the final playing out of a species about to become extinct.

After the curtain, we went backstage and commiserated with all the actors and the backstage crew. We had developed a sense of community, like a huge family, which is one of the extraordinary things that happen in the theater, music, and sports, when you have a gifted, committed and principled person in charge, like Bobby Lewis. Many were crying as they spoke to him. He was gracious and supportive to everyone, as he had been since the very first day.

"David, enjoy your family. Go home and write more music. And keep up your love of the serious theater. This experience will make our next work together more glorious. I'm sorry the producer forgot the values I try to instill in all my students. To retain truthfulness, a purity of purpose, a sense of joy, and the realization that great art done correctly is also always great entertainment."

We went home and turned on my little black and white TV set to watch the television commentators' review. Stewart Klein, a knowledgeable and humorous reviewer, always on the money, was the first to come on the air.

"The major mistake the producers of *Harold and Maude* made in tonight's opening on Broadway was to have my seat facing the stage," he began. Lora Lee, her father Ralph, and brother Tommy looked horrified and hurt, so I changed channels. All the other reviewers had a similar opinion of the production. They liked the actors, the music, and the original film, but all saw that the play itself had been massacred by the production.

I went down to buy the early morning edition of the *New York Times,* and calmly read the blasting review.

"What did they say?" said Lora Lee, looking forlorn.

"There's some great recipes on page forty-seven," I said, trying to cheerfully change the subject.

"I thought it was pretty good," said my father-in-law, Ralph.

"Me too," said his son Tommy.

"Well," I said, "there's always next time."

"The music was so beautiful," said Lora Lee, looking as if she were about to cry.

"Don't worry. No one got to hear the 80 percent of the score that was cut, and since the play probably won't run more than a week, I'll use some of the themes in a concert piece some day. When Alana is a grownup, she'll hear something in a symphony that is based on what I was writing while she was sleeping here on 6th Avenue when she was one year old. What's beautiful stays beautiful!"

Eventually the first part of the overture to *Harold and Maude* became the introduction to my saxophone concerto *Ode to Lord Buckley*. The melody of one of the lyrical, Renaissance-flavored songs, written for Janet Gaynor to sing, which was cut from the show, became the principal theme of the second movement of the concerto. *Ode to Lord Buckley* premiered a year after *Harold and Maude* closed, and has been recorded and played around the world.

And since the producer had no money to pay me my royalties for the remaining three performances before the show closed, I got to keep the banjo.

I still look back with pride and pleasure on working with Bobby Lewis and the cast of *Harold and Maude*. If it had been presented the way Bobby Lewis envisioned it, it would still be running.

In retrospect, the overproduced fiasco of *Harold and Maude* was a forerunner of what has been happening to the Broadway Theater during the last twenty-seven years since the close of the play in 1980.

Today, at the time of this writing in 2007, serious drama, sophisticated comedy, acting values, musical excellence, brilliant choreography, socially significant stories, and shows reasonably priced are being presented all over the world and in many small theaters in New York City. The producers who used to bring world-class theater are being replaced by a new generation of entrepreneurs who think that *Batman, Jerry Springer,* reality TV programs, kung fu, ultimate fighting, porno movies, and shows designed to look like video games are what Broadway needs on stage to satisfy as well as to attract audiences. Over the years, the essential elements for most of the hit shows on the Great White Way have begun to include helicopters, outrageous special effects, and over-amplified sound designers blasting the audience into a catatonic state of submission, accompanied by music assembled by tone-deaf hacks and written by an army of ghostwriters and orchestrators, replacing talented musicians with the soulless, sterile sounds of synthesizers and computers. And enormous sets and technical displays dwarf the play and the actors.

Much of what you see on Broadway today is as dull and businesslike as the attaché cases carried by the army of lawyers, accountants, technicians, and agents who have taken over the Great White Way.

Fortunately, this is now all changing. With the tremendous growth of regional theaters all over the country, and the splendid work being done in tiny venues all over the five boroughs of New York City and the entire Eastern seaboard, there is a renaissance of small theater companies springing up every day. This will eventually force Broadway to return to its high standards of the past.

Broadway will be reborn again.

In the meantime, New York is now just one of *many* places where you can go to see exciting theater throughout the United States. And a new generation of playwrights, actors, composers, dancers, and all who work in the theater, as well as those who love to be in the audience, can experience a lifetime of joy without ever coming to Broadway. Still, there is a special thrill to the Great White Way, and like conducting or performing at Carnegie Hall, it always gives you, at the very least, a salutary blast from the past whenever you can be there.

After *Harold and Maude* closed, I was so busy composing my saxophone concerto, *Ode to Lord Buckley,* conducting young people's concerts at the Brooklyn Academy of Music and with the Vancouver and Montreal Symphonies in Canada, and performing with my quartet, that I was able to overcome the disappointment of this beautiful play's early demise.

When I told Bobby Lewis that I could salvage a few snippets of the overture to *Harold and Maude* and one of the songs cut from the play and use them as themes for the saxophone concerto, he was pleased and chuckled appreciatively.

"It makes me feel like I have become a veritable patron of the arts, like the Margrave of Brandenburg commissioning Bach to write what the German royalty referred to as *tafle musik*. You know, David, that this *tafle musik* Bach wrote for the Margrave of Brandenburg was supposed to be used for dinner music at one of his picnics and ended up becoming the six glorious Brandenburg Concertos, played for the last two hundred and thirty years, ever since the picnic was over. So out of the ashes of *Harold and Maude* will rise some shining moments from the music you composed for me in your new saxophone concerto.

"But don't give up working in the theater. Live theater, like live music, is the most challenging and enriching experience for the artist as well as for the audience. And Broadway is one of the many venues where we hope it will survive in some fashion, even though it is a shadow of its former creative self."

On March 17, 1981, Adira was born a few hours before *Ode to Lord Buckley,* dedicated to her birth, was premiered by Kenneth Radnofsky and the Portland Symphony under the direction of Bruce Hangen. I flew from the hospital in Schenectady, New York, to Portland to hear the exciting world premiere performance, and handed out cigars to the soloist, conductor, and members of the orchestra, as the piece received a standing ovation. I could see Adira, pink and placid, sleeping in her white comforter in the hospital, surrounded with an ethereal glow, like a giant halo of light that seemed to emanate from her and fill the room with sunshine.

During the years when she was growing up, I played Adira a tape of the world premiere performance, so beautifully played by saxophonist Ken Radnofsky. She heard some of the themes used in *Harold and Maude,* and I told her about Janet Gaynor, in all her dignified loveliness and strength, inspiring all of us who worked with her to be bold and devoted. I hoped Adira could carry on that same spirit in some way, whatever she decided to do in her life.

Adira has become an accomplished singer-songwriter, actress, comedienne, narrator of Kerouac's writings with me backing her up, as I did with Jack, and also a free-associator scat-rap performer in her own right.

This has made me feel that the music I wrote for *Harold and Maude* and the positive energy of the production created by the actors and Bobby Lewis's direction has had an afterlife that is still part of the world and survived the disastrous production. I think this sensation is much like the descriptions of people in near-death experiences who describe hovering above the accident, bathed by light and filled with joy as they are liberated from the shackles of earthly cares, wishing to tell their mourning friends that they should not despair because this rebirth after death is a happy experience.

In the fall of 1981, after coming back from some concerts I did in San Juan, Puerto Rico, with Lora Lee, Alana, and Adira, I received a phone call from the producer and director Bob Whitehead on my answering machine. I played the message back to my daughter Alana, so she could hear his well-modulated voice and impeccable diction. She was now two years and three months old and loved to talk, meet new people, and listen to grownups speak to one another.

"Alana, listen to how beautifully Mr. Whitehead speaks," I said. "He has worked in the theater all his life and was brought up in Canada. Listen to him. His talking sounds like music."

I played her the message three times, and she was fascinated.

"Daddy ... Daddy!" she said, as I turned the machine off.

"Yes," I said.

"Do he really got a white head?" she asked.

"Kind of," I answered. "He has very distinguished gray locks."

"Oh," she said, looking disappointed. "I thought he look like Mr. Potato Head."

"No," I said, "he's much better looking."

I called Bob back at his office. I had worked as the composer and music director with him from 1963 to 1965 when he, along with Arthur Miller, Elia Kazan, Harold Clureman, and actors including Jason Robards Jr., Faye Dunaway, Salome Jens, Ralph Meeker, and Barbara Loden, founded the Lincoln Center Repertory Theater. He was one of the mainstays of the American theater and had a long history of producing classic dramas on Broadway. He was married to the award-winning, Australian-born actress Zoe Caldwell.

"Bob," I said, "it's great to hear from you."

"David, it's wonderful to hear your voice again, plus the two little voices I could hear yelling into your answering machine while you were leaving your message.

"We really enjoy your *No More Walls* album. In addition to your symphonic compositions that you conducted, we love hearing the extended version of 'Waltz from After the Fall' that you did for our show nine years ago at the Lincoln Center Theater. Zoe and I listen to it every morning while we are doing our exercises."

"Well," I said, "The composer Paul Hindemith always talked about *gebrauchts musik* (music used for useful functions), so I guess I inadvertently created something for the home physical fitness market."

"The reason I'm calling you, David, is to see if you'd be interested in working with Zoe and me in a production of *Medea*. It's going to be done at the Clarence Brown Theater in Knoxville, Tennessee, and I hope it can come to New York some day. You know, of course, that Broadway today is so risky that our only chance to bring *Medea* into New York is a slim one at best. I know you are so busy composing concert pieces, conducting, and performing. I'll understand perfectly if this is something that no longer interests you. I want to add, however, that Dame Judith Anderson, now in her eighties, is going to be performing the role of the nurse. Robinson Jeffers adapted *Medea* into English for Judith Anderson, and she created the role of Medea herself in the original Broadway production way back in 1947. Now she is passing the torch to Zoe. It should be a memorable experience in the theater, and we want to include some of that marvelous Middle Eastern flavored music we have heard you perform. Do you think you might be interested in working with us?"

"Yes," I said, without a moment's hesitation. "Give me the dates, the deadline, the number of musicians I can use, and I'll be there."

"Splendid, David. And there will be no conflict between the producer and director, because I'm both the director and the producer, so I'll see the producer is sympathetic to all of our artistic needs."

"Thank heavens," I said. "I wish you could have worked with Bobby Lewis a year and a half ago and been the producer for *Harold and Maude*.

"Well, David," said Bob, "we won't have the same problems that Bobby Lewis had. We have a masterful script in place. And we don't need any extraneous specialty effects. This production will concentrate on the intrinsic values of the play and the artistry of the actors. Ben Edwards has designed the set, based on his original one he created many years ago. It is simple, functional, and helps the actors and the audience to all be part of a theatrical experience. The costumes, the lighting, and, of course, the music, will all support the actors and the play, rather than overwhelming it. And with Zoe and Dame Judith in the cast, we should have an exciting time in Knoxville."

"The South will rise again, Bob. I'll be there."

I hung up and took the kids for a stroll in Washington Square Park, and when I came home, the script had arrived by messenger. It was a magnificent play, and I started writing music in my head.

A few days later I went to the small rehearsal space to begin our work together. The first reading was spellbinding. Zoe Caldwell sent shivers down our spines as she moved in her portrayal from a regal woman in love with her husband and children to a victim so traumatized that she murdered her own children out of revenge. Zoe was so intense and consumed by the role that after we had finished the reading of the play, we were all speechless.

Dame Judith Anderson, who had created the role of Medea in the original production decades ago, turned to Zoe after a minute of hushed silence and said in a low voice, "Well done, my darling. Let's have some tea." She embraced Zoe, and we all breathed a sigh of relief and took our lunch break, still in a daze from the power of the first reading.

Zoe came over to me before we all went out to lunch.

"I'm so glad you're with us, David. We need some music to evoke the fiery, smoldering passion of the ancient Greeks, the music of the slaves, the different kinds of music brought by the visiting people to the seaports of Athens, and the sounds of pagan rituals. You can dig deep into your collective unconscious and create something magical for us."

"Zoe," I said. "Your reading was so powerful, I'll just try to do what's needed without getting in the way."

"No, no, no. Be daring. Be creative. And this was just a reading. In a few weeks, I'll be able to begin to delve deeper into the character, and with all of us evolving together, I'll give a performance. And having Judith Anderson in the production, playing the role of the nurse, thirty-five years after she created the role of Medea herself in the original production on Broadway, is a thrill beyond belief. She is so marvelous and supportive."

I had never witnessed any performance more powerful than Zoe's first reading, so I knew we were all in for a treat. I was struck again how a great actor or actress could literally create and become another person, and moments later, return to the person you have known for years and sit and talk to you, drinking tea and eating a sandwich.

It reminded me of when I met Charlie Parker for the first time backstage at the Howard Theater in 1952 in Washington, D.C., after he had blown us all away with his one-time-only genius improvisations. When we were introduced to him, he was sitting calmly in his dressing room in his suspenders, as he leaned back on the back two legs of his chair and reminisced about being a teenager in Kansas City and taking up the saxophone. He talked to us in a warm down-home way that made us feel as if we were at home with him on his back porch.

Over the next few weeks, I attended rehearsals and wrote music that included the use of the *shanai*, a double reed Middle Eastern ancestor of the oboe that I had been playing since 1978 when I came back from concerts in Egypt, the Middle East, and Southeast Asia. I also used the *nay*, an ancient form of the flute I had acquired in Isfahan, Iran, that is played from the side of your mouth between the teeth and has a unique sound, like an ethereal voice from an ancient tomb. And my ceramic *dumbek* and clay Moroccan drums also created sounds that evoked the feelings of the past.

I brought some of the instruments to rehearsals and played them for the cast. Mitch Ryan, with whom I had worked in many productions of Shakespeare in the Park, came over to look at my array of instruments.

"You've got some new sounds, David. I can hardly wait for the jam session for the cast party when we open in Knoxville."

"It's great to see you again, Mitch. I've seen you in films and on TV, but I still remember you in Joe Papp's Shakespeare productions. The theater performances stay in your memory for a lifetime."

"That's what always brings us back," said Mitch. "Even when we make a fraction of the money we do in films, the theater nourishes our soul. And that's a vitamin you can't buy in any health food store."

When I recorded the music, I played ten instruments myself and had George Mgrdichian, the master of the *oud,* play a part I had written. George had a degree from Juilliard as a clarinetist, but was self-taught on the *oud*. We had played together since 1960, and in addition to being able to perform every style of Middle Eastern, Turkish, Armenian, Greek, Israeli, and Arabic music, George performed a Handel Concerto he transcribed for *oud* and orchestra, which I conducted. He was a true master of many genres of music. I also created sounds for the play, using all acoustic instruments, rather than going to a sound effects library and using electronic sounds created by machines.

When I completed recording the music in New York, I flew to Knoxville to oversee and edit the music. After landing and checking in at the hotel, I immediately headed to Buddy's Barbecue for some down-home Southern food, like they used to have in Washington, D.C., in the 40s when I lived there. Similar to the scrumptious eats of Savannah, Georgia, where my great-great grandfather landed and my cousin David Byck and his family still live today.

I told the cook at Buddy's Barbeque about my family members who are still in Georgia when he asked me if I had been South before, and told him about all the years I had lived in the South.

"Welcome home, son," he said. "I'm giving you some extra sauce. Come see us more often, and bring your whole family next time."

I had a delicious barbecue plate and went to the Clarence Brown Theater. All the stage crew were gracious and hard-working. During the rehearsal, no one raised their voices, and all the attention we paid to whatever Bob Whitehead requested us to do contributed to the energy which took place on stage. The sets, the lighting, the music, and the costumes all seemed to be part of the whole picture. Everything of importance in the theater's atmosphere was created by the actors, and our contributions were supportive to what they were doing, not intrusive.

Zoe was riveting. She had added new dimensions each day to the character she was creating in her voice, body language, and timing.

Bob Whitehead came over to me. "David, your music is wonderful as always, but I do have one request. While we're here in Knoxville, I want you to find one real truly authentic southern place to take us to. We all know how you always seem to wander into interesting out-of-the-way places wherever you go in your travels, when you take your instruments along with you and make friends. Zoe and I are working so hard we couldn't possibly have time to find one real Tennessee experience to take home. If there are no jazz clubs anymore in Knoxville, perhaps there's an old-fashioned southern eating-place that's really authentic that would give us a memory of this lovely experience of being here in Tennessee. I know you've spent a great deal of time in the South. We'll rely on you to be our tour guide for at least one genuine southern experience. Something authentic."

"Okay, Bob. I'll do my best to find someplace," I said.

The next night, one of the stagehands, who was a student at the University, came over during a break and began to talk to me. He had read my book *Vibrations* and was interested in Charlie Parker and Kerouac, which was unusual for most teenagers in 1982.

"Let's hang out after rehearsal, and I'll share whatever I know," I told him.

We went out and I told him Bob Whitehead and Zoe wanted to go someplace outside the Chamber of Commerce Best Bets circuit some night before they left Knoxville.

"I know a far-out place, man. Bring your instruments and you can play, even though it's not a music place. And it's the best barbecue in Knoxville. I'll drive you there right now."

We got in his car, went through town, parked in front of what looked like an abandoned shack, entered through a tiny doorway, and walked down a flight of stairs into a grotto full of smoke and the intoxicating smell of meat being barbecued, accompanied by the crackling sounds of succulent sauces simmering over coals in metal pots. The sizzling fats dripping on the coals emitted stomach-rumbling smells as they exploded into the fire. The slowly turning sides of beef and pork cooking on the spits looked like the set for King Henry VIII in Merry Aulde England, transposed to the South.

As we entered, we were eyed by men sitting at three rickety tables, slowly savoring their barbecue plates, chomping away in silence.

On the darkened musty walls, handwritten in dripping paint, were the three house rules:

No Spittin'.

No Cussin'.

No Hair Combin'.

I knew I had found the right place.

"Awright, boys. Welcome to mah place," said the chef, as we entered. "Tonight we got some fine ribs. There ain't no sauce can equal mine. Everybody try to steal it, but they can't. It's mah secret. Nobody make it like me. Ain't nobody can cook meat like me. I'm the only one. The best. The greatest the South ever had. Everybody come and want mah recipe. No way, Jose. It's mah secret and it gonna die with me. They bring in that World's Fair to Knoxville soon. They say they gonna tear down mah place—they stupid! The fools! I'm the best, can't never have another me, no way. I am the master! Try this."

He stopped his monologue long enough to give us each a rib, dunked in the excruciatingly pungent sauce of his secret recipe, dripping with grease and down-home southern magical flavors.

"How 'bout that, boys? You ever tasted anything could equal mah food? Who you know can cook like that? I see you got your horns with you, son. Play us somethin'. I know you must be a bad cat, but you speakin' to *Mister* Bad his self. In the newspaper, they call me the Babe Ruth of Barbecue. They say I'm the Sultan of Sauce. I'm the man! That's right! How you like them ribs? You never ate nuthin' like that in your life, I know that for a fact. You ask my boys here. Who's the best they is and ever goin' to be? I can answer that mah own self. Me! Am I right, fellahs, or what?"

"Un, hungh," murmured the men at the tables, softly intoning the age-old affirmation of approval that was like the call and response to the Babe Ruth of Barbecue's sermon.

We each ordered a rib, sausage, and chicken combination special, and slowly savored each unforgettable mouthful, standing and mopping the grease dripping from our chins as the proprietor continued his nonstop monologue.

"He may not be modest, but he sure can cook," whispered my companion, as we slowly ate the final mouthfuls from our paper plates, which, like our chins, hands, and shirts, were now totally soaked with grease and sauce.

"Amen," I answered. "I know this doesn't fulfill the requirements of the fat-free, vegetarian organic health food type of diet I try to be on, but anything this delicious has to be good for you, at least from time to time."

"Play us something, brother," said the chef, after we finished our meal. I began playing my French horn, pennywhistles, and dumbek, and an hour later, everyone was singing and clapping and the chef was beating a pair of sauce spoons against the pots, keeping terrific time.

"I was a bad-ass drummer once. But I like to stay in one place. That road life ain't for me. I like to stay put so I can cook every night. I ain't never going no place where I got to eat no restaurant food. They ain't got cooks out there. Them fools think they got it, but they can't do it right. They can't never cook like me. I'm the man! Right, fellahs?"

"Un-hungh!"

We stayed another hour and a half and split another combination plate, along with a giant extra helping of homemade potato salad and coleslaw, washed down with sweet tea and a dessert of two small homemade pies. I played some more music. Every time a new customer came in, the Sultan of Sauce went into his monologue again, often segueing to the beginning of his prepared statement from wherever he was and rambling on until the next customer arrived and then starting again.

The following day I told Bob and Zoe I had found the place.

"We'll go at the end of the week, David," said Bob. "Zoe will love it."

I continued fine-tuning the music, and the rehearsals kept getting better and better. Each night, I went back to the barbecue place and began sitting down at the table with my friend from the university, telling him how small places like this were precious in the lives of artists like Charlie Parker and Jack Kerouac. How all of us evolved from real-life down-home experiences and were inspired by people like the chef, whose barbecue infomercials were like Muhammed Ali's pre-fight rants—poetry and music in themselves. I explained to him that working in the theater in Knoxville and hanging out in all the different locales in Tennessee, the fantastic small towns like Bucksnort, Bulls Gap, and White Pine, could give him something he'd never learn at Harvard, or experience on Broadway or in Hollywood. And that all of us lucky enough to travel ultimately felt that places like this were the theater of life.

"Well, that sounds pretty highfalutin, but it makes me feel like less of a hick," he said.

"Remember, people in New York over and over again told Charlie Parker and Jack Kerouac they looked like hicks, and the same thing was often said to me when I arrived in New York in 1955."

"Maybe so, but I still dream of working on Broadway someday."

"Someday you will," I said.

I didn't know that two months later, *Medea* would open on Broadway. None of us did. We were trying to have the best production possible in Knoxville, and that was our only concern. The final dress rehearsal left us all feeling fulfilled and proud.

"Let's go out, David, and celebrate," said Bob. "We have a great show. The student stagehand you have befriended is now a big fan of yours. He says you are now the composer-in-residence for Knoxville's leading underground barbecue emporium, and give a command performance each night."

"Well, Bob, it's different than an after-the-theater late-night snack at Broadway's own Sardi's Restaurant, but it's more fun."

"I can hardly wait," said Bob, smacking his lips.

"Yum, yum," said Zoe. "I need something besides hotel food. I can already taste that barbecue sauce you've been raving about all week."

Bob had a black Lincoln Town Car he had rented to drive Zoe and other cast members to the theater and back to the hotel. After the intense work, day and night, they appreciated the comfortable ride. As we approached the barbecue place, there were two pickup trucks and a beat-up jalopy parked outside and several good ol' boys camped on the sidewalk, eating barbecue, and drinking beer from cans and Jack Daniels from a communal bottle.

"Look-ee here. Yankees in an Abe Lincoln Town Car. Ya-hee! Have some beer!"

"I think I'll stay in the car and have some barbecue to go, Bob, my darling," said Zoe in a theatrical whisper. "I'm not sure I can handle a community dinner right now. We open tomorrow."

"Of course," said Bob, always gracious. "I'll go inside with David and we'll have them wrap up us up a meal to take out."

"It has a fabulous aroma," said Zoe, as we opened the car door and the gourmet smells wafted our way.

"That's the musician who's got kin folk in Savannah," said Slim, one of the outdoor diners I had met on previous forays to the Babe Ruth of Barbeque's headquarters. Slim handed me a can of beer he was drinking from. "Have a drink on me, Dave. Take your friend downstairs and get him some of our finest barbecue. Have you come from a funeral?" he asked, pointing to Bob, who, as always, was impeccably attired, wearing a tasteful dark suit with a neatly pressed shirt and tie. He looked like a head of state, naturally elegant.

"No," said Bob. "I'm Robert Whitehead. "We're here in Knoxville and we've just completed our final dress rehearsal for *Medea,* which opens tomorrow night at the Clarence Brown Theater. I hope you can come."

"Thank you, Sir, for the invitation. I never been to the theater here in Knoxville," said Slim. "I did go to the Grand Ol' Opry once in Nashville, but I don't like all them people squished together. Maybe I'll catch your show when it gets made to a movie and see it when it comes to a drive-in. I like to set comfortable and drink mah beer when I see a show."

"Excellent point," said Bob.

Slim chug-a-lugged his beer and Bob followed me through the door and downstairs into the barbecue emporium in the basement. His eyes lit up as he saw the motto on the wall, as I had described it to him.

No Spittin'.

No Cussin'.

No Hair combin'.

"I wish Zoe could see this," he said.

Since it was Saturday night, business was booming, and the chef was in the middle of his monologue, extolling his genius greatness with even more fervor than he did during the weeknights.

"He's quite a performer," said Bob. "He doesn't need to book a theater. He has his own right here. What would you recommend from the bill of fare, David?"

"Ask him for the special combination with extra sauce. That's enough to give Zoe extra energy for a month."

The chef paused at the end of one of his five-minute sentences as he wrapped up a huge order to go for the final customer that preceded us.

"Dave, my man, the music cat. Here again. I have to start to charge you rent. Hey, I see this time you brang your main man with you. Welcome brother, you come to the right place. I see by that suit you a man that's hip to the happenins. Well, this is where the hippest happenins happen. Your boy, Dave, told me you comin' by sometime. Try this here! You never had nuthin' like it, 'cause there ain't nuthin' like it nowhere else in the world. It's the best there is."

He slapped a whole rack of ribs on two paper plates with slices of bread and handed it to Bob.

"Don't worry 'bout spillin' on your suit. My sauce makes that jacket cloth breathe!"

Bob gingerly accepted the gift, adjusting his body to avoid the sauce and grease that was dripping from the edge of the folded paper plates that served as a wrapper.

"Do you take plastic?" he said quietly, opening his wallet to a row of credit cards and extracting a Visa card.

"Do I take plastic?" bellowed the chef. "Hell, no. I take money. Green money. Silver change. Copper pennies. I don't owe no one person nuthin'. No person don't owe me nuthin'. I'm straight up money only. I could be a million dollar man if I sold my sauce recipe. Cats want to steal it and bottle it. Nobody can't make no barbecue like I do it. I'm the onliest one. I'm the main barbecue man on the planet Earth. Am I the cat who backs up what he say?"

"Un-hungh," intoned the ever-present congregation of his gourmet fans.

"You see. I'm only sayin' what everybody already know."

Bob was immobilized by the soliloquy, and during the one-second pause, I realized this was the cue from the chorus of yea-sayers for him to go to the beginning of his monologue.

"Three combo specials to go," I said.

"Ain't you gonna eat here and play some?" said the chef.

"I wish I could, but Mr. Whitehead's wife is waiting in the car and she has to get back and rest for her opening tomorrow night," I said.

"Well, let me give the lady some greens," he said, and filled a container with collard greens.

As he prepared the three specials to go, along with the extra greens, he launched into his opening monologue, which Bob hadn't heard yet, slowly wrapping the food to make sure Bob didn't miss any information. As we paid and left, another customer entered.

"See ya' in a minute," he said to us, and started from the top of his speech, casting his spell on the new customer.

We stepped outside. Slim was still drinking and dining with his friends on the sidewalk.

"So long, you all. Come back soon, you hear? There ain't no better barbecue than what you can git right here. You tell them folks in New York they don't know what they're missin'. Good luck with the show. Give 'em hell!"

"Thank you, Sir," said Bob graciously.

"Hell, jes' call me Slim," said Slim, taking a big hit on his Jack Daniels bottle.

"What a heavenly aroma," said Zoe, as Bob and I stepped into the Lincoln Town Car, loaded down with steaming, dripping barbecue. Zoe eyed the ribs, peeping out of the top of the greasy brown paper wrapper, which had been folded over the paper plates.

"I think perhaps we should wait until we get to the hotel to unwrap this," said Bob. "If you could be kind enough, David, to hold the package over this copy of last Sunday's paper, the car rental service would appreciate it. Otherwise they'll have to replace the rug."

I wrapped the entire Arts and Entertainment section of the *Knoxville News-Sentinel* around the barbeque special. The headlines of the paper were quickly becoming decorated with droplets of sauce oozing through all the wrappings.

"You're right, Darling," said Zoe. "The creative juices are already flowing."

As we drove back to the hotel, Zoe talked about Dame Judith Anderson and how her devotion to the theater had inspired generations of actors and actresses to persevere, no matter how hard and difficult the road that they had chosen often seemed to be.

"In Australia, we had very few role models or heroes. Judith showed all of us that it could be done. You know, David, acting is very much like music. The words paint the audience a picture, just as the notes or tones that are played create images in the listener's mind. How you paint that picture determines its outcome, and every actor and musician has their own brush and palette. And we transcend geography, sex, race, nationality, and social position. Making *Medea* alive to audiences in Tennessee is magical! We can put all the elements of our collective experiences together."

"It is exciting," said Bob. "I'm a Montrealer. I never dreamed when I was growing up in Canada that the theater would enable me to have such a fulfilling life. Through the theater, I met Zoe and we have our two marvelous boys. And all the shows on Broadway that I'm so proud to have been a part of gave me experiences we'll always treasure. And on this trip, we have brought together two of Australia's greatest artists, Zoe and Judith. And ancient Greece's classic play, adapted by Carmel, California's Robinson Jeffers. The show has a stellar cast of New York's finest actors. We have, in addition to me, a Montrealer-in-exile directing it, and you dear David, bringing Middle Eastern music and sounds together. It shows how the theater brings the world together."

"It certainly is powerful," said Zoe, opening up a window of the town car to let some of the potent fumes of the barbeque escape into the balmy Knoxville nighttime air.

We arrived at the hotel, and as I got out of the town car, I unfolded the Real Estate section of the *Knoxville News-Sentinel* that I had folded over the Sports section and Arts and Entertainment section to staunch the flow of juices, sauces, and grease, threw all three in a nearby garbage can in front of the of the hotel, and rewrapped the barbeque in the Travel section.

As the three of us entered the hotel, I saw two stray cats race towards the garbage can, leap inside of it, and lick up the excess heavenly juices of the Sultan of Sauce's all-grease culinary masterpiece.

"Good night, dear David," said Zoe, as I handed her the freshly wrapped barbecue, which was still warm. "Bob and I are now going to have a late dinner for two in our room."

The next night, the Clarence Brown Theater was humming with excitement. All of the hard work and collective energy made it possible to have a performance that had a natural flow where there was no feeling of time or place.

From the entrance of Judith Anderson as the wise old nurse until the devastating end, the power of the mythical Greek tragedy swept up all of us. I felt I was seeing it for the first time, and kept praying that Medea would decide not to murder her own children.

Zoe's performance was riveting. Because she and the entire cast worked so well together, the audience became part of the experience, rather than being spectators. I kept imagining I was transported back 2,500 years to one of those outdoor stone theaters that still exist in Athens, where the play was originally done. There was no time lag. *Medea* was still modern, because in this production, the dedication, truthfulness, and artistic brilliance of all involved made the play come to life, and we all felt we were part of it actually happening each night. It seemed real. Every show made this experience from the past become contemporary. Ancient Greece became right now. Like all great works of art, *Medea*, when done right, is timeless.

Fans of Zoe and Bob and Judith Anderson had come from all over the country to see the production, and Bob spoke to all of us a few days later.

"We're going to the Kennedy Center with *Medea*," he said, his eyes sparkling with excitement. "Everyone's hard work has made this possible. Zoe and I thank each and every one of you."

"Wow," said my backstage friend and barbecue tour guide. "I'm glad the show's going to continue. What a nice cat that Mr. Whitehead is. I didn't know that there were any folks like that in New York that still have some manners and consideration. We see a lot of blowhards and phonies come through here, screaming and shouting, that couldn't direct traffic in the parking lot of an abandoned shopping mall. And he even thanked all the actors and the backstage crew."

"You all deserved it," I said. "And if you hadn't taken me to that barbecue place, the fates might not have smiled on us."

"Everything happens for a reason, Dave. You surely know that."

"I surely do," I said. "Please tell Slim and the Babe Ruth of Barbecue we'll remember them always."

"I know you will. And Knoxville will always welcome you back. We'll be your second home. Sock it to 'em in Washington."

The atmosphere of the JFK Center was completely different from the down-home warmth of the Clarence Brown Theater. Restaging had to be done, and the lighting had to be re-adjusted. But what had already been accomplished remained, and with more tireless work, the play came together in a new way. By opening night, the Kennedy Center Theater became intimate and personal. Zoe, Judith Anderson, and the cast filled the huge theater with so much energy that the audience seemed hypnotized by the power of the production.

Lora Lee and our two little girls came down from New York and I took them in their strollers during the scary parts to a corner backstage. I could still feel the excitement of the audience and see the actors on a TV monitor. Then I snuck back into the balcony with the two girls, after the murder scene. Adira was asleep in her stroller, and Alana lay in my lap, giving her toy rabbit an imaginary bath. I had seen the entire show many times and I wanted Lora Lee to see it without having to worry about the kids. After the final curtain, I took the girls down to the lobby and we found her. She looked pale.

"My God," she said. "That was fantastic! It was so beautiful. I've never seen anything like that in my life. Zoe Caldwell and Judith Anderson are amazing! Are the girls all right?"

"Mommy," said Alana, putting down the toy rabbit. "When are they showing the cartoons?"

"That's on TV, Sweetie," said Lora Lee. "This is the theater. This is real live people."

"I'm tired," said Alana, and she fell asleep as soon as I put her in her stroller.

Lora Lee and I went into the outer lobby, each of us pushing a stroller. We listened to conversations among members of the audience as they were leaving, and all of them loved the production. We went backstage and celebrated with the actors and crew. We all knew how good it was.

Both the reviews and response of the audience were so favorable that two young producers, Fran and Barry Wexler, decided to bring the production to Broadway. A month later, *Medea* opened on Broadway, and Zoe's spectacular performance won her a Tony Award. At the opening night party, Lora Lee and I came alone. The cast was surprised not to see our girls in their strollers, because we never got babysitters, except for members of our family. They always came with us, everywhere we went. But I wanted Lora Lee to be at a Broadway opening that could show her an alternative to the disaster of *Harold and Maude*.

"In the old days," I told her, "you didn't come to Broadway with anything until you had it together. Shows would be done out of town, sometimes for years if necessary. When you came to Broadway, you were ready! The same as when you gave a symphony concert at Carnegie Hall. Leonard Bernstein used to tell me how unfair it was to have four rehearsals, then give a different concert every week in New York City with the New York Philharmonic. Other orchestras around the world could take a program on tour, play it thirty times, and then come to New York for a night. Bernstein always told me that the theater had the right idea. To take it on the road, fine-tune it, adjust, correct, and then bring it into the merciless spotlight of New York City. When *Medea* came to Broadway, by opening night we were ready! When *Harold and Maude* opened on Broadway, we were not ready."

When I spoke to Bobby Lewis years later, he said, "David, I dreamed that *Harold and Maude* could be our triumph. But you know the motto of the Boy Scouts:

Semper Paratus—Always Be Prepared. That's the key in the theater, as well as in life. Always be ready. We were never given the time or the chance to fix the play and the production. We could have used six weeks out of town before New York. Both of us chalk that one up to another learning experience, and move on to greener pastures. I hope our producer learned a lesson. After all, he was my student."

♪

Chapter 6

The Dutch Treat: The Genesis of *Offbeat: Collaborating with Kerouac*

In the spring of 1998, I got a letter inviting me to the Roosevelt Study Center in Middleburg in the Netherlands for a conference about Beat culture, scheduled to take place June 3–5, 1998.

I couldn't pass up the chance to return to Holland, so I accepted, and a week later I received a long distance phone call from Holland.

"Hello, Mr. Amram, are you there? I'm calling on behalf of the Roosevelt Study Center. We are happy to have received your prompt response accepting our invitation for our conference, which we are calling "Beat Culture: The 1950s and Beyond." We would like you to play a concert, give musical examples of your pioneering work in presenting world music for so many years, and accompany some readers who will be attending the conference in recitations from the works of Jack Kerouac, as you did with Mr. Kerouac himself in the 1950s ... are you still there, Mr. Amram?"

"Yes I am. Please wait a minute, let me take notes," I said. "I'm in the middle of writing music."

I moved the manuscripts in my shed in back of the farmhouse, which is where I write music when I'm not on the road, went into the house, and sat down at the kitchen table to take notes.

""Except for a brief visit to Goes in the Netherlands for the *Meer dan Woorden* festival last year, I haven't been to Holland since 1955, when I sailed back on a student ship, the *S.S. Groote Beer,* to New York. I love it there. Please give me a list of exactly what you want me to do."

"Well, first of all, my name is Cornelis A. van Minnen, but please address me as Kurt. It's much easier to say. We are so grateful you can accept our invitation. There are distinguished scholars from many countries who will be attending. In addition to your concert, we would like to have you be part of a panel discussion about this most special period. Your friend Joyce Johnson will be there from New York. Also Professor John Tytell, an outstanding scholar of Jack Kerouac's work. We also have invited Professor Morris Dickstein and his wife Lore Dickstein, who is also a distinguished scholar. Your friend Regina Weinreich, who is so brilliant, as you know, said she will attend. Mr. Christopher Felver of San Francisco will be filming and photographing the conference.

"When speaking to him on the telephone, he sounds like a very charming, if somewhat eccentric, character. But he seems enthusiastic and has been highly recommended by Professor Douglas Brinkley and everyone else I have spoken to. I realize you are sixty eight years old and that all this traveling here and back with no time to rest and then speaking and being on several panels might be somewhat rigorous. We hope of course that you can also perform at a special concert for us. Would that be too taxing?"

"Well Kurt, music is my main calling, so if I get a heart attack while I'm playing, at least I can say I died on the bandstand."

"That is quite humorous," he said dryly. "We want this type of levity and your personal reflections, as well as your quite unconventional philosophy when you present your ideas to the conference on one of our panels."

"I'll do my best," I said.

"Excellent. That's all one can ever do. There is one more request. Could you write a scholarly paper, in your own way of course, that you could present to the entire audience about all the work you have done with Jack Kerouac and what you are currently doing to keep this tradition alive today? Professor Douglas Brinkley suggested that I ask you to do this. He told me you are privy to much information that has yet to be documented."

"Well, I'm not sure I'll have time to write anything down on paper," I said. "Can I just rap it out?"

"What do you mean? Do you want us to engage a rap group to accompany you while you deliver your paper? I'm afraid we don't do that type of thing here in Middleburg."

"No. I mean I'll just talk. I don't need notes. It's all in my head. It all happened. I'm always telling my own kids and other people's kids around the world of what Jack and I and others did together. How we all supported and encouraged each other and collaborated together. I've been telling these stories since 1959. That's when everything seemed to change. The stories are the same as they were then. It's all in my head, memorized. Like the desktop of a computer. I don't use a computer, but my friend Jean Sweezey has one. She files everything in order and has a desktop with categories of all the different subjects she needs to access. My father helped me to train my mind to organize my recollections in the same way she organizes her computerized data. I have a special little room at our farm with file cabinets, folders, notes, old programs and flyers, letters, and diaries about what I did with Jack. They're all in a special room. I go through them all the time. I have them memorized. I can just rap it out at the conference."

"You should write another book," said Kurt.

"I'm going to," I said.

"It will be about what happened from 1956–69, from when Jack and I worked together until he passed away. The second part of the book will be about what I am doing today with a new generation who has a better understanding of what our era was about than most of our contemporaries ever did. It will address my continued efforts to keep the legacy of our collaborations alive, in order to encourage this new generation to persevere. I'm going to call it *Offbeat: Collaborating with Kerouac*.

"That sounds fascinating," said Kurt. "When is it being published? Perhaps your publisher would give permission to print an excerpt."

"I don't have a publisher," I said. "I haven't written it yet. It's all in my head, and in my notes scattered all over the side of my shed where I write my music"

"Oh ... I see ..."

There was a long transatlantic pause. I could feel Kurt thinking and sense his disappointment.

"Well, Professor Douglas Brinkley told me he will fly with you from New York to Amsterdam and perhaps he can help you to prepare a scholarly paper to deliver that we can publish after the conference."

"That sounds fine," I said. *"Dank U wel Doktor van Minnen. Het was aangenaam met U kennis te maken. Tot zien.* (Thank you Dr. van Minnen. It was nice to make your acquaintance. Good-bye.)"

"Oh, I didn't know you spoke Dutch," said Kurt.

"I don't speak that well" I said. "I remember what I learned from my visits there in the Army in 1954, and then when I returned to Amsterdam from Paris in 1955 to sail on a student ship back to New York, and when I was there last year."

"Did you like it? If so, you will love Middleburg. It's most picturesque. *Tot zien,* Mr. Amram. May I call you David?"

"Ya. astobleef (Yes, please)," I said.

"In that case, David, *tot zien.* We'll look forward to your presence in Middleburg."

I called Doug Brinkley in Bay St. Louis, Mississippi, where he lived. He was always up at 1:00 a.m., often having just completed a three-mile run on the beach, always working on two or three books at the same time, preparing courses that he was teaching, doing research for new projects, and organizing events of all kinds. His extra-curricular activities ranged from leading tours around the country for kids from Louisiana who lived in the projects, showing them the history of the civil rights movement, to hosting the seventy-fifth birthday party for George

McGovern in Washington, D.C. He was such a dynamo that he made me feel like a retired person.

"Hi Doug. It's 1:45 a.m. and all my chickens, turkeys, and children are asleep. The top of the morning to you, Professor Pops. Just got called today by the conference in Middleburg. How's the busiest man in America?"

"Couldn't be better. Thank you. What are you going to do in Holland? Did Kurt read you what I suggested you do?"

I went over my notes with Doug, including Kurt's suggestion that he help me prepare a paper for the conference.

"That would be no problem," said Doug. "You don't really need to write anything. I've heard you speak. Just tell those stories about what you and Jack did together and what you're doing today. We'll go over it together on the plane ride. We'll have a chance to really talk on the plane and on the three-hour train ride from Amsterdam to Middleburg. No phones, no faxes, no computers, no mobs of people. I'm looking forward to it. How is your family? Can any of them come?"

"Not this time. They're all in school. I'll see you at the airport."

Before driving to JFK Airport at 9:00 p.m. to fly to Amsterdam, I was scheduled to appear at the St. Mark's Church on the Bowery in New York's East Village at 7:00 p.m. to read the first chapter for an all-night marathon reading of *On the Road.* I was invited to eat supper with Jack's brother-in-law, John Sampas, now the executor of Jack's estate; Sterling Lord, still Jack's literary agent after all these years; and David Stanford, who was then the editor at Viking who had the responsibility of getting Jack's books back into print in paperback.

Helen Kelley and Ed Adler from New York University also joined us. Both of them had made the 1994 NYU Beat Conference an event that was changing the way a whole new generation of scholars and students were looking at Jack and his work. It was wonderful sitting at a table with people who were all devoted to Jack's literary output, rather than to his legend.

"I have to leave right after I read the first chapter of *On The Road,* I said. "I wish I could stay all night, but I have to go to JFK at 9:00 p.m. and fly with Doug Brinkley to Middleburg in the Netherlands for a big conference. I'll present the Roosevelt Center and the Dutch government with copies of both of Kerouac's *Some of the Dharma* and the anniversary edition of *On the Road* for their International Library. They'll get Chris Felver to photograph the presentation. They will use the photos and videotape of the whole event to encourage scholars around the world to study these two books. I've memorized my presentation in Dutch for when I present the books."

"Now we've got to work on your English," said Sterling, smiling. "You're still Jack's advocate after all these years."

"So are you, Sterling," I said. "So is everyone at this table."

As we ate supper and shared each other's company, I felt as if I were part of a tableaux or painting similar to *The Last Supper,* with Jack's spirit sitting at the empty seat at the end of the table.

"It's almost like Jack is here with us," I said, just before dessert.

"He most certainly is," said John Sampas. "That's why we're all here. All I want is to see him appreciated for what he was. A great American writer. He deserves credit for what he has accomplished. And he's going to get it."

I left supper early and went to the reading. The church was packed. I saw a few old friends from long ago, but the majority of the audience consisted of young people who obviously were born after Jack had passed away in 1969.

None of them were dressed up like Beatniks. They were a diverse group, judging from their appearance ... punk rock devotees in black studded leather jackets, young executive Wall Street types in fashionable Armani suits, a Guatemalan delivery man with a group of young kids, all of whom I had met and rapped with in Spanish at the Nuyorican Poets Cafe. There was a posse of Ed Adler's art students from NYU and several young up-and-coming jazz musicians and freelance symphonic musicians I had worked with. Several young folk musicians with guitars strapped to their backs sat next to a group of young men in their 30s, with whom I rapped just before the readings, who told me they were off-duty firemen who loved Jack's books. Several friends from the American Indian Community House also were there.

It was like the audiences I am used to playing for when I do my jazz and world music concerts today, and like the ones I performed for during the twenty-nine years that I directed the free Parks Concerts and Young People's concerts with the Brooklyn Philharmonic in Prospect Park and at The Brooklyn Academy of Music. Seeing all these people gathered together reminded me of the memorable summers that I spent composing new music for Joe Papp's Shakespeare in the Park productions from 1957–67.

It wasn't a typical literary soiree-type crowd at all. It was like the New York and the America that Jack Kerouac loved and wrote about. This was a perfect event to honor him. All races, all nations, all coming to celebrate something positive and beautiful—a reading of Jack's classic novel.

I opened up the show, welcoming everybody, and apologized that instead of being the first to come and the last to leave, I had to rush to the airport to catch a transatlantic flight to Amsterdam, en route to Middleburg in the Netherlands. I also said, as I always do, that I hoped all the young people who came would be inspired by Jack's struggles and never give up pursuing their dreams, try to remain positive, share whatever blessings they had, and never give up trying.

I didn't feel any cynical, angry, negative feelings coming back towards me. For years, sharing any of these positive kinds of feelings with anyone fixated on Beatnikdom produced derision, suspicion, or sarcastic replies.

It seemed from the late 60s through the early 90s there was such an inordinate amount of Full-Greed-Ahead philosophy assaulting all of us that only anger, infantile behavior, and sociopathic forms of expression could capture the attention of audiences.

Now it appeared that there was either a rebirth of some kind of humanistic searching for a higher level of living one's life, or at the very least, a crack in the callousness that our society was encased in from decades of abuse. The night of this marathon reading, there was no sign of any New Age rip-off artists, Gurus with Limos, or sadomasochist neo-Nazi post-beatnik wanna-bes. I didn't see anyone in the audience with the desperate look in their eyes of someone ready to charge the stage and shout obscenities into the microphone while being videotaped by their managers, in hopes of getting noticed. Everyone seemed to be there to celebrate a beautiful book and the legacy of its author.

The same was true of the readers. They were an astonishingly varied group of all ages, from Sterling Lord in his late seventies to college students, all of whom shared a love for Kerouac, and all of whom were thrilled to have the chance to read a small portion of *On the Road*.

I wanted to stay, but couldn't remain a minute past the end of my reading of the first chapter. I waved goodbye, rushed out the door and jumped in my van, and drove like mad to JFK.

I checked my bags and went to the ticket counter to look for Doug Brinkley. I kept looking. I finally boarded the plane after trying to ingratiate myself with the airline hostesses by speaking Dutch. Then I walked the length of the plane to find Doug.

He was nowhere to be seen. I sat down in my seat, had a cup of English Breakfast tea and decided maybe I'd make an outline for my upcoming spontaneously rapped scholarly paper. Just two pages of subjects to rap about, like chord changes in jazz to use as guideposts for improvisation.

I had a bag full of unanswered mail to answer from the past three years, so I pulled out a pile of blank paper to rest my notes on. As I drank my tea and stared at the blank paper, while the plane slowly ascended over the New York skyline and out over the Atlantic Ocean, I thought about what Lawrence Ferlinghetti had discussed with me in a recent phone call. We talked about some of the tabloid-style inaccurate trash material recently written about Jack by people who never knew him, and how upsetting it was to those of us who knew and respected him and his work, as well as what a drag it was to the millions who had read his books and loved them.

"Just ignore all that. Don't get involved. Write your own book," said Lawrence. "You were there and part of it. Don't get fancy or exaggerate. Just tell the story. I'll write you a blurb when it's done."

"I don't know if I could ever find the time to do that," I said to Lawrence.

"Don't procrastinate. Just do it," said Lawrence. "Keep it simple."

"Maybe I will," I said. "I would call it 'Collaborating with Kerouac.'"

As the hostess brought some Dutch delicacies to munch on, I decide that at the very least I'd have the time now to make a few notes to riff on for my spontaneous rap when I spoke at the conference. Since Doug Brinkley wasn't on the flight, I might as well write two or three pages about what Jack and I did together.

I polished off all the pastries, had another cup of tea, and began writing straight through till the plane landed in Amsterdam. I couldn't stop. All the memories, the conversations, the places, the sounds of the voices, the smells in the air, the great times, laughter, shattered dreams, triumphs, and finally Jack's death all returned. I hadn't planned on starting and now I couldn't stop!

When we landed in Amsterdam, I took the train to Middleburg. During the nearly four-hour ride, I went back to writing again. By the time I got to Middleburg I had about eighty pages of manuscript. I put the pile of papers in my Mexican shopping bag with the unanswered letters, small percussion instruments, and everything else I could squeeze into it and was welcomed at the train station by the energetic, peripatetic, joyously manic Chris Felver, waiting to greet me with his ever-present cameras.

"Hold it, baby!" he hollered in his crazy high pitched voice. "Professor, you made the gig! I knew you could do it. How was the fight? Just a minute, let me get this. This will be the picture the world has been waiting for. Hold it, Professor. Stand right there. No, no ... right there. That's it. Now hold up your French horn and your *dumbek* drum, whatever the hell you call that thing ... that's it, hold it, hold it. Give a smile. Turn your head slightly to the right. That's it. HOLD IT! Beautiful (snap-snap-snap). One more, one more. Work with me, baby, work with me ... one more! Now turn a little to your left ... a little more ... PERFECT ... hold it ... work with me ... Professor ... that's IT! David, how are you?"

"After a grueling photo session, I'm suddenly wiped out," I said. "I'm fine. How are you?"

"Fabulous, Professor," said Chris. "Dig these great shots from Boulder of you and Amiri Baraka and Cecil Taylor and Anne Waldman and your kids and Ken Kesey. I'm doing a new book. I'm nearly done with my documentary film on Lawrence after twenty-four years and now I'm going to work on a documentary about you."

"That means if it takes you twenty-four years to make mine I'll be eighty-nine when it comes out."

"Perfect," said Chris. "You'll be mature enough to appreciate it. We'll have everything you do with symphonies, with jazz and all the other music you've always been into, your compositions, what you do on Jack's behalf, I'll edit in the footage I shot a year ago of you climbing that bell tower in Goes to play "Pull My Daisy" on the town carillon. Rememeber how their regular carillon player played it every hour for the three days we were there? It was wild, man! You and Jack having your song played on that bell tower. I'll shoot even better stuff here on this trip. I'll edit in you playing "Pull My Daisy" a year later for all these gals in the kitchen.and I'll shoot photos of you giving Jack's books to the Dutch government for the opening ceremonies.. Let's go see Brinkley. He's over at the center. I'm in love, man. The women here are *amazing*! They're all so cool and they don't hate men. They know how to laugh. I'm in love with five of them. They all think I'm nuts. What do they know? They have to visit America. Then they'll see who's *really* nuts. How come you're being so quiet? Oh, by the way, just for your information, Howard Hart and Philip Lamantia both send their love and ..."

After writing on the plane and the train for nearly eleven hours, it was relaxing to hear Chris's nonstop monologues punctuated with conversations he had with passersby on the street en route to the center.

With his ever-present beret, Toulouse Lautrec–type long flowing scarf, navy pea jacket, sneakers, and cameras slung around his neck, he was able to be anywhere in the world and have everybody in his presence become part of his documentary movie set and photography studio. The world was his visual oyster.

We arrived at the Roosevelt Study Center and I met Kurt van Minnen.

"I understand you never saw Professor Brinkley on the plane. He told me he took a later flight. Do you have anything prepared? Would you rather not deliver your speech?" he asked.

"Surprise!" I said. I reached in my Mexican shopping bag and pulled out the eighty-page pile of papers I had just written.

"My goodness," said Kurt, "are you writing a novel?"

"No," I said, "I'm going to shock all my old friends, like Joyce Johnson and Professor John Tytell and Regina Weinreich and all the younger folks I know who are here. Rather than just rapping it out, I'm going to read something I actually wrote down on paper."

"That's why I call you Professor," said Chris Felver. "You've graduated from the world's oldest rapper to the world's oldest-youngest born-again professor of bebop French hornist's prosody."

"A delightful turn of the phrase, Mr. Felver," said Kurt. "I think you and Mr. Amram will add much spice to our very serious group of scholars. I would now like to have both of you please join us for dinner. Please show Mr. Amram where he can get some vegetarian food and introduce him to our volunteers in the kitchen."

"Common man," said Chris, "You've got to meet the cooking staff. These Dutch babes are something else. They're not only great cooks, they've got great looks and they're *smart*! They don't miss a trick. They've all seen *Pull My Daisy*. They want to meet the real Mezz McGillicuddy. I told them you're better looking now than you were thirty-nine years ago when you played Mezz in the movie, and that you never were an actor anyway. Bring your horn and play them a tune. Do some scat singing and sing a few bars of "Pull My Daisy." It'll be a great moment for my documentary. First I show you playing the horn while they pour you stew and flirt. Then we cut to a year ago when you were at the Meer dan Woorden Festival in Goes. I'll use my fantastic footage of you climbing the bell tower with John Tytell and crawling up the ladder at the top, like Sir Edmund Hillary climbing Mount Everest, and playing "Pull My Daisy" on the carillon. Then we show you today, a year later, back in the Netherlands again, reading your encyclopedia length scribbles to Doug Brinkley and Joyce Johnson. Then we have you presenting Kerouac's *Some of the Dharma* and the new edition of *On The Road* to the Dutch government. Then a shot of you holding up the old picture taken of you and the original cast of *Pull My Daisy*. The beat goes on! You're a survivor, Professor! Let me get another picture. Stand right there for a minute. Perfect.....don't move an inch. Chin up. That's it. Perfect.Work with me, baby!"

Chris kept talking, snapping pictures and filming everyone else in sight with his small video camcorder until we reached the kitchen.

"Chris, let's cool out the documentation for a while and relax," I said.

"Good idea," said Chris, strapping all his cameras over his shoulder, and adjusting his beret and scarf. "Let's socialize."

Chris walked into the kitchen ahead of me and started talking to everyone, as if he had been there for the last hour. The small kitchen was filled with a group of serious looking young women serving delicious-smelling home-cooked food to an equally serious-looking group of scholars. As soon as Chris entered, the whole room brightened up. Everyone called greetings at once.

"Hi, Chris."

"Oh my God, it's Crazy Chris!"

"Chris, don't take any more pictures. You've photographed my soul away."

"*Hy is gek* (He's crazy)."

"Here comes the one-man world media center."

"*Hij is gek maar hij is schattig* (He is crazy but he is cute)."

"It's the peripatetic paparazzi."

"Everybody stay *right* there," said Chris. "Don't move. Before I introduce you to the professor of ethno-funkology and hangout-ology, as he so aptly describes himself, I want one group photo. Stay right there. Easy. That's it. THAT'S IT! One more. You're beautiful. Work with me baby, *work* with me. All right, as you were. Let's eat! I'm starving. This is David Amram. Don't ask to marry him unless you get his wife's permission. He's here. Say hello."

Chris charged to the hot table and filled up a tray of food.

"*Ik ben bly om in Nederland te zyn* (I am happy to be here in the Netherlands)," I said to the gracious and charming women who were making a good old-fashioned Dutch vegetarian stew for all of us. They smiled and restrained themselves from giggling because of my Feasterville-Washington, D.C.-Greenwich Village accent when I spoke Dutch, but told me they admired my courage. I entered the dining area and saw Doug Brinkley, Joyce Johnson, John Tytell, and surprise guest Ron Whitehead, the Kentucky poet who had a reading in Europe and stayed over to come to the event to narrate passages of Kerouac's work at my concert. There were also a lot of prominent scholars from all over Europe and the United States, and listening to them talk as I chowed down was like a college education.

"David, glad you could join us," said one of the visiting scholars. "I'm giving a talk about the role of women in our era. I tell a lot of my younger female colleagues that it is not fair to judge you guys by today's standards. You were as oppressed as we were, but you were *fun*! If any of the desirable young men back then knew we had ever had even one affair, they thought we were whores. You guys understood we all needed some love and excitement. You wanted us as companions in your struggle, like soldiers by your side. You were romantic and represented rebellion and excitement and adventure. You weren't boring. You would *talk* to us. You would show your emotions and even cry in front of us. We knew we'd never marry any of you, but you were our escape from the dreary Eisenhower white picket fence Doris Day suburban nightmare we were told we had to cherish. I hope you don't find all this world of academia too stuffy. What do you think Kerouac would have thought of all this? Being analyzed like Dostoevsky or Charles Dickens, by a bunch of scholars?"

"He would have loved it," I said. "All he ever wanted was to have his work taken seriously and judged on its merits."

"I'll look forward to your talk. You and Joyce Johnson are the only ones here who actually knew him."

"I'll do my best," I said. "I hope I'll be able to honor Jack and help others to gain even more respect for what he was about, and clarify not only *what* we did, but *why* we did it."

As I was able to actually sit down to a quiet home-cooked meal, I really felt at home. Being back here in the Netherlands again reminded me of the great afternoon Chris and I spent in this special part of the world in the little town of Goes in 1997, just a year ago at the Meer dan Woorden Festival.

Chris was my guide and motivator during my third day there, and as always, radiated torrents of energy as well as non-stop repartee as we climbed the bell tower with John Tytell so that I could play "Pull My Daisy" on the town carillon. Chris, a former professional golfer and still a great athlete, scamapered up the tower, simultaneously snapping still photos, recording video on his camcorder, and regaling us with some of his stream-of-conciousness monologues, which were so funny that I forgot how tiring it was to climb up so far on a rickety set of stairs and an old ladder that looked like it might collapse at any moment.

"David, did you bring an oxygen tank? Can you make this last seventy five feet up the ladder to the top?" asked John Tytell, hearing me gasping for air as we reached the last leg of our ascent to the top of the bell tower.

"Everything's cool," I said. " I'm still breathing, but I'm afraid to look down. I'm terrified of heights, so if I pass out and die from acute acrophobia when I start playing the carillon, tell your students, 'He died while he was on top.'"

"I'll promise to do that for your euology, if my leg cramps don't kill me first," said John.

"You can make it, Professor," yelled Chris Felver, not even panting as he bounded up the stairs ahead us, lugging all his equipment. "You used to be a gym teacher. Show us some of that stamina. Look up here. Right at me, right into the lens. Don't look frightened. John can catch you if you slip. That's it. Relax. ReLAX! Hold it. One more. Beautiful. Keep climbing. You're almost there. Now comes the tricky part. I can get a great shot if you look up from the ladder. Work with me, baby."

We hauled ourselves up the last tortuous seventy-five feet on a narrow rickety ladder to the cramped bell tower. After catching my breath I played a few choruses of "Pull My Daisy" on the carillon. It had a huge keyboard, like a giant toy piano, and it sounded like a bunch of crazed bell ringers at a jam session, but it was fun hearing our song floating out over the old towers and stone buildings of Goes to the peaceful Dutch countryside in the distance. The song had come a long way from Alfred Leslie's grimy cluttered studio on New York's old Lower East Side, where we shot the film in 1959. Now on this sunny afternoon in 1997, the song was part of the brightly colored flowerbeds and peaceful farms that were a work of art in themselves: the bucolic and immaculate landscape of the Netherlands. I realized, as I looked out at the people way down below listening to our song being played on the carillon, that one of our collaborations was now becoming part of people's lives on another continent.

"I don't know if Jack would have even recognized the song, the way it sounded on the carillon, but it's a beautiful idea to do this," I said.

"I recognized it," said John Tytell.

"It was beautiful," said Chris. "I got some great shots. Let's go down and meet Frank Messina, Richard Deakin, and Ron Whitehead and sample some of that fine local Dutch beer."

We slowly climbed down the tower and spent the night talking to people from all over who were now arriving to attend the Meer dan Woorden Festival. It was as if Jack were a new young writer being discovered by a new generation.

His dream was finally coming true. People were reading his books and judging them by what he had written.

I recalled all this as I was eating my meal. I realized how lucky I was to be back in the Netherlands a year later, and that this time, I didn't need to climb any more bell towers. I spent the rest of the night thinking about what I was going to say tomorrow at the Meer dan Woorden Festival and decided to simply read what I had written and not improvise as I usually do.

The next day, I was ready to give my presentation about my work with Jack. After my climb to the top of the Bell Tower a year earlier, I knew I could handle anything. An hour before I was due to speak, I reread the pile of papers I had written on the plane and the train and realized that they were way too long to read at the conference. I told Kurt to signal me when I had two minutes left and I would draw to a graceful conclusion from wherever I was.

I hoped that the professional scholars who were there would not be taken aback by the conversational tone of what I had written.. The speakers I had heard were all excellent, but they were delivering papers that were meant to fulfill scholarly standards. Mine was more of the 3:00 a.m. informal-hangout-at-the-all-night-cafeteria post-concert spontaneous philosophy style of speech that was an unforgettable part of our era, but not exactly academic.

I wanted to convey all of the seemingly inconsequential experiences and unusual mileus which created, amidst all the chaos, a certain ambiance that fostered creativity during the period of the 50s when all the arts and artists seemed to join hands, and equally important, make everyone who was attending the conference feel that they could share that sense of community today.. I could no more talk about all our precious experiences in a true scholarly style to which I was not accustomed than I could translate my talk into Latin.

I began to read, shuffling through my enormous pile of papers, which I had organized in order. In the back of my mind, I worried that in this room full of brilliant people, I might seem out of place.

Three outstanding writers, Joyce Johnson, John Tytell, and Regina Weinreich, were all good friends with whom I had worked. They knew how to say what they had to say with clarity and didn't ever waste a word when they were writing or speaking. Reading their books was always illuminating. I thought that they might feel that I was like the old characters we grew up listening to in the Village: in the early 50s. People like Joe Gould, the nonstop speed rapping author of "The Oral History of the World," who never actually wrote anything down but could talk until you were lulled into a trance; Maurice the newspaper man, the self-appointed Mayor of Greenwich Village who carried a dinner bell and regaled anybody within earshot with stories about Edna St. Vincent Millay and the Village in the 20s; Jake Spencer, crazed artist who lived by his wits and swam five miles to shore when his rowboat capsized in the ocean off the coast of Provincetown, and after swimming to shore partied for three days, telling everyone what survival was all about. . . . These nonstop rappers created a foundation for the atmosphere of downtown New York that affected and influenced Jack and all of us.

Joyce Johnson, John Tytell, and Regina Weinreich all were able to deal with the sea of chaos that was such a part of our era. They created and published works that made students aware of how our artistic achievements and intellectual contributions came to pass and how we and our work managed to survive. The three of them were ambassadors for Jack's work, as well as their own. I hoped what I was reading would reinforce their years of devoted labor and not set the clock back forty years, by my talk sounding like the ravings of an overly enthusiastic nut case.

I peeked up for a second behind my mound of papers and saw Joyce smiling. I got an instant blast of energy. If she approved of what I was reading, I knew I was on the right track. I began to enjoy reading aloud what I had never committed to paper before. I could feel warmth from the people in the room and even hear some moans of approval. Then I heard the precious sounds of laughter. I began to feel comfortable. The whole conference room begin to change and become like a coffee house or jazz club or the old loft-studios of painter Alfred Leslie or saxophonist-actor Gary Goodrow back in the 50s, when we all hung out, playing music and talking till dawn.

This was one of the only times in my life I had actually read anything I had written down on paper in front of people. Since 1968, when *Vibrations* was published, all my speaking about the people I was blessed to cross paths with in my life and what we did in the arts and what was happening as a result was always delivered in an extemporaneous fashion and geared to the moment and the people who were listening at that moment ... when I would be asked to speak as well as play at all kinds of events I participated in over the years, I just spoke from the heart. At the most I would have an outline of two pages of topics to discuss.

Hundreds of hours of interviews, talks, and seminars, which I always let people record, have been written down by others. Much of what I have said and shared with others has been broadcast and published, but like all the music I improvised, I simply took it out of the memory bank and let it flow downstream, fly away in the air, and forgot about it. I would go on to the next thoughts, work on new musical compositions which I *was* laboriously writing down, and deal with whatever life led me to each day.

I kept on reading. The room was silent. They were *listening*. I looked at Kurt. I must be past thirty minutes, I thought. I never went overtime unless requested. In a symphony concert or a recording, one minute of overtime can cost thousands of dollars. When performing in a live concert with others, going over your allotted time can ruin the whole evening and cause pain and resentment to those who follow you.

I saw Kurt signaling with his hands to *continue*! I kept on reading. Every time I looked up he kept signaling me to continue. Finally I decided to stop anyway. There was a huge applause. Even the most formal and reserved people were smiling and laughing.

"David, you got what Jack and all of you were about," said Joyce Johnson. "You should publish that. Not as a speech to us. As part of a book."

I flashed back to my conversation with Ferlinghetti. Maybe what I had written could be part of a book about all of us, then and now—the one I had thought I might write someday.

"David, you've got to expand this and write a book about all these experiences. *Vibrations* touched on some of it, but this could be more extensive, and include all you have done and are doing now to keep this spirit alive with a new generation. I'll write an introduction and try to help you get a publisher. Sterling will, too," said Doug Brinkley. John Tytell and Regina Weinreich said the same thing.

I had played music for John, Regina, Doug, and Joyce when they read from their own works, and also when they recited Jack's work. It never occurred to me that they would ever speak to me about writing about all of these experiences myself.

Since I was now being interviewed almost every day due to the amazing resurgence of interest in Jack's work as well as my own work in music through the years, I thought the information I shared with others about our adventures would suffice. I was, and knew I always would be, happy to be a primary source for anyone interested in documenting the whirlwind of energy that filled the air of the 50s.

But on that sunny afternoon in Holland, I realized that what I had written on the plane and the train a few days before was the beginning of a new book.

Even with all the composing, performing, and family obligations I had, I knew I would have to get it done. I owed it to Jack and all the others who were no longer here to speak for themselves to tell these stories.

This was the genesis of *Offbeat: Collaborating with Kerouac,* which was published in 2002 (to be reissued in early 2008 by Paradigm Publishers).

It took me three years more to complete it.

Chapter 7

Words and Music: Scat and Make-up Songs, the Art of One-Time-Only Rap Reporting

"How do you create those rhyming scat-raps, that you call make-up songs, on the spot?" This question has been asked so many times since I started doing this as a kid, I wish I knew the answer. I don't have any system except to start the first line, and let it happen. Usually, the last word of the first line gives me rhyming ideas. (For example, "I always dreamed that someday I could cook at least one dish" would automatically trigger "fish.") Then I would have to build something on the spot and fill in the blank space to lead up to the upcoming word "fish," thus:

> "I always dreamed that some day soon
> I'd learn to cook at least one dish,
> I feared I'd never find the way
> Until I sautéed beer and fish."

This little quatrain could be the foundation of the story about a would-be cook raiding the icebox when surprise guests appeared and said that they were hungry. The necessity of feeding them something required taking half an opened can of beer, some margarine, mayonnaise, garlic, peppers, a recently thawed out bluefish, and whatever else was lying in the fridge and creating an improvised recipe in a microwave since the gas bill hadn't been paid.

Letting your imagination soar without the constraints of good taste or other literary refinements, you could move along with your song-story-rap-reportage and include references to other foods of the world and the guilt of reverting to being a fallen vegetarian after you and your guests finished eating a whole plate of sautéed seafood, including the fish roe. Roe from a fish sounds the same as a row of people.

A row of people could lead to the possibility of veering off in a new direction and describing the rigors of a shopping trip to your local grocery store to replace the items of your now-empty icebox, standing in line with a row of other shoppers, waiting patiently to replace what had been scraped up from the ice box, which is now empty.

You could then describe the empty feeling of having a bare cupboard while ogling all the different kinds of barbecue sauces on the supermarket's shelf that you could use for future sauté experiments, and then describe telling the cashier at the checkout counter about your new recipes, hoping she wouldn't think that you were fishing for compliments. You could describe your fear that the cashier knew how desperate you were to receive her approval, which could then provide a natural launching pad to the next stop on your free association highway. You could reveal the fear you also had for your next-door neighbors' welfare, after they called to tell you that they received a fish head wrapped in newspaper left on their doorstep by a Cosa Nostra–connected representative of the same beer distributor you had purchased your can of beer from, as a warning because they hadn't paid their bill on time. Then you could return to describing the fish that the beer was cooked in, and talk about the Native American tradition of planting a fish in a hole next to the seeds, all placed gently in the ground to grow crops in any kind of soil.

This would modulate directly to the greatest fish story ever told of Jonah and the whale, followed by mention of the whaling industry in early nineteenth-century Nantucket and Provincetown and the saga of Moby Dick, written by Herman Melville, who loved to drink beer. And then end by having the audience sing along on a mantra of Herman Melville's favorite recipe to serve when people dropped by unexpectedly.

The infinite number of ideas that a key word or short phrase can trigger in a well-seasoned brain is the basis of many forms of rap reporting and on-the-spot poetry. This process is not a way to create a finished product but rather a way to make you tap into your creativity, which is the first step toward making any form of art.

These first-draft efforts are often the basis of various forms of make-up songs that are spontaneously chanted or sung in many cultures around the world. And often, unless they are documented, they are a one-time-only experience. They are judged for their value at the moment, and then serve as a basis for formal work. Sometimes, they can suffice on their own, without any revision.

I am sure that many would feel that the above example of a one-time-only story is already one time too many, but inspired listeners can often spur you on to creating more interesting material than you ever thought you possessed, and free you from writer's block. And most important, it can stoke the fires of your creativity and make you go home and write, paint, or play something with a spontaneous feel that, unlike the stream-of-consciousness silly story idea above, can be worked on painstakingly until it becomes structured, well crafted, and of lasting value.

It is also valuable to remember that two of the great tools of modern technology, a pair of scissors and a wastebasket, are also a way of organizing, editing, and refining the first draft that comes naturally as your mind soars unabated down the highway of your imagination. into something that sounds and feels extemporaneous. By reworking patiently, you can end up with a story or poem or song that is mean and lean with all the fat trimmed away.

I came from a family where stories, jokes, monologues, and long conversations were a staple of life whenever friends and relatives gathered together on our family farm. The other source of my exposure to endless repartee and uninterrupted monologues was at Wally Freed's gas station on Bustleton Pike, across the road from our farm, which was the social hub of Feasterville, Pennsylvania's, 1939 communal gatherings. Since I mowed Wally Freed's lawn, I was part of the inner circle of the gas station elite and was allowed to sit and listen to all the local philosophers tell tall tales and gossip, hearing them rail against the government, the weather, and their wives, and watch them as they shared their dreams, heartaches, and old jokes with one another.

When my father sold our farm in 1942, we moved to Washington, D.C., and lived in what was then referred to as a checkerboard neighborhood, where African-Americans and Caucasians lived next door to one another. I heard all kinds of southern storytelling, rapping, scatting, rhyming, and jovial insults, in what is referred to as playing the dozens, twenty-four hours a day, until I went into the Army ten years later in 1952. Segregation was still the law during these ten years I lived in Washington, but no law could separate all of us in the neighborhood from talking, yelling, joking, and playing games and music with one another.

All this prepared me for my first and most memorable one-time-only rap reporting field trip. It occurred during a furlough in the U.S. Army, when I visited Athens in 1954. I saw a man in a cafe drinking from a glass of retsina wine with one hand and holding up a Greek newspaper with the other. After a few sips of the powerful tar-flavored wine, he pointed to a headline and began rapping, with his eyes closed.

Everyone in the place stopped talking and listened intently. He was obviously improvising on whatever it was the headline said.

All during his rap, there were shouts of approval. And if it was a super thigh-slapper mega-laugh punch line, a few coffee saucers, plates, and wine glasses would be smashed to the floor as a sign of appreciation.

"*Stradiotis Americanus* (American soldier)," yelled one of the customers, pointing to me, saluting me in a friendly way, and nudging his friend.

"*Stavros, metafrase tou ta anegthota kai ta paramithia* (Stavros, translate those jokes and stories for him)."

I was joined by Stavros, a portly energetic man, who sat down beside me and drained his glass of wine in one gulp. He had tears in his eyes, which were red-rimmed from the retsina wine and laughter.

"Mr. soldier boy. Me name Stavros. You like this? You understand him jokes?"

"*Then milau kala Hellenica, alla thelo namatho* (I don't speak Greek well, but I'd like to learn it)," I answered. This was one of the first expressions I always learned in every language of every country I have ever been to, after first learning how to say "please" and "thank you."

"Hey. You speaking a nice Greek, soldier boy. He taking newspaper, make jokes off that. You and girlfriend have good time. *Thelo na sou agoroso kai tousthio ena poto. Steeniyiasas kai na ziseesi!* (Let me buy you both a drink. To your health! Long life!)"

The scat-rap reportage continued, and when the first man with the newspaper stopped his scat-rapping, he was instantly replaced by another reader/rapper who did the same thing, reading from a magazine and pointing to a photo on the cover and going into a speedy monologue that sounded like an auctioneer, including what sounded like different characters arguing with one another, using different voices and different pitches.

He was soon replaced by another reader/rapper who seemed to try to outdo his predecessors, and the crowd loved it. The sounds of glasses and dishes crashing to the floor continued to punctuate the various comic improvised rhymed monologues as the retsina flowed throughout the night. Stavros accompanied each performer with cheers and more orders of retsina and plates of tarama, a delicious form of Greek caviar, served with fresh home-cooked bread.

At about 4:30 in the morning, I staggered back with my companion, a lovely art student named Rango whom I had met in Sicily on the way over to Athens, to the fleabag hotel where we were staying in downtown Athens. Just in front of the entrance, I saw a newspaper lying in the gutter.

"What do you suppose it says?" she asked me. "You seem to have an affinity for languages. Can you read Greek?"

"I never tried to," I said. I stared at the headline and wished that it were written in English. Then I could attempt to do what the rap-reporters had been doing all night in the café. Since I couldn't figure out what even one letter was in the Greek alphabet, I made an imaginary translation from the headlines:"U.S. Army gives away all its ammunition and throws a bring-your-own bottle party and jam session at the exclusive Chateau de Fleabag in downtown Athens, hosted by that sentimental gentleman of swing, David Amram."

To the bemusement of my companion, I started making up a song/story from this imaginary headline, and I've been doing it ever since.

Often, in concerts and festivals when the situation seems to allow it to happen without disrupting the flow of whatever kind of program I am participating in, I'll ask the members of the audience for four topics and include each idea in a song made up at that moment, often using the 12-bar blues pattern for a musical foundation.

After making up a few rhymed verses that include the four topics that have been suggested by the audience, I get them to sing back the four topics, one at a time. Then I give each of the four sections of the crowd a simple phrase to sing or chant. Once the first group in the audience has sung their part, I add the other three sections, one at a time, until all four sections are singing their different patterns together. It creates an instant four-voice chorus that sounds like a jazz orchestra except that words are also part of the mix.

This is what Count Basie often did musically, in the middle of his carefully written arrangements, to add a special energy to the evening's musical bill of fare. So did all the great territory bands in the Midwest and South in the 1930s. They didn't use words, but they created a musical structure of many different melodies playing together as a base for someone to solo over. The bandleader would create a simple melodic phrase, called a riff. The bandleader would sing or play the riff, which the saxophones would then repeat and play over and over. Then the bandleader would give the trumpets a second riff or counter melody. Then the trombones would play yet another counter melody. Then the piano and sometimes the guitar would play a fourth riff, and more riffs could be added by dividing up the saxophones, trumpets, and trombones.

These riffs were all satisfying to hear individually, and they all fit together when played in conjunction with one another.

After years of doing make-up songs anywhere I was at the moment, when people felt like being cheered up, I started doing them at various concerts where I would involve the audience singing. I would cue them to begin their participation during the middle of the song/story I had made up. After all four topics which the audience had suggested had been introduced in the song, I would have them become part of the music by encouraging them to sing their individual parts.

But instead of just having everyone singing little nursery rhyme melodies, the riffs I created for everyone to sing would always include the words that they had suggested to me as topics for the song. I would sing these topics to them, until they could sing them back to me.

It gave a chance for everyone in the audience to be part of the band and feel what it was like to be a musician.

I began using this technique on special occasions for symphony concerts I conducted, usually for kids' programs or as a lighthearted encore for a regular concert, when a spontaneous moment of fun was in keeping with the rest of the program. I was made aware decades ago that I would have to find a way to do this without shocking any members of the audience. I always had to do this in gracious fashion, to help the audience to enter into the world of spontaneous words, sounds, and audience participation.

In the era I grew up in, society in general assumed that classical concerts of the twentieth century no longer included improvising, one of the key elements of the eighteenth and nineteenth centuries concert experience. In this bygone golden age of European classical music, every concerto for a solo instrument and orchestra had what was known as a *cadenza*. This was a part of the composition where the soloist had to make up something on the spot at a designated point in the concerto.

During his lifetime, Bach was just as famous as an improvisor as he was as a composer. He often would take suggestions from the audience of random notes of the scale and make up a fugue on the spot from what the members of the audience had suggested.

Until recently, improvisation was no longer part of every musician's training. In addition to being told by our teachers that classical musicians were interpreters only and therefore not creative, the general public assumed that most musicians were only interested in their special area of expertise and had no ability or interest in anything else except how to play their instrument or develop their vocal technique if they were singers.

I first encountered this stereotypical and limited view of musicians, held by those who never were blessed with the magic of a true musical experience themselves, when I attended a party in New York City after I had just moved there in 1955. I was playing with Charles Mingus. He invited me to an elegant brownstone house on the Upper East Side, where he was a special guest at a late-night party. The home was elegant and the walls were crammed with a stunning array of original works of art. I told the hostess how much I appreciated her original Degas, which was hanging on the wall between a Renoir and a Cézanne. I told her how much these three beautiful paintings reminded me of the year I had just spent in Paris, where artists, writers, musicians, and everyday people would all gather at cafes. As she stared coldly at me, I thanked her again for the pleasure of being in a warm, inviting home where you could feel through those paintings the atmosphere created by these three great nineteenth-century French artists, who somehow captured that indescribable sense of communion that still filled the air one hundred years later throughout Paris. And I told her what a thrill it was to be in her home in New York City where such treasures were there to be admired and how grateful I was to be her guest, thanks to Mr. Mingus inviting me to come there with him.

"Talk through your horn," she growled at me, as she glowered at my French horn case, as if the horn was going to break out of its case like a rabid raccoon and destroy her home.

"I'm not interested in your views on art. You're a musician. I'd rather hear you talk through your horn."

That particular experience in the fall of 1955 made me understand that, unlike most people I had met in Europe, some people here in New York City would always feel that my role in life as a musical person would not allow me to interact with the adult world except when I was performing for people. It prepared me for people I met later on who assumed that all musicians, at best, are amiable morons who, like perfectly behaved children of Edwardian England, should be seen but not heard once they stopped playing their instruments.

All of these somewhat depressing experiences helped me to understand, years later, that classical composers were also often regarded as having a very limited role in our culture. We were supposed to have our music heard, but were not to be heard from ourselves, or even seen, except when we had reached my current senior-bopper age group, the late seventies. By the mileage on the speedometer, you were now qualified as a grand old man of music and were more acceptable.

In the forties and fifties, I occasionally saw those lucky few composers who had not yet expired, but whose works were often played. It was exciting to have them there at the performances of their music. Especially Stravinsky's public appearances, when he would sit in a special box seat in a tuxedo and gracefully take a bow when acknowledged by the conductor after his work had been performed. In the late fifties when I was one of a handful of people privileged to meet him, he was as much fun to talk to and listen to in person as his music was to listen to.

The orchestra that presented his work never invited him to speak to the audience during the concert or made it possible for him to meet and greet most of the audience after the concert.

For those of us lucky enough to have had the chance to meet him, I think most would agree that he would have enjoyed an interchange with the public as much as the people who were dying to meet him would have enjoyed his wit and brilliance as a raconteur and social critic. All who ever heard him speak will remember some of his fantastic raps, which were as incisive as his music. Robert Kraft's timeless books with interviews of Stravinsky are a precious reminder of what a great mind this musical master possessed.

I was honored when Eugene Ormandy invited me to join him on stage at the conclusion of the first performance of my symphonic work *The Trail of Beauty*, premiered by the Philadelphia Orchestra in 1977, and at subsequent performances at the Kennedy Center in Washington D.C. Out of respect to Ormandy and the traditions of the Philadelphia Orchestra, I followed the accepted role of being a silent partner during the tour of the orchestra when my piece was played. I spoke when spoken to, and remained as invisible as possible.

Having my music played by the Philadelphia Orchestra, the New York Philharmonic, the Chicago Symphony, and other orchestras around the world was and always will be all I could ever have hoped for in my life and a reward beyond description. I didn't need to be the center of attention. My music was what was being paid attention to. But today, I am more concerned that other composers and musicians will have the opportunity to communicate with the public, as a way to foster creativity for all artists and make the general public feel that they are a vital part of today's artistic community. When *The Trail of Beauty* was premiered by the Philadelphia Orchestra, I would have loved to have had the chance to thank all the members and staff of the orchestra, the conductor, the audience, and all the Native American people who inspired me to write this piece, and to encourage young composers and all artists to persevere and to honor some of the hidden treasures of our everyday culture. But in 1977, when the piece was first presented, I understood that doing this would have been impossible without offending those who were presenting the programs. It would have been considered to be self-serving, grandstanding, or just plain gauche.

Leonard Bernstein broke down many of those barriers with his historic televised concerts for young people. He always spoke eloquently, even at many regular subscription concerts, and he always did it in a down-to-earth, warm, and loving manner. Thanks to him, doors were opened up for all of us to transcend the limitations of only being allowed to speak through our horns. Adults loved Bernstein's televised concerts and lectures as much as their kids did. And Bernstein, in addition to being a bona fide genius in so many areas of music, was also one of the most brilliant public speakers and educators that America has ever produced. He was also one of the most literate public figures in America.

When I took what Lenny did a step further in my symphonic programs, which I conducted and narrated, I often included audience participation and occasional scat-rapping reportage. I never wanted to shock or offend those who felt that by definition, any composer who was also a performer, conductor, and improviser was a menace to tradition. That's because I knew for a fact that in the eighteenth and nineteenth centuries that's what most composers did. But in the sixties, when I also began using words as part of an evening's musical presentation, when introducing compositions, or when I would occasionally end the evening with a make-up song, some arts administrators felt that I must be either mentally unbalanced or a schizophrenic.

This has all changed now, but forty years ago, I accepted the fact that I might appear to some to be like a trespasser about to be arrested for breaking and entering if I even dared to finish a sentence in a conversation that dealt with anything other than music. You can imagine what some administrators thought when they heard me making up a ten-minute song on the spot with the audience and members of the orchestra participating, in the ways I have described, at the conclusion of the concert.

This was especially the case when my scat-rap make-up song followed my more serious moments, when I would talk to the audience about the composer's life whose work we were playing, as well as the importance of having an orchestra as part of building a healthy community.

Fortunately, the make-up songs I did always seemed to send everyone home smiling. It was certainly not a career choice to pioneer this, but I was only doing what comes naturally, whenever it seemed appropriate. I hoped the good feelings it created would make people feel that something special was being done just for them, and make them want to support their local orchestra and find a new appreciation for the musicians. To my surprise and delight, I was often asked to come back to guest conduct and end the next concert the same way. One of my biggest thrills was seeing the manager of an orchestra and the president of the board both sing and clap the rhythms I assigned everyone in the audience, and watching them smile. I knew that they had the hardest job of all in music, being responsible for keeping the ship afloat. I felt that they deserved a moment of fun as well.

In 1966, when Leonard Bernstein chose me as the New York Philharmonic's first composer in residence, one of New York's most prominent members of the Literary Glitterati cornered me at a cocktail party.

"I know you are probably some kind of protégé of Lenny's, David, but I have to ask you why he is always so intent on discussing a plethora of topics outside his area of expertise. Whenever he is with us, he often spends a whole evening regaling us with his observations about society at large, analyzing world politics, and then relating specific political conflicts to the wars among various factions of the art world: the abstract expressionist painters, the magic realists, the hard-edge school, and Pop artists. He often insists on dominating our conversations by discussing trends and feuds among today's novelists and the battles of lyric poets versus those poets who call themselves the New York School. Why does he intrude on our turf? We don't lecture to him about music. He seems to feel that he is qualified to give discourses on anything and everything! After all, he's a *musician*! How does he dare think he is so smart?"

"Because he is," I answered. "Lenny is living proof that participating in music doesn't lower your IQ, it raises it.

"Ask anyone who runs a bookstore to tell you how many musicians are among their best customers. Remember that understanding music is a gateway to appreciating literature just as literature is a gateway to music. And that music and words together are a gateway to civilization. I was a history major in college. We studied the Renaissance for a whole year, and we were told that's what the Renaissance was all about. It was a rebirth of the connection between mind, spirit, art, science, and an understanding of the relationship between the past and the present.

Our history teacher told us that during that era, a thirst for knowledge was a prerequisite for the leaders of their society, and that Renaissance had great meaning for the hi-tech society of our day, because it too had become an age of overspecialization.

Our history teacher also told us that an educated person should realize that there was more to life than just perfecting skills. Otherwise you would spend the majority of your time on earth attaching the left fender to a vehicle on an assembly line for forty years and then retire without ever understanding how the rest of the car was built. He said that the age of overspecialization was the reason why the forty-year veteran left fender man would spend most of his life of hard work without appreciating the importance of the car itself, his role in our modern society in helping to build it, and the aesthetic as well as the utilitarian value of the car itself.

He told us that we don't have to stop developing our minds and ignoring our thirst for knowledge by allowing ourselves to be defined solely by what we all have to do in our daily lives to pay our rent. And he said that today, we can apply the same principles to our lives as Leonardo da Vinci did in his life, as a way of constantly learning. Our history professor made us see that da Vinci didn't come out of a career councilor's program, and that da Vinci wasn't a schizophrenic or a dilettante, but rather an extraordinarily evolved human being who was emblematic of that rebirth known as the Renaissance. He told us that way back then, becoming an educated person meant a lifetime of development and constant cultural and social interchange. Nothing of beauty was considered off limits. Science, the arts, and knowledge of history were the guideposts on the path towards becoming a better-educated person.

"We musicians would never tell a brain surgeon to give up playing the bassoon. Albert Einstein played the violin. So did Thomas Jefferson and so did the emperor Nero, even as Rome was burning down," Bernstein said to me after a concert when we were talking about music and life outside of music once the final visitor had left the Green Room at Avery Fisher Hall, having congratulated him on an outstanding performance.

"Don't ever stop learning. Never allow yourself to feel that all of us who call ourselves musicians are supposed to spend the little free time we have in our lives reading comic books, watching TV, and ignoring everything else. Develop your ability to express yourself in words as well as music. Like everyone else in society, we musicians all have something to say about a lot of things, as well as a lot to learn every day from others. Don't be afraid to speak out when you feel you have something important to say. We have to make a connection with the world in every way possible as one way of keeping all this precious music alive. We are not only creators; we are keepers of the flame. We have to make our audiences feel welcome and at home when they come to a concert."

In spite of Lenny opening up the door for all of us, the symphony world of the 50s and 60s was still more comfortable with the idea of the maestro as someone who was an unapproachable authoritarian autocrat, except when appearing at a fundraising event, at which time the conductor was required to press the flesh and schmooze on a level equal to a presidential candidate. So the fact that Bernstein was comfortable speaking to the audience in a serious way about the music met with some resistance. But that never fazed him and attitudes have changed.

Unlike the exciting world of symphonic music today in 2007, when new vistas are opening up, my earlier forays in breaking down these artificial barriers by saying a few words about each piece and occasionally creating make-up songs for the audiences at the end of the concert was met with some trepidation. In the 60s, musicians in the orchestra as well as members of the orchestra's board of directors were surprised to see me, dressed like the traditional conductor in white tie and tails, leap off the podium after the final piece on the program and go to the piano and start expounding rhymed verses on the spot, and then include members of the orchestra as well as audience participation, to send everyone home smiling.

Often, after I had the audience singing the riffs I had assigned them, based on the topics they had suggested, I would play a solo on my French horn, the piano, or the pennywhistles, creating new melodies to complement the figures that I had assigned the audience to sing and the orchestra to play.

On occasion, when it was comfortable for members of the orchestra, I would invite musicians who felt like it to come up to the podium in front of the orchestra to join me, and have them create an improvised instrumental solo of their own, always to the delight of their colleagues, as well as the audience.

The members of the orchestra always enjoyed participating in these make-up songs, because they were always constructed in a way that was musical, simple, and enjoyable. They also often gave some members of the orchestra a chance to shine by giving them the opportunity to create an improvised solo.

The musicians saw that these scat-raps, combined with brief improvised instrumental solos, were a great way to end the evening. It brought the audience closer to the music and the musicians. By participating themselves, the audience got visceral contact with what musicians do when they are playing in a group and what it felt like to make music with others.

The musicians sensed that when we did this, I was always coming from a musical place, rather than trying to be cutting edge or avant-garde. I never included this in a concert unless it felt right and honored the entire concert, the audience, the orchestra, and all its members. It worked for special occasions. There were many times when I never said a word or included improvisation. I only ventured down this path when it seemed that it would enhance the evening. Symphony musicians are some of the most skilled people in the world, and can find the value in just about anything. But you can never fool good musicians for very long. They are always interested in quality, not labels, packaging, or gimmicks.

In the 60s and 70s, orchestral and chamber music players had to spend a considerable amount of time in their careers playing pieces where they were often asked to nearly wreck their instruments, hitting or abusing them, and playing what was certifiably unplayable and generally agreed to be totally unmusical.

Often, they had to sit for endless rehearsals as well as performances of these pieces, suffering in silence as they watched a gifted soloist attack a grand piano with hammers, or stuff it with objects designed to destroy the infinite variety of subtle sounds for which a grand piano was painstakingly built to project. These supposedly cerebral exercises in what have now become defunct procedures were usually accompanied by four pages of written instructions and explanations to the orchestra of how to recreate the wheel, but with no musical material for them to actually play, much less interpret.

Pages of instructions on how to make all kinds of extra-musical sound effects can be intellectually stimulating, just like reading the instructions for how to assemble a model airplane. But musicians already know to play at an extraordinary level by the time they are able to get a job in any orchestra nowadays.

Today's musicians can play just about anything put on their music stands that they are asked to play. All they really ever need to have, in order to feel creative, is some good music to play. If I was adding an unexpected scat-rap spontaneous encore piece to a program, I would always try to make the musicians in the orchestra know that this was not supposed to the musical equivalent of "The Ten Days That Shook the World," but rather a chance for all of us to be creative together and give the audience a chance to be part of our world.

"Ladies and gentlemen," I would always tell the orchestra. "You know from playing my compositions that my publisher, C.F. Peters, agrees with me on what I try to share with you as a composer. Everything they print of mine is always written down so clearly that I don't have to show up at any performance of my music to have it played correctly.

"I also don't ever want to give any heavy philosophical musicological lectures about the decline of Western society since the Industrial Revolution to explain what my music is or isn't about. In all my compositions, everything you need to know is all clearly written down on paper in each of your parts, the same way Brahms and Beethoven and Bartók wrote theirs down. I am very old fashioned.

"But the last piece we will play on the program as a surprise encore has very little written down at all. It will be primarily a spontaneous piece, which I call a make-up song.

"I'll cue everybody every minute so it won't be chaos. We'll be doing it tonight as an encore. This evening's adventure into the unknown will be its first, last, and only performance, but it should be fun and show the audience that all of us are not only champs of discipline, but also spontaneous and creative. I'll cue you when to come in and sing you your part on cue after the audience has their singing under control. The sketch you are provided with on your music stands is written down and is accurately notated; it's an outline of the fun to come.

"I'll be making up rhymed verses on the spot from topics suggested by the audience. You'll enter when I signal each section of the orchestra, one at a time, and I'll make it clear where we end."

I have done this all over the world, in five languages, and it has never offended even the most conservative players or members of the audience.

Invariably, these simple moments where the audience and orchestra all have a few minutes of spontaneous fun together is a great way to end a program. Often when I return to conduct the same musicians a year later, many of them will come up and show me poetry they have written, paintings they have done, and music they have composed, and they feel free to tell me great musician-traveler stories.

Musicians of all disciplines are creative by nature, just as most other people are, even if these natural gifts are often stifled in all of us as we are told that growing up means shutting up.

Telling stories, with or without music, is liberating and energizing for anybody and everybody.

The largest audience I ever made up a song on the spot for was in Lincoln, Nebraska, September 19, 1987, for forty thousand people in a stadium. It was the first of many times I played the benefit concert for family farmers known as Farm Aid. Willie Nelson had invited me to perform with him. He and his band backed me up as I rattled out verses about being here on time in Lincoln, Nebraska, after returning from conducting a symphony concert in Fairbanks, Alaska.

Just like the man in Athens I heard in 1954 rapping about current events and news stories taken from the headlines of a Greek newspaper as a guideline, I used my recent experiences to make up a story/song on the spot. I started by recounting my recent guest-conducting of the Fairbanks Symphony in Alaska, where I hung out afterwards at the Howling Wolf Saloon in Fox, Alaska. I sang about staying up all night and being shown how to call moose by a group of Indians who had attended the concert. Then I recounted the nerve-wracking traveling experience of making three changes of planes and racing through airports to make all the connections in order to arrive in Lincoln on time for the Farm Aid concert.

I described the empty feeling after missing the final connecting flight late at night and renting a car with a farm activist and driving three hundred miles, getting to Lincoln Nebraska with no sleep, just in time to join with Willie and his band. Then I segued back to the time I first played with Willie in the early 70s in Austin, Texas, at the Opery House, when I was invited to perform with Steve Goodman, the great Chicago singer-songwriter. I mentioned how Steve had invited Willie to join the concert with Jethro Burns and me, where we all did make-up songs together for hours, ten years before Willie asked me to play with him for Farm Aid in Lincoln, Nebraska. And finally how happy I was to be there just to play this little song for all the family farmers of America. I ended the travelogue by making up two more verses about what farming had meant to me as a kid in the 30s growing up on our 160-acre farm, and what this vanishing way of life means to everyone in today's world when our family farmers, who feed us, can barely survive. All this came out in a rhymed scat song, using the twelve bar blues as a musical foundation. The whole stadium sang the different parts I assigned them to sing.

Everyone had a good time, and I was careful to look at my watch as I sang to make sure that I didn't go one second overtime. Brevity is the soul of wit, especially when you are on a program with many other performers, who depend on you not to go any longer than your allotted time.

For twelve years, I had the privilege of doing all kinds of musical events with Steve Goodman. We played at major music festivals, recordings, television specials, benefits, coffeehouses, and even at the reception of my own wedding. Steve loved to scat and rap and when we played together, he would always have me start my make-up song alone and accompany me playing his guitar.

After I had rapped out about fourteen choruses of what became a story based on the topics that the audience had suggested, Steve would sing one killer chorus that summed up the whole song. That's because as a master songwriter, he always knew how to cut to the chase.

When we performed together at the Mariposa Festival in 1974 in Canada, I made up a song from four suggestions from the audience, which included the request of including Moby Dick as a topic. The song was long but somehow sounded structured, mostly due to Steve's brilliance. Everyone told us we should do more together and we did for all the years he was still with us.

A few months later, Steve sent me a cassette of a new song he had written, called "Moby Book," which credited me as a co-writer. I listened to the song about Captain Ahab and the great white whale. It was beautiful. I called Steve in Chicago.

"Steve," I said, "that song is great. But I didn't write any of it."

"Yes, you did, Dave," he said. "You just make it up off the top of your head and forget about it 'cause you can write symphonies, so you have other things to remember and think about. You had some wonderful lines in the live recording they made of our concert together, which the Mariposa Festival sent me to listen to. I used some of those choice phrases and built the song around them. I'm a songwriter. Every word I end up using in a song is as crucial to me as the notes you are writing for your new symphony *Trail of Beauty* for the Philadelphia Orchestra.

"When I came down to stay with you at your pad on 6th Avenue a month ago, I saw you slaving away at the piano for the whole night, just trying to get one chord right, as I was trying to get some sleep. I do the same thing with words. One word can change the whole story or viewpoint of the song. I took your choice lines and used them. And the others I discarded. I know how particular you are, the way you choose every note you use in your symphony composing. I'm the same way when I write a lyric. I am a ruthless editor with my lyrics for my songs. Every word counts, just like every note counts in your symphonies."

"Wow," I said. "The song you came up with is so clear and simple. You're like a haiku poet."

"The haiku poets always knew what to leave in, and what to leave out," said Steve. "They knew how to tell a story and make you feel that you are part of it. So did Hank Williams, Merle Haggard, Lead Belly, Otis Redding, Richard Rogers, Bessie Smith, Cole Porter, John Prine, Willie Nelson, and Ira Gershwin. You have to say it all in a short amount of time. Every word has to make the listener feel that you're talking right to them, and that they are part of the song.

"You're more of a scat rapper jazz/poet who makes up songs the way you play jazz, with a lot of time and space and wandering down dark alleys and finally coming back to what it was supposed to be about. You're a lot like Jack Elliott, when he goes into overdrive and tells all those wild stories that go on and on. That's why he's called 'Ramblin' Jack.'"

"'Moby Book' is a real song," I said. "There's no rambling at all. I thank you for giving me credit for something I already forgot I did."

"You deserve it. I just edited out all the hyperbole and hot air and kept the choice parts, and tightened everything up. We always have a good time playing together, but I take songwriting very seriously. It's an art."

Steve's songs, like "City of New Orleans," have become part of the American repertoire of song-poems that are enjoyed all over the world. Mine have always been throw-always, unless someone records them. Occasionally, people have sent me recordings of these spontaneous moments. A few have been released on records through the years.

One of them was recorded at the end of a session in New York on January 6, 1996, while I was making a CD with Randy Crafton for Lyrachord Records, entitled *Duologue.*

Randy is an innovative musician and composer who can play anything that is written down, as well as improvise a whole night of music spontaneously. Randy can do both so well that you can never tell whether what he is playing is written down and rehearsed or made up on the spot. He is a musical natural.

Randy and I first met when he played percussion in the orchestra I conducted for a performance in New York of my opera *Twelfth Night,* which I composed with Joe Papp providing the libretto. I was amazed that such a young musician could be such a master and play such difficult percussion parts with ease and expressiveness.

He subsequently played in my ballet score *Chakra* for Jacques d'Amboise National Dance Institute, and I found out he had an enormous interest in all kinds of music from around the world, as well as the compositions from the classical and contemporary concert repertoire.

Randy and his wife, clarinetist Amy Platt, presented a concert of their own at an art gallery in New York City, with guest artist Glen Velez, master of world hand drumming styles. John Cage also participated, and I was invited as a guest composer and soloist. We played in the traditional concert style, performing composed works by Joan Tower, Cage, and myself. Then we changed gears and the written-down pieces were followed by pieces that were totally improvised.

Later on, at the reception, I was requested by old artist friends of John Cage's and mine from the Cedar Tavern days of the 1950s, to make up a post-concert crazed critique in rhyme about the occasion. They had all come to Randy and Amy's concert for a reunion, and I couldn't say no.

Randy played a rich tapestry of percussion sounds, playing with his fingers to create some scintillating rhythms on the empty silver serving bowls used at the reception. I made up a scat-rap-reportage-travelogue about John Cage going on one of his famous mushroom hunts in Rockland County, and how his landmark piece "Seven Minutes of Silence" might be a good encore to calm things down after my seven minutes of rapid-fire scat-rapping.

"This is so much fun, having a concert together at a little art museum in the Village," said John. "Let's do it again. So many of our old friends came to join all the young people here. Next time we'll make up a song together."

I never got the chance to do that with him, because that happy night was the last time I saw John Cage. He left us in August of 1992.

Three and a half years later, Randy invited me to play some instrumental duets with him for his recording *Duologue.* We recorded a spontaneous duo using the Native American courting flutes Sky Walking Man-Stick had given me at the Kerrville Music Festival, and a second improvised duo where I played my *shanai* in a piece based on the *hijaz* mode, a popular Arabic scale.

I put on my coat to rush out to Grand Central Station and take a train back to our farm to see Lora Lee and the kids for a special celebratory supper. It was the night before our seventeenth wedding anniversary, and I didn't want to be late.

"Dave, can you do one more piece? This is my last day in the studio," said Randy.

"I've got to catch the train for our anniversary supper in half an hour, and I've got all the instruments packed," I said.

"Then do one of your spontaneous raps," he said.

"You mean you want the senior-citizen James-Joyce-goes-to-Birdland ska-voot-o-reenie fourth-grade-reading-level special?" I asked, warming up to the challenge.

"Do it," said Randy.

We sat down. I knew I had only ten minutes before I had to run and catch the train. I made up something on the spot, and what is printed below is exactly what was recorded as I did it, including my mentioning a wrong date. On the recording I said January 6, 1995, was the date we were making the CD, and actually it was January 6, 1996. Randy mentioned this in his liner notes, but said everything else was accurate and done in one take with no preparation.

When I listened back to the CD *Duologue* a year later, I liked the scat-rap. I certainly would never perform it again or consider it a finished song or a poem, unless it was completely revamped. I believe in editing.

But sometimes spontaneity can have merits of its own, excesses notwithstanding, especially if you are speaking from your own experience and feelings. Here is the rap as it was done on the spot, which can be downloaded to hear from the Internet. Hopefully, it will inspire you to make up a better one. And then develop it into something coherent without a wasted word.

> Well, here we are with Randy
> January 6, 1995
> And all these years later
> I'm glad that I could survive
>
> Now you might think making a record
> And doing it spontaneously in one take is insane
> But I gotta leave in ten minutes
> Cause I gotta catch the train
>
> To see my dear wife Lora Lee
> We've been married tomorrow seventeen years
> If you miss an appointment like that
> You bring on a lot of tears
>
> Because time is only the friend you know
> And really all that we have got
> Because honoring the past and the present
> Helps out the future a lot
>
> Now rapping and rhyming on the spot
> Happened a long, long time ago
> When Homer did the *Iliad* and the *Odyssey*
> But he didn't do it on a rock-and-roll show
>
> He did it on a boat accompanied by a lyre
> With some guys singing along

Fourteen hundred pages later he created
The first big rap song

Well, I did it in 1957, the first jazz poetry-reading ever
In New York with Jack Kerouac
And all these years later
We're finally looking back

And seeing that what we did forty years ago
Had a future as well as a past
Jack and Charlie Parker and Dizzy Gillespie and Thelonius Monk
Are appreciated at last

And Bela Bartók, the painter Franz Kline, and Edgard Varese
The composer, you know?
All had something they ordered
From the great hot house in the sky—to go

They took out an order rather than giving it
To share with all of us today
The beautifulness that we know which means
Those blues might not go away

But if they're here for a good reason
It means the season time is now
Cause Charlie Parker said that "Now's the Time"
And he meant it ... and how!

Because the present, when combined with the beauties of the past
Makes the future secure
So for all the folks who feel uptight
You've got a little more you have to endure

Cause paying those dues is only normal
And in the sound-bite society of today
You're never gonna have the freedom and love
And make those blues go away

If you expect solutions to problems,
That never existed in the first place, you know?
Well, it means that finally all those clichés'
And bromides have to go

There was never a beat generation
There was never a generation X
It's only a way of labeling people
Just like they used to do in the Puritan days with a hex

But the hex sign in Amish country meant
Good luck, not bad vibes, you see?
So finally we're understanding that all those terminologies
Get in the way of spontaneity

Spontaneity means freedom,
You can ask Randy Crafton if you don't believe me
Cause he said, "Let's rap this all in one take, Dave,
And throw away the papers," you see?

Well, that's the way it's supposed to be
So for all the young folks who like world music today
Remember ... it's something that happened
A long, long time ago, so they say

When the first person hit a stone and sung a song
And heard the bird's heartbeat-prayin'
They knew that the flowers of springtime
Were coming once again

Because the rhythm of the seasons
Was God's rapping to all of us
So let's all join, rap along, and make up our own poems
On the freedom bus

You don't have to be uptight
You don't have to be full of misery
You can write a poem and rap a song
You can even write a symphony

'Cause I've done it, I've played with Willie Nelson,
Dizzy Gillespie and Attica Prison as well
Conducted symphonies at Carnegie Hall
And really lived to tell

That you can have a beautiful life
If you dare to fulfill your dreams
And avoid other people's suggestions
If they're full of nefarious schemes

Just be honest and true
And follow what's in your heart
Remember there is such a thing called art
You don't have to be the board that gets hit by the dart

You don't have to worry about someone else's desires
And dreams of what you're supposed to be
Just try and do what's better than expected
And you'll always be happy, you see?

Because if what's expected is never really good enough
And since I never wrote this down in the first place
It only means that you can also try to create
Your own rhyme and reason in this same space

So ... on January sixth
In the time that does remain
I gotta split from Randy now
I gotta catch the seventeenth anniversary train

So ... I wanna say to all the people
On this record who played so well
Old Howard Levy playing his harmonica
What a story he had to tell

And Randy I knew when he first played
My opera *Twelfth Night* about ten years ago
Later came to the Brooklyn Academy of Music and played with Jacques d'Amboise
As I wrote music for an Indian show

It was called *Chakra* and Randy held it all together
He's an important part of my life
And that's why I'm here on this record
Dedicated to his wife

To his wife and my wife and all the wives and husbands
Sons and daughters as well

All of us have a story
All of us are grateful to have something to tell

And what we can tell all of you is
To believe ... believe
Don't worry about all those others
Who won't give you a reprieve

But daring to dream and daring to live
And daring to survive
That's why I'm glad I lived this long
And glad I can still be alive

Because if you want to play with someone
Who's talented and risky and handy
You're lucky if you can play
With the rap meister Mr. Randy!

Scudda doo-bah dee-bah do-bee dee-bee doobie
shiddy-a-doo-bah dee-bah diddy-bit
Doo-den-doo, den-doo-dah, diddy diddy doobie doo
Dee-ba-dee shoobie-doo. ... That's it!

I ran to the station when it was over, and just made the train.

My first recorded songs, where I wrote every word down beforehand, came about by chance. It happened unexpectedly. In 1971, I was signed and made my first of three recordings, *No More Walls,* for the classical branch of RCA Victor, RCA Red Seal.

No More Walls was a double album, with two LPs in the same package. The first LP contained three orchestral works: *Autobiography for Strings, Shakespearean Concerto* for oboe, two horns and strings, and *King Lear Variations* for wind symphony. I conducted a once in a lifetime orchestra assembled from all the best symphonic players on the East Coast. Every note on the first LP of the double album was written down in the traditional classical way in which composers of the European tradition have notated music for the past few hundred years.

The second LP of the double album was music inspired by West Indian, Lebanese, and Brazilian music, as well as the jazz waltz I had written as part of my score for Arthur Miller's play *After the Fall,* which was the opening production in 1964 of the brand-new Lincoln Center Theater company. I also recorded the title song from my score for the silent film *Pull My Daisy,* narrated by Jack Kerouac. The lyrics were by Jack Kerouac, Allen Ginsberg, and Neal Cassady. For this RCA recording, I recreated the original performance of the song as it was done for the film. Anita Ellis sang the version used on the 1959 soundtrack. For the 1971 re-recording of "Pull My Daisy" on the *No More Walls* double album, Lynn Sheffield sang the song with my jazz quintet, augmented by a chamber music ensemble.

There was even a duet I composed, with Ramblin' Jack Elliott and me playing guitars, with Jack yodeling at the end, while his huge dog Caesar lay on the floor of Studio A, in a blissful state, panting and wagging his tail in counterpoint.

All of my instrumental solos were improvised, as were most of those by the other outstanding players.

The first half of *No More Walls* contained three of my most successful symphonic works that were already being performed internationally, which I conducted. The second LP of the double album consisted of jazz and world music pieces that I composed and for which I performed on a bunch of instruments.

It created quite a stir and lots of head wagging and confusion for many of the merchandising moguls of RCA recordings. In 1971, nothing remotely like this had ever been done before. Today in 2007, the world of classical music has opened its doors, and world music is now a merchandising term. There are now interdisciplinary college courses entitled *No More Walls,* named after my double album. The whole idea of this double album was shocking to people in the record business in 1971.

"Is he some kind of schizophrenic nut?" I overheard one of the executives say in a loud voice as I passed his office. He was projecting to be sure that I heard him.

"RCA is a business, not a mental health clinic," he added, waving his cigar at me as he emerged from his office. "What in the hell are you doing? You're all over the place. What are you? What are you trying to accomplish?"

"I'm a musician. I'm trying to make the best music I can," I answered.

I passed Dennis Katz's office next door to my critic's office. Dennis had just been put in charge of finding new performers for the pop department of RCA.

"David, have you thought about the idea I suggested to you two years ago?" said Dennis.

"What idea?" I responded.

"You know, making an album of those crazy songs you make up all the time at the drop of a hat. You've been doing it for years. You could make a whole LP in one three-hour session. Come into my office for a minute. Let's talk."

Dennis reminded me of an event in 1969, during one of the many nights he heard me carrying on with friends after I had finished playing with my jazz group and joined the small army of folk musicians and songwriters standing in front of the Gaslight Café on MacDougal Street after someone had just played us one of their newest songs, at an impromptu sidewalk recital.

"Do you remember that night in the fall of 1969, after Jerry Jeff Walker took out his guitar in front of the Gaslight and asked you to make up a love song for the waitress he was secretly in love with who was standing between you both eating a *souvlaki* and spilling the onions all over you?"

"How could I forget that?" I said. "I remember after I finished my serenade to her on his behalf, Jerry Jeff and the waitress disappeared into the night, and I had to spend five minutes cleaning up all the onions and *souvlaki* juices off of my French horn case. And that's when you first suggested to me that I make a recording of some of my spontaneous raps, like the one I had just done for Jerry Jeff's heartthrob. That was three years ago, before the classical department of RCA signed me. I was flattered that you asked me.

"I also remember I told you I couldn't do it. I still can't. I have too many friends who are great songwriters. I enjoy accompanying them. That's what I'm best at. I remember that night that after you went home, I went with Ramblin' Jack Elliott, Odetta, Kris Kristofferson, and Roland Moussa, the Native American poet-singer, to go play music together."

"Before you and I bumped into each other outside the Gaslight, they had come earlier that night to hear my jazz set at the Village Gate down the street. After you left the Gaslight, we all went to go find a place to make music. We found an old coffeehouse down the street from the Café Wha. I played backup for their songs at this tiny place where people would come in after hours and jam. Billy Mitchell ran the open mike sessions, and he used to play hot guitar licks using his toothbrush instead of a guitar pick. It was a great night."

"Well, with all the things that happened to you that night, I'm glad you remember our conversation. Have you given it any further thought, David? The offer still stands. I am producing records for the pop department at RCA and Peter Munvies of the classical branch of the label told me he will lend you to me so that we can do a special project together."

"Dennis, I play backup for all these great songwriters," I said. "I'm not a songwriter. I'm a spontaneous scat/rapper. There's a big difference."

"That doesn't matter, David. I like what you do. Just go in the studio and make it all up. If nothing else, it would be different. Remember, one of RCA's best-selling records was the dogs barking in different pitches that was edited together as a hit version of "Jingle Bells." I'm sure you could end up with something better than that. Let's try. I'll book some studio time. I know you can do it."

"I'm happy you would want me to do that, Dennis, but I can't inflict that on the American public. It would constitute cruel and unusual punishment," I said.

"Okay, then write some words down. You've written two operas, two cantatas, and a book. You can certainly write a few songs. I have a big enough budget in the pop department to allow you to hire the best players in New York. You write any kind of arrangements you want. Do whatever you want. Just go with the flow. I'll book a studio for next month."

I spent three weeks writing songs for a whole album, based on all the things I loved about New York City, and called it *Subway Night.*

Since I was given complete freedom to do whatever I wanted, I wrote lyrics for each of the twelve songs on the album, and then spent endless hours editing them to make them as short as possible. Each song had a completely different ensemble for which I created orchestrations to serve as the accompaniment.

For the song "Ballad for Red Allen," an homage to the great old-time trumpeter, I had a Dixieland orchestra.

For "Mean Dean," based on the terrifying personality of a famous European conductor who told a fifteen-year-old student of mine who once smiled during one of his rehearsals, "These eyes can kill," I composed a song using folk, rock, and jazz players Joe Henderson, Pepper Adams, and Thad Jones.

In the song "Credo," I wrote a short piece about what most musicians believe is their calling and hired friends from the Metropolitan Opera Orchestra to play. In the song, I mentioned Bartók, Bach, and Charlie Parker in the lyrics, and proudly sent the lyric sheet to everyone in the pop department, hoping that they would be impressed by my including these three giants of music in a song.

For "Horn and Hardart Succotash Blues," I assembled a Middle Eastern ensemble from many of the great players I had worked and jammed with in the Village since the 1950s, including George Mgrdichian playing the *oud,* Ali Hafid playing *dumbek,* and Collin Walcott on *tablas.*

For "The Fabulous Fifties," which was released as a single, I assembled a doo-wop vocal quartet, including Hilda Harris, who later sang with the Metropolitan Opera, and Randy Peyton and Carlene Ray, both of whom were singers who had performed in my classical choral works and who could sing 1950s doo-wop style with equal fluidity.

For the two songs "East and West" and "Little Mama," I organized a bluegrass group with guitar wizard Dave Bromberg and mandolinist/clarinetist Andy Statman.

For the "The Professor and the Panhandler," my jazz group was augmented by four French horns.

The song "Dunkin Donuts," which paid homage to Brattleboro, Vermont's, late night clientele, was scored for a big band.

In addition to writing the words and the music, and singing all the songs, I was able to use a completely different orchestra for almost every song, and I orchestrated and arranged them all without any interference.

"Man, this is some far-out material. It sounds like James Joyce on an acid trip," said one of the musicians who came to record the arrangements I had written, when I sang him some of the lyrics.

Dennis Katz, who made it possible for me to do this, loved it all. He was a free spirit as well as a brilliant young lawyer, and a friend of musicians. Otherwise I never would have dared to embark on such a new venture. And I am sure that no one else would have ever asked me.

Dennis somehow convinced his associates to bring me in as a forty-two-year-old to make an entire album of my own songs. Peter Munvies, who had signed me to RCA Red Seal as a composer and conductor of my symphonic works, also loved the idea as well as the songs.

"It's an extension of *No More Walls*," he said excitedly. "I don't know how they'll ever sell it, but it's great stuff. Next year we'll record your *Triple Concerto for Woodwind, Brass, and Jazz Quintets and Orchestra* with David Zinmann conducting the Rochester Philharmonic.

"I hope these crazy songs you have recorded for Dennis can help to get a whole new generation interested in symphonic music, as well as getting symphonic performers and listeners interested in jazz and folk styles from all over the world. And it might even encourage poets to get out there and read their works with music the way you and Kerouac did in 1957.

"David, you're ahead of your time, as usual, but keep it up. Someday there'll be an audience for all of this. I hope I'm alive to see it."

When I saw Peter Munvies in February 1997 at the National Academy of Recording Arts and Sciences (NARAS) luncheon before the Grammys in New York City, he remembered our 1972 conversation, and bubbled with his usual enthusiasm.

"I am still very much alive, and I'm seeing it," he said. "And now everyone's finally getting a chance to hear what you do. With the music industry's recent discovery of world music and the relationship of jazz and symphonic music, the interest in American Indian music and the rediscovery of Jack Kerouac, instead of being considered a mad man, they're calling you a pioneer. They thought I was crazy for signing you way back then. I'm proud I discovered you and recorded you in 1971 and 1973, after knowing about you since the 1950s. Promise me you'll never become stuffy and complacent or act your age. Remember, we're from a generation of true believers."

During the past thirty-five years since it was first recorded, there have been bootleg copies made from the original LP *Subway Night* appearing all over the world. Now, in 2007, it is receiving a new life because people can download it via the Internet, along with almost everything else I have ever recorded.

Shortly before I recorded *Subway Night,* I spent an afternoon with Bob Dylan when he came over to my apartment on 6th Avenue to play me some new songs he was writing.

"Are you still making up those long songs?" he said to me.

"Believe it or not, Bob, I'm actually writing down the lyrics ahead of time for an album called *Subway Night*. And I even wrote a short one."

I handed him a typed copy of "Credo." It was the shortest song of all twelve I had written. A few months later, after *Subway Night* was completed and ready to be released, Roland Moussa told me that he saw Dylan on MacDougal Street and told Bob that he sang some back-up vocals for some of the songs on the album. Roland then mentioned to Bob that the song "Credo" that I had written as a statement about a lifetime commitment to music was a song he thought that Bob might like to hear. Roland told me that Bob smiled and pulled the copy of "Credo" that I had given to him several months earlier out of his back pocket.

Like Steve Goodman, Jimmy Webb, Hoagy Carmichael, Fred Neal, Willie Nelson, Jerry Jeff Walker, Gary P. Nunn, Townes Van Zandt, John Prine, Nanci Griffith, Ira Gershwin, Lorenz Hart, Cole Porter, Buffy Sainte-Marie, Jimmy LaFave, Woody Guthrie, Arlo Guthrie, Harry Chapin, Billy Joel, Peter LaFarge, Johnny Cash, Merle Haggard, Tom T. Hall, Kris Kristofferson, Bobby Bridger, Dave Frishberg, John Lennon, Paul McCartney, Carlos Santana, Pete Seeger, Tish Hinojosa, Butch Hancock, and Bono, Dylan had the ability to tell a story in a few words that made you feel that you were part of the song.

I'll always remember when Dylan called me one afternoon in 1971, a year before I ever thought about recording any of my own songs, much less writing any of them down. He invited me to go with him to New York University in Greenwich Village to hear Allen Ginsberg and Gregory Corso read their poems.

Bob mentioned again how much he liked the film *Pull My Daisy,* which Allen, Gregory, and I all appeared in. He also told me, as he did many times, about how much he loved Kerouac's work, which he agreed was being woefully ignored in 1971.

During intermission at the poetry reading with Ginsberg and Gregory Corso, I told Bob about the carefree spirit and tremendous creative energy that was shared by poets, painters, musicians, authors, dancers, actors, and anyone who would listen to us during the 1950s.

"I wish I could have heard you and Jack together," said Bob. "I know that was for real."

Allen saw us at intermission and implored me to bring Dylan over to his apartment after the concert and play some music with him. "I've been trying for years to get Dylan to play some music with me. Please see if you can get him to come over. I have a guitar at the house."

Later that night, I took Bob to Ginsberg's place. Allen greeted us at the door, handed Bob a guitar, took out his harmonium, and we spent the night playing music together. Allen chanted his poems while alternating between bashing a pair of finger cymbals and playing one note on his harmonium. He was beaming.

November 17, 1971, the day of my forty-first birthday, and the next day, we recorded some of Allen's songs. Dylan played guitar, and I played many of my instruments. We both tried to help Allen find a way to organize his endless energy and fine speaking voice into a musical statement. Over the years, Allen kept getting better, and working with the superlative musician Steven Taylor as his accompanist, created some fine music. Allen wrote some lovely songs, especially his settings of Blake's poetry, which he learned to sing beautifully.

Dylan inspired Allen to dare to do this. I told Bob that I wished that Kerouac could have been with us that night, since Jack was such an accomplished jazz singer and knew so much about all kinds of music, as well as being able to play the bongos and the piano. And Jack had a deep understanding and respect for the work of the jazz masters of the twentieth century, which he incorporated into his always-musical style of prose. Jack's stories were like hearing music when he read them aloud.

I always felt Dylan was one of the few singer/songwriters of his era who understood the enduring value of Kerouac's unique prose/poetic depictions of the treasures of everyday American life that were ignored by much of the literary establishment of the 1950s and 60s.

Like Kerouac and myself, Dylan was brought up in a small community outside the cultural mainstream, with zero expectations of ever having a life in the arts. His discovery of what the world had to offer was harder to come by as a child, and more precious as a result, just as it was for Kerouac and me. Like all of us who had to work hard to discover and find a way to express the beauty that surrounds us, these early struggles gave Bob the strength to compose many of his most memorable songs.

In the summer of 1969 he was out at Bayberry Dunes at Fire Island with his family and we jammed together at the beach for hours on end almost every day.. He encouraged me to try to bring the old jazz-poetry style of free-associating out of the past and recreate the spirit of spontaneity and collaboration that culminated with the film *Pull My Daisy*. I always had fun playing with Dylan. Like Steve Goodman and so many other songwriters I have known over the years, he exhibited a generosity of spirit and encouraged me to write songs and take up the guitar, as well as dare to perform in public the make-up songs I had done whenever the spirit moved me, although never in a regular concert.

In 1972, we had the opening night record release party for my song album *Subway Night* at Malachy McCourt's The Bells of Hell bar, only two blocks from my Village apartment.

Charlie Chin played guitar with me, Malachy McCourt and his brother Frank recited Irish poetry and Shakespeare, and a steady flow of jazz, Latin, Middle-Eastern, and symphonic musicians came by to play a tune or two. We were also joined by singer-songwriters and poets. We performed just about every type of music that was played in New York, with all the visitors who came by and sat in with my band.

It was a two-week jam session and the only song I played each night from the album was "The Fabulous Fifties." The rest of the time, I was improvising words and music in an endless series of make-up songs, with the audience singing along through the night, as well as listening to all the talented people who came by to join us.

"You're not plugging your songs," said one of the many RCA executives who came by The Bells of Hell, expecting to see a carefully produced show, choreographed like an infomercial that hawked the new album every minute.

"Look," I said, "The album is already being played on the radio, and I'm singing "The Fabulous Fifties" on *The Today Show* in two days and on *The Mike Douglas Show* next week. The several million people who watch these two national TV shows and listen to the radio will know about *Subway Night*.

"These two weeks at The Bells of Hell should be a once-in-a-lifetime experience for everybody who comes to hear us. We are in Greenwich Village in New York City. This is live music, not a taped television commercial. People want to see and hear something that they know is just for them and won't ever happen again in the same way. Of course I want people to buy the record, but I'm never going to be a human jukebox. I'll play any of my songs if I'm asked to, but there's a lot of other music worth hearing and I want to do new things every time I play."

Making *Subway Night* helped me to become more sensitive when accompanying other singers, poets, and narrators. Whether I was playing an instrument to back up dramatic readings, conducting an orchestra as soloists sang operatic or choral music, playing for actors when they read poetry, or leading various musical ensembles while narrators recited with orchestral accompaniment, I found I could breathe with whoever I was accompanying and felt an enhanced psychic connection, as if I were singing or reading at the same moment myself.

Whenever I accompany other artists reading or singing or playing their work, I flash back to that wild opening night party for *Subway Night* at the Bells of Hell in 1972. Charlie Chin and I backed up a veritable army of performers and it all sounded rehearsed even though none of it was. Charlie Chin was a master accompanist as well as a spellbinding singer/songwriter, composer, raconteur, and multi-instrumentalist. And his description of how to approach combining words and music, and then make the soloist shine, was an approach that I always try to put into practice every time I play with anyone.

"When I back you up, Dave, or anybody else, I'm like a jeweler, setting a stone. I try to enhance the beauty of the stone, so that the gem shines with more brilliance, without drawing attention to its setting or the person who set it."

Charlie Chin and I had two wonderful weeks in 1972 performing at the Bells of Hell. Malachy McCourt and his brother Frank performed extemporaneously with us nearly every night. Frank was a high school teacher, so he usually left The Bells of Hell before midnight, but the rest of us stayed up, creating words and music nonstop until the last revelers had left during the wee hours.

"In Ireland a real poet has to galvanize his audience by reading in a pub. Only then is he considered to be a true poet," said Malachy. "Never lose your touch, David, my lad. No matter what you do in the symphony world, stay in touch with everyday people and don't lose your spontaneous spirit. Otherwise you'll become a shriveled up old fuddy-duddy like some of my customers, who have lost their zest for the pursuit of romance, beauty, and adventure."

He gestured to a booth in the back, where a white-haired geology professor and his third wife were sleeping with their heads on the table. "Obviously the liquid spirits overcame their intellectual appetites. The top of the morning to you!" he shouted to them. "Wake up, Professor! Wake up so you can have another drink and listen to this Brendan Behan poem I just discovered, which I'm going to read especially for you and your lovely bride."

The professor and his wife continued to snore but Malachy bellowed out the poem and then launched into recitations of James Joyce, Shakespeare, and led the whole bar singing traditional Irish songs.

Malachy himself was a born improviser, and twenty-five years later in 1997, his brother Frank McCourt wrote *Angela's Ashes,* a number one bestseller about his childhood, written in the warm and spontaneous way that sounded exactly the way he and Malachy spoke when they recited with us. They both had the ability to make listeners or readers feel that they were being talked to directly.

This quality is present in the work of all great authors, composers, and playwrights who are able to maintain a visceral relationship with the oral tradition.

"Continue to use your mind, David," said Frank McCourt to me one night. "You only live a block from the Jefferson Library. Go there more often. God didn't give you a brain to let it rot away sitting in front of a TV set."

I told Frank and Malachy that contrary to what many people believed, most musicians appreciate poetry and fiction.

"You always see musicians reading," I said to Malachy.

I said to him that since we were told in my era that we were all a bunch of inarticulate, illiterate morons, we were usually ignored in intellectual circles, which gave us more time to pursue our underground scholarly efforts, without having to let anyone know that we were trespassing on turf deemed off limits to us. We knew we weren't, and we felt that if we could develop ourselves, we could provide an alternative place of refuge from the snobby, uptight, stale environment of those who wanted to make literature and all forms of high art an exclusive experience for a select handful of cognoscenti. Malachy agreed that these feelings were shared by almost everyone else as well.

"Words, music, dance, cooking, languages, painting, and romance are all part of the total world that all of us live in. We all want to feel all these things of beauty belong in a place where we should always feel welcome. That's why I love having a bar. I can make it a home for everyone who comes by and everyone can share the finer things of life with us"

I told Frank and Malachy that while I always admired the stunning craft of poets who could create a haiku, a sonnet, or a brilliant song using a minimum of words in a short space of time, I realized that my own abilities lay in the much longer scat-rap reportage style that came more naturally to me.

Two of my favorite of the songs I wrote for *Subway Night* in 1972 came close to the raps I have done most of my life spontaneously. But I had time to make them structured and write them down.

The first one, The Fabulous Fifties, was written as an ironic comment on the glamorization of the greaser mystique of those bygone days. The weird nostalgia for the 50s in the early 1970s was bizarre for those of us who were part of the 50s, and I wanted to comment on that. Here are the lyrics from the 1972 recording, which are heard more today, thirty-five years later, than they were when the song first came out.

THE FABULOUS FIFTIES

Some folks seem to want us to dream
The fifties are here again
TV shows deal psychic blows
And take us to way back when
I was there when those Fabulous Fifties began
Korea had just begun
I was no fool, I stayed in school
Through '50 and '51.

If you want to hear about 1952
Those fabulous forgotten days of
na-na-na-shoo-bee-doo
Remember when you grease your hair that
Nixon greased his too
I don't despair that I was there
You're lucky it wasn't you.

August sixth of that same year
The Army captured me
They shaved my head and gave me a bed
And sent me to Germany
Many brothers went east instead
Some rested there forever dead
Pete Seeger and Woody were scuffling for bread
In 1953.

Joe McCarthy reared his head
And seared us with his stare
Best friends turned in each other's names
Gray fear was in the air
Returning veterans hooked on smack
Were desperate for a score
Korean ghosts were hosts for swinging 1954.

1955 held hopes for
Better days to come
I packed my bags and left the land
My ancestors had come from
We landed on Hoboken's piers
With no hellos to greet our ears
The haunted subways showed their years
Grim silent faces spoke of fears.

New Year's Eve of '56
I worked with Charles Mingus, played all my licks
Searched for jazz on the radio
Couldn't find Coltrane, Dizzy, or Monk on one show

Where did American music go?
Senate payola investigations let us know
Facts confirmed most musicians' fears
The people's airwaves belonged to racketeers.

True rock and roll just like jazz had a goal
The Platters, Flamingos, and Coasters preached soul
Chuck Berry and B.B. King all did their righteous thing
Screamin' Jay Hawkins could really sing
They were the masters who started it all
Listening to them and watching them was a real ball
They all got cheated, ignored, and abused
If you think that's fabulous you are confused.

Chorus:
Oh no-no-no no-no
Yeah yeah-yeah-yeah, YEAH
May may-may-may maybe
Def-i-nit-nit-nit-nit-nit-ly.
Some folks seem to want us to dream
The fifties are here again
Oh no-no-no no, yeah-yeah-yeah
May-may-be definitely.

Jails were full of men whose sin
Was getting high on grass not gin
The drinkers swore not to give in
They would have killed us all to win
Changes stirred but those who heard
Were warned, "Conform, look what happened to Bird."
On the Road sent out the word
But '57 refused to be stirred.

Many couldn't appreciate
The date was nineteen not 1858
Some went down South to integrate
But their homes up North were still filled with hate
Intellectuals screamed and fumed
Ghosts of the twenties were exhumed
Hemlines went up and hair was groomed
But most of America was Pat Booned.

(Chorus)
Life was the middle road's endless white line
You followed it silently in '59
Canasta and watching TV was real fine
You could rent a beatnik and pay him to whine
Rockefeller went abstract
Converting Franz Kline's dreams to fact
Artists, poets, composers sighed
And quietly cheered as the Fifties died.

Now this song shouldn't make you sad
The 1950s weren't that bad
We had lots of cars and no depression
But it was an era of silence and repression

So if you worship the good old days
Beware of returning to the bad old ways
'Cause NOW'S the time! Don't look backwards in fear
It takes work to bring peace and justice here.

Some folks seem to want us to dream
The Fifties are here again
TV shows deal psychic blows
And take us to way back when
Remember when you grease your hair that
Nixon greased his too
I don't despair that I was there
You're lucky it wasn't you
I don't despair that I was there
You're lucky it wasn't you
I don't despair that I was there
You're lucky it wasn't you.

The second song that was a much shorter reportage of New York life was "Horn and Hardart Succotash Blues," a portrait of old New York. There was a chain of restaurants called Horn and Hardart Automats, where you could insert nickels into a slot to buy whatever was in a little glass container on display, lying there waiting for you to order it. Then, for the price of some spare change, you could remove whatever you had paid for, put it on a tray, and sit down in the spacious caverns of the cafeteria and eat, drink, and sit around all day for practically nothing. The Horn and Hardart on West 57th Street was one of the best automats in the city.

The colossal rents of 2007 in New York City would make it impossible for places like Horn and Hardart to survive today. Even back in 1971, escalating rents were already sounding the final call for the small mom and pop businesses that gave New York City such an infinite variety of flavors.

The neighborhood candy store, the family-owned butcher shop, the local grocery store, and the thousands of little coffeehouses, bars, and tiny convenience shops were all feeling the rising waters of what has become the tidal wave of exorbitant rents which now force so many major cities around the country to lose their character. The small intimacy of neighborhood meeting places that these modest enterprises provided has been replaced by giant corporate, faceless businesses that have no individual flavor or local history.

Horn and Hardart was a venerable chain of cafeterias throughout New York, as well as many other parts of the United States, but they somehow retained the small-town flavor that made each block of New York City's concrete megalopolis a special place. They were like free-form social clubs.

Articles were written about the decline of so many small businesses in 1972. One in particular appeared, lamenting the fact that 57th Street's beloved Horn and Hardart was on the verge of becoming an extinct species.

A man named Jack Tafoya appeared as the man on the white horse to single-handedly rescue this landmark automat from a premature demise. Jack Tafoya was beyond categories. He attained success as a talented jazz singer/record producer/TV host/entrepreneur/published author of books on numerology/all-around visionary and beloved eccentric.

Every time he made some money in ventures that everyone else deemed hopeless, he would plunge into the next event and pull the rabbit out of the hat again. Jack decided that he would single-handedly rescue Horn and Hardart from becoming an extinct species.

After hearing my song "Horn and Hardart Succotash Blues" on the radio, he called me and told me of his idea of preserving the 57th Street Automat, using my song as the rallying cry, and engaging many of the jazz greats he had supported through his bevy of concerts, recordings, and independently produced TV shows.

"Listen man, they've been trying to kill off jazz since the 1920s, but we refuse to be stomped out. The jam session and everything in the music shows the rest of the world that the true soul of America is all about democracy and community. So are the Horn and Hardarts.

"Anybody and everybody are welcome there. They're soulful, just like the neighborhood jazz clubs used to be. There are only a few Horn and Hardarts and a handful of jazz clubs left in the whole city. Let's get some great jazz and Latin artists together and hippify the masses. Get Pepper Adams, Elvin Jones, Ray Barretto, the guys from Gil Evans's band, and all the cats you play with and we'll have a parade from Central Park to the Horn and Hardart on West 57th Street to stir up the public's imagination.

"Isaac Stern saved Carnegie Hall. We'll save Horn and Hardart, the one right down the block from Carnegie Hall. Beboppers to the rescue. Damn the real estate torpedoes. Full speed ahead.

"You can get classical cats and kitties to come and sit in with your band, and invite all the folk musicians and songwriters and poets you hang out with to join in, and we'll wake up everybody. I already have a parade permit for the opening night two weeks from today.

"You told me when I saw you last week that you are working on your violin concerto for Charlie Castleman. Can you take a few days off? Charlie digs jazz and he plays solo concerts with orchestras at Carnegie Hall. I'm sure he likes to nosh at the Horn and Hardart there when he's in town. Ask him to come and play too. Have him play Bach or the blues with your band, or whatever.

"You've got to think big to survive. Take a break. Taking the time off to do this would be another milestone in your checkered career. How many symphony composer-cats have ever played in the front window of an automat? This could be huge.

"I already have a sponsor. Everyone gets paid each night. The owners of the chain love "Horn and Hardart Succotash Blues," that insane song you wrote. They really want you there. And you and all your friends who come by to jam with your band can have all they want to eat for free. This is definitely another first."

"Sounds like a solid business plan to me, Jack," I said. "I'll have the first movement of the violin concerto orchestrated by the end of next week, so I'll take a few days off to celebrate."

Two weeks later, I marched with a group of wonderful musicians from Central Park down to the 57th Street Horn and Hardart. Elvin Jones played a field drum and sported an American flag ensemble with an Uncle Sam hat. Pepper Adams marched along, playing atonal variations on John Philip Sousa marches, interspersed with quotes from Stravinsky, Ravel, and Bartók, famous show tunes about New York City, and New Orleans second-line celebratory old-time marching songs.

Jack Tafoya led the parade, keeping time with a huge baton as if he were the grand marshal of a band that was playing for the halftime show during the Super Bowl. He kept up an animated series of conversations with everyone within range of his rapping radius, bellowing through a bullhorn while delivering on-the-spot public service announcements about jazz, classical music, Horn and Hardart's history, numerology, many of his other upcoming projects, and anything else that crossed his overactive mind.

By the time we reached the automat on 57th Street, there was a huge crowd behind us including curiosity seekers and kids holding balloons that Jack distributed during the march with his left hand from his shoulder bag full of buttons, flyers, and other goodies. Meanwhile he continued his oratory and never missed a beat, pumping his baton with his right hand like a psychedelic drum major. Jack's multitasking abilities invigorated us all.

"We're going to save the world," Jack yelled into the bullhorn to the crowd, as if he were delivering the State of the Union address.

"We are gathered here today to keep jazz and all great acoustic music of the world alive at one of New York's great cultural institutions," said Jack. "Dig into your pockets, get all the spare change, and come on in to New York's hippest jazz club and have a meal and hear the greatest music. No cover. No minimum. No MSG.

"And remember, this is 1972. What does seven and two add up to?"

"Nine," piped up a little girl, wearing a papier-mâché Uncle Sam hat and carrying some of Jack's balloons.

"Perfect," said Jack. "You heard it. The voice of our future has spoken. Nine is a power number. Nineteen is an energy source that has the circuitry completed when the seven and two are added up and attached to it. This means that 1972 is the year that numerologists have already deemed as the time for action!

"I have the instructions on how to order my book on numerology on my card, which I will hand out when you enter, after you have gotten your food and are seated. Come on in and hear the music, eat the food and drink the coffee. It's the best in the world."

"This dude's really *wired*" whispered one of the spectators to me. "What's with all this numerology weirdness? Is he whacked or what?"

"No," I said. "He's just enthusiastic."

Our series of concerts at the 57th Street Horn and Hardart Automat were even more fun than listening to Jack Tafoya rant and rave. Musicians strolling by from every genre came into the automat to join us, including symphonic musicians from visiting orchestras who were performing at Carnegie Hall, a block away.

There was a view of 57th Street from the front window of the Horn and Hardart Automat where we set up our bandstand. Each night, we saw a parade of musicians and music lovers passing by who smiled and waved at us as they went to Carnegie Hall. Crowds often gathered outside the automat to watch us playing and eventually came into the cafeteria out of curiosity to join the Horn and Hardart regular customers.

The year-round patrons of the Horn and Hardart Automat on 57th street were mostly refugees from Central Europe who used the cafeteria as a social club for senior citizen, old-country schmoozing seminars. My song "Horn and Hardart Succotash Blues" honored the feelings and shared memories of survivors of a gentler time who were able to create their own harmonious environment in a New York which now seemed increasingly disinterested in caring for its old people.

No matter how diverse the evenings of words and music got, we performed the song at every show.

The *New York Times* wrote a thoughtful article about the passing of an era and quoted some of the lyrics of the song.

The last Horn and Hardart in New York City closed in 1990. Those of us who experienced the warmth and friendliness of these cafeterias will always have a fond place in our hearts for the people who spent many of the happiest hours of their days and nights in these welcoming refuges, finding solace and companionship, as well as a place where they could afford to eat, in the heart of the city that they loved and called their home.

Here are the lyrics to the song.

HORN AND HARDART SUCCOTASH BLUES

Horn and Hardart
Succotash blues
Central European
Immigrant dues.

White bread and coffee light
Blend with the Polish night
Drivers from Krakow
Survivors from Dachau.

We all nosh on automat
Late evening stews
Horn and Hardart
Succotash blues.

Salads and hot foods
Cold bread and rolls
Drive minds and stomachs
Through tunnels and tolls.

Slide the old brain waves
On trips to Croatia
Serbian cab drivers
Sit like crustacea.

Horn and Hardart
Succotash blues
Fresh liver and bacon
Old tortured beef stews.

It's really hip
To go back into time
See 1930
For only a dime.

One cup of coffee
Will buy you a flight
Into a Czechoslovakian night.
Horn and Hardart

Succotash blues
Central European
Immigrant dues.

Black hats and coats
Ancient white socks and ties
Sway with the rhythm of
Small talk and lies.

Catsup and tea water
Make a fine drink
Hard times are closer
Than most people think.

Photos of surfers
Jump out of the walls
Spraying white water
As we eat meatballs.

What a relief from
New York's hectic pace
Forty-five cents gets
You out of the race.

It's really hip
To go back into time
See 1930
For only a dime.

Horn and Hardart
Succotash blues
Central European
Immigrant dues.

To my surprise, as well as to the astonishment of everyone who worked at RCA, this song and "The Fabulous Fifties" from the album *Subway Night* were both played on the radio, and *Rolling Stone Magazine* interviewed me and published a hilarious article written by Ed McCormack about my foray into scat-rap reportage.

I began playing festivals throughout the 70s and 80s but continued to make up one-time only songs, rather than cranking out the ones that I had already completed. And all this helped me to combine singing and improvising lyrics as a part of my presentations of jazz, Latin, and what was now called world music. And in my make-up songs, I was able to free associate in English, Spanish, French, German, and smatterings of other languages whenever I was in a country whose languages I could speak enough to make some kind of rhyme.

Still, the majority of my time was spent writing orchestral and chamber music, with all my songs written on the run when traveling to and from concerts around the world. By the 1980s I had so many piles of lyrics and song/stories written when traveling that I had to buy a file cabinet to store all of them.

By this time I had three kids. I'd forgotten about *Subway Night* until they became teenagers in the 90s and found some old copies of the LP recordings and finally heard it.

"Daddy," said Alana, my eldest, "That's hysterical. How did they ever dare let you record an album like that?"

"I've often wondered myself," I said.

"Maybe they should have put you in a time machine, or frozen you, and then thawed you out so you could finally make some money, now that people are doing stuff like this," said Adira, my second daughter.

"No," I said, "I loved doing it then. And I love what I'm doing now."

"I like the one called 'East and West,'" said Alana. "It sounds like Dr. Seuss freestyling at a bluegrass festival. And you snuck in the names of people you always tell us about."

"East and West" was done in a bluegrass style, influenced by the daydreams I had as a little boy when I would walk down to the Summerton Springs railroad station near our farm in Feasterville and put a penny on the tracks and wait for the train to roar by without stopping, heading for New York, a mythological place I thought I might visit some day. I used to sit by the tracks with my neighbor, Artie McCrae, and make up stories, speaking faster and faster as the train approached, and then run with him down the rails to see what the penny looked like after the train wheels had redesigned it.

I thought it would be good to sing someday for kids, like a Gilbert and Sullivan high-speed patter song. Now all these years later, since Canadian songwriter Raffi mentioned me in his peanut butter and jelly with jam song, young people and their parents have discovered "East and West."

EAST AND WEST

East and West
They're both the best
There is no front or back
Heads and tails
Ties and rails
Just a penny on the track.

Cup and saucer
Beowulf and Chaucer
Sit like Jack and Jill
Up and down
Cap and gown
On graduation hill.

In and out
Ale and stout
We drink to fantasies
Wash and dry
Laugh and cry
We dream at Santa's knees.

Lemon and lime
Space and time
Old radiators groan
Spring and fall
Hear summer's call
As winter sits alone.

Towns and farms
Toes and arms

Tramp the fields of summer
Sleet and rain
Joy and pain
Cats scream cream's a bummer.

Bird and Trane
Love and pain
Walk the lonely valleys
Ramblin' Jack
And Kerouac
Portray forgotten alleys.

Free and tight
Love and might
Dance to Adam's oboe
Eve and dawn
Doe and fawn
Paint the walls of SoHo.

Ups and downs
Saints and clowns
Circle through the changes
Phones and poles
Bones and souls
Graze on barren ranges.

Mom and Dad
Sweet and sad
Call us to the table
Haves and hads
Girls and lads
Feast if they are able.

Skies and waters
Sons and daughters
Flow like streams to rivers
Knights and knaves
Squaws and braves
Teach takers to be givers.

Sticks and stones
Skins and bones
Pray for understanding
Slaves and kings
Chains and rings
Need no more commanding.

Earth and skies
Birth and lies
Need no separations
Thought and speech
Shout and preach
Love not reparations.

East and West
They're both the best
There is no front or back
Heads and tails
Ties and rails
Just a penny on the track.

In 1996, at the age of fifteen, my daughter Adira began reading Kerouac in public, while I backed her up on piano, flutes, and French horn, as I did with Jack in 1957. I always told her how being with Jack was like being with another musician. He relied on ESP a lot to communicate when there weren't other people around, and he was always down-to-earth and conscious of other people's feelings.

He used to love to improvise verbally and combine words, music, and sounds when we would scat-sing together. Whenever we would visit his old friend Lucien Carr's place, or go to my 6th Avenue apartment or a loft party, we would often carry on for hours. Sometimes we'd switch off, and he would sing and then play the piano while I would make up scat songs with him backing me up. Jack was such an accomplished jazz singer and scat singer that he was able to transfer the very ethos of jazz into his writing. He made you able to hear the music when you read his books or heard him read excerpts from them.

Just like other musicians I traveled with often did, when I played with Dizzy Gillespie, Lionel Hampton, Oscar Pettiford, and my own band, Jack would break into song at unusual moments when on the road, just to cool things out. We all did this as a way of entertaining ourselves and keeping our creative fires stoked during endless hours in cars, trains, buses, planes, ships, and when waiting around for sound checks, motel registrations, or sitting offstage for hours when all schedules went haywire. No matter what was happening, you could always make up a song or sing a fragment of something you would like to be able to play someday or use in a future composition.

Scat-rapping was part of the culture of the 40s and 50s for many of us, and while it might be defined today as a subcultural form of expression by some social scientists, scat-rapping was never subcultural or sub anything for any of us. It kept our heads above water.

Even the most Eurocentric scholars in the world could never accuse Kerouac of being someone whose intellect was limited to what they dismissed as being the subcultures of his time and place. Kerouac had an enormous knowledge of French literature, nineteenth-century English authors, contemporary American poetry, and the works of twentieth-century novelists. And he was equally knowledgeable and appreciative about all kinds of music, art, sculpture, sports, and world events that occurred each day of his life.

Musicians loved being with Jack, especially before *On the Road* came out when he was not under the pressure of instant fame.. He shared admiration for all the poets whom all the musicians loved. Dylan Thomas, reading "A Child's Christmas in Wales"; Delmore Schwartz, reading his poems from memory at the White Horse Tavern; Joel Untermeyer, reading at the Lion's Head Bar at 3:00 a.m.; and Bob Kaufman reading in Washington Square Park. And Diane di Prima, reading with fire and drama at one of our all-night bring-your-own-bottle extravaganzas at a painter's loft. All of these poets could make anyone a fan of poetry. They were all disciplined writers and excellent readers of their own work. So was Jack, and he could also make up raps and scat on the spot.

Howard Hart and Philip Lamantia, who, with Jack and me, did the first-ever jazz poetry readings given in New York City at the Brata Gallery in 1957, both spent a lot of time with musicians. Howard Hart started out as a professional drummer.

Philip Lamantia could have been a jazz journalist if he had chosen to be one. He had a vast knowledge of contemporary music as well as the treasures of the European classical tradition and understood how they were related.

Many of us in music also read the poetry of Baudelaire, Rambaud, Kenneth Patchen, William Carlos Williams, Langston Hughes, and T.S. Eliot. Their writing had a sound, even when you read it in silence, and when it was read alive, it *was* music. And I read Jesse Young, author of "Man with a Bull Tongue Plow," to everyone who would listen. He was a big favorite of mine. His southern Ohio poetic style was unique and close to the way people spoke in what was still a rural area where our farm was in the 1930s. And I would often read poems by Saint-Jean Perse in French and Edna St. Vincent Millay with Jack accompanying me on one of my hand drums, or playing on an upside down wastebasket or with a fork and spoon on an empty coffee cup in some all-night eating place until we were asked to knock it off.

Jack introduced me to the writings of Gary Snyder and Lawrence Ferlinghetti, as well as the work of poets Phil Whalen and Guillaume Apollinaire. These four poets were among musicians' favorites, because of their honest, soulful, musical styles.

When Jack improvised the narration to the film *Pull My Daisy*, doing a different version on each of the two takes, I wasn't even surprised. The narration is scat-rap at its best and is also a perfect example of how this way of letting it all flow can become an instant piece of reportage. Jack's narration for the film *Pull My Daisy*, preserved in the film's soundtrack with my musical accompaniment, is a perfect example what we did together all the time. I remember how much fun it was playing for him when he did it that spring evening in 1959. I wasn't surprised by the results. We did it all the time whenever the spirit moved us, usually for our own enjoyment.

However, as outstanding as Jack's spontaneous narration was for *Pull My Daisy*, the best make-up songs and scat-rap that night occurred after we were done with the two takes of recording Jack's narration for the film. Jack and I threw ourselves an all-night marathon victory celebration at Jerry Newman's studio, where we both made up words and music till dawn. Jerry recorded it all for hours as we carried on.

After Jerry died, all his tapes disappeared. I wish I could hear them now.

I never realized how amazing Jack's improvised narration was for the film until my kids' friends saw it at a festival at NYU in 1995. They had heard the song "Pull my Daisy" that Jack, Neal Cassady, Allen Ginsberg, and I wrote together, but they had never heard Jack narrating in his spontaneous style. As I listened with them when we watched the film, and heard it through them, I was reminded of his brilliance all over again.

Jack and I both came out of the tradition set by King Pleasure, the premiere jazz-poetical singer, Lord Buckley, the poet-philosopher-comedian pioneer of scat-rap-reportage on the state of the universe, Carlyle Macbeth, the poet who everyone thought was a musician even though he never played an instrument, and many extraordinary performers, like Harry the Hipster, scat singers Slim Gaillard and Joe Carroll, and the peerless Mighty Sparrow, who could improvise a thirty-minute poem to calypso music.

The fertile soil of the 1950s underground sowed the seeds for the twenty-first century to be more receptive for all artists to allow themselves to celebrate their own creativity and spontaneity, and to incorporate the beauty of colloquial speech and improvised flights of fancy. Much of this energy came from the spirit of jazz.

In the 1990s, I rewrote a short tribute to Kerouac, entitled "This Song's for You, Jack." I first played it in 1982 for the twenty-fifth anniversary celebration of the publication of *On the Road* in Boulder, Colorado. Almost all the lyrics were improvised. Ten years later I finally wrote the best ones down at the suggestion of Townes Van Zandt, when we were playing Farm Aid together with Willie Nelson. Since Townes was a master craftsman in the art of songwriting, I knew he was serious, and felt that I should write down the essential lyrics, tighten it up, and write something short and to the point. I sat down immediately backstage for an hour and wrote it down on the back of an American Agricultural Movement flyer.

In 1994, I rewrote the final version of "This Song's for You, Jack" for New York University's celebration of beat culture, honoring the thirty-seventh anniversary of the first-ever jazz poetry reading in New York City with Jack Kerouac and me at the Brata Art Gallery on East 10th Street.

Poet and publisher Ron Whitehead of Louisville, Kentucky, liked it so much he made a poster of the complete poem for Whitefield's Press. At the top of the poster was a photograph from 1984, taken by Chris Felver, showing my daughter Adira climbing up my back during an outdoor concert while I was attempting to switch from French horn to piano.

Here are the lyrics. Each of the five verses is constructed using the twelve-bar blues pattern.

THIS SONG'S FOR YOU, JACK

As long as there's a tree
A flower
A river
Or a stream
As long as there's a swallow
A catfish
A storm cloud
And a dream
As long as there is summer rain
And early morning dew
This song's for you, Jack
This song is for you.

All the times you talked of Texas
As the sun set in the west
Across New Jersey skyline
Those stories were the best
People from all over
We got to know through you
Cross the Rockies, down to Mexico
Far from New York 6th Avenue
Two floors up, one room, scat-singing
Laughing-dancing-poetry all night through
The good times and rivers roll along

So I wrote this song for you.
Moonlight bright October night
In Lowell, Massachusetts
Birds fly south
On their winter way
Casting moonlit shadows
On the road
You traveled
Yesterday
The wind blows east
From Denver
In San Francisco
Clouds are turning gray.

You stayed and left
A thousand places
Searching for Buddha
Brittany and Spain
Walked through Colorado holly
Heard the ancient South Dakota drum
Of Sitting Bull
Drank Oklahoma rain
You wrote us stories
By your brakeman's shining lantern
Through the night on rusty tracks in Texas
On the roadside by the train.

The road
You shared with us
The road you showed us
We can ride on too
We share the ride
You're by our side
Jack, this song's
For you
Together on the road tonight
We share the holy highway light
This song's for you, Jack
This song's for you.

A year after the NYU conference where this song was done at the end of the festival, I composed the music for *A Little Rebellion: Thomas Jefferson,* for narrator and orchestra. I used the words of Thomas Jefferson, selected and narrated by E.G. Marshall, commissioned by the Library of Congress and premiered at the JFK Center in October of 1995 in Washington, D.C.

I conducted members of the National Symphony, and it was easy to put together. Because of singing and playing backup for singers, I could apply the same principles of trying to enhance Jefferson's spoken words with formally composed music. Rather than overpowering the natural musicality that the words of Thomas Jefferson already possessed when spoken, I tried to complement them, just as I did when accompanying Kerouac's words.

In the 1960s, E.G. Marshall and I had performed a series of spontaneous word and music events in the parks in New York City, along with Kurt Vonnegut and actor Kevin McCarthy reading. So when E.G. Marshall renewed our collaboration thirty years later at the Kennedy Center, it was an especially joyous time.

"Now we're finally doing it indoors, David, and getting paid," said E.G. Marshall, after our final rehearsal with the orchestra, the day before we gave the world premiere of *A Little Rebellion*. "Even though we're in white tie and tails with the National Symphony, let's not lose that spirit we had when we played in the parks for free. Remember Jefferson's great quote, which gave us the title for our piece, 'I like a little rebellion now and then.'"

For the second half of the concert program, I wrote two orchestral accompaniments for two passages from *On the Road*, which I had done with Jack so many times when I would simply make up the music and play myself. Jack and I had always talked about doing these readings with a symphony orchestra and I was finally able to do it, thirty-nine years later. I wish he had been there, but his words were. E.G. Marshall read Jack's words in his own way and everyone was moved. The words and the music became one.

For the second half of the concert, I also programmed *Theme and Variations on Red River Valley for Flute and String Orchestra*. I called up the Luckenbach, Texas, General Store and spoke to Marge the Sheriff, a tall gracious woman who always sported a gigantic cowboy hat and tin badge. Since Hondo Crouch had appointed her to this post, and since Luckenbach didn't have much crime with a population of seven people, she appeared at the general store whenever she could, outside of her real job in the medical field.

"Luckenbach General Store. Sheriff Marge speaking. What can I do for ya?"

"Marge, this is Amram calling long distance."

"Hey boy. Haven't heard from you for quite a while. Almost a year since you came by after Kerrville. Long distance? Lessee, lemmee guess," said Marge, not missing a beat. "You're either in Pakistan, Cairo, Kenya, London, or Cut 'n' Shoot, Texas."

"No, Marge, I'm here in Washington, D.C., at the Kennedy Center. We're doing words of Thomas Jefferson, Jack Kerouac with music, and *Theme and Variations on Red River Valley*, the one you heard at Kerrville in 1991, written in memory of Hondo. It's going to be broadcast nationally so everyone in Luckenbach can hear it. Tell everyone in Luckenbach that Kerouac and Hondo both made it to the Kennedy Center."

"Well, it's about time," said Marge. "Like they say in the Bible, 'all things come to those who wait.' By the way, I've got that pennywhistle you forgot to take back with you last year right here by the cash register. I sure can't play it, so we'll keep it warm for you till you come back and visit with us. Give those Yankees hell and tell President Clinton to give all us Texans less taxes and to spend more time practicing his saxophone. I don't want to have to send a posse out to arrest him for playing out of tune."

In the beginning of 1997, a year after the premiere of *A Little Rebellion: Thomas Jefferson*, I conducted the Nashville Symphony for the world premiere of my symphony *Kokopelli*. Just before I came down to rehearse with the orchestra, Mickey Raphael of Willie Nelson's band called me and suggested that I make a recording of some of the make-up scat-rap songs he had heard me do over the years.

"A bunch of great pickers are coming to hear your new symphony, David. Why don't we make a record with you on your off hours, when you are not conducting rehearsals? Vassar Clements told me you were both in the army together in 1953 in Germany and you used to jam together in the barracks all the time. He's coming to hear your symphony. He can play with you for the CD of your songs, and I have a whole bunch of friends who would like to play as well. You can do all the songs you always do about Texas and the South."

"I'm flattered that you'd suggest that, Mickey," I said. "You're my favorite harmonica player in the world, but I don't think anybody would want to hear my songs."

"We would," said Mickey. "I'll get all the musicians. My friend Fred Bogert has the original RCA Studio B, the best one in Nashville. We can record there. Just get some songs of yours together and we can do the whole CD in two sessions. If you don't have time to write anything down, just come anyway and make them up in the studio."

"This is the first time anybody has asked me to do this since 1972," I said. "I did a bunch of them in Canada in the late 70s for RCA Canada, but no one has asked me to do it here."

"Well I'm asking you, so you be sure to do it," said Mickey. "I'll get you Nashville's finest pickers. And Fred Bogert can release it on Chrome Records or put it out on the Internet or both."

I went through piles of jumbles of pages torn out of old notebooks, scraps of papers, restaurant menus, laundry lists with lyrics on the back from hotels and motels, stationary from airplanes, and manuscript music paper with musical sketches for orchestral pieces on one side and words on the other and found enough material to record all the songs I could fit on a new CD. I called it *Southern Stories*.

I included "Kentucky Southern Gentleman," the short poem I wrote honoring Hunter Thompson, which appears in the first chapter of this book. Mickey Raphael and Vassar Clements knew exactly what to do, and almost the entire CD was done with only one take of each song.

One of the songs, "Down Home Sunday in the South," was a tribute to my own southern roots, and I tried to simplify everything and tell the story as clearly as possible.

DOWN HOME SUNDAY IN THE SOUTH

Soul fire preaching, crying, teaching
Hear the congregation shout
That's what southern down home Sunday
Soul is all about

Constant scenes of tambourines
Struck for the living and the dying
Flowered hats and cotton dresses
Souls on fire, laughing, crying

Grits and greens, fresh pecan pies
Melt so slowly in your mouth
Homemade wines from dandelions
Down home Sunday in the South

Ancient voices sing their songs
In Cherokee and Seminole
Mockingbirds, whippoorwills
Join the chorus, heal the soul

Southern Sunday sun goes down
Born again a brand new week
Strength to be in harmony
Love thy neighbor, heal the meek

Down in Georgia on a Sunday
At the dock in 1857
All my family landed in Savannah
Felt they were in heaven

Ate grits and greens, fresh pecan pies
Melting slowly in their mouth
Hear their voices calling me
Down home Sunday in the South

Ate grits and greens, fresh pecan pies
Melting slowly in their mouth
Hear their voices calling me in my dreams
Down home Sunday in the South

Another song I wrote for the CD, "New Orleans Horn Man," was a story song about a composite of so many musicians I had known throughout the years who tried to balance their love of music with their love of their family but couldn't quite do both. It was also done to honor the musicians from New Orleans, the city that has given the United States and the world music so precious that the whole planet is made more harmonious by its existence.

When the tragedy of Katrina occurred years later, I gave the proceeds for my seventy-fifth birthday concert to the Musician's Emergency Fund to try to do something to show support for everyone from this beautiful place. When we did the song at the seventy-fifth birthday bash in 2005, I thought of all my old friends from New Orleans since I first visited it with my uncle David in 1943. Like so many others throughout the United States and the world, I say a prayer each night for a rebuilding of the city and a return of every one of its people and for all the musicians, past and present, who have graced the world with their special Crescent City spirit.

In the song, I tried to tell the story without too many excursions into the unknown. Again, I used the classic twelve-bar blues structure.

NEW ORLEANS HORN MAN

He's traveled through the wilderness
He's played with all the bands
His only dream is home
His wife and baby's outstretched hands

He's seen a million headlights
Cut across a thousand nights
Mississippi summer highways
Drive-ins and mosquito bites

His horn's still his companion

On his never-ending ride
All the cheers and tears are memories now
His one true love's his bride

She wanted him to stay in town
And be a file clerk
And play on weekends when he could
And get some extra work

He told her that he had to play
He didn't have a choice
He loved her more than anyone
But music was his voice

His only chance for playing
Was to go back on the road
His wife said she would leave him
His life had become a load

Their baby was just three weeks old
When he was called to play
He packed his horn and
Hasn't seen his family till this day

We didn't leave you, you left us
Is what the letter said
There's nothing left in New Orleans for you
Except your empty bed

His horn's still his companion
On his never ending ride
All the cheers and tears are memories now
His one true love's his bride

His wife and baby still inspire
What's left of his art
Their picture in his wallet
Stays right by his heart

His wife's sister called him
Left her message on the phone
We still love you
But you made your choice to be alone

He travels all year through the South
He plays with all the bands
He dreams of New Orleans
And his wife and baby's outstretched hands

I still continue today to make notes, when different experiences move me to do so. I either do this when I have a piece of paper available and the time to do it, or I make them in my head and file them on my brain's desktop to be accessed whenever the circumstances dictate.

But with my current sixteen-hour days of composing music, writing words for articles and new books, and traveling around the world in various roles as a musical performer, conductor, and speaker, I usually write down ideas while I am on the road.

When performing at Lowell Celebrates Kerouac, the annual celebration of Jack Kerouac's writings and his hometown, I end the festival each year with what is called an Amram Jam. Everyone visiting the festival and all Lowell residents in the neighborhood who want to recite a poem, sing a song, or create a rap on the spot are welcome. I accompany them spontaneously as I did with Jack until the last participant has performed.

Sometimes the Amram Jam goes on as long as seven hours, but it is a great way to end the festival on a high note. At Café Paradiso, an exceptionally gifted tall blonde-haired woman wearing a black beret performed a blues piece and then joined me in scatting and making up words on the spot. She was as good a singer as anyone I had heard or performed since I last worked with the late Betty Carter.

When she left, before I packed up my instruments to drive back to the farm, I went out on the cobblestone street in front of the Café Paradiso on Palmer Street, to thank her for making the finale of the festival so outstanding.

I couldn't find her, but as I was walking back to pay my final farewells, I saw the black beret she was wearing lying in the middle of Palmer Street. I told the owner of the café.

When I got back to the farm at 1:00 a.m., after the long drive from Lowell, I wrote down what I felt, and put the paper in a part of the house where I could find it again some day.

THE WOMAN IN THE BLACK BERET

In Lowell where Jack's heart still beats
We gathered for some poems and eats
The joy we shared was worth the cost
Paradise was no longer lost

Paradise is found and so were we
With music, song and poetry
I'd done this six-hour jam before
The way Jack shared his open door

Young and old came to hear and see
The way it was and will always be
When joy meets spontaneity
All hearts connect and minds feel free

On that October afternoon
Our trio played a brand new tune
I saw someone come through the door
I knew I'd seen her face before

She wore an old-school black beret
But not in the Beatnik cliché way
Rather like the French still do
Like Dizzy did in '52

Bird and Dizzy both told me
That they knew someday they would be
Appreciated in the way
That they finally are today

It all took years and sometimes tears
And they're not here to hear the cheers
But their music's here to stay
As classic as that black beret

Worn in a natural 50s style

That made all cats and kitties smile
When Bird and Diz and Monk were kings
With black berets and diamond rings

But Bird told me that Now's the time
To live without the Now's a crime
He said this back in '52
So someday I'd know what to do

Said, "Here's a thought for you to share
The hippest thing's to be a square
My beret's what I love to wear
'Cause I love Paris when I'm there

I don't wear it any more
Other cats who do don't know the score
They think that fashion's what makes art
Our music just comes from our heart"

Bird's words came back to me again
As I slipped from Now to way back then
But realized that Now's still the time
To share what's precious and sublime

And see that in some special way
The presence of that black beret
Was Now the voice of yesterday
Saying I'm still with you here today

Hours later just around seven
Like a voice that came from heaven
The woman with the black beret
Sang and blew our blues away

With perfect pitch and natural grace
She brought a smile to every face
We felt we were Now on a trip
As her voice sailed us on her ship

Now day was night I had to drive
Two hundred miles to arrive
At my next port of call to play
Some music on the very next day

I said goodbye to everyone
Another festival was done
I packed my bags and paid the band
I hugged and shook my final hand

I went to say one last goodbye
To the woman who made our spirits high
I talked to her about her singing
And all the joy that she was bringing

How she made the precious past
Alive and Now and built to last
And how her very special way
Could help us all live for each day

Inspiring us with her special gift
To heal all lonely souls and lift
Our spirits and bring all joy back

As we all honored Kerouac

There was no more that I could say
We'd said it when we played that day
I watched her as she drove away
On dusky Lowell streets now gray

Laying there before my feet
On that rainy old-bricked Palmer street
Resting there as if to say
Take me, I'm your black beret

Now I'm on the road again
I really don't know where or when
I'll give her back that black beret
Which she wore in that special way

She wrote me said just keep it warm
And wear it if you're in a storm
Put it on a hook or on a shelf
Till I wear it once again myself

I told my son when I got back
The way she sang for Kerouac
How when she drove away I found
Her black beret there on the ground

Next year in Lowell where Jack's heart still beats
I'll bring my son for poems and eats
He'll meet and hear the final day
The woman in the black beret

In the summer of 2004, at 3:00 a.m. on my last night in Chengdu, China, at the end of the "Beat Meets East" Conference, I stared out the window of my room on the fifth floor of the small hotel I was staying in. I saw a young woman riding by on the back fender of a bike, sitting sidesaddle, holding onto a young man in the bicycle seat, pedaling away. As she looked up, I saw an extraordinary looking young woman whose eyes seemed to go right through me, and I suddenly flashed on some kind of subconscious past life experience and jotted down this poem on the back of the hotel stationery. I wrote this as a spoken introduction to a talking blues piece where the audience sings a phrase in Mandarin in the middle of the song, called "Meanderin' in Mandarin."

People hearing the song liked the spoken introduction so much that "My Buddha Angel in Chengdu" has been published as a poem by itself.

MY BUDDHA ANGEL IN CHENGDU

It's 5:00 a.m. in Chengdu China
I can't sleep
A wink
Staring out the window
Water drips on dishes
In the sink

A bicycle goes by
A young gal sits
Sidesaddle on the back

Looks like Buddha's angel daughter
Sent from heaven
Dressed in black

She glances up
Her dark eyes
Make the morning come to life
Suddenly I realize
Long ago this angel
Was my wife

Wanted now to tell her
When we married
Many years ago
That I never would have left her
If I knew then
What I now know

Waited for what seemed
A thousand years to see
Those eyes again
Hoping someday I could tell her
That our love
Would never end

Never dared to tell her then
Because of all the love
We shared
It was more than I could handle
Even though
I really cared

Now it's many lifetimes later
Here in Chengdu
5:00 a.m.
My favorite wife
From an earlier life
The sweetest one of all of them

Once she told me in our lifetime
Our true love
Would never die
And that even if I left her
Buddha's angel
Still would fly

Now she tells me broken hearts
Will all heal themselves
In time
And that all the pain I caused her
Now is gone
Except for mine

Now in Chengdu
Through the window
She's come back to me again
Riding on the back seat
Of a bicycle

Sidesaddle with her friend

Guess that since she passed me by
There's only one thing
I can do
Get myself a new gal
And a bicycle
That's built for two

When in this reincarnation
When I've found
A brand new bride
Maybe I'll find out
It's Buddha's angel
Riding by my side

Telling me wherever
We have been
And through whichever life
Through all our reincarnations
She has always been
My wife

Now it's 7:00 in the morning
Chengdu streets
Are filled with light
I'm still staring out the window
As the day
Is growing bright

Waiting by the window
Need to see
My true love's eyes again
When she rides by
On her bicycle
Sidesaddle with her friend

Then I'll tell her that I love her
This time I know
What to do
Waiting by the window
For my Buddha angel
In Chengdu

In addition to my work as a classical composer, my collaborations with Kerouac and scores of authors, poets, folk and jazz artists over the last fifty years made it possible to finally be able to go to China as well as many of the other places I have been and still go around the world. I realized when I returned from Chengdu that if I hadn't played for free with Kerouac and an army of others a half a century ago, this never would have happened.

Ninety-nine percent of my education came and still comes from being with others and paying attention to what they say as well as what they do. For all the people who told me that even trying to do anything artistic was a waste of time, and that artistic expression was only a pursuit for other people, I always was lucky enough to meet someone who took a minute to encourage me to persevere. They always found a few minutes to share a little of what they knew and tell me how others had enabled them to find a way to pursue their own way and make their impossible dreams become a reality.

As a way of acknowledging those gifts bestowed upon me, often from people who never received the recognition they deserved for their own achievements but who had such big hearts and generosity of spirit, I try today to encourage people I meet to tap into their own creativity. My hope is that one of my contributions to the world I live in, in addition to my own work, is to make people of all ages feel that *they* have a contribution to make. Because we all do.

Every human being has something of value to offer. If anyone finds the events I do to be energizing, I only hope that whatever I do will make them want to dare to tell *their* story in whatever way they feel best able to tell it.

In 2002, after his spectacular performance of the world premiere of my flute concerto *Giants of the Night*, which he had commissioned me to write for him, flutist Sir James Galway and I went out to celebrate.

In the wee hours before he went to sleep, he said to me, "Ya know David, after a night like this, or whenever I have some kind of triumph and standing ovation like we had a few hours ago, I go home and feel that if only one person in the audience, after they get home, can feel for five minutes that maybe what I did at the concert meant something to them and added a little something to their lives, then I've done a good job, and that their feeling that way for even five minutes makes it all worthwhile."

That's the way Sir James has always spoken to me about everything he does, and why he does it that special way of his.

He is always down to earth and articulate, regardless of the situation. And he can sum things up verbally with the same panache as when he plays music. The warmth and positive energy he emanates, as one of the world's most popular concert artists, is a reflection of who he is as a person when he is offstage.

I have seen him when he appeared as a soloist with the New York Philharmonic. After the concert, he appeared in the green room to talk to all well-wishers. He was as warm, loquacious, and gracious to one and all in New York City after a major concert as he was when he was in New Orleans, Louisiana, leading a mass two-hour workshop, three hours before playing the world premiere of the thirty-minute concerto, *Giants of the Night,* that I had written for him.

Most world-renowned virtuosos, on the day of a concert and most of the rest of the time, would be as unapproachable as the head of state or president of a giant corporation. But Sir James, on that late afternoon, just hours before performing the world premiere of my concerto, played, coached, conducted, and charmed a room full of flutists of all ages, talking to them about music, demonstrating how to produce a sound, and leading them in playing together. And he didn't need to use a script to express himself when he spoke. He spoke from the heart without wasting a word.

Just like the great jazz poets and scat-rap energy-sharing people I have described in this chapter, Sir James has a higher purpose in life than looking in the mirror. He shares his music and himself just as Kerouac, Charlie Parker, and Dizzy Gillespie did in their words and their music during their lives. That's why I dedicated the three movements of the concerto to the three of them as well as to Sir James.

It was so moving watching him motivate the three hundred flutists with his words and music that I forgot I was in New Orleans to hear the debut of my concerto. What Sir James said to all those musicians was a textbook for how all of us should approach music and life.

After finishing the workshop, he was mobbed by almost everyone in the room and stayed there for another hour, signing autographs, answering questions, and telling stories and anecdotes while being photographed by almost every one of the three hundred flute players who had a camera. It was getting close to concert time, but Sir James was indefatigable, making sure that he snubbed no one.

"Well, I'd better go and take a shower. I've got to play the concert in two hours," he said after posing for a final picture with an eighty two-year-old flute player and his ten-year-old flute-playing grandson from nearby Lafayette, Louisiana.

"You will please excuse me. I've got to go now. You both keep on practicing every day. Remember to breathe properly and always try to produce a beautiful sound with every note you play. Be like a singer when you play," he said.

As he left the room to go to his hotel to get ready for the concert, he told me about his foundation to help kids be able to acquire instruments if they couldn't afford to buy them so that they could study music as a way of expressing themselves, whether they wished to pursue music as a profession or not.

The way Sir James spoke to all the aspiring flutists that late afternoon in New Orleans was the same way he shares his thoughts and ideas with a group of friends or alone with you in a room. It became clear to me that afternoon, as he inspired three hundred flutists with his irresistible repartee, that he is as good a rapper and storyteller as he is a world-class virtuoso. And when Sir James speaks to the audience before playing Mozart and other masters of the classical repertoire, his unrehearsed spontaneous raps are a crash course in public speaking as well as a scat-rap reportage and a Ph.D. seminar in what the spirit of classical music is all about.

Sir James, like Yo-Yo Ma and other top concert artists of today, has helped to bury the myth of the musician as a non-communicative mumbling cretin who needs a script to express himself. When they speak, their words are like music.

Sir James never allowed himself to become jaded and cynical, or stop searching each day for new ways of bringing the music of the old masters to life and creating the possibilities for new music to be written and performed. His concerts and his presence are invigorating to everyone because he keeps the hard and gem-like flame alive within himself and others. Burning with that hard and gem-like flame is what Walter Pater said all artists must do all the time.

Sir James does that all the time at every concert and workshop and every time he speaks, telling his wonderful spontaneous stories. He is an advocate for the importance of sharing ideas, telling stories, and practicing self-expression.

There are infinite ways to express yourself, whether by making something new in words, music, dance, painting, photography, theater, sculpting, filmmaking, carpentry, farming, or just collaborating with others to help them as they do their work. Doing anything creative and being around other people who are creative is a reward in itself. And it's good for your health.

As an antidote to the rigors of survival, and as a way of documenting the sunny side of the street, everyone can be some kind of historian in action, and a part-time rapper-poet-philosopher-advocate for the arts and positive thinking.

Rather than succumbing to *televisionitus dementia,* people of all ages can turn their TV sets off and find much more fulfillment and renewed mental health by enrolling in courses at their own regional tuition-free University of Hangoutology, which guarantees daily hands-on instruction in the art of being able to communicate with at least one other person every day of your life.

No prior experience is necessary in order to be a student or a teacher at the University of Hangoutology, nor is any tuition required to attend any of the worldwide series of campuses of this tried and true university. No building fund is required, because the campus is wherever you are at the moment. No degrees are awarded, but your disposition is improved and you are becoming more receptive to the messages of really accomplished artists because you are now attuned to allowing yourself to tap into that mysterious but very real part of what we are all born with, but usually lose in childhood. Socrates was one of the first outstanding alumni, and the list of distinguished graduates since his time fills libraries around the world and continues to grow every day.

Maturity does not mean that you have to stifle your own special creativity. It means that you have to tap into it in a responsible and sharing way, and try to foster it in others.

People of all ages can find fulfillment in making up stories or poems or songs on the spot, just as kids do, and then either write them down, read or recite what you want to say extemporaneously, or just have a conversation with other people and share ideas.

Scat-rapping, jazz-poetry, formal poetry, and songwriting are all part of the foundation of today's form of spontaneous poetic expression that is called freestyling. There is an explosion of freestyling among our young generation. Participation in this vital new form of intergenerational rhymed storytelling with music is an ancient way of communicating, brought up to date, which enables us to share our collective dreams of a better world, personal history, and reaffirmation of our individual humanity. Long after the commercial rap industry becomes obsolete, the new skills of the hip-hop world's unsung practitioners will remain intact, and the world will be a better place because of the new work created by an army of outstanding young rappers in languages all over the globe.

Every culture has a tradition of creating and maintaining its own oral history.

Scat and make-up songs, the art of one-time-only rap reporting, is one of many ways of keeping this tradition alive. It is an enriching experience. We can all do it.

Try it!

♪

Chapter 8

Postcards from the Road, 2002–2007

During my travels, which come about as a result of where the music leads me, I always try to write my kids, Alana, Adira, and Adam, and my sister, Marianna, at least a postcard from wherever I am. When there is enough time, I'll send them a letter, to let them know that wherever you are on the planet, there is always something new and exciting to see each and every day, and that every place offers its own special flavors to be savored, people to meet, and special feelings that you can't find anywhere else.

Playing concerts for and with people from every walk of life, in opulent eighteenth-century concert halls, junior high schools, baseball stadiums, private salons in luxurious living rooms, maximum security prisons, coffeehouses, and outdoor festival grounds all over the globe makes you realize that even when you always feel that every night is Carnegie Hall, small is just as beautiful.

Eventually, you realize that wherever you are and whomever you are with, the telepathic one-on-one catharsis of playing music for people is just an extension of the feedback people share with you in everyday life.

Traveling and participating with others around the world makes you see that you must always treasure the people whose company you are in at that very moment, and learn from them, by opening yourself up to how *they* feel about the precious everyday things in *their* lives.

Kerouac always used to talk to me about living in the Now. Charlie Parker's anthem for all of us in the '50s was his classic song, "NOW's the Time." It still is, and will always be. What might seem old-fashioned or unfashionable often has a lot to offer. You don't have to be an anthropologist in order to appreciate how the "Then" is always so much a part of the energy of the "Now."

All you have to do, to feel at home around the world, is to always pay attention to what is happening, and allow yourself to become part of wherever you are. And never judge what is unfamiliar, but rather try to understand it.

As I have previously mentioned, my father's brother, my uncle David, a former merchant seaman, for whom I was named, taught me this when I was a little boy living on a farm in Feasterville, Pennsylvania, in the 1930s, dreaming of seeing the world some day.

That someday is now everyday. Here are some reflections of recent times I spent on the road, which I shared with my own three kids, Alana, Adira, and Adam, and my sister Marianna, and which I can now share with you.

Miami, Florida, December 22, 2002

Dear Marianna:

Since you are the truly literary member of the family (your stunning achievements as an editor, translator, et al.), I have enclosed a letter I just wrote to a young writer, who took some courses with my old friend, Dan Wakefield.

Dan had me as the writer-in-residence (!!!) at his literary festival at Florida International University. He is not only a great writer, he also has the gift of teaching and making his students feel that they can express themselves in their own way and find their own voice.

Dan's student, J.J. Colagrande, sent me an incredible letter written on a bunch of napkins, while he was sitting in an airport, where he discussed his ideas of what being creative was all about, and asked me for some of my thoughts.

Here is what I wrote to him.

I send brotherly hugs and want to see you soon!

David

Dear J.J.

Thank you for your wonderful Napkin Note. I am going to copy it on a piece of paper so that it does not "go gentle into that good night" (quote from Dylan Thomas), although Dylan Thomas might not have been referring to a similar sketch for a piece of genius poetry he was scribbling, on the same kind of napkin, fifty years earlier at the White Horse Tavern in Greenwich Village, where Dan Wakefield, Jimmy Baldwin and I used to go in 1956, after Dylan Thomas had his final drink and left us for good before we ever got to meet him, back in the early '50s.

I don't know if any Napkin Notes of Dylan Thomas exist anymore, but your Napkin Note to me (with your poem at the end) was such a great letter, I read it aloud to my eighteen-year-old son, Adam, who said, in the middle of my reading it…

"That guy can really write. He's a great writer; he thinks fast."

I agree.

You have all that you need to develop a whole lifetime of work, because writing, like composing music, is being able to DO IT, daring to know that YOU have something to say, and being able to say it. Also having a sense of structure, so that no matter what it is about, there is always a beginning, a middle, and an end.

And knowing that if what you write is honest, and done from the heart, (and then, if necessary, revised, thrown out, put back, spliced, erased, added to, and finally ends up being the very best that you can do), it is worth all that hard work to make it seem effortless, because you will make those reading it feel that they are having a natural conversation with you.

You already have something of your own, the gift of telling a story and painting a picture of a place and time ... all coming through loudly and clearly to me, the reader, on the Napkin Note you sent to me!! If you have even ONE READER who can dig what you are saying on paper, you are on the way to a lifetime of writing, even if you don't immediately have a mega-book/film/Blockbuster explosion or a Moses to take your own J.J.'s Ten Commandments and publish them in stone (the first hardback edition in history).

You don't need to instantly become a number-one best seller as the first step towards creating The J.J. Colagrande Foundation as a tax write-off for your brand new entertainment empire. And you don't need to hire an entourage of advisors to accompany you when you appear on the Oprah Winfrey Show, to complain how lonely it is to be an overnight millionaire and no longer able to be creative.

You don't need all, or any of that. You are already a writer. So all you need to do is write on! And on and on!!!

None of us can control the whole business scene in the arts, but we *can* control the level of our life's commitment to excellence and hard work and devotion to what we do, and you, like me, are the beneficiary of knowing Dan Wakefield, who is a master. I am sure that for you, the blessing of having Dan for a teacher is the same blessing I receive by having him as a lifetime friend.

Dan PAYS ATTENTION TO WHAT IS HAPPENING. Dan is INTERESTED IN OTHERS, and compassionate enough to have the people he is with at any moment feel secure enough to be themselves, and allows them to share their feelings with him. Dan SPEAKS TO YOU, rather than being a literary jukebox, delivering the same series of prepared statements to everybody. Dan checks out WHAT IS HAPPENING, HOW IT HAPPENED, WHO IT AFFECTS, and WHY IT IS THE WAY IT IS. He knows how to observe and, when he writes, how to put together what he has observed. He always does this in a selective way, combining experiences from real life with those which occur in his imagination, and then paints a picture for us all to see.

That's because like Charles Dickens, Ernest Hemingway, Dostoevsky, Jack Kerouac, Carson McCullers, Kurt Vonnegut, the McCourt brothers, Thomas Mann, and Faulkner, he is always a storyteller-journalist-truth-seeker, straight out, no B.S. chronicler of the human condition, and everything he writes and says comes from an honest place. Cats like Dan who come from Indiana and the Midwest in general either say what's on their minds as simply and clearly as possible, or they KEEP QUIET!!! (This is a level I have yet to reach, but I admire it in others!! At the very least, when I am not delivering a crazed and often unsolicited monologue, I also listen and try to pay attention.) Often, I go into my free associative raps with other people to make the environment more fun to be in, so that I can stand being there myself.

I dare to suggest all of the above to you because I am just back from a week in Los Angeles, the world capitol of writers and composers who all end up with writer's block.

Since I decided in 1962 that I would forgo the temptation of moving there, after my five weeks while composing the score for *The Manchurian Candidate,* I can visit there and enjoy its unique charms. Dan was there for a spell, and he was able to avoid getting strung out and seduced by the charms of the pots of gold, glitter, and gorgeous gals.

I think you would really dig it for your next napkin note series of observations about contemporary American cities. It is ten times more fun than a week in Disneyland and the free entertainment is available twenty-four hours a day.

You must check out the freaked-out Hieronymus Bosch-like jumble of bleached blondes; silicone implants (in men as well as the gals); low riders; seriously debilitated vagabonds and homeless street-people, beyond anything Beat; gigantic limos; convertibles driven by angry-looking middle-aged New York hustler rejects in Gucci shades, stalled in the smog-filled miles of backed-up traffic, being harangued by their driving companions; loudmouthed prune faced never-to-be starlets with fake jewelry and layers of garish makeup, often stalled and shouting at other drivers overlooking plastic palm trees leaning over funky falling-down motels with the neon signs busted, spelling out part of the name of old trysting places for transvestite hookers who dreamed of movie stardom.

Ya gotta love it!!

I hope you have great holidays, and I send cheers from the frozen hills of Putnam Valley, N.Y., where I have just returned.

Please send my love to Dr. Dan.

Keep being creative. Write on, Write on!

Best cheers

David

Paris, France, July 15, 2003

Dear Adira:

I'm just back from the City of Light.

After forty-eight years, this was my first time back in Paris since I left there in 1955 to return to the United States, after a year of living and working there in France as a musician. Obviously, a half century later, Paris has changed enormously, and some of the places where I lived and worked for the year I was there are totally unrecognizable, but the *esprit Parisien* and the burning energy and sense of *joie de vivre* are still as strong today as they were when I left Paris back in the fall of 1955.

The warmth, craziness, high energy, and individualism of Parisians remain the same, in spite of all the physical changes that the city has undergone. I immediately noticed the enormous amount of traffic, and the different styles of clothing, which are now much less French and way more American, especially among the young people of your age.

The Shakespeare and Company bookstore was the presenter of their first annual Festival of the Arts, and they invited me as a featured performer and speaker. Their old building is the same four-story jumble of books and papers, with endless hordes of people filling the store, quietly reading in all the dark rooms. They are joined by others who stroll through the rooms.

You also see other visitors who have spent a night or two as temporary guests of the bookstore during the past fifty-two years. They usually look bleary-eyed, and often scratch themselves. They move in and stay for a few nights in the famous guest rooms above the store, still replete with bedbugs and flying insects, which during the warm weather soar in and out of the grimy open windows, where you hear the sounds of klaxon horns (like the ones Gershwin used in *An American in Paris*), from the endless traffic overlooking the Seine River, where people sit in outdoor cafes, as well as in front of the bookstore for hours, eating, drinking, smoking, talking, and people-watching.

The bookstore was the command headquarters for the whole festival, which had many of the events held in a tent in a nearby park, as well as in theaters, cafes, jazz clubs and concert halls around the city.

The organizer of the festival was Sylvia Whitman, who is only twenty-two years old!!!

(Sylvia Whitman is the daughter of Shakespeare and Company owner George Whitman, and George is now ninety.) Sylvia spent months planning the entire eight days of nonstop events, (concerts, plays, readings, panel discussions, tours, etc.) with two other young women her own age, who ran the whole show.

The three of them were extraordinary, and people came from all over Europe, the United States, and Canada, to attend the eight-day event. You would have loved it.

I had a bunch of programs of my own, and was able to involve a lot of musicians, poets, actors, and readers to participate with me, using people I bumped into, as well as those who were invited by the festival. As you know, I always love to get people to participate with me, whenever possible, wherever I go.

This particular time, while in Paris, I also had a chance to sit down between non-stop activities, (at least once a day) and eat a meal at any of the hundreds of outdoor cafes, RELAX for at least a few minutes, and enjoy life!! Something I guess we all forget to do in our hectic way of living here at home.

And I got to hang out with all kinds of people, speaking French and other languages with people from all around the world who live in or were visiting the city. There seemed to be no political bad feelings or anti-Americanism of any kind towards any of us from the United States, contrary to what you would expect. The French don't really like any politicians, and don't seem to confuse politics with people.

I have already received requests to come back to Paris for concerts, literary events with music, readings from my two books, and to conduct performances of my classical works. I feel now, after a forty-eight-year interlude, that I have never left Paris. I had a chance, the day before I left, to go with Nikoletta to visit my old building at 50 Rue Mazarin where I lived in 1955 (which is now part of a bustling upscale tourist area), and the jazz club, the Caméléon, which I wrote about in *Vibrations,* where I led my own jazz quartet, and which is still at the same location, even though jazz hasn't been played there for decades.

The present owner, Pierre, knew of the history of the cave in the basement, now a vacant room long closed down. He took me down a dark set of stairs into the dungeon-like cellar to see where I played with my quartet for several months in 1955.

It was like visiting a tomb!!!

I had a copy of *Vibrations* with me, and read him the part of the book where I described playing there, and the musicians who played with me at the time, as well as those who came and jammed with me there, like Lionel Hampton, with whom I recorded in Paris during that year.

It was an amazing kind of reunion, and the owner's sixteen-year-old son, a rock guitarist, joined us when we climbed back upstairs to the bar from the cave and spent time talking about the influence of jazz from fifty years ago on his generation of young French musicians today, who play rock inspired in part from the music we played a half century ago.

It was a wild feeling for me, as the returning kid musician of the 1955 Paris scene, finally coming to the place where I played nearly fifty years ago, and now speaking as some kind of an elder statesman to all the people in the bar about what it was like there before they were born!!

Paris is still an inspiring place, and I feel blessed to finally have gotten back there again. It makes me appreciate America more than ever and makes me proud of all of our artists, poets, painters, sculptors, musicians, composers, actors, and others, our true ambassadors whom the French appreciate and love sometimes more than we do.

I hope to go back every year from now on. Next time, you, Adam, and Alana have to come with me.

With monstro hugs, *et beaucoup d'amour toujours.*
Ton pere
Daddy

Chengdu, China, June 7, 2004

Dear Alana and Adira:

I am just back home at the farm for about eighteen hours, from an incredible week in Chengdu, China, before unpacking and repacking to fly to my next adventure with the Pittsburgh Symphony from Tuesday, June 8, till James Galway plays my flute concerto *Giants of the Night* with them in Pittsburgh on the tenth.

I have had such a great time in China with so much nonstop activity that I didn't even have enough time to get any jet lag while I was there or since I have returned. As usual, I didn't have much time to sleep during the week I was there (and of course I didn't want to go to bed, because I was afraid I would miss something if I did). Now that I am back at the farm, I have enough time to sit for a day and relay the feelings of all that collective energy of a billion people all living together in one country.

The leader of the conference, which was called "Beat Meets East," was Professor Wen Chu-an of the Department of English of the School of Foreign Languages at Sichuan University. He has translated *On The Road* into Chinese, and he and Professor Bill Lawlor from Stevens Point, Wisconsin, organized the whole extraordinary festival in China. Bill Lawlor somehow coordinated getting a few Americans to come as panelists and was a wonderful representative of the United States. Both he and his wife are real scholars, who love to teach and love sharing their knowledge with students, as well as oldsters like myself who still take occasional courses at the University of Hangoutology that I always tell both of you and Adam about.

I was bowled over when Professor Wen Chu-an told me that he is interested in translating *Vibrations* and *Offbeat: Collaborating with Kerouac* into Chinese! I told him I was honored, and that after he had completed this monumental task, we would have to find someone to translate them into English (but I didn't get a chuckle, except from some of the European professors who overheard my conversation with him, but told me that they appreciated my including in these two books the poetry of bebop phraseology, combined with an occasional dash of everyday vernacular and enthusiastic hyperbole.) They asked me if I had read Hemingway's short stories and when I indicated that I had, whether or not I liked his short sentences.

"I sure do," I said.

Then they asked me why my two books and my raps at the conference always used such long sentences.

"That's the way I think," I said.

So at least I completed two short sentences during my stay there. Many of the Chinese poets and prose writers use *really* long phrases, and much of their traditional music had lyrical weaving of melodies that take you on a journey that is comforting, because their art is not about hysteria as a way to make the reader or listener feel energized. Their approach in literature, music, and the visual arts is a spiritual one, and I think that's why they like Kerouac, Walt Whitman, and Edna St. Vincent Millay, as well as our music, all of which is now increasingly available to the Chinese public.

Professor Wen Chu-an treated us like royalty, and his students and all the people and scholars he assembled created a festival that was a dream come true. I only wish both of you and Adam could have been there.

I was one of the keynote speakers, as well as the featured performer, doing the opening and closing events at the conference. Both Professor Wen Chu-an and Prof. Bill Lawlor told me that they wanted to emphasize how Kerouac and our loosely knit group of artists all celebrated spontaneity as one of the key elements that influenced some of the best work done in the 50s. And they wanted me to relate how this spirit could be maintained in today's world.

Almost everyone at the conference told me that they felt this spirit was personified in Kerouac's writing, as well as in the work of many of the artists of the period ... painters, poets, jazz musicians, innovators in the theater and film, and in my own work as a classical composer.

To my amazement, a small army of college-aged kids, only a year or two younger than both of you, knew about my life's work, as well as what Kerouac and I pioneered almost fifty years ago. Even more important, the young people I met in China told me that they feel that what we did in the 50s and what the handful of us still alive are continuing to do today, gives their generation inspiration to spread their wings and find a way to pursue their dreams in their own fashion.

Professor Chu-an had prepared everyone about all of us and our work ahead of time, and is a true ambassador for spreading awareness about the true spirit of all of us then and now.

There were no nouveau beatniks or prematurely jaded postmodern *poseurs* who attended (the kind you both can't stand and imitate so well in your comic routines). The visiting scholars from around the world and the students were there to learn and to share. They were for real. It was a milestone event.

The young people who came were all openhearted, hard-working, and serious about what they wanted to do, and the same was true of the scholars from many parts of the world who attended. All of my old friends who were honored at the conference (most of whom are no longer with us), were celebrated as artists whose enduring work and devotion during their life's journey had set the stage for this new generation to dare to express themselves and to know that they never had to give up.

I only wish that so many whose memory we celebrated in Chengdu, like Kerouac, Charlie Parker, painters Franz Kline and Joan Mitchell, composer Edgard Varese, poets Langston Hughes and Gregory Corso, and so many others from our era were still alive, to see how much their work means today to young people in Asia, as well as to the rest of the world.

The whole marathon of events made me really proud of America, because it painted a picture of the beauty part of the shared humanity of our era, reflected by all the outstanding work that had been created by our true artists, and was being honored. The conference served as an antidote to counteract all the swill that we have dumped on the world with our corporate entertainment industry's merchandising of mediocre TV shows and films and soulless music. Instead, we were honoring the best of what America has to offer.

The work we celebrated nonstop at the Beat Meets East Conference seemed as fresh and communicative in 2004 in China as it appeared to be in America for the handful of us who were our own cheering section when we first created and shared it among our tiny group of friends a half a century ago. Everything still felt fresh and bursting with energy.

During the whole week I was there, young people attending the event in Chengdu told me over and over that they consider what they are having jammed down their throats by our invasion of their culture is an additional form of pollution, but that they are all using the Internet and Web as an antidote to this poison, to find the treasures that America is *not* exporting, including a lot of American creative work done today by young artists like both of you and Adam, which is not packaged and sent around the world, but which they find infinitely superior. And through the Internet, they can search for themselves. They have told me that they feel most advertising directed towards them is brainwashing. And that they are also proud of their own myriad forms of cultural treasures of the past several thousand years and want to create new art reflecting their own feelings in today's chaotic times which come from their own experiences and heritage, and not become enslaved by conforming to what our industrial approach to entertainment tells them that they must become.

They told me over and over that they can love us without having to become us. They told me that they felt our WORK (rather than the stereotypical image of the moronic beatnik), during the era of the so-called Beat generation, reflected that same spirit of wanting to reach out and create something personal and honest, and not become trapped into blindly following changing fashions, or being dictated to by trends the way a stockbroker must watch the market reports every day in order to survive.

In addition to all the things I was scheduled to do, I played with Chinese musicians, accompanied readings of *On the Road,* read in English and Chinese, with readers from the United States, Australia, Thailand, and Turkey, and exhibited my caricatures of Kerouac, Dizzy Gillespie, Ferlinghetti, and Neal Cassady, played a concert of world music, had little informal jam sessions all over town, saw Chinese opera, visited the world's largest giant panda preservation center, and visited the site of the recently rediscovered lost empire of the Shu Dynasty from the Bronze Age (3600 B.C.), with mind-blowing artifacts, including designs of ancient temples and restored masks that are EXACTLY like the ones that we see today in the Mayan culture of Mexican Indians of the past, very much like the temples we saw twelve years ago when we all went to visit Brooks Jones in Tepoztlan and took the trip to see the temples. All of these same styles of artifacts, made during the Shu Dynasty, were discovered in China a few years ago.

I also spent nonstop time with students and teachers and composers, and introduced some of the music of Charlie Parker, Monk, Gillespie, Charles Ives, Copland, and Gershwin, as well as sharing with them some of my own symphonic works, especially those that were based on my life's experiences, using folk rhythms or fragments of traditional melodies or chants which ended up becoming the basis of formal works, after I had performed them and lived with them for years.

I tried to present the positive, soulful, humanistic part of America that we don't export ... the art, music, poetry, painting, and down-to-earth humaneness and generous life-affirming spirit. All of which is the best America always has had to offer the world. I tried to share these most precious attributes of our culture, which are not shown around the world by our entertainment industry, an octopus which often portrays us as boorish Philistines, yearning to become even more decadent, self-indulgent, selfish, and infantile mini-versions of narcissistic greed-mongers, i.e., Ugly Americans, when in fact almost every person I met from Chengdu, as well as those from many countries who were visiting China, all seemed to have a more positive image of America than we ourselves often do. We are so much better than our entertainment industry tells us we are through the negative portrayals of ourselves which we are bombarded with, which tell us who we are supposed to be.

Almost everyone I met in Chengdu seemed to have a yearning to know more about the kind of artistic expression that reflects the true nature of America. This was the case among the Chinese of all ages, because they are emerging, since 1978, from repressive times and now becoming a more open society every day, celebrating their own return to some of their traditional humanistic values.

To see a young man riding a small bicycle with his girlfriend, his grandparent, or male friend perched on the back, to see people young and old walking down the street holding hands, to witness people of all economic classes often smiling and laughing, and seeing crowded streets where the sense of family and community is always present, is overwhelming. Every day in Chengdu was life-affirming.

The appreciation of being alive was something I sensed among all the groups of people I met everywhere I went. The way everybody always seems to be observing everything around them in a quiet way is a guide for all of us in the West to practice as an additional way of how to approach life.

Like the sprawling city of Chengdu itself, China is a country with enormous problems. It is now in a time of rapid change and could be another society where all its own values could be thrown out the window, due to the globalization that is affecting everyone's life.

But I was told over and over that's not what they want to see China become. Everyone I spoke to is aware of this loss of individual history and destruction of culture taking place in the world. I sensed that whatever happens, the Chinese are quietly determined to keep their humanity and identity, no matter how Western things appear to be in much of the clothing, neon signs, and blasting heavy metal junk music that assaults innocent citizens as they walk by and shield their ears with their hands from the blasting payola-driven trash music roaring out from the bars where tourists go. As they hold their ears until they are out of range, you get the feeling that the Chinese learned millenniums ago how to deal with the external, and keep the internal strong.

From the emperors and various invaders, up to the Mao regime and now during the birth of a new form of Wild Westernism, you sense that the soul and spirit part of the Chinese people has been preserved and is so strong that it will never be squashed or strangled to death by tyrannical leaders calling themselves communists or by rip-off artists calling themselves capitalists. They have a culture, a language, an alphabet of more than four thousand characters, and pride in who they are. And they have terrific symphony orchestras, folk ensembles, graphic arts, and literature, dance, and sports groups that already are combining Western elements along with their own historic roots in everything they do.

There is a spirit in China in 2004 that is so strong, that even when sleeping, you know you are somewhere that has a lot to teach us all about how to live our lives. None of us who participated in the conference are dumb enough or self-indulgent enough to glamorize, romanticize, or try to form an opinion of a country of more than a BILLION people, but Chengdu and all the people I met and interacted with nonstop since getting there on this sleepless marathon made me want to come back. I felt as at home there as I do on our farm in Putnam Valley or when I visit my own personal meccas ... New Orleans; anywhere in Texas, Colorado or Canada; Lowell, Massachusetts; Louisville, Kentucky; Orlando, Florida; Cairo, Egypt; Israel; Brazil;

Sri Lanka; New York City; London; San Francisco, and Venice Beach, California.

In Chengdu, China, I feel like I now have a new second home.

And in addition to all else, the extraordinary sense of good manners and respect to old people and affection for the young is touching to see. Kids and old folks are looked after and appreciated, and families hang out together everywhere, just as we always did when the three of you were growing up.

The conference also cleared the air of years of misrepresentation and degrading of true spiritualism, something which plagued our society since the sixties, when the Gurus with Limos I always refer to invaded America to franchise the divine.

I told the co-chairman of the conference, Professor Wen Chu-an, the energy-packed scholar and visionary who has championed our era, that certainly Kerouac and me, who were respectively Roman Catholic and Jewish, had an enormous respect for Buddhism and Taoism, but never would dare to claim anything other than our admiration for these ancient philosophies and religions, which require a lifetime of study.

I made it clear to everyone at the conference that we admired Gary Snyder, the only one of us who really understood and could teach others about these concepts, because Gary, like Philip Whalen, has devoted much of his life to this, and that Gary is so modest and un-self-serving that he would never say this about himself.

And I made it clear that neither Kerouac nor I would ever have endorsed today's hucksterism and BurgerKingization of sacred Eastern religions, or the Jimmy Swaggartization and New Age rip-off versions of the sacred teachings of the Kabbalah or Native American spirituality. This message from me was always received with laughter and appreciation by all the people I met in Chengdu, because the Chinese, who have lived and survived by practicing the principles of the Golden Rule for many millennia, through every nightmare history can provide, know what is real and what is jive. When any people from any part of Asia see their culture or spirituality ripped off, repackaged, and merchandized by Westerners in a form that is screaming FAKE, it is just as offensive and hurtful a feeling for them as it is to all the Native Americans like Floyd Red Crow Westerman and other Indians you knew when you were growing up, when they see their own artifacts inaccurately reproduced and imported from Hong Kong.

I think if you could come to China, you would also notice how much the people value the work ethic, their family, their history, and the simple pleasures of life … enjoying sitting down for a meal or hanging out and rapping, drinking, playing cards, sharing stories or jokes, or quietly observing what is happening around them.

Professor Wen Chu-an and Stevens Point, Wisconsin's, Professor William Lawlor's seemingly impossible dream came true, with the Beat Meets East Conference. It was a triumphant East/West celebration of cultural, spiritual, and humanistic enduring values.

It was an historic occasion, and I believe it will open up the doors for many more events to take place in years to come.

As I told you when I called you from the airport in New York as soon as our plane got in from China, it looks like after waiting for seventy-three years to finally get there for the first time, I will be able to return to China with symphonic, jazz, and world music presentations of my own and other composers' works I admire, as well as doing more of what I did at the conference with Professor Chu-an and his colleagues, and I can hardly wait to do so. And I'll bring you my conversational Mandarin book so the three of you can get started, and you can join me on the next trip there to do some meanderin' in Mandarin.

I realize that this is longer than a haiku-length post card, but I wanted to write you my thoughts before crashing out and getting up in a few hours to get on a plane to join James Galway performing my flute concerto in Pittsburgh, and then off to a festival in Texas, the International Theater Festival in Bonn, Germany, and the Montreal Jazz Festival.

I am so proud of what both of you and Adam are doing with your own music, in your own way, and feel lucky to be your father. I can hardly wait for Adam and all of us to get together, and for all of you to tell me about *your* adventures!

I send endless love and big hugs to you both.
Daddy

Windber, PA, Discovers *On the Road,* October 18, 2004

Dear Alana:

This has been a great action-packed thirty-two days with hardly a minute off. Glad my cell phone works so that I can stay in touch and hear about what you are doing in the wilds of Brooklyn. I think of you and your endless energy, whenever I think I might be dozing off.

Had a great time when I did my annual series of events at the Lowell Celebrates Kerouac Festival in Lowell, Mass., where I performed with my trio, accompanied scores of other musicians and poets, read from my books, hosted screenings of *Pull My Daisy,* played at an art show where my caricatures of the era are being shown, and did programs with John Cassady, (the very much alive and always energetic son of Jack's road buddy and inspiration for *On the Road,* Neal Cassady).

I also did a program at U Mass Lowell, and a bunch of interviews (in three languages) for people from around the world who come every year to Lowell to participate in this joyous grassroots event that also celebrates Kerouac's hometown, where twenty-seven languages are currently spoken.

The old French, Greek, and Portuguese communities have been replaced with new immigrants from Vietnam, Cambodia, Laos, and many countries in Central and South America, and most of the people who were born here still have a strong regional old New England accent. It is like music to hear, because so many other regional accents are rapidly disappearing throughout much of the country.

Even the way people dress and relate to one another feels like a much earlier time, and the stark beauty of the old abandoned red brick mills, the rushing waters of the Merrimack River, and the old wooden frame houses and shops with fading handwritten signs in many languages are magical in comparison to most plastic chain-store franchised miles of monotonous malls that make more and more cities in America all seem like the same place.

Wish you could have been there, to see all the people gathered from all over to celebrate Jack's life and the enduring value of his life's work ... the beautiful books he left us.

Like Woody Guthrie, John Steinbeck, and all the oral history books you have read that document the actual speeches of Native Americans during the past two hundred years, Kerouac embraced America in a way that makes us all open up our eyes and our hearts to the beauty part of this fantastic country of ours that still has so much to offer and so much that is often overlooked or ignored.

After my Lowell pilgrimage and two concerts in New York, I went to a festival in Windber, Pennsylvania, which culminated in a marathon reading of *On the Road.* I was the guest of honor (Senior Bopper-at-Large).

Driving with Nikoletta from our farm in New York through the Western Pennsylvania mountains to Windber, Pennsylvania, was a trip you would have loved. The roadside was dotted with small truck stops. One had a huge red neon sign saying "The Holy Road" posted on a small clapboard chapel for truckers to come and pray. It was a blast from the past to enter the truck stops and watch and talk to the people working there and see the local farmers hanging out, speaking with the same rural accents of my boyhood's farmer neighbors of sixty-five years ago in Feasterville, Pennsylvania (population two hundred). Most of the people in the truck stops looked the same as those people from long ago that I grew up with. I felt as if I were in a time machine and now had re-entered the late 1930s.

I spent the first day in Windber giving concerts and hosting a screening of *Pull My Daisy*, prior to a marathon twelve-hour reading of *On the Road*, the next day, for which I provided some of the music, as well as playing between and during the readings with local musicians. I also had a show of my caricatures I had painted of everyone from that era.

The festival was held in an abandoned hotel, which had been purchased for $10,000 from eBay by a wild guy named Blair Murphy who loves Kerouac's work, and who was our tireless and gracious host.

During the one break I had in the two-day marathon event in Windber, we went a few miles to eat a celebratory meal with Nikoletta, John Cassady, and others at the one place I wanted to take everyone to. I told everyone who came along with us that eating at Nathan's Coney Island in nearby Johnstown would be the same transcendental experience for them that it had been for me thirty-five years ago.

As we drove from Windber to nearby Johnstown to dine, I told everyone in the car how in 1969, when my horn concerto was played in Pittsburgh, the more adventurous members of the Pittsburgh Symphony, joined by local jazz players and poets, took me on a ride to eat at Nathan's Coney Island in Johnstown for a 2:00 a.m. chow-down.

I told our hungry crew from Windber how after all these years, I could still remember feeling like I had visited Johnstown, Pennsylvania's, equivalent of Mecca, the Taj Mahal, or the Vatican. I told them how I also wanted them to experience having a meal at one of the world's Seven Culinary Wonders ... Nathan's Coney Island hot-dog emporium in downtown Johnstown.

I told them that I could still taste that grease in my sleep to this very day. I mentioned that I hadn't been back there to eat in thirty-five years, but I knew that I would always remember the sight of the waitresses bringing twelve hot dogs balanced like newborn puppies on their outstretched arms, like some great late-night ballet, with hordes of hungry workers from the nearby mattress factory storming in for their night shift 2:00 a.m. lunch break. And how I could still see the faces of some of the wild-eyed old timers who sat in a near catatonic state sipping coffee, whom I was told were still suffering posttraumatic shock, from the great flood that took place many years before in Johnstown, which they had survived but from which they never had recovered.

And like an intoxicating perfume, all the subtle variety of various burning grease aromas, intertwining with the smell of spilled beers and used coffee cups with cigarette butts ground out in the bottom of them, old pie crusts and syrup stains caking the Formica tables, along with the pickle juice, mustard, and relish scattered on the tables, chairs and floor, all combined to build up your late night/early morning appetite. No master chef or interior designer could ever construct such a temple of late-night/early-morning chow-downing.

As we approached downtown Johnstown for our only sightseeing moment of the festival, I told John Cassady that I was sure that it was worth the three-thousand-mile trip he had driven from California to the East Coast, if only to eat a meal at the Johnstown branch of Nathan's Coney Island. I described to all of the gourmets in the car how they could look forward to seeing the fluorescent lights cut through a perpetual light cloud of smoke inside the cafeteria, like a drifting fog ... a haze of onions, peppers, gristle, pork, beef, and chicken fats, combined with cigar, cigarette, and pipe smoke, all slowly rising to the ceiling, which after many decades was encased in various lumps of what appeared to be petrified fat, looking like some giant abstract-expressionist Renaissance Sistine Chapel mural of various greases, caked there over the years, and exuding its own subtle smells, adding to the total ambiance.

When we pulled up to the landmark cafeteria, the place was packed. The doorway and sidewalk outside were jammed with a crazy assortment of Saturday-night Johnstown bon vivants in various stages of intoxication, eating hot dogs, dripping French fries, hamburgers, fried onions, and stale pastries while drinking beer, whiskey, soda and coffee, shouting, arguing, laughing, and releasing various exploding sounds of heavy digestion.

Somehow, in spite of everyone in the car enjoying this late night/early morning outdoor action, like a medieval passion play's first rehearsal, I could sense that this was a different place from the one I remembered. As we eased through the crowd of diners and drinkers on the street outside Nathan's and entered to eat, I sensed that like the family farmers for whom Willie Nelson and all of us play benefits each year at Farm Aid, and like so much of what Kerouac and other lyric writers chronicled about a vanishing America, the Nathan's Coney Island in Johnstown, Pennsylvania, in the month of October of 2004, was now becoming gentrified in comparison to its glorious days and nights of 1969. I realized that I had been there in its Golden Age. The ceiling mural of grease was still there, but the waitresses no longer delivered either the hot dogs or the Sundowners (a terrifying heart-clogger cheeseburger with a greasy fried egg on top of it) on their outstretched arms to the tables.

Nathan's Coney Island was now a regular twenty-four-hour day/night cafeteria, although what looked and smelled like black crankcase-oil where the fries were cooked appeared to be unchanged from thirty-five years ago when I last dined there, and about which I later wrote a song called "Greasy Spoon."

I asked the oldest looking person behind the counter what happened to the waitresses serving meals with the hot dogs on their arms.

"The Health Department don't allow it no more. That's what made them hot dogs taste so good for all them years. You remember, you always looked for the table where the fattest waitress was serving. The bigger the waitress arm was, the better them dogs tasted. That's all history now. Like the coal miners in Windber. They ain't here no more either."

"Well, I guess that's progress," I said.

"Tell your friends how it used to be, 'cause it ain't that way no more, and never gonna be," said the man behind the counter. "But we still got the world's best hot dogs."

After our sojourn of chomping down the quadruple-bypass specials, we returned to nearby Windber and I was asked to read the final pages of *On the Road* to end the festival, to be filmed and then intercut with the old video of Jack reading the same passages with Steve Allen playing the piano from the 1958 telecast of Steve's old show in black and white.

There were people of all ages who attended this event, and it was a heartwarming two days, seeing how much young people like you, Adira, and Adam love this great book and the spirit it conveys.

I can hardly wait to see you and send love. We'll have a good time for my seventy-fourth birthday when I get back from Texas, and you, Adira, Adam, and your Aunt Mari and I can all hide out in New York together and have an anonymous meal and all congratulate one another!

With naches and Nachos, and an extra serving of love
Daddy

Texas, October 31, 2004

Dear Alana:

I'm writing you from deep in the heart of Texas, just before I return home.

I had a fabulous time here, as I always do in the Lone Star State.

I started out by doing a marathon residency in Denton at Texas Women's College, barnstorming the Denton/Dallas area with a series of concerts, workshops, and collaborations with dancers, actors, choral groups, writers, poets, and composers, and even playing a concert for their jazz society with a senior citizen Dixieland band where the players were even older than me!! That doesn't happen too much any more. And they played beautifully.

I stayed in Denton at an old bed and breakfast close to the university. The owner was also a professional storyteller and regaled us with all kinds of funky Texas folklore. It was a refreshing step back in time, eating meals with strangers who were staying there, many of whom were not from Texas, and some of whom were and stayed there for their vacation so that they could hang out and hear all the owner's tall tales.

Regardless of where the guests came from, all of them were enjoying the openness of the little oasis that the bed and breakfast provided from big city madness, and the owner and his wife exemplified the sunny spirit of this unique state.

During my nonstop marathon of activities in Denton, I had the chance to spend time rapping with a small army of native Texans of all ages, who have such an unforgettable bunch of stories, regional accents, and a poetic way of expressing themselves. They make their down-home Southern-Western everyday style of speaking a musical feast to listen to. Texas is still a treasure chest of individuals, and there is nothing that can beat being in a roomful of Texans and listening to them as they share anecdotes and observations about their lives. What they say and how they say it is always unpredictable, often humorous, and consistently delivered full speed ahead with loads of energy and a special farmerly rural *joie de vivre*.

After my nonstop events in Denton, I drove one hundred miles to Wichita Falls to conduct their orchestra in rehearsals and the October 30 performance of *Giants of the Night*, the flute concerto that I composed for Sir James Galway, and my *Theme and Variations on Red River Valley for Flute and Strings*.

When we had our first rehearsal with the orchestra, to my astonishment, they played both pieces really well. It was really fun conducting them, and the flute soloist in my concerto, Pam Youngblood, was excellent. She played the solo part so well that she made it sound easy. She knew every note, and had a lot of spirit. So THERE IS HOPE IN THEM THERE HILLS!!!

As you know, the three movements are dedicated respectively to Charlie Parker, Jack Kerouac, and Dizzy Gillespie, all of whom I knew and jammed with, and all of whom knew one another. I know you remember Dizzy, when he used to talk to you when you were five years old and puff out his cheeks and get you to do it as well. He always asked me about you, and he remembered every time I saw him about when I took you when you were three weeks old down to the Village Gate when I played with him there, so that you could meet one another.

I spoke to the audience during the concert about Diz, Bird, and Jack, and about how the enduring creations of Charlie Parker, Jack Kerouac, and Dizzy Gillespie are more appreciated now than ever. After the concert was over, people, young and old, came up and talked to me. It made me really happy to know that many of them, not only liked the concerto, but knew who these three men were, and told me that they were also inspired by their work.

The positive energy and enthusiasm I saw in the faces of the audience and the musicians of the orchestra made me realize how fortunate I was to have had the chance to honor these three people who have meant so much to so many others. I was so lucky to have known them and played music with them.

Seeing the increased appreciation of their work is a constant source of joy, proving the old adage that a thing of beauty IS a joy forever. I know you always hear me talk about them, but they were supremely gifted and gave us all something to aspire to creatively and humanistically. Each of them always took the time to share their gifts with others. They were generous and fun to be with, even during the hard times they went through.

You are that way too, and so are Adira and Adam, and that alone makes me so proud of the three of you, because you are generous and gracious to everybody you cross paths with, and you always try to make others feel better when they are in your presence, and you can't do better than that!! As you know, being a miserable, whining, negative, exclusive ingrate is an overcrowded field and NOT a growth industry.

That's another reason it's always so nice to come back to the Lone Star State and get re-Texified! People here still are aware that everyone needs each other. And Texans generally accept the most outrageous eccentrics, as long as you exhibit good manners and act remotely human. And they love music.

The concertmaster of the orchestra had a surprise gift from the orchestra for me, which he gave me after the concert. It was a small ceramic amulet in the shape of the state of Texas to add to my beads. He also gave me a book, *How to Talk Texan,* to add to my collection of languages to learn.

He told me when *Giants of the Night* received a standing ovation, that this was the first time in the Wichita Falls Symphony's history that they had ever had a standing O for a contemporary piece. I wrote Sir James to thank him again for making it possible for me to write the concerto, and told him that hopefully *Giants of the Night* will have a life of its own, and continue to honor the memories of the three people I dedicated it to.

The other two works played on the program, in addition to the two of mine, were Stravinsky's *Firebird Suite* and Darius Milhaud's *Creation of the World.*

Sorry that Wichita Falls, Texas, is not closer to your apartment in Brooklyn!!

So with all this crazed activity I had while here in Texas, I didn't have any time to get into trouble. My little free time was spent working on my new book, composing new orchestral music, and trying to answer mail!!!

I send cheers from that never-ending road, and am so proud of all the wonderful things that you are doing!

In seventeen days, we will all chow down for my big seventy-four, and I can hardly wait to see you.

I'll bring you back some killer barbeque sauce and jalapeno peppers.

As they say in Ozona, Texas...

Yipee ki yay, OY VEY!

Love and chuckles

Daddy

Portsmouth, New Hampshire, Jazzmouth April 20, 2005

Dear Alana:

I am writing from the airport, while changing planes on the way to Braga, Portugal. When I called you a few days ago, I was in Portsmouth, New Hampshire, where I kicked off the first-ever Jazz/poetry festival ever held in New England and had a chance all weekend to collaborate with some wonderful musicians and poets. Almost all except for me are from this beautiful seacoast area of New England. The name of the new festival was Jazzmouth, the first-ever Seacoast jazz/poetry festival.

The organizers picked a perfect space to premiere a jazz/poetry festival. I flashed back to the raunchy dives that Kerouac and I and so many others frequented when we would do our spontaneous unsolicited presentations until we were asked to leave or were thrown out. It seemed historically in keeping when I entered the sagging unpainted stage door of a great old 128-year-old theater, with a coffee machine backstage all full of rust, surrounded by half-eaten bags of moldy, stale potato chips, rotted salads, containers of yogurt with green hairy penicillin fungus, and one unopened can of SlimFast that I opened and drank, because I figured it was the only hepatitis-free nourishment available (and drinkable), all of which was right out of the Lenny Bruce textbook 1950s descriptions of decrepit back stages on the endless trail of American provincial rundown show-biz venues.

But the audience was not backstage, and the interior of the theater oozed with a back-in-the-day flavor, with a musty user-friendly ambiance of World War II pre-plastic refuges from the rigors of survival. These old theaters were gathering places, like churches and town halls, and now the building was initiating a new event for a new community within a community.

Both jam sessions before and after the screening of *Pull My Daisy* were fantastic. I preceded the screening by giving a thumbnail anthropological account of how we all somehow got the film made, and then played, sang, and scatted the title song with a band of fine young players from Portsmouth.

All the local musicians played their hearts out, including a teenage bass player and a seventy-three-year-old ex-airline pilot playing some lyrical 1950s Chet Baker-style trumpet. As we made music together, the atmosphere of the old theater gradually changed from a ghostly relic of the late nineteenth-century into a 1950s Saturday night in New York party at a painter's loft studio, like the ones we all went to, and like the one where I met Kerouac at a bring-your-own-bottle weekend celebration. Because of the music, everybody got in that heavenly zone and the film took on a whole different tone, following our jam-out introduction before *Pull My Daisy* was screened.

Having it screened on a big movie screen with a really fine sound system made the film more impressive than usual, and Kerouac's spontaneous narration filled the theater. His Lowell, Massachusetts, accent was almost the same one that 99 percent of the audience in Portsmouth still uses today, since Lowell is so close to Portsmouth. This way of speaking has a special style with a soulful sound all its own.

After the film was shown, I played some more and then went out in the lobby to sign books and records and spent two hours hanging out with people even older than me. And then hung out with others of all ages, even high school students. Whatever age they were, all were movin' and groovin' for the very first-ever Seacoast jazz/poetry festival, called Jazzmouth..

It was all organized by a musician, Larry Simon, who, in addition to his regular concerts as a bandleader, has presented poetry/music readings throughout New England for years. Larry has created a whole network of musicians and poets, and cultivated an appreciative audience as well as attracting some terrific artists, ranging from renowned writers like Pulitzer Prize–winning poet Charles Simic to high school kids and retirees, many of whom, like Charles Simic, are participating in this festival.

Because I had done the first-ever jazz/poetry readings ever done in NYC in 1957, with Kerouac, I was asked to come to this one as the featured musical guest. Because of this new awareness of what Jack and I did in '57, I am now being invited to other festivals of this nature in Europe, Asia, and across the United States and Canada, in addition to the ones I have always done. I hope you can come to some of them with me, and sing some of your songs.

Still, here in an old nineteenth-century refurbished theater in Portsmouth, New Hampshire, an hour from Lowell where Kerouac was born and brought up, it was a special feeling to be part of a new festival based on what we did so long ago, and the completion of yet another circle and the start of a whole new series of adventures. Almost fifty years later, it was another first.

I told the audience how I was sure that so many from our era, most of whom are no longer here, would be happy to see this kind of local festival being created in 2005, and presented and received in such a joyous, celebratory way. And that all of us would hope that what we did a half century ago (and what those of us lucky enough to still be here are still doing today), would hopefully inspire everyone to be creative and work hard at whatever they love to do in life, and to keep developing their skills and encourage creativity in others.

There was also a series of other events, all of the same high quality. People in the audience and on stage ranged in age from teenagers to those older than me, and none dressed like beatniks.

It seems that finally, the sediment of the Beat stereotype, which diminished us all fifty years ago, has finally settled to the bottom of the sludge pile of our junk culture's landfill.

Now only the beauty part remains.

The work and the spirit are still here, standing on their own merit, to illuminate the cultural landscape, all of which should encourage all to pursue excellence throughout life and realize that you never give up, because ... a thing of beauty IS a joy forever. I know you have heard all this before ... but it's TRUE!!!

After the marathon was over Sunday afternoon, April 17, I drove back 265 miles to the farm, and the next day went to see all the folks at the Guthrie Foundation to finalize details about the new composition, *Symphonic Variations on a Song by Woody Guthrie,* that they have commissioned me to write for them.

I just made it to the airport in time to fly to Braga, Portugal, for the festival, and finally GOT SOME SLEEP (on the plane ride), after I made corrections in my score of *Symphonic Variations on a Theme by Woody Guthrie,* which I did while the other passengers were snoring.

I'll write Adira when I get to Portugal. Please send my love to Adam as well and save a whole bunch for yourself.

You have been a light in my life since the day you were born.

I'll try to find at least one good recipe while in Portugal and make you a new scary dish when I get back.

Xxxxx
Daddy

Braga, Portugal, April 25, 2005

Dear Adira,

I am just back from a great whirlwind trip to Braga, Portugal, and as usual didn't sleep much because there was so much to experience in such a short time, but it was so fulfilling, I feel energized!!

I am happy that I have paid all my taxes, because it was our very own U.S. State Department that sponsored my appearance at an international event at the university in Braga, Portugal, where I presented (in Brazilian-Philadelphia-Greenwich Village-accented Portuguese) how the loosely knit community of all of us who loved music, painting, and the written and spoken word were all part of every other artist's and any other interested person's life, during the middle 50s in New York, San Francisco, and Paris, and how all this was the foundation of what later was called the Beat Generation.

And that Kerouac was our reporter, in addition to the brilliant work he did in revealing his own roots in the 30s and 40s, and his self-discovery through his journeys in life. Everyone there, young and old, seemed to grasp the essence of his writing, and the spirit of many of the other artists from this period.

There were no morbid wallowers of gloom and negativity looking for beatnik stereotypical trash. They all seemed to know that Jack and all of us were part of a much larger picture. It seemed that everyone who attended the programs I presented was interested in our era in terms of what we had to offer as *artists*.

It looks like that at long last ... the times are more than just a'changing.

It seems that the times have changed!!!

In 2005, we have finally caught up with the 1950s!!!

And when a good thing happens, it is never too late. It is always right on time.

On the final day of the conference, I hosted a screening of *Pull My Daisy*. It is always fun to do and I never get tired of doing it. I wish you could have been with me so that we could do our spontaneous scat-singing free-styling after the screening to cheer everyone up. You are getting so good at it that I can barely keep up with you!

While many of the professors and students in Braga spoke impeccable English, they all said after watching *Pull My Daisy* that they had never heard anything like Jack's wild improvised narration before, where he plays different characters, using his voice to compliment the images of the silent film, making up everything on the spot as he went along.

After the screening of the film, when I performed for them, I improvised rhymed lyrics, and explained to them how this was part of the culture of our era, when musicians would travel together and sing and scat to one another during endless hours on the bus or when we were packed into a car, driving hundreds of miles to a gig in some far-off place, and that Jack was drawing on that tradition as well. And how this constant daring and living in the Now made it possible for us in our formal written-down work to be much better editors of what we created, because we could revise what we did by having a sense of whether or not it appeared to be spontaneous and natural, because we had a sense of the natural by spending time *away* from writing it down and *living* it, before committing anything to paper.

I also gave a concert of world music and jazz, showing how classical composers from Tchaikovsky, Dvořák, and Brahms, to Bartók, Gershwin, Copland and me all lovingly honored folk traditions in formal classical works.

And I read sections from my books, *Vibrations* and *Offbeat: Collaborating with Kerouac,* both of which are going to be translated into Portuguese!!!

I also read from the new book I am writing, *Upbeat: Nine Lives of a Musical Cat.* They also had a little exhibit of my caricatures from the recent New York show at Molly Barnes Gallery. I made a few caricatures on the back of menus and napkins and gave them to various people who wanted some made of themselves.

I also performed with local poets, accompanying them, as well as playing with local musicians.

I told everyone, in a little rap I wrote out in Portuguese, that at seventy-four, I am blessed to be able to share with others some of what has been shared with me, and I feel honored that I can represent some of the beautiful contributions that have been made by American artists of many disciplines and genres, as well as with the young artists of today from around the world.

Braga and the surrounding countryside of Northern Portugal is a wonderful place to be. It is close to the border of Spain, with special feelings of the past that go back to pre-Roman times.

Braga still retains much of this ancient feeling, with its cathedrals, churches, narrow cobblestone streets, calm pace, and fabulous wines from the lush vineyards that surround the town. Braga is surrounded by rolling mountains and an ever-present feeling of pre-Roman ghostly spirits that are reflected in the quiet but intense warmth and passion of the people from there, who seem to have an inner flame that is always slowly burning, combining an ever-present deep sadness from long ago with a quiet sense of joy when in the company of others.

A lot of the communication between people takes place in a non-verbal way, by looking into people's eyes, as they look at one another and then look at you, and when it is clear that you are comfortable in being part of this way of communicating, you are no longer a foreigner but become part of the family.

The hearty handshake is replaced with a gentle kiss on both cheeks as a way of sharing a hello or good-bye.

And having a meal is almost like a holy ritual, where good feelings are shared by all, and done at a leisurely pace, with dish after dish of fabulous food and lip-smacking tasty red wine from nearby Porto.

A group of traditional dancers performed one evening at the three-day event, presenting the *pauliteiros,* an ancient Celtic-based stick dance, where men do synchronized and complex group dancing that resembles the English Morris dances, combined with sticks being struck by the men as they weave through various mazes of dance patterns, striking each other's sticks, while doing steps that are a cross between the highland fling and Balkan and Central European folk dancing, accompanied by old bagpipes that combine Arabic scales with Celtic melodic patterns.

Songs are sung in *Mirandesh,* an old dialect from the town of Macedo de Cavaleiros in Northern Portugal. *Mirandesh* is also spoken in Galicia in Spain. It is the remains of an ancient language, and like the dances and the music, is a history lesson that raises more questions than it answers, leaving you eager to know more about this special place. I can hardly wait to go back, and there are plans to have me do more there in the future.

Now that I am back from Portugal, I have to work in Denver, Florida, Wisconsin, Chicago, and then this summer at a bunch of festivals, but finally will have more time at home where I can put in nonstop days to finish my new symphonic work (which I am writing and orchestrating on the road as well as in hotel rooms and airports between performing and speaking).

I feel blessed to be able to do what I love to do, and hope to do it better!

Some day I hope you, Alana and Adam can come to Portugal with me to see where the Amrams came from five hundred years ago, before all of us were requested to leave in 1492. It sure was nice to come back, and we'll all go there together some day.

As they say in Portuguese......

A te logo

Um beijinho grande e até brêve

Hugs and kisses,

Daddy

Denver, Colorado, May 15, 2005

Dear Alana:

I am just back from Denver, after a marathon series of events, and had such a great time, I forget that I haven't slept in nearly a week! I remember when we first went to Colorado together in 1991, and I thought about you and how proud I am of you and your brother and sister, and what a blessing it is to be the father of the three wonderful, independent, and creative people that you have all become. Adam was able to come with me, and it made me so proud that he could participate in all the events as well.

I was invited to Denver by a group who called themselves the David Amram Collective, composed of a group of students and parents, joined by members of the University of Denver's faculty from the departments of music, sociology, history, literature, biology (!) and urban studies.

The reason I was invited was in large part because of my collaborations with Jack Kerouac, as well as because it was a way for me, as someone who was there and part of it all, to honor other outstanding work created by many of the trailblazing artistic innovators of the 1950s, including the collaborations many of us have had and continue to have with one another.

Amazingly enough, the word *beatnik* and even the word *Beat* itself didn't ever appear in any of the information about what we did during this week, because the organizer of the event, Dr. Audrey Sprenger, felt that what Kerouac chronicled, as well as what so many other artists and visionaries of the period created, was now considered by many to be work of enduring value which seems more alive and meaningful today than ever before.

Dr. Sprenger felt that much of this work no longer needs that clichéd stereotype of "Beat," to define the art of our era. She understood that it was a catchword that automatically limited or dismissed so much of what we did then (and still do now) with a label that implied mediocrity, infantilism, and whining narcissism.

For the past four years, Dr. Audrey Sprenger, the young Canadian sociologist who teaches at the University of Denver, has created her own courses. Acknowledged as an outstanding scholar, scientist, and innovator by her colleagues, she uses the arts as a kind of barometer and pathway to gain a better understanding of our society, giving us all a fresh new look at the whole era of the 50s by examining where these various works of art were created, and the social conditions of each locale during the time in which they were created.

This sociological perspective helps to make the literature, music, visual arts, film, dance, and poetry of this rich period of artistic expression become more meaningful, and enables you to feel more at home with the origins of these ways of expression, as well as learn about where the artists who created the work came from, and what they had to deal with because of the conditions of the society in which they lived.

When *On the Road* was published in 1957, all of us who were part of an informal community of painters, poets, musicians, composers, actors, dancers, and free spirits spread across the United States, Canada, Mexico, and Europe, were all overjoyed that a book had been written that celebrated the joy of living your life to the fullest, pursuing your dreams, acting in a humanistic egalitarian way towards others, and rejoicing in the simple pleasures of life, wherever you were.

These seemingly old-fashioned values appeared to be vanishing, following the euphoria of the triumphant victory of the Allies in 1945 when World War II came to an end. *On the Road* reminded us of the enormous energy and sense of adventure that was part of our collective psyches.

In 1947, Kerouac, like all of us, was searching for a way to keep the flame of this spirit alive when he joined Neal Cassady in Denver.

In the New York literary establishment of the 50s, Denver in 1947 was the last place anyone would dream of as being anything worth writing about, unless you were writing a report for school about vacationing or what it was like to attend a rodeo. It was referred to by many as Cowtown, even though I imagine that the majority of people who felt this way had never even been to Denver.

Dr. Sprenger, through years of painstaking research, has created a framework to understand the social structure of the Denver of 1947, when Kerouac and Cassady first met, and how that influenced their lives, their interpersonal relationship, and Kerouac's work later on when he wrote about it.

During the recent urban hike that she conducted through downtown Denver, she incorporated information about Denver during the 40s and then moved us forward from the Denver of sixty years ago to the Denver of today, creating a new frame of reference, which helped us to see, feel, and hear what Kerouac and Cassady experienced when they walked down these same streets in the late 1940s. And it made us all feel more appreciative of the Denver of 2005.

I wish they had events like this when you were in college a few years ago.. They certainly didn't when I was in college. It was really an eye opener.

Being part of this hike reminded me of what it was like when I visited the Beethoven House in Bonn, Germany. That experience made me feel even closer to Beethoven's music.

When visiting the Beethoven House, you could hear recordings of some of his work played over the sound system in the room where he wrote it and see the old piano he used. When you left the Beethoven House, his work now had an extra contemporary significance as you walked away from the old house into the business district of the huge bustling metropolis of modern-day Bonn. Your urban hike there now made you realize that you were walking down the same streets Beethoven did.

I think that everyone who has visited the Mozart House in Salzburg, Hemingway's house in Key West, and Dvořák's summer residence in Spilleville, Iowa, where some of his great works were composed, or the town of Lowell, Massachusetts, where Kerouac was brought up, all have had similar experiences, where the past and the present become one.

During our recent hike, we were all seeing Denver in this same way, by walking the same streets that Jack and Neal did, accompanied by occasional readings of what Kerouac wrote about these same parts of town. This experience enhanced our collective appreciation of Kerouac's words, in his loving descriptions of a time and place that he cared so much about. Hearing these words read aloud in the very place where he was inspired to write them, reminded us that real works of art, like the magnificent mountains which surround the city of Denver, remain timeless. And that everyday life is full of surprises and moments of beauty and passion that are usually not documented but are what makes life worth living. Hearing Kerouac's words read aloud on the streets of Denver was an unforgettable experience for all of us.

Dr. Sprenger is one of the group of young scholars who are now creating their own new ways of presenting as well as enjoying artistic expression that, like the work of Kerouac, is pure in intent, and created in a natural and personal way. Many of these new scholars attend the annual world-renowned festival, *Lowell Celebrates Kerouac,* which features an academic conference every other year under the direction of Dr. Hilary Holladay, an outstanding teacher and poet in her own right. Professor Holladay has created a whole studies program at U Mass Lowell, where students can learn to appreciate Kerouac's work while living in his own hometown, and experience the same sights and sounds that influenced him in his early life, during the years before he first came to Denver.

For her conferences, Dr. Holladay invites a wide assortment of academics who are committed to furthering the understanding as well as the appreciation of the work done during this special time, and the invited scholars are equally committed to having their programs and courses presented in a new way, based on factual information, rather than pop mythology or caricatures like Maynard G. Krebs, the imaginary airhead "beatnik" who was a character on the *Dobie Gillis Show*.

These young scholars, many of whom I have met during the past five years at Professor Holladay's conferences, all have their own approach to teaching and their own areas of expertise, but all of them seem to feel that most of the artists from our era whose work has endured, while still referred to collectively as Beat, were for the most part much more than that term implies.

They tell me that rather than seeing us as being members of some kind of deviant subculture or an organized social movement, they recognize that we were all a loosely knit collection of individualists and artists who were also friends.

I always say to this new generation of teachers that each of us tried to tell our own stories in our own way, while hoping to engage the reader, listener, or viewer and bring *them* into the picture, even inspiring others to go out and find a way of being creative and adventuresome themselves. We were NOT trying to torture other people or leave the world a laundry list of our despair or mental problems. And I tell them that we always celebrated our surroundings and the people who inhabited them.

Most of these young scholars seem to feel that Kerouac was the engine who pulled the train, and that his work stands alone, independent of any "Beat" category, which is why his books speak to more people around the world today than ever before. They agree that since his death in 1969, his work speaks to the heart of each new generation of readers, and that few authors have ever articulated so well the beauty part of America.

Kerouac's positive message is what they say energizes their students, many of whom have never shown interest in contemporary literature until they read his books. When many of these scholars visit Kerouac's grave in Lowell, they tell me that they are all moved by what Jack's wife Stella Sampas so aptly inscribed on his gravestone, "He honored life."

I tell these young scholars that as children of the Great Depression, we didn't feel a necessity to wallow in despair. We understood that while Dostoevsky spoke of salvation through suffering, our American ethos was rooted in the hope that we could overcome adversity and save ourselves and one another from the jaws of disaster, and always find a way to make things better.

This Whitmanesque yea-saying life-affirming philosophy, necessary for survival, which the work of Kerouac personified, helped us all to remember that no matter which idioms we embraced or pioneered, we should always remain aware of our responsibility to share our dreams, as well as whatever blessings we had, with others.

We all understood what Duke Ellington meant when he said: "It don't mean a thing if it ain't got that swing." We never had an "A" table seating arrangement or advance reservations during our informal collaborations and get-togethers. Anyone and everyone was welcome to join us, including those who didn't want us to join them.

Dr. Sprenger hoped that all the events of our mini-marathon week in Denver would help to clarify these older ideals for young people brought up today with the merciless merchandising designed to make them addicts of junk consumerism. She was aware that the majority of Youth Culture exploitation emphasizes greed and selfishness as the basis for being a successful person. She designed the programs for my visit to the University of Denver in a way that enabled students to get a feeling of the egalitarian spirit of the era Kerouac personified through his work. She also presented all the programs that we did in a way that never made any of what we did become holier-than-thou rants or self-righteous tirades. Everything was presented in a down-to-earth fashion with an inclusive spirit.

One of the highlights of my marathon of events during my residency for the University was the final three-hour urban hike we took through Denver (5,280 feet above sea level) in the blazing sunshine. It was exhausting but exhilarating. It was a thrill to hear passages of Jack's work being read with my music on the streets of Denver in May of 2005.

As I accompanied students reading Jack's work, playing my instruments on the sidewalk, I realized that many of the passages being read from *On the Road* were the same ones that Jack and I first performed together in 1956 when we were at loft parties, coffeehouses, or walking around the streets and just felt like doing it. All of us on the hike enjoyed hearing these readings from Kerouac's novels, *On the Road* and *Visions of Cody*. The hike made it clear to us that many of the highlights of these two books of excellent fiction were based on actual events which occurred here in Denver sixty years ago.

This lit a light bulb in our imaginations, making us aware that all of us could create art based on what surrounds us each day of our daily lives, and celebrate and understand the people we interact with every day, just as Kerouac did.

As he probably told you when he phoned you yesterday, Adam had a great time and played hand drums with me on the hike, and although I'm sure he didn't tell you, all the students loved him, and also were crazy about Adira's songs, which they heard on the Internet.

After the hike, most of the students told me that one of the things that makes *On the Road* so appealing today to people of all ages all over the world is its joyous and celebratory nature, emphasizing that we should all embrace life, no matter how hard some situations might be to deal with. They told me that after the hike, they felt energized and inspired, NOT BEATEN DOWN!!

In addition to the hike, much of what Dr. Sprenger and I worked on during our marathon series of events during the week of our collaboration was finding a way to present to young people how an older generation dealt with the challenges of the stark nitty-gritty realities of the late 1940s and mid-50s, and specifically how Kerouac, like Dostoevsky, when faced with the grim realities of his time, was able to find the hidden treasures which society at large dismissed, by ALWAYS PAYING ATTENTION TO EVERYBODY AND TO EVERYTHING AROUND HIM. And how today's generation, who live in a different society with a different set of challenges, could do the same thing, in order to create their own legacy.

During the week in Denver, in all my various presentations for the kids, I also tried to honor the memories of the small army of my other contemporaries no longer with us, all of whom during their lives treasured bonds of enduring friendships.

These lasting friendships were one of the hallmarks of our era. We also celebrated hard work, devotion, respect, sharing whatever blessings you have with others, and appreciating life!!! I told the kids that when we honor the memory of those who gave more than they received, we all profit as a result. We were told by our elders during our youth of the 1950s, that these old values would always remain relevant.

I reiterated to the students how we were all open and eager to live and learn fifty years ago, and remain so today.

Finally, I told everyone that all these high ideals were ones that have endured as the basis for all civilizations, not something created fifty years ago by some nonexistent and highly exclusive Beat Movement, similar to a secret organization like Skull and Bones, the Masons, The Trilateral Commission, The Ten Days That Shook the World, or al-Qaeda.

Dr. Audrey Sprenger told me that she feels that because of my being a person from another generation, who was a primary source as well as a participant in what was now being studied, and that since I was not a social scientist, my subjective perspective, combined with her expertise as a social scientist, could help to open up doors for other educators to share their interests and disciplines with people from other fields, even if they came from outside the academy.

I found it interesting that Dr. Sprenger, just turned thirty-six, and having traveled the world, had a better objective understanding of what Kerouac and all of us were about than many of us ourselves did. This is in part because she has studied the literature, visual arts, music, and social history of the last fifty years, and is able to present this information in a well-structured way, enabling her students to understand the relationship of the 1950s to today's world.

I told Dr. Sprenger that her approach of having her students appreciate the value of our era by participating in events like the hike enabled them to see our past and present as one reality, rather than perpetuating a mythological aura of who we were supposed to be.

I asked her in the future to remind her students that the reason why Charlie Parker made a point of naming his landmark 1945 composition *Now's the Time* was because he felt that every minute of his life was precious, and that we must all feel the same way about using every day to continue to grow. I also told her that since I met and jammed with him in 1952, Charlie Parker's devotion to perfecting his art and embracing people through his work remains a major influence in my life as a classical composer and reminds me that each day and every moment of life is precious. I also told Dr. Sprenger that in 2005, I felt that her enthusiastic approach to teaching by involving her students in the Now was *right on time*.

Many us who have spent our lives in the arts are also interested in science, politics, history, and philosophy, but usually don't have the chance to participate in events where we can collaborate with someone in a different field in an academic setting. This experience in Denver of collaborating with a social scientist gave me hope that many others in the arts will now, like myself, also have the same chance that I did to finally sit at the table with what our parents, during the Great Depression would have referred to as "the grownups," i.e., those bright and learned people whom society deemed members of a profession that teaches something *useful and essential*, and who have a *real job!!!* As opposed to those of us who wanted to go into the arts for life, and were considered to be mentally unstable for wanting to do so. Before the term *beatnik* was invented, those of us who dared to try to be artists were often referred to as "No Goodniks."

Fortunately, the older artists who mentored us always told us to remember that whether or not we were deemed to be No Goodniks by others, we should always know that above all else we must remain hard workers and perfectionists and remember to love our chosen trade every day. Our mentors encouraged us to remain committed to trying to enrich our society with work of lasting value, and to inspire future generations to be creative.

They also made it clear that we must never succumb to accepting the role of being inventors or vendors of luxury consumer items, whose work as artists was designed solely for snob appeal or tax write-offs.

And they made us aware that accepting the nineteenth-century tradition of glamorizing the image of the starving artist as a hopeless victim only guaranteed all of us a lifetime of low expectations and even lower wages.

I felt really honored in Denver to be able to speak for all the musicians, visual artists, poets, novelists, composers, folk singers, filmmakers, dancers and even the many brilliant street philosophers who enriched the otherwise barren years of the 50s with their ideas and ideals which now reverberate around the world. So much of what they left us has given your generation hope and energy to work hard to achieve its own goals. The University of Denver's invitation to me to join professors in various fields was an exciting as well as a memorable experience.

Now that Adam and I are back from Denver, when I receive my Honorary Doctorate of Music from Five Towns College in Long Island this May 21, I am going to give a little rap to the graduating class about how we can all become educators of sorts by continuing our educations every day of our lives the way Kerouac and so many of the people he wrote about also did.

I also hope I can continue to give all those I meet a desire to tap into their own creativity and pursue their dreams and never give up!!

I send my love as always, and hope you enjoyed my travelogue about Denver, and the sleepless four days and nights I spent in the sunny mountains of heavenly Colorado. I really hope you can come with me the next time I go back there, and look forward to you, Adira, and Adam all getting together soon at your apartment in Brooklyn or at one of Aunt Mari's *fantissimo* home-cooked hot meals so you can all tell me about *your* latest adventures.

Now I have to go back to work and practice what I preach, in order to finish my new book and to work on *Symphonic Variations on a Song by Woody Guthrie* in the wee hours, when normal people are sleeping, and I also have to take care of the farm!!!

Of course I miss you as much as I am proud of you.
Love you always
Daddy

London, England, July 22, 2005

Dear Alana,

I'll be coming into the city for your twenty-sixth birthday and we'll celebrate! I'll bring a pennywhistle to play happy birthday to you (or maybe play it on my French horn, like I always used to do at the farm when we would have all your friends come over and bash down the piñata).

Know that I love you so much, with all my heart, and that will never change. You, Adira, and Adam are the light of my life and we will all three play a special farmerly birthday song for you at the 4-H Fair, when we roast corn together at the farm booth. I'm home again tomorrow, after eight wild days in London of non-stop adventures.

After hearing English spoken the way it originally was spoken before we created our own styles here in the United States, my week in London has upgraded my Feasterville, PA/Philadelphia/Florida/Washington, D.C./NYC accent, my English diction is now SUPOIB, and each day I sound more like William F. Buckley than he himself ever did, although my newfound cultivated speech style is fading fast.

I know our dog Tony and your brother Adam, who both have always had a hard enough time figuring out what I am saying, will be totally nonplussed when I lay my Laurence Olivier Old Vic Shakespearean bebop phraseology on them when I get back tomorrow night from Jolly Aulde England.

When I stand in the shade, I now look almost like an Edwardian gentleman (speaking in a well-modulated voice only when spoken to, not chewing food while talking, and never inhaling my salad while expounding). I feel I have finally learned to restrain myself after dealing calmly with the nutty time I had for eight days in England with no phone, no e-mail except for funky Internet cafes, and keeping my couth as all the appointments I had arranged were changed or were canceled or put on hold because of freak-outs resulting from the subway bombings, escaped bombers, and outrage over the death of the poor soul who was mistaken for a terrorist and was shot in the subway by mistake.

Three days before I left London to return home, as a relief from all this, I had an afternoon and evening off and David Sambrook a fine Australian journalist who interviewed me took me to see an amateur cricket game played by all his friends, who spent most of their time drinking beer, smoking cigarettes, eating sandwiches, and drinking tea for an hour before starting the game. During a thirty-minute intermission, in the middle of the game (called between innings), they partied even more, until the outside field smelled like a tavern at 3:00 a.m. with beer and wine spilled all over the grass and cigarettes and cigars all filling the fresh air with acrid fumes as they laughed, swapped tall tales, and discussed their strategy for the final half. What innovative training techniques!

As they staggered out for the second half, everyone was bombed out, and I realized that cricket could become the sport of choice for every stoner in all the bars in the United States, since tip-top conditioning did not seem to be a necessity, at least not for these weekend warriors, whose obvious love for the game and sense of fair play and fellowship was the only reason they play this game, which was originally a pastime for gentlemen only.

After the game was finally over, both teams spent another hour drinking, lying in the grass, smoking and drinking some more, and then giving each other prizes and awards and toasting the opposing teams, shaking hands, and drinking even more, before tottering off.

I was invited by David Sanbrook who had interviewed me to go out to eat with him, his girlfriend, and his teammate (a six-foot-four disc jockey with a crew cut) and his Jamaican wife, for Turkish food, in a grease-filled smoky bar/cafeteria which was just like the funky Turkish cafeteria on Houston Street in downtown NYC next to Katz's Delicatessen that we go to late at night. While Greek music (not Turkish) was blasting away, the Australian guy's friend told me about his being a third generation Marxist radical of Welsh descent (like Brooks Jones, only this guy was really BEYOND FUNKATISSIMO) as he expressed his desire to end capitalism (even though he was a full time DJ aspiring to a right-wing lifestyle) ... and he assured me that the place where we were eating and the whole neighborhood was the new home for all the Turkish radical Muslims who were kicked out of Turkey and are now living in England and waiting for the Revolution!

His Jamaican wife ignored him whenever he explained how he himself was going to overthrow the government, in between describing his own history as a DJ at parties he worked around the world. She told us how she was a makeup artist, and described how, whenever she did the makeup for fashion shows in England, she would raid the pantry and eat all the food, which had been prepared by big time gourmet chefs for the models.

She explained that because the models were all more or less anorexic, they almost never touched their food for fear of gaining a pound or two. She told us how once she ate so much that her front button fell off her dress onto the silver sandwich tray and then bounced into a bowl of salad, and how she received a standing ovation from all the models for her good appetite and lack of fear of being pleasingly plump.

Her husband, who kept knocking back more wine while she told stories, was beyond sloshed by this time, and he ended the evening by telling me that he was glad to meet someone like me, who seemed to understand why he was a genuine radical eagerly awaiting the day when he could see the Revolution smash the establishment ... an interesting conclusion, since I didn't understand most of his stoned-out rants or have a chance to say much of anything during the course of the entire meal, except to thank the waiter, ask for a glass of water, get directions for the subway ride home, and tell him of my hopes that he and his wife could visit America some day, come and hear some of the music being made by a new generation, and see what a wonderful country we had and what an infinite variety of people live there, who have come from all over the world to try to have a better life for their families.

So now you understand why I'd rather drink ginger ale most of the time! When you finish draining your bottle of booze, there is never salvation at the bottom of the bottle. And there is always a hangover the next day.

The rest of the time in London, I was working about fourteen hours a day on all the projects I will be doing there in the future, and taking the subways (called tubes) everywhere, often detoured because of the bombings. The English were characteristically cool through it all, considering what a drag this all is, but they seemed to hang in there, and their tenacity is a shining example of their true grit. And whether or not they like our current government (I didn't meet ONE person who did), they still like Americans and are hospitable, friendly and full of a dry humor that complements their good manners.

Being in the city of the great classical composers, from Henry Purcell to Benjamin Britten, and the modern-day popular brilliant artists like Elton John, Sting, U-2 (Irish but adopted by the British), Eric Clapton, and the surviving members of the Beatles, and the home of Charles Dickens and Emily Brontë, and of course of the beloved works of Shakespeare, I have always admired the British artists of the theater, music, literature, and the visual arts. I can hardly wait to go back.

I hope you are thriving, and send love and birthday cakes of joy to you, kisses to Adira, and new conga drum rhythms to Adam.

Big hugs with a side order of English muffins to go to my angelic, big, bouncing, talented, delightful, charming, brilliant daughter from your ever-lovin'...
Daddy
a.k.a. The one-man laugh factory

Okemah, Oklahoma, August 1, 2005

Dear Mari:

Your brother, the often tardy (but always ever-lovin') correspondent here, letting you know that even though Shakespeare referred to encroaching maturity as "... age with his stealing step," the plethora of senior boppers around the country who are sitting at home watching TV may be of value to retirement home directors and morticians, but I know that two of America's most hyperactive workaholics, you and I, WILL NEVER RETIRE!!

The old Amram work ethic, which we both embody, is still "burning with a hard and gem-like flame" (like Walter Pater himself said all artists themselves must do,) and imagine how Willie the Shake would have described the Golden Years if he had ever had the chance to chomp down handfuls of MSG organic vitamin concoctions to ward off aching bones, or Emergency C to give energy, or Ginkgo biloba to make the brain cells tingle.

This past July 16–18, just before my week in London, I spent four round-the-clock days and nights at the Woody Guthrie Folk Festival, held in various venues throughout the community of Okemah, Oklahoma, Woody's hometown. Only eight years old, the Woody Guthrie Folk Festival is one of the most enjoyable musical events that I have ever participated in, and as I approach my big seventy-fifth this coming Nov. 17, I have had many great times at many great festivals all over the world to look back on. Now, after being at this year's Woody Guthrie Folk Festival, I know that I have a lot *more* to look forward to, and can hardly wait for July of 2006 for the next one.

The festival embodies the egalitarian spirit, high ideals, and celebration of beauty of the simple things of everyday life that Woody Guthrie himself is remembered for. Being there in Okemah, his place of birth, with members of his own family, as well as musicians and devotees from Oklahoma to Australia, made me think back to the first time that I crossed paths with Woody.

It was forty-nine years ago, on a cloudy afternoon in 1956 on the Lower East Side of New York that I first met Woody Guthrie. Ahmed Bashir, a friend of Charlie Parker, Sonny Rollins, and Charles Mingus (with whom I was playing at that time), took me over to meet Woody at his friend's apartment a few blocks from mine.

Woody was lean, wiry, and brilliant, with a farmerly way that reminded me of the neighbors we grew up with in Feasterville during the late 1930s. I know you remember how in the late afternoons after long hours of work, they would often congregate to chew the fat in the side room of Wally Freed's gas station, across the street from our farm. Remember how proud I was that I used to get fifty cents to mow Wally Freed's lawn? And best of all, when I was done and stayed around the gas station, I never got caught while eavesdropping on all the conversations of the local farmers and out-of-work men who would commune at Wally's for their late afternoon bull sessions after their chores were done.

They always told it like it was, without wasting a word or a gesture, leaving space for you to think about what they were saying, and in spite of the grinding, seemingly endless horrors of the Great Depression, they had better jokes and stories than most professional comedians or politicians. Woody had this same quality, and I felt at home with him the minute we met.

As Woody, Ahmed Bashir, and I sat swapping tales and drinking coffee at the tiny kitchen table from noon until it was dark outside, Ahmed and I spent most of the time listening to Woody's long descriptions of his experiences, only sharing ours when he would ask, "What do you fellas think about that?"

The rest of the time, we sat transfixed as he took us on his journeys with him through his stories. Woody didn't need a guitar to put you under his spell, and you could tell that when he was talking to us, it wasn't an act or a routine. Like his songs and books and artwork, everything came from the heart.

Looking back at these memorable first few hours with Woody, I still remember the excitement in his voice, as if he himself were rediscovering all the events and sharing them for the first time, as he told Ahmed and me his incredible stories of his youth and subsequent travels. Both Ahmed and I marveled at his encyclopedic knowledge of all kinds of music, literature, painting, and politics, which he wove into his narratives, all delivered in a poetic country boy style that was all his own.

During these descriptions of his travels and adventures around the country, he often included references to events of his early boyhood days in Okemah.

Ever since that day we first met, I have always hoped that someday I would get the chance to go to Okemah, but with my crazy schedule I never had the opportunity to do so. When I was invited to the festival, I realized that I would finally be able to see his hometown and be able to meet his sister, her husband, and his remaining old friends from long ago who were still living there. By doing that, and by playing music and spending time with people who were also natives of Okemah, I knew that I would be able to understand Woody and his work in a deeper way, just as I have gained a deeper understanding by visiting, performing in, and spending time talking to people in the hometowns of Beethoven, Mozart, Thomas Wolfe, Jack Kerouac, Hunter S. Thompson, Harry S. Truman, Charlie Parker, Bob Dylan, Rembrandt, Duke Ellington, Socrates, Charles Dickens, Billie Holliday, George Gershwin, Dimitri Mitropoulos, and many other men and women from around the world who were defined to a large extent, as all of us are, by their roots. Like Jack Kerouac's hometown of Lowell, Massachusetts, Okemah, Oklahoma, was Woody's gyroscope.

Since first meeting Woody half a century ago, over the years I have played countless times with his great friend Pete Seeger, who has always kept the flame of Woody's true essence alive by honoring everything that Woody stood for as an artist and as a person. Pete's unflagging devotion, as well as his own peerless artistry and idealism, have enabled several generations to have Woody's legacy become part of their own lives.

Over the years, I have also spent nice times with Woody's late wife, Marjorie. I have played numerous events with his son, Arlo, over the past thirty-five years, as well as knowing his sister, Nora (for whom I am now composing *Symphonic Variations on a Song by Woody Guthrie*).

I have seen Nora's great kids grow up, and have performed at various festivals over the years which featured the fine family of young musicians that Arlo and his wife Jackie have raised. After being invited to the festival in Okemah, I learned that three of Arlo's daughters would be performing there, as well as the daughters of Willie Nelson and Peter Yarrow.

Adam was invited to come to the festival with me to play drums. I knew that like Arlo's kids, and those of Willie and Peter Yarrow, Adam would feel right at home in Okemah as part of the new generation of musicians who are creating new ways of sharing good music and high ideals with their contemporaries.

Adam and I left the farm at 6:00 a.m. for the airport for another crazy day's traveling. We had a seven-hour plane delay from New York spent sitting in the airport. After barely making it to St. Louis, following missed bags and canceled connecting flights, Adam and I finally arrived in Oklahoma City fourteen hours later and were met at the baggage claim area by an old Kerrville Music Festival buddy, Phil Lancaster.

I kept waking up Adam as we drove through the glorious countryside on I-40 towards the town of Okemah, so that he could see the panorama of the Oklahoma countryside, with cattle grazing in rolling fields that seemed untouched by modern times. All the names on the small green signs, Kickapoo, Tecumseh, Shawnee, Pawnee, Okfuskee, Creek Nation, Thlopthlocco Tribal Town, Cherokee, and Okemah were a reminder that Oklahoma was a state that still honored its Indian heritage.

After a lifetime of hearing Woody's songs and reading his books, I saw when we pulled into town that Okemah is just what you would imagine it to be—small, homey, and as pristine as the movie set from a classic 1930s Western feature film.

Old weathered buildings were gently nestled together, framing the wide main street where you could imagine hearing the sounds of horses still clopping and whinnying as they came into town, hitched up while their owners ran their errands at the library, bank, pharmacy, and dentist's office.

There were no McDonald's, Starbucks, Wal-Marts, sushi bars, massage parlors, head shops, tattoo parlors, or videogame emporiums.

The town had an unearthly but welcoming quality that made you feel that you were suddenly in a time machine, being gently escorted into another era where everything slowed down, surrounded by a sense of peacefulness and grace, with the spirits of Shawnee and Cherokee Indians, old cowboys, farmers, and oil drillers still there, all about to emerge from any of the old buildings to greet you.

The brilliant singer/songwriter and bandleader, Jimmy LaFave, whom I have known and admired since 1986 when he won the new songwriter award at the Kerrville Music Festival, became my guru of the regional history of Okemah and old-time Oklahoma, during my four days at the festival. When we weren't playing music, Jimmy shared with me the musical and social history of this unique part of the West.

Jimmy was born in Texas but raised in Stillwater, Oklahoma, and therefore was blessed himself by growing up surrounded by the mystical character of this special part of the world, where Indian spirits remain so strong, joined by the heritage of the hardy settlers who were members of the last of the American frontier.

In between the marathon nonstop round-the-clock jam sessions, preceding and following concerts, Jimmy took me all around Okemah, with a special visit to Lou's Rocky Road Tavern, an old fashioned bar with a sign outside saying:
ROCKY ROAD TAVERN
HOME OF WOODY GUTHRIE AND THE COMMON FOLKS
GOD BLESS AMERICA

Jimmy introduced me to the owner, Lou Johnson, a tall, slim woman with deep eyes that reflected her lifetime of hard work. Even before she said hello, you could feel a glow of confidence, strength, and satisfaction that emanated from her, making you know that she was a strong, special person who stood tall and proud, because of all she had overcome, in order to have created a place of her own.

She carried herself with that special grace that is pure Oklahoma ... a mixture of pioneer-farmer and Indian-warrior. Her voice was full of energy and her down-home poetic descriptions of her life in the special accent of old-time Oklahoma made you feel that you were suddenly a resident of a new hometown.

In between her stories and observations of the old days and the new ways of life in Okemah, Lou explained to me, as so many others did while I was in Oklahoma, that the word *Okie* was always used as a way of defining strong people of good character, but that when John Steinbeck's *Grapes of Wrath* became a best seller, "Okie" suddenly meant something else to people who knew nothing about the history of this unique place and the people who lived here.

The three of us talked about the similarity of how the words "Beat" and "Okie" both lost their true poetic meaning, following the publication of Steinbeck's *Grapes of Wrath* and Kerouac's *On the Road*. Jimmy explained to me how the name "Okie" was a source of pride to those whose families had settled there, and was used to identify a special group of people in a positive way.

I told Jimmy how Kerouac always told me that he felt Beat was about the search for the spiritual and the practice of Beatitude, but that eventually Beat became eclipsed by the derogatory word, beatnik, after *On the Road* was published. With the book's enormous popularity, the word "beatnik," and eventually the word "Beat" itself, both became pop-culture merchandising terms, used in a derogatory way to stereotype a new generation of artists and visionaries as nothing more than a bunch of untalented, infantile, whining, self-loathing blameologists and worthless losers, whose only value to society was to spawn sales of berets, bongos, paste-on goatees, and dark glasses, even though in all the pictures of us, none of the original "Beats" ever looked like beatniks, or any other group who all wore matching uniforms. I know you remember when you visited the madhouse studio of Alfred Leslie when we were filming *Pull My Daisy* in 1959, and how each of us bore not the slightest resemblance to one another, and certainly didn't have an iota of "Beatness" about us. (Unless you would attribute that dumb term to Gregory Corso's behavior when he asked you to marry him thirty seconds after I introduced you to him.)

As you know, most of us who had an artistic association and personal friendship with Kerouac (who was supposed to be the king of the Beats) were suddenly told that we should now call ourselves Beats. Of course we thought that this was ridiculous, and those of us still alive explain to all who are interested that what we were about was much more than the total misrepresentation of what "Beat" meant when John Clellon Holmes and Kerouac first used that word long ago.

Jimmy LaFave told me that the word "Okie" was used for years with loving pride by some of the hardiest and most humane people in American history, as a way of defining themselves and celebrating their identity. Suddenly "Okie" became another stereotype, like Beat and beatnik, similar to the crude stereotypes of rural southerners in the hit TV shows, *The Beverly Hillbillies* or *Hee Haw*.

In spite of Steinbeck's moving portrayal of the tragic days of the Dust Bowl and the Great Depression, where extraordinary and courageous people were honored, it wasn't long before the awareness of their heroism was turned into an opposite image by people who probably never even read Steinbeck's book. All these brave people were lumped into the stereotyped version of the Okie, which then became a way of defining hundreds of thousands of people who dealt with the tragedy of losing all they had and somehow found a way to persevere and flourish. Suddenly all these brave survivors of the ecological catastrophe known as the Dust Bowl were now depicted as shiftless illiterate morons, incapable of dealing with the modern world, dependent on the charity of others.

Because of Woody Guthrie and other Oklahoma geniuses like Will Rogers, there is a different picture painted which has endured beyond the stereotypical one, and like Kerouac's, Woody's message touches the hearts of many young people in 2005 who are now discovering what both "Beat" and "Okie" really mean. This can only make people of all backgrounds feel more optimistic and proud of themselves and their forbearers who survived the Great Depression, regardless of where they came from.

When Lou Johnson and Jimmy LaFave, both Oklahomans, spoke affectionately of someone as being "pure Okie," it indicated to me that this was the highest compliment you could receive.

Lou shared her joy of now being able to plan a celebration this coming October for having paid off every debt and payment due for her bar, which also serves Okemah as a kind of community center.

Lou told Jimmy and me the story of all her struggles in creating Lou's Rocky Road Tavern, making a place that was now such a valuable asset to the community as well as to the festival, and told us how much she loved to be around the Tavern herself, because she enjoyed communing with the customers and making them happy year round, in the same way that neighborhood bars were once gathering places, serving as an oasis in earlier days throughout the country.

"It makes me feel good when I see people happy when they come in here. My customers are like my family. When folks sit outside and pick guitars on the terrace, and sing songs they wrote, just for the enjoyment of it, it makes me feel like this place is worthwhile. It's nice when you all come in each year to visit us for the festival.

"Some folks in town were against the festival at first, because they thought Woody was some kind of Communist, but that's changed now. The festival brings in people from all over the world, and it makes us all proud to find out how much Woody gave the world, and that no matter how big he got, he never forgot Okemah. And he puts a lot about Okemah and Oklahoma in a whole bunch of his songs. Well, some customers here want some attention, so I've got to get back to work. You boys both have a good time and I'll come out and give a listen to you when I get a break."

Lou went behind the bar, and I went out on the terrace, which was now packed with a standing-room-only crowd of early-morning diners, patiently waiting in line for the annual presentation of Mary Jo's Pancake Breakfast, a fundraiser for the Huntington's Disease Society of America.

As the small army of early morning diners chowed down piles of scrumptious, aromatic, overflowing plates of fresh cooked pancakes and bacon, Jimmy and a group of excellent songwriter/singer/players all squeezed up on a tiny stage, and we played for two hours without a break, while seeing the joyous faces of people from four-month-old babies to those in their late eighties and beyond, all smiling, laughing, clapping, and singing along, while still eating even more pancakes. It was like a picnic/revival meeting/early morning family outing that you could not imagine would ever still be happening in 2005.

When we were done playing, and the crowd as well as the supply of pancakes and bacon thinned out, I sat down at a table with a man in a black cowboy hat tilted at a rakish angle (as if he were a combination of a country boy and a rapper from 1875) who was drinking from a bottle of beer with one hand, and seemed to be swatting an imaginary fly with the other. When he talked, he punctuated his monologues with a downward swat, as if he were chopping cornstalks for silage.

Motioning to my long double D whistle, he spoke to me in a boozy, gargling voice, highlighting each sentence with his fly-swatting gesture.

"What the hell's that thing you playin'? Some kinda oboe or sumpin'?"

"No sir, it's an Irish double D pennywhistle, similar to the kind that the great Irish flutist Sir James Galway often plays," I said.

"Well les hear you *play* that sucker," he said, taking an enormous swallow and draining his remaining half bottle of beer in one gigantic chugalug, letting out a sonorous belch, and after punctuating the belch with a fly swat to the table, he picked up another full bottle and held it up like a coach about to fire off a pistol to begin a track meet, and swatting again, cued a guitarist who had wandered in and was sitting at the table next to him to play some songs. Like a natural born impresario, he let us both know that it was show time for the command performance for his enjoyment.

"Awright boys, you pick me sumpin' nice," he said, taking a swig from his fresh bottle.

I played my flutes and pennywhistles and *dumbek,* accompanying the guitarist, who was singing a wonderful song. When he finished it, I asked him who had written such a great song.

"I did," he responded. "That's mine."

"Could you play some more of yours?" I asked. "That was terrific."

"Sure can," he said. "I seldom get asked to do that."

He played three more of his songs, all about his life in rural Oklahoma, and they were beautifully constructed, telling soulful stories about the old ways and bygone days and the bittersweet price that we pay for what we call progress.

I finally got up to leave, because I had to go to play on an old baby grand piano next door for a two-hour session accompanying twenty-three Oklahoma poets, all brilliantly organized by poet George Wallace, who came all the way from New York for the festival's first-ever poetry/music/spoken word event.

As I was leaving Lou's Rocky Road Tavern with Jimmy, the man in the black cowboy hat drained his bottle, and with a swat that now had an added lateral motion (like an Italian gesture of approbation), he saluted me with a toast from his empty beer bottle.

"Ah don't know what the hell you were doin'," he said. "But Goddam ... ah LOVED it!!!!!"

"David," said Jimmy, when we walked out onto the street. "Did you hear what he said? You've got to use that in your brochure."

"I already wrote it down, Jimmy," I said. "I'm using it in my next book."

The poetry readings were all delivered by outstanding poets from Oklahoma, and many introduced themselves as being proud of being Okies, often prefacing their poems with touching stories of their families before and after the Dust Bowl.

Somehow I was able to make the piano, whose soft pedal didn't work, soft enough not to drown out one word of the poets' recitations. I also figured out a system of which notes to leave out entirely, because of the keys that were stuck and made some of the other notes that they were stuck to keep on ringing. I also found which keys not to play at all, because some only produced a clunk since the parts inside were broken. I also had to avoid using other keys that produced notes that were so out of tune that they sounded like a Micronesian folk orchestra or an avant-garde quarter tone festival.

Still, as we used to say in the 1950s when most jazz clubs' pianos were old wrecks that were seldom if ever tuned, half a piano is better than none. I played my *ocarinas*, flutes, French horn, and percussion instruments as well, and the two-and-a-half hours of readings seemed like a few minutes, as each poet read their works beautifully.

All the poets, while different from one another, shared the musicality and the unique sounds of Oklahoma speaking styles, different from the regional accents from Texas, Arkansas, Colorado, or Nevada. I was sorry when the last poet finished. I could have listened to them for hours.

Many of the poets were professors at universities, and none of them sported fake English accents, but spoke in the special way that Oklahomans speak, rather than sounding like poetry slam dropouts from the Old Vic Theater or British Royal Academy of Bad Acting. None presented their fine work with histrionics and screaming. It was both a challenge and a treat to accompany them all.

After the two-and-a-half hour session was over, I went to the table to talk to Woody's sister and her husband, both of whom were at almost every event of the festival, speaking to everyone and encouraging all the artists and visitors to feel at home in Okemah.

"I stay around to see everybody," said Woody's sister. "I don't want to miss any one person. It's good to meet somebody who knew Woody as you did. I'm sure having fun. Let me tell you some stories about our family."

In the next hour, she told enough stories for someone to create a novel or history book. Now in her eighties, her memory was like that of the master storytellers and oral historians in Africa known as *griots*. She recalled and recited minute details of her family's life and how they dealt with tragedy, as well as the good times and the community's ups and downs. As she spoke with love and enthusiasm, she painted a picture of a time gone by, all done with a delivery and turns of phrase that were pure poetry. Her eyes sparkled as she regaled me with the detailed history of Woody's early days and the Okemah of her parents' generation during the last years of the nineteenth century.

Finally she and her husband and I were the only people left in the room. Throughout her irresistible monologues, her husband counterpointed her stories and observations, laughing delightedly and interjecting stories of his own, as if he were hearing them for the first time. Almost everyone at the festival referred to them as national treasures, and I second the motion.

I said good-bye because I had to go back to the OK Motor Lodge where all the musicians were staying, make a quick change of clothes, and pick up Adam to go out to the industrial park where the outdoor concerts were being held on the main stage.

Adam got the drums set up while I rounded up a makeshift band I had solicited during each of the 2:00–6:00 a.m. nighttime jam sessions that were held every night after the concerts on the black asphalt parking lot in front of the rooms where we all stayed at the OK Motor Lodge.

For my concert, I played and sang the traditional Lakota round dance melody "Mastinchele Wachipi," to open up my forty-minute set. Then I invited Jimmy LaFave and Marie Burns of the Burns sisters, both of whom gave magnificent readings from *On the Road*, which I accompanied. Then I sang "Pull My Daisy." The closing number was "Meanderin' in Mandarin," the talking blues sing-along about my adventures last summer at the first Beat Meets East Festival in Chengdu, China, in which the audience sings along with a phrase in Mandarin. I invited Karen Mal to play mandolin, Terry Leonino to play her harmonica, Darcy Deaville to play her violin, and Jimmy LaFave to scat-sing on cue, in the middle of the song.

I told Jimmy just to sing whatever came into his head at the moment, and since it was in the twelve bar blues structure, he couldn't go wrong. As he always does, Jimmy blew everyone away, and his improvised lyrics brought down the house, as did the instrumental solos from Terry, Karen, Darcie, Adam, and bassist William Landin.

Afterward, many people came up to me, saying that they felt that Jack's lyrical homage to the American landscape, in the short excerpts we did, was in the same spirit as Woody's celebration of an America that seemed to be vanishing but whose spirit would always endure.

Arlo Guthrie's daughters, Sarah Lee, Annie, and Cathyaliza, all performed that night, as did Willie Nelson's daughter Amy, and Peter Yarrow's daughter Bethany. During the rest of the evening, I was invited to sit in and play with other groups.

Afterwards, we all returned to the OK Motor Lodge to participate in the 2:00 a.m. jam session in the parking lot until the sun came up. Adam stayed up even longer than I did, and I never saw him have a nicer time, meeting and playing with people his own age, as well as performing with us old-timers.

Every musician I spoke to at the festival said that there was no other event quite like this, and many old friends from the Kerrville Festival in Texas, whom I ran into at the Woody Guthrie Folk Festival, all felt that this younger festival was a continuation of the pioneering efforts of Kerrville's own memorable thirty-five years of groundbreaking music made in the Hill Country of Texas, for which I have appeared twenty-seven times since 1976. Now a world-class internationally renowned festival, the Kerrville Music Festival started out in the same way as the Woody Guthrie Folk Festival, and retains the same purity thirty-five years later.

Since the concerts for the Woody Guthrie Folk Festival are free, and all the musicians come each year just for travel and lodging expenses only, with no salary, everyone felt unified with an egalitarian spirit that filled the air day and night. All the staff who work as volunteers throughout the year were not only perfectly organized but were unfailingly gracious to all the musicians and made us all feel so at home that none of us wanted to leave Okemah. If our government were run as well as the Woody Guthrie Folk Festival, we would never have a problem.

The Woody Guthrie Folk Festival is a perfect tribute to the spirit of Woody Guthrie and his beloved hometown of Okemah, and an important cultural event for all of America, setting an example of how to do things right, and celebrate the arts in a joyous way where the community and the artists all join hands to give our young people standards of excellence to aspire to, for whatever they do in life.

Just as all of us who play with Willie Nelson every year for Farm Aid feel, being part of The Woody Guthrie Folk Festival makes us proud to be musicians.

Adam and I can hardly wait until July 12–16 of 2006. I hope to bring the girls with me next summer, and if I do, we'll call ourselves the Amram Family Band.

And it would be great if you could come too.

I'll come into the city soon to see you.

Until then,

With brotherly love

From that never-ending road

David

London, England, November 28, 2005

Dear Mari:

Greetings from London. It was great to hear from you, and please pardon my late response to your nice note. I am finally attacking all the correspondence I have been trying to answer, whenever I could plug in my laptop, between all the places I have been going to nonstop, including all the seventy-fifth birthday celebrations (in San Francisco; Davis, California; Chicago; DeKalb, Illinois; NY, and London), while still finding time to write music as well!!

Through the holidays, I'll be working around the clock on my new symphonic composition and my new book, after three months of gigs around the country, topped off by a hectic week of nonstop activities in London. I'll mail you a flyer of the two London events, so that you can see actual copies of the formal programs I presented, along with the following travelogue of other more spontaneous adventures which took place while I was in this jewel of a city.

The first structured program presented was called "Shakespeare in the American Imagination," held at the Globe Theater Center, where I gave a two-hour rap in a rehearsal room in the building where various events about the history of the Globe Theater take place. I started out by telling the kids about the terror of appearing in a high school production of Shakespeare's play *Richard II*, when I was fifteen years old, and all the chance connections I have had with Shakespeare since then, including a 1951 production of *Hamlet,* at Howard University, for which I wrote the score. It starred Earle Hyman, who became world-famous forty years later when he played

Bill Cosby's father on *The Cosby Show*.

I talked about the very beginnings of the New York Shakespeare Festival, held in a park on the Lower East Side and then a few months later in a church in 1956, also on the Lower East Side of Manhattan, a few months before the triumphant first summer of 1957 in Central Park.

I also told them about the long road that the festival's founder Joe Papp took from his childhood in Brooklyn, coming from a family who only spoke Yiddish and Polish, and how discovering Shakespeare in the nearby public library gave him a gateway to entering into the English-speaking world, as well as a dream of having a festival in Central Park some day where all New Yorkers could come for free and see and hear Shakespeare.

A student for the University of Denver sang some of my settings of Shakespeare's words from my two-act opera, *Twelfth Night,* for which Joe Papp wrote the libretto. I ended up the program by playing a recording of my saxophone concerto, *Ode to Lord Buckley,* since part of the concerto used a portion of the music for *As You Like It,* which I composed for a long-gone 1961 production at the Stratford, Connecticut, Shakespeare Festival forty-four years ago (!!!).

And I told them how Lord Buckley himself used to come to the productions in the park, often with members of Oscar Pettiford's big band, with whom I played. Lord Buckley and Oscar were friends, and when we had an off night from playing at Birdland, we would all go to Central Park to see the productions presented by The New York Shakespeare Festival for which I had composed the scores. Lord Buckley himself revamped the famous speech in *Julius Caesar* as part of his comedic poetic bebop monologues, and would astound the actors who were appearing in Joe Papp's Shakespeare in the Park productions when he would give impromptu monologues when we all hung out together after the shows. We did his fantasy version of Marc Antony's speech from *Julius Caesar* when we performed together for the last time at George Plimpton's apartment in New York in 1960 at a gala for Buckley the night before his Lordship died the next morning.

After I completed my two-hour presentation for everyone in the rehearsal room, I was invited by the education director of the Globe Theater, with students from Denver University and drama students from the Globe Theater, and assorted tourists who had wandered into our lecture room, to walk outside and visit the newly restored replica of the Globe Theater's original outdoor stage, where Shakespeare himself had his plays held during his lifetime.

It was like entering into a dream, going back more than four hundred years in a time machine, as I went through the doors of the modern building and entered the courtyard where the groundlings (the people with no money) all stood for hours to watch Shakespeare's plays (the way young folks today stand for hours in a mosh pit to watch a rock concert).

Above the back of the stage, about fifteen feet high, held up by pillars and decorated with ornate carvings, was a small second story, where the musicians sat during the show, surrounded on either side by where the nobility sat (so that the titled elite could be seen by the common people during the entire show).

Then I was invited to climb up onto the stage itself, in the same way that Shakespeare once stood as an actor when he performed in his own plays, and suddenly felt that I could hear the voices of the actors from so long ago, reciting those same wonderful words I heard out of doors during the twelve years I composed music in Central Park, writing music for Joe Papp's free Shakespeare in the Park productions in New York.

Being on that stage was like the completion of a circle.

I suddenly flashed on the idea of having my opera, *Twelfth Night,* for which I composed the music with Joe Papp's libretto, being performed here at the Globe Theater someday, just as Joe had wanted it to be performed at the Delacorte Theater in Central Park, when we wrote it in 1964–68.

I also took a group of American students to a free concert in St. Martin in the Fields, a beautiful old church next to Trafalgar Square, where homeless people and recently arrived immigrants were welcomed and even provided for.

I told the students, as we stood at the entrance of the church, that when they looked behind them, they could see the statues of King George IV and a bunch of famous English generals, all of whom had subjugated the great-grandparents of all the immigrants during the heyday of the British Empire. Now the descendents of these formerly colonized people lived in the same neighborhood as the church itself.

I told them that now, in 2005, both the descendants of those oppressed people and the great-grandchildren of the soldiers who were sent around the world to conquer and control the colonies, were welcomed to sit side by side and attend these free daily concerts and lectures. Those in need were provided free meals, with a homeless center next door to the church, a few hundred feet from the public square, which honored the military heroes of the occupying forces with statues of the old generals from the era when England colonized much of the world.

I mentioned this to them, not as some political polemic, but rather to show them how understanding history and relating what happened in the past to what was happening around them today could make the music they were going to hear more meaningful. I explained to them that Mozart and Hummel, whose music was being played at the concert, both lived in Europe during the heyday of the British Empire, and that both of these brilliant composers were dependent on the European court system to survive. I explained that in 2005, both Mozart and Hummel were long gone, just like the statues of the men in the adjacent park, as well as the aristocracy they were beholden to. Still their music was just as alive and youthful as ever.

I finally suggested to the students that when they returned from their overseas study program in London to go back to school in Denver, they should continue to check out the history of their surroundings in Colorado, and always pay attention to everything.

The free concert we heard at St. Martin in the Fields was extremely well played, performed by eight young English musicians playing Mozart's Serenade in C Minor and Hummel's Partita in F.

On the night of November 24, I went to a gala reception for my old friend Frank McCourt at the Irish Embassy in London, celebrating his new book, *Teacher Man.*

The Irish ambassador to London, Daithi O'Ceallaigh, told me how fondly he remembered the same group of people we both knew in the 70s, when he was the ambassador in the Irish embassy in New York.

We reminisced about how we all went to The Bells of Hell Bar and the Lion's Head Bar, where Frank, his brother Malachy, and many of us all hung out together thirty-five years ago in Greenwich Village. The ambassador was as down-to-earth and warm as he was brilliant, a real *menche,* just like Frank and Malachy, and he made all guests in the elegant posh surroundings of the embassy feel like we were all having a real party, celebrating Frank and his new book. It was an evening of rejoicing, not a snobbish uptight Who's Who ego fest.

Toward the end of the evening, I was asked to play a solo on my Irish double D whistle, and afterward Frank told me he is finally ready to resume work on *Missa*

Manhattan, an ecumenical setting of the Mass he has been planning to have me compose music for, which he couldn't really complete during the past five years, since he was writing his new book, *Teacher Man.*

It was great to see him and his wife Ellen again, both enjoying the well-deserved accolades, surrounded by well-wishers from London's most elegant literati, all congratulating him while having him sign their copies of his splendid new book.

Then, for a startling change of pace, I left and took a cab to where I was invited to attend a concert which, to my surprise, was presented by an insane trio who did 1920s raunchy X-rated blues, complete with a wild New Orleans-born blues belter expatriate singer who dressed like Mae West, complete with a squirrelly white wig like the one Mozart wore in *Amadeus.* She belted out outrageous songs, starting out with soft groans, combined with low mental institution–style growling and moaning, and ending each number in a huge operatic voice, bellowing like a Wagnerian diva on an acid trip, with super-campy double takes that made most people think that she was a female impersonator.

I had been invited there, having no idea of what the trio did, because she had heard that I was in London, and since my jazz/poetry night was to be held in a venue with no piano the following night, the singer was kind enough to offer to lend me her electric piano and sound system for the concert I was scheduled to give. She left a message that she wanted me to hear her perform, as well as to show me how to assemble the sound system.

When I met her after her show was completed, she told me that earlier in her checkered career, she had sung in opera productions in Italy, sponsored by the church, before marrying an American film producer who lived in both Italy and in England in exile, after he was forced to flee the United States because he was caught for counterfeiting money to finance his own films, and how after his death eight years ago, she came out of retirement, and rather than returning to the operatic field, reinvented herself, drawing on her New Orleans roots to become a born-again blues belter, renting out rooms in the house in London her husband had left her, so that she could have enough income to find places to play and present her incredible versions of Mae West, Judy Garland, and other divas of the past. Her recreations of these great old-time stars made it appear they were now reincarnated as opera singers stranded in the deep South of the 1920s, singing on a street corner for spare change, all dressed in Elizabethan Eurotrash costumes, with wigs, garish makeup, stiletto high-heeled boots, and endless scatological ad-libs, accompanied by ultra-campy slithering gyrations.

The tenor sax player in the trio was a physicist who teaches at Oxford University, but when appearing off duty as a performer, dresses like a 1960s Austin Powers-style rocker, complete with a lamé gold jacket and Beatles hairdo, singing old time X-rated songs in a raspy voice completely the opposite of his well-modulated Oxford University speech style when he is off stage. He is also an excellent tenor saxophonist, as well as a fine accompanist. He demonstrated his ability to enhance the songs she sang by playing subtle complementary counter melodies, always in excellent taste, making himself supportive to her at all times, even when being groped by her as part of her all-out theatrical performance.

The pianist looked like a classic chubby English lord, kind of like a young Winston Churchill, with sandy curly locks, a ruddy complexion, and wearing a bemused expression when being bombarded from both sides of the stage by the heavy porno lyrics and non-stop theatrics of the singer and the sax player. Still he was clearly a spectacular virtuoso when he soloed and seemed to enjoy accompanying these two most unlikely performers.

In the middle of their show, they invited me to come out of the audience to sit in with them for a tune. Since I had my pennywhistles with me, and I knew it might be a long time before I would ever play with a group like this again, I joined them and had a great time.

During the entire outrageous performance, the audience of smartly dressed Englishmen and women all sat in silence, with perfect postures, hands folded on their laps, except when delivering polite applause, and looked as if they were attending a recital of Haydn string quartets, not even registering a gasp of disapproval or shock when the singer pranced into the audience to bury men's heads into her enormous décolletage as she brayed out her songs of sexual submission. If the men were bald, she would plant huge rings of bright purple-red lipstick on their pates, or leave smooch marks all over their faces, all of which received polite titters and mild applause from the rest of the audience.

After the show was over and the trio was packing up, the singer and tenor player both showed me how to hook up the portable sound system, which they were kind enough to lend me. The singer asked me if I wanted a job for a night, later in the week, playing with her at a transvestite bar, but I gracefully declined, telling her that I already had a full schedule.

She was actually really talented, goodhearted, smart, and a fascinating person, as were the other two members of the trio. Seeing three middle-aged people doing what they did, and having so much fun doing it, was in keeping with a lot of the street performers I saw in Covent Garden, all of whom, like the trio, are politically incorrect, often tasteless, but always spirited, energetic, brilliant performers and never mean-spirited, giving the English audiences a special kind of relief from the rigors of everyday life.

Also, I realized that appreciation of the madhouse antics that took place during the trio's performance and with most street performers throughout London was a reflection of the English tolerance, as well as affection, for true eccentrics of all varieties.

All this made me see that in London, the English people's great sense of humor and appreciation of true eccentrics is similar to the acceptance held by so many folks I have crossed paths with in parts of Texas, Arkansas, and Maine. I realized for the first time that both the British and rural American's love of these seemingly bizarre performances, as well as the outlandish people who create them, is a way of preserving an old tradition of family get-togethers from an earlier era. Before homes had TVs or radios, most social gatherings included homemade entertainment, with special moments when kids would put on a show for the older relatives after dinner at family gatherings, or the elders would sit around the table telling jokes or singing songs, before television and mass communications enslaved us all into a state of zombiehood.

Thanks to Dr Howard Cunnell, British-born scholar and editor of the original scroll for *On the Road,* I was invited to participate in a memorable jam session in Brixton, the old West Indian section of London, which was like playing at Minton's or Small's Paradise or the 125 Club in Harlem, when I moved to New York fifty years ago in 1955, and would go uptown with Charles Mingus and his band, of which I was a member, to sit in and play with musicians that none of us had ever played with before.

The jazz club in Brixton was in the back room of a bar, and there was no admission fee, no cover charge, no microphones or sound system, but a wonderful inviting atmosphere and a room full of people who really enjoyed the music as well as each other's company. It made you really feel like playing.

The outstanding drummer in the group, Kenrick Rowe, joined us for the concert-readings we did on Friday called "Kerouac in the British Imagination." This program served as a sequel to "Shakespeare in the American Imagination." Everyone involved outdid themselves, and I saw, to my delight, that for the people young and old who attended both events, the miserable stereotype of "Beat" could now be replaced in the minds of young people in England by appreciation of Kerouac as a writer, as well as a reporter of a unique time and place, just as Shakespeare was, rather than as a leader of some morbid depressing "movement."

We were joined by Richard Turner, a highly accomplished twenty-year-old English trumpet player who proved, by the great response he received from the kids in attendance, that jazz and classical music have new directions, new people to travel these uncharted waters, and a new audience. A special surprise guest was the actress Adjoa Andoh, who sang "Lover Man" and brought down the house.

In addition to jazz and music from around the world, we had readings from work written by Kerouac fifty years ago, accompanied by music, readings from my *Offbeat: Collaborating with Kerouac,* and recitations with music of the poetry of two teenage students from the University of Denver, reflecting their feelings about visiting London in the fall of 2005.

I hoped that this event helped to make a connection between the spirit of artists of yesterday and today by showing what we were about in the 50s, when musicians of all ages, as well as painters, actors, dancers, novelists, sculptors, poets, composers, and everyday people who all wanted to see a more compassionate and egalitarian world, would get together and create a moment in time, specifically to reenergize one another.

I also had the chance to visit Carolyn Cassady at her home outside of London for a reunion. A few students came with me. She graciously shared her priceless recollections of what really happened when she, Kerouac, and Neal Cassady all lived together.

She told us about the new books that both she and her son John are writing.

Her insights will be an invaluable addition to a better understanding of what actually happened during this exciting period of Jack's early days as an unpublished writer.

My grand finale in London (my only night off) was attending a Bangladeshi cooking class in Brick Lane, the largest Muslim neighborhood in London.

None of these events in London would have ever happened without the tireless work of Dr. Audrey Sprenger, who created all the courses and somehow managed to organize all the events I have described. The students all agreed that she was a teacher who made everyone want to find a way to continue their education for the rest of their lives, and never stop trying to develop themselves after they left school. We all decided that for her, the campus was wherever you were every day of your life. And as one of the young sophomore men said to me, "She's a real teacher. She makes learning new stuff fun."

I can hardly wait to see you and bring the kids over and have another high IQ evening with our favorite most Fab Upper West Side sweetheart ... my very own big sister!!

Until then, I hope you have joyous holidays and that 2006 will bring peace, happiness, good music, laughter, fewer blogs, more eggnogs, and unrequited love to you.

Wishing you an all-inclusive gender-free macrobiotic Buon Natale, Merry Christmas, Happy Chanukah, Joyous Kwanzaa, Roaring Ramadan, Swingin' St. Patrick's Day, Independence Day, May Day, Labor Day and BILLIE HOLIDAY!!!

In the words of the prophets of old...
To do is to be. —Descartes
To be is to do. —Voltaire
Do be do be doo. —Frank Sinatra
Shoobie-Eel-ya-coo,
That's all the news that's new
This *belle lettre* to you
Is on the way, I'm through!!!!
Your loving Bro'
David

P.S. For a final salute to the winter of 2005–06 ... an arctic blast from the past, with a poem by John Dryden (1697), surely one of the hippest of the seventeenth century's most beatific cats.

In Genial winter, Swains
Enjoy their Store.
Forget their Hardships,
And recruit for more.
The Farmer to full Bowls
Invites his Friends,
And what he got with
Pains, with Pleasure
Spends.
John Dryden (1697)

Florida, February 3, 2006

Dear Mari:

It was so nice to hear your voice when I spoke to you from the airport (my second home away from home nowadays).

I have been meaning to write since then to tell some of my latest adventures, but my nutty schedule and limited secretarial skills make me an infrequent flier in the correspondence department.

This year of 2006 is already one of my busiest in decades. Fortunately, except for my concert in Olympia, Washington, in early January, I had a brief respite from the endless series of events of last fall and had a chance to hide out at home in precious isolation, writing music and working on my third book. I ended my hiatus driving through a snowstorm from the farm to LaGuardia Airport in NYC, where I last called you January 25, just before hopping on the plane and arriving in sunny, eighty-degree temperatures in Fort Lauderdale, accompanied by Adam, who played percussion with me in three classical concerts I conducted with a fine orchestra in various venues throughout the state.

The members of the orchestra were an energetic group of young virtuoso soloists and chamber music players who love to play, and each gets a chance to shine during the concerts. We programmed some of my favorite treasures of classical music, each played in their own correct traditional style, as well as some of the treasures of contemporary music, including works inspired by jazz, Latin American influences, and new pieces using elements of what is now called world music.

Much of the week, during rehearsals in Fort Lauderdale, Adam and I traveled by van, with the members of the orchestra, where I was able to practice speaking in Spanish, Portuguese, French, and German with the international group of musicians.

On the way to and from rehearsals, we drove through areas where there are bands of wild monkeys, escaped from a zoo thirty years ago during a hurricane, who run around, safe from us, in a patch of remaining wetlands squashed between the Fort Lauderdale airport and the nearby surrounding industrial parks and funky boat yards. At dusk, possum- and raccoons run across the dirt roads into the wild impenetrable foliage, ignoring all of us two-legged interlopers.

We finally left Fort Lauderdale to go to our concerts in Sanibel Island and the Keys. Driving to the West Coast from Fort Lauderdale to Fort Myers, through what is known as Alligator Alley, you can see giant alligators sunning themselves, oblivious to the roaring traffic passing through their turf, looking like huge abandoned black rubber tires as they lie curled and motionless in the midday sun, nestled halfway with their tails in the brackish swamp waters and their heads buried in the dense foliage.

You can imagine Cabeza de Vaca and his army of perspiring conquistadors, in a time warp, all trying to hack their way through the same twisted roots and uprooted stumps of tropical trees, unchanged for thousands of years, as they discovered Florida, long before the existence of the sky-scrapered, condo-clustered, traffic-jammed state of Florida that we know today.

Crossing the bridge from Fort Myers to Sanibel Island made me feel that I was re-entering the paradise that it was when you and I first went there in 1937 with Mom when we lived in Passagrille, Florida, for a year, and Pop came down to visit us and we all went to Sanibel.

I know you remember how we had to take the small leaky boat from Fort Myers that delivered groceries to Bailey's General Store, which also served as a ferry to get there, before the giant bridge was built, and before the population explosion engulfed Florida, as it has during the last sixty-eight years since we first went there. Even so, on Sanibel in 2006, there are still huge stretches of unspoiled swampland and a gigantic bird sanctuary at Ding Darling National Wildlife Refuge that remains pristine and timeless.

For the opening concert in Sanibel, in addition to Bach, Mozart, Telemann, Borodin, Scott Joplin, and Duke Ellington, we did a selection from *On the Road*, where the narrator read the final page of Kerouac's timeless book, accompanied by the orchestra, for which I composed and conducted original music for a concert at the Kennedy Center with the National Symphony, narrated by the late E.G. Marshall, which we did together in the mid-nineties. It was a program where E.G. Marshall narrated words of Thomas Jefferson with music that I was commissioned to write by the Library of Congress. On the second half, E.G. read Kerouac's words and I composed the music for that too. I wish that Jack had been alive to hear E.G. then, and know he would have loved to have heard it with the wonderful narrator, Jose Pacheco, who did it in Sanibel.

Jack and I first began to talk about doing work together with a symphony when we started collaborating with his words and my music, when I began playing for him back in 1956 at our jazz/poetry forays, before *On the Road* was published, and before we gave our official first-ever jazz/poetry readings in New York at the Brata Art Gallery in 1957.

Since I had no orchestra to conduct in 1956, and no orchestras were playing my music, having Jack recite his work with an orchestra where I would compose music and conduct it was just something we talked about doing, but even though it was never a possibility back then, at least we had the idea! Now, fifty years later, in 2006, I am able to do it. And I'll be doing it again in a lot of places in the future.

The one piece of mine that included setting Jack's words with orchestra and that he did hear during his lifetime was first done in 1965, when I composed the cantata *A Year in Our Land,* with passages from Jack's *Lonesome Traveler,* scored for tenor solo, chorus, and orchestra. Jack helped me to find other authors to include in the cantata, giving me a list of fifty books to read. I ended up using words by James Baldwin, Dos Passos, Thomas Wolfe, John Steinbeck, and Walt Whitman, as well as those of Jack. Jack and I had all kinds of plans to collaborate again, using his words with orchestra, where he himself would be involved doing the narrating, just as he did when I would play for him myself, and he also wanted to do a baseball opera.

Another Kerouac-connected orchestral work that is now being played is my flute concerto, *Giants of the Night,* which you came down to hear when Sir James Galway premiered it in New Orleans in 2002. It is getting played all over now, and as you know, the second movement includes two French Canadian folk songs Jack used to sing to me. They want to play it here in Sanibel—they don't yet have the budget to get a large enough orchestra, but they are working on it. And a lot of other flute soloists and orchestras are planning to play it this year and in 2007. Next week I go to Hilton Head, South Carolina, where the phenomenal twenty-four-year-old flute wizard, Mimi Stillman, is playing the concerto with Mary Woodmansee Green conducting.

The following night in Sanibel, I did a concert without the orchestra, called "From Cairo to Kerouac, Classics of Jazz and World Music, and the words of Jack Kerouac."

This event was as equally well-attended as the classical concert, and we did the whole evening with a trio. Adam played percussion, joined by a fine bass player from the area and me playing all my instruments. Jose Pacheco narrated again and was terrific. He is a fine poet in his own right, and also read one of his best pieces about the night he heard Charlie Parker play at the Montmarte, just before Bird passed away in 1955.

After this concert, prior to leaving to conducting two more classical concerts in the Keys, Adam and I took a fourteen-mile bike ride through the Island, and then packed up and were driven to catch the express ferry from Fort Myers to Key West. As I hobbled on board the ferry, nursing my leg cramps from the bike ride, I felt like you must have after you ran the New York marathon. But it warmed me up for the boat ride to the Keys.

Riding on the brand-new high-tech ferry was a real treat for Adam, who enjoyed seeing a boatload full of camera-toting seniors. All of them were dressed in their Florida tourist finery, revving up their engines by having a few alcoholic-laced snorts of booze hidden under their jackets and poured into soda cups on board to prepare themselves for cruising the nonstop party-hearty jammed streets and sidewalks of Key West, where Ernest Hemingway's once peaceful fishing village is now a tourist madhouse.

When we landed in Key West, we followed the throngs of tourists into the maelstrom of vacationers on parade. We milled slowly through the streets. The salty nighttime air of the Keys was filled with the pounding cacophony of rap, disco, and heavy metal white noise. You couldn't escape the thumping of electronic earsplitting torture that was blaring nonstop from the shops and food stands, all of which were trying to outdo each other, using their sound systems as weapons to lure tourists off the streets and into the shops, by showing that their CD recordings were played louder than any other store in town. Adam and I had to watch our footing, because if the sound waves didn't knock you down, or the mobs of revelers didn't push you off your feet, you could easily slip because of the condition of the street itself.

It was just like McDougal Street on a Saturday night in Greenwich Village in the 50s. You could feel your feet sliding over the grease from hundreds of discarded fried-in-crankcase-oil fast food delicacies. If you stumbled, you would fall face first into small mounds of seafood shish kabobs, crab shells, rancid shrimps, crushed Key Lime pies, melted ice cream with squashed cones, candy bar wrappers, and piles of paper cups, plastic spoons, and soggy napkins.

As we walked away from the mob scene toward the Hemingway House in a quieter part of town, I told Adam about the plots of as many of Hemingway's stories as I could remember. We arrived at the black wrought iron fence which surrounds Hemingway's old house, which is now a museum. The lawns are inhabited by stray cats, the descendants of his old house pets. They run wild, much like the descendents of the escaped monkeys of Fort Lauderdale that we saw the past week as they hid during the daytime, waiting for all the people to leave.

In the dark, we couldn't enter the house, since the museum was closed, but could both still feel Hemingway's spirit filling the outdoor porches of the house and imagine him walking right by us in his shorts and fishing sandals to his old neighborhood bar for a nightcap. I told Adam that even though Key West will never be the same as it was in Hemingway's lifetime, that long-gone time will always be with us, preserved through his books. We stayed with my old friend Russ Scavelli and his wife, who had moved there from Mahopac, New York, and worked as musicians, as well as running fishing tours. They had known Adam since he was born and were thrilled to see him soloing with the orchestra in the Duke Ellington piece I orchestrated.

The concerts in Key West and nearby Marathon were sold out and the presenters in Key West said that ours was the most successful artistically and financially in their thirty-four-year history. Most important, the audience really enjoyed what we did and gave us standing ovations, the musicians all played with spirit and enjoyed doing it, and we programmed the best music possible.

After our final concert the next night in Marathon, we left at midnight and drove from the Keys to Miami to give a program the next day. It was called "Spirituality and the Beat Generation," held at Florida International University, and hosted by my old friend Dan Wakefield, author of *New York in the Fifties*. He is a professor of creative writing there, and considered a treasure by all the faculty and students, as well as by the many readers of his books. They constantly surround him for advice and encouragement and the joy of hanging out with him. He somehow finds time to mentor a small army of writers, between his daily writing stints. He is still the same unspoiled Indianapolis appreciator of life that he was when we first met in the madhouse of New York long ago, and he hasn't changed in the last fifty years. I am so glad that Adam could meet him. Dan also had us do a world music program where Adam and I played and showed students and visiting oldsters how all this music from around the world relates to roots music of classical composers of the past, and influences modern classical composers to explore new ways of expressing themselves.

We finally went home, and Adam got a good night's sleep, as did I.

It was a wild nonstop schedule as usual, but every event came off well. Adam was terrific and everyone loved him. He played beautifully and was gracious and enthusiastic, charming everyone with his natural unspoiled way of relating to people. Between Adam, your two daughters, and my two daughters, we have some fantastic children, so we must have done something right in our lives, and also have been extremely lucky to have such wonderful kids. Children are really the ultimate blessing in life, and they tune you in to all the other children of the world, once you have had some of your own. We'll have to find a way to all go to Florida together, for an Amram invasion of the South, and show our kids and grandkids where we lived in Passagrille, way back in 1937, in that old rickety bungalow with the scorpions under the porch, if it's still there.

I'll try to see you this week before I go out on the road again, and sitting here by the woodburning stove in the freezing snowy hills on another winter night in Yankee land gives me a chance to think about you.

I send brotherly love to you as always.
David

San Francisco, February 10, 2006

Dear Alana:

I'm here in San Francisco for a day and a half to perform a concert tonight for and with Dennis Banks and Floyd Red Crow Westerman, the American Indian founders of a special event called the Sacred Run. It is a cross-country run to raise awareness, as well as money, for Gulf Coast victims of Katrina and support Native American educational programs.

As you know from all the times Floyd and I have told you whenever he visits us, Dennis Banks, Floyd, and I have played together since the late 60s for countless Native American events, and it was another great reunion to be with them, as well as Oneida American Indian comedian and old friend Charlie Hill and actor Peter Coyote, who was the host. Charlie Hill remembers visiting the farm twenty years ago when you were little and sends his love. So do Floyd, Dennis Banks, Dennis's sister, and a bunch of other people who are here.

The concert tonight will include Native American performers, local musicians, an amazing Japanese drum ensemble, English rocker Pete Sears (formerly with Hot Tuna and Jefferson Airplane), and performers from all across the country, as well as Europe, Asia, and Australia. It is already a sold out house (unlike the events we did in the late 60s, 70s, 80s, and early 90s, when only a handful of people would attend events for American Indian benefit concerts when Floyd Red Crow Westerman, Dennis Banks, and I first began doing programs together nearly forty years ago). In 2006, there is an interest and desire to support the needs and goals of our Native Americans that includes a true cross section of our society.

Last night when I got off the plane, I went directly to North Beach. I mingled with a wild assortment of poets, rock musicians, painters, unemployed actors, bearded bandanna-wearing Che Guevara look-alike revolutionaries (with trust funds), and Bay Area boulevardiers looking for a Saturday night good time (as a reward to themselves for putting in their forty hours during the week of hard work).

After being smothered by San Francisco's special crazy charms until dawn, reveling in the atmosphere created by a small army of local bon vivants outdoing me until the sun was coming up, I flashed back to what Charlie Parker told me in 1952 when I was a twenty-one-year-old kid, and he was visiting my crowded basement apartment in Washington, D.C. After one of his fans had spilled a glass of wine on Parker's shoes while kneeling down on the floor to pay Parker homage, then losing his balance and collapsing onto the floor, Parker calmly said to me, while cleaning off his shoes, taking it all in stride, that no matter how wild the late night/early morning environment of the jazz scene was, "Ignore foolishnesss. Just stay with the music."

Even so, in the midst of all this good-natured merriment last night, I realized that even if Charlie Parker was right, North Beach remains an irresistible, as well as nutty combination of laid-back living, fun-loving people, and genteel suburban-style Beatness. It remains a little patch of urban heaven. I love being back here, even if only for thirty-six hours, and know what a good time you would be having, as you did when you were here a few years ago when you spent the afternoon with Lawrence Ferlinghetti.

North Beach and many other old neighborhoods in San Francisco are places where, in spite of the astronomical cost of living, the artists of my youth a half century ago who worked and lived there, as well as those like myself who visited there whenever they could, are still celebrated today, even though the life of an aspiring artist in the late 40s and early 50s wasn't nearly as comfortable or acceptable to the society as a whole, as it is now for the new generation in today's boho North Beach scene.

Returning to San Francisco always brings back precious memories of when I first was there for three months in the summer of 1948, when I hitchhiked out from the East to visit my high school sweetheart, worked as a carpenter's helper, played music at night after work, and spent time on the weekends wandering around North Beach, meeting artists of all disciplines who were such outsiders that while they were nearly invisible to society at large, they were accessible to anyone who wanted to meet and learn from them, even to a teenager like me.

Fifty-eight years later, while everything in America seems to change every month, the beauty of San Francisco remains timeless, and North Beach still remains a mecca to people from all over the world as a place where artists of all disciplines are honored. Streets are named after poets, and Jack Kerouac's original scroll for *On the Road* is currently being exhibited in the city and is getting a tremendous amount of attention. People all love seeing it!!

I still have the picture Chris Felver took on the wall of your old room at the farm from when you were in North Beach in San Francisco and you and Lawrence Ferlinghetti were hanging out and Chris Felver took that wonderful photo of the both of you communing. When I get back home in two days, I'll look at it and feel like I'm back in North Beach with you.

Lawrence Ferlinghetti asked all about you, and I told him that you liked the poetry/music collaboration CD/ DVD *Pictures of the Gone World* that he and I did together a few years ago. His reading was great, as are his words. He wants to hear your songs, so we have to send him a CD of your latest. Chris Felver sends his love too and wants to hear your new songs as well. And so do I!!

I send you love along with the sweet sounds of seals calling to you from the Bay, floating over the foggy San Francisco hills to the rolling slopes of Brooklyn where I know you are being creative as always and helping to save America with everything you do.
Daddy

Mobile, Alabama, March 5, 2006
Dear Adira,

Greetings from sunny downtown Mobile. It was so nice to get your lovely letter two weeks ago and I would have answered PRONTO but since I am my own secretary, I can't fire myself or ... I WOULD BE SUED FOR AGE DISCRIMINATION!!!!!

I am just on the way back from several sleepless days and nights of events in Florida and Alabama. We had an exciting bunch of concerts in the northern part of the state of Florida, which is still farmland, where you hear southern accents, even the fast food places still serve grits, and strangers greet you with smiles. Many refer to it as

Old Florida. The Florida Panhandle is more like William Faulkner's descriptions of Mississippi than the Florida seen on *Miami Vice*.

In northern Florida, there is not yet a preponderance of snake-eyed real-estate developers, snarling New Yorkers, or frenzied tourists. You actually meet people who were born here and who want to stay and don't want to see strip malls, fast food emporiums, and condo-mania take away what little rural paradise they still have. There are huge trucks parked along the highways, stacked full of fresh vegetables just picked, selling customers crates of giant strawberries, bags of oranges, grapefruit, and mangos. Truckers still pick up hitchhikers, and there are country music stations playing trucker's songs you can hear at the truck stops as their drivers stop to savor some super-delicious truck-stop high cholesterol delicacies, washed down with high octane black coffee, accompanying huge off-the-charts high-calorie home cooked pies, cakes, and pastries.

The television shows that you can see in any of their funky motel rooms have more religion channels than you ever knew existed, and include some of the fieriest, hoopingest-hollering old-time soul savers. The fuel crisis doesn't seem to stop the huge motor homes and pickup trucks towing gigantic, often homemade, trailers from driving from all over to come and camp out in this part of the deep south which is still so beautiful and unspoiled.

Our tour ended with a Saturday night special concert in Mobile, Alabama, where I conducted an excellent chamber orchestra in music of Mozart, Telemann, Borodin, Haydn, Pachelbel, Scott Joplin, and Duke Ellington (I played piano, *dumbek*, and pennywhistles with the orchestra as well as conducting them), including the appearance of a special guest, Mobile native Lil Greenwood. She is a national treasure and revered in her hometown. At the age of eighty-two, she sounds as vibrant as she did during the years when she sang with Duke Ellington. She joined us on *Summertime*, which I arranged for orchestra. I'll come back to Mobile this summer to record with her. She sings with a remarkable energy and passion and is a one-woman encyclopedia of music, combining spontaneity, sanctified church styling, classic jazz phrasing, and something indefinable of her own. Somehow, we are going to make a CD together this summer called *Lil Greenwwood and David Amram: Back to my Roots*. She will get all great local musicians, I'll bring Adam down with me to play congas, and we'll make a live in-the-studio recording that will sound like a real live performance, with almost everything done in one take. She is magical and we had such a natural rapport I am already hearing what we can do in my head.

During the brief time we spent together, she told me of her journeys when leaving her hometown of Mobile to go out in the world to try to make music and her adventures that led her to traveling the world with Duke Ellington and his orchestra for years, finally coming home to Mobile and being rediscovered, becoming a hometown hero, and doing community work to try to show kids about a higher path in life through the music and the history of those who created it.

This concert was the finale of David Amram Week in Mobile, where they showed films for which I composed the scores, as well as an exhibition of photos, articles, etc., about my life and music. It was like attending my own memorial ... WITHOUT THE DRAG OF EXPIRING!!!!

The orchestra for this tour was a group of terrific young virtuoso soloists, now all living in Florida. It was a true international group, and I was the only member on the tour that was born in the United States. The players came from Rumania, Mexico, Israel, Brazil, Honduras, Venezuela, Japan, Uzbekistan, and Mexico. They were as enthusiastic and as thrilled as I was to be seeing new places and bring great music to communities where live music of any genre is a rarity. When we all said good-bye after the final concert, I felt like they were my own kids. Many of them have solo careers and don't usually play in orchestras, and I am never sure who will be playing in our next concert, but the rewarding thing is that when you go through a grueling tour and play great music together, it forms a special bond for life, and now I have that with a group of musicians who for the most part are fifty years younger than me.

I have to leave at the crack of dawn tomorrow morning to get back to New York but hope the next time to stay longer. Even with the devastation of Katrina, Mobile is still a gem, and the ghosts and enduring spirits of the great blues and gospel pioneers, as well as the jazz and country masters of the past, are still part of that southern magic that fills the night air.

We can all get together when I visit the three of you in Brooklyn, and I want to hear some of the new monologues, comedy sketches, and songs you are writing!

Big hugs from your senior-bopper fan base president
Daddy

Denver, May 17, 2006

Dear Adira, Alana, and Adam,

This is a letter to all three of you to let you know that I am still the same promising young composer who thinks about the three of you every day wherever I am and wish I were in Brooklyn right now to join you for some Middle Eastern food or Polish delicacies.

When I get back from Denver, we'll do that!

I just got back from Latvia, and it was worth waiting seventy-five-and-a-half years to get there for the first time. The symphony concert I went there to conduct was in the town of Liepaja, a two-hour drive from Riga, the capitol of Latvia.

An oboe player from the Liepaja Symphony met me at the airport after a LONG series of connecting flights and drove both the cello soloist, Yosif Feigelson, and me from Riga to Liepaja at about one hundred miles per hour on a two-lane highway through some of the prettiest farmland I have ever seen. I closed my eyes every time he passed another car whose driver was only going ninety miles per hour, especially when there was a car coming the other way, with only one lane for each direction. But we made it and I was told that this is the Latvian driving style, since everyone seems to have faith that they will always get to their destination if they drive fast enough.

Liepaja is right on the western tip of the country, and the fresh salt sea air from the Baltic fills the old streets with a the smell of the ocean that makes you feel like you are on board an old fishing boat way out beyond the horizon, like an old nineteenth-century whaling town in New England.

Invigorated and energized by the salt sea air while walking all over town, I saw some three hundred-year-old brown buildings made of wood that have been boarded up but still preserved, which were miraculously not bombed by either the Germans or the Russians, when they were fighting one another during World War II.

Even though there is a huge Russian population in Latvia (in some towns as much as 95 percent), the original Latvian people have somehow been able to preserve their language and history, and all the signs are in still in Latvian, even when the businesses are owned by Russians.

In Liepaja, old houses and churches sit as they have for ages on the small winding side streets, and a few Russian monster gray office buildings that were used by the KGB and government officials of the old Soviet empire sit like menacing fortresses or angry watchdogs, still exuding bad totalitarian vibes. (Whether right or left wing, the old repression still casts a pall when you walk by these huge depressing structures.) They are counterbalanced by many young people who wear a mixture of Eastern European clothes and a wild assortment of mismatching 1960s London Soho accessories, faded jeans, and even straw cowboy hats made in Taiwan.

I passed a young woman on the street who was rapping away in Latvian to her companion while pushing a baby carriage, and she was wearing a faded East Hampton Beach Club T-shirt that matched her dyed purple hair, so the United States is slowly having some of our cultural contributions appearing in these parts.

One small video store had an earsplitting sound system with rap music being screamed in Russian and Latvian, as office workers walked by on their way back from work, seemingly paying no attention.

I didn't see one McDonald's or Starbucks, and the little shops, the fishing boats that line the canal going out to sea, and the old streets all seem to still be suspended in time. When eating the best fish dinner I have had in years, the waitress, who looked like the Latvian women bobsledders and weight lifters you see on TV during the Olympics, burst into a beatific smile after I said a few sentences to her in my three newly acquired Latvian phrases, and a few seconds later raced off to watch the TV set in the restaurant, following a series of bloodcurdling screams from the other patrons, who were watching the broadcast of the ice hockey championships.

These primal squeals of ecstasy and shouts were the first loud voices I heard here, as the Latvians are very reserved (at least before drinking hours at dusk), but I was told that they all freak out when ice hockey is being played, especially when their country's team is involved.

I wish I could have stayed longer to see the whole country. I have been told that there are still two hundred original natives called the Liv people, who still have their own language and reside in three little villages in Latvia. A handful of old-timers are preserving their ancient culture, which was predominant from the tenth to the thirteenth centuries. I will try the next time I get here to Latvia again to see if I can learn at least one tune of their old music.

The capitol city of Riga, 150 miles from here, is a boomtown now, with Russian tourists flooding the streets, as well as other people from around the world who come to party, but Liepaja still retains the old-time style, and is a true Latvian blast from the past!!

There are wrecked remains of abandoned crumbling buildings that were synagogues throughout towns all over Latvia, and now descendants of these people are returning to live there again.

Now there is a new Jewish community returning there, and this concert is to celebrate both the rebirth and cultural contributions of the past and a new beginning.

I was asked to be the conductor for this special concert, doing works by Mendelssohn, Ernest Bloch, Leonard Bernstein, and my own symphony *Songs of the Soul* as well as my piece "Sinai Desert Song" based on the traditional Middle Eastern classic dance melody "Aya Zehn." For this piece, following a conventional symphony program, cellist Yosif Feigelson (who has performed the solo cello in Bloch's "Schelomo") improvised in the Middle Eastern style and I played the *shanai, hallil, tambor,* and *dumbek* with the orchestra accompanying us for the grand finale.

Our concert was memorable, and the Jewish communities we honored through the music we performed were remembered and celebrated that night as part of a tribute to the contributions of all those of the Jewish faith who were decimated during World War II. Hopefully, the concert will remind everyone how these people helped to build many of the urban areas in the entire country of Latvia. In the town of Liepaja, the whole Jewish population was killed in World War II, so this was a special night for the city, as well as for Yosif Feigleson, whose family was from there.

As always, the music was a healing force that brought everyone together. It was a warm and wonderful hard-working group of musicians who love to play, and the symphony orchestra was WAILIN' at rehearsals, and at the concert they were SMOKIN'!!!!! We got six curtain calls and three encores. It was incredible!!

And for the party after the concert for the musicians, I found some members of the Liepaja Symphony who could play jazz, so we had a small jam session after a heavy night of symphonic music, and I was able to share with the Latvian cats (and kitties) some of THE SOULFUL BEAUTY SIDE of America, when we played music by Thelonious Monk and Errol Garner together.

After the concert Saturday night, May 13, I left the next morning from Latvia, got off the plane at JFK that night, and then left NYC six hours later at dawn to get back to the University of Denver in time to kick off a program on Monday night called "The Mysteries of Jewish Music," for Judaic Studies scholars from all over the country, who all came to Denver. I was the opening speaker and performer, having arrived in Denver just in time to get off the plane, change clothes, and then host this event at the university a few hours later.

With all the upcoming events until June 3 at the University of Denver and in the community, I am still finding time to finish writing the last few two chapters of my new book and compose every day!

It is a privilege to try to spread something positive through music in these difficult times, and I know you all feel the same way when you perform your music. I'll be doing a program in the same yea-saying spirit as I did in Latvia this coming weekend—a whole different kind of concert in a whole different part of the world—conducting members of the Austin Symphony at the Kerrville Music Festival, where my *Theme and Variations on Red River Valley for Flute and Strings* will be performed there again, returning to where it was first played fifteen years ago. We will also be doing pieces by Jimmy LaFave, Bobby Bridger, and various Texas songwriters accompanied by the orchestra. It will be different than conducting the orchestra in Leipaja.

Most folks don't speak Latvian in Kerrville, Texas, or Denver, Colorado, but ... they ALL SPEAK MUSIC!!

So until our paths cross in Bushwick, Brooklyn, when I drive into Big Town to see you all again for a another hot meal and more cool conversations, I send all three of you lots-a Latvian love from all the places music still takes me to on that endless road around the world. Liepaja, Latvia, was one of them ... a FAR OUT as well as a FAR AWAY place

Again, with lots-a Latvian love from the recent memories of being in downtown Liepaja, the high cholesterol capitol of the Baltic nations, I send the three of you my 2006 Putnam Valley, NY/Denver, Colorado/Kerrville, Texas-style Nouveau-cowboy-ology/Fatherly hugs...
Daddy

Putnam Valley, NY, September 30, 2006

Dear Alana and Adira:

I'm back, and as Adam must have told you, we had a great time with Willie Nelson, Neil Young, Dave Matthews, John Cougar Mellencamp, and all the other musicians and supporters of Farm Aid. You know how I have done it for the past twenty years, but I don't know if I ever told either of you about how I ever came to play for the first time at Farm Aid with Willie in Lincoln, Nebraska, on September 19, 1987.

A few months prior to the Lincoln, Nebraska, concert, I was in Austin, Texas. I had been invited to Austin by Jerry Jeff Walker to conduct members of the Austin Symphony and play with him at a fundraiser at the Paramount Theater. Willie Nelson was also playing at the same fundraiser with his guitarist Grady Martin. After the concert was over, Willie invited me to come and play with him in Lincoln, Nebraska, for Farm Aid III, and I have been doing it ever since.

In addition to the joy of playing with Willie Nelson and his band, this year's concert in 2006 was a really special one for me because it was held in Camden, New Jersey, only half an hour drive from across the river to our old 160-acre family farm in Feasterville, Pennsylvania, where I grew up between 1937 and 1942, before your grandfather Philip Amram sold the farm and moved to Washington, D.C. I have showed you both pictures of it many times, and have told all three of you all the stories and adventures that your Aunt Mariana and I had growing up there.

Now there are no more farms in Feasterville or any of the surrounding areas of that part of Pennsylvania at all, but the memories stay with me so strongly that every time I get within a few miles of our old farm, as I did at this latest Farm Aid concert in Camden, I can still feel that special magic of those boyhood days and nights in Feasterville. The fields, full of vegetables and rows of corn, were as beautiful as any painting in the Louvre Museum in Paris, with the colors of the rolling summer landscape, all shades of green and tan blending into the clear blue sky and puffy white and gray clouds with the bright colors of the farm equipment.

When we finished the last of our chores, the evening air was so sweet with the smell of newly mown hay, accompanied by the music of the crickets, frogs, cows mooing, and chickens clucking through the night, followed by a rooster crowing out a wake-up call at dawn.

These are some of the indelible memories of growing up on our farm that I still carry with me through the sixty-five years since we left. I remember how at midnight, when I lay in bed, dreaming that someday I would travel to some of the far-off places that Uncle David always told us he had been to when he was shipping out as a merchant seaman, I looked up at the old wainscot yellow walls of my room and felt a constant sense of motion, almost as if I were on an ocean liner at night, slowly but steadily moving through some invisible sea, but rather than relying on engines or sails, I felt that I was actually on board, traveling somewhere, powered by the energy of the crops growing slowly but surely.

During those late summer nights in Feasterville, back in the late 1930s, I was sure I could *hear* the corn and soybeans I had planted actually growing by the minute, before going down in the morning to see how much taller they were. The farm, during the growing season, had a special energy of an indefinable life force, as the crops miraculously rose from the soil, complemented by the daily growth of the livestock.

That's one of the main reasons I wanted all three of you to grow up on our little farm in Putnam Valley, so that wherever you went later on in your life's journey, you would be connected to that spiritual part of life that is the gift of living in the country on a farm, no matter how small the farm is. I remember the first year our corn came up in 1985 when you were both little. I carried Adam on my shoulders and we walked between two rows of sweet corn we had all planted together, with the corn stalks towering above us. You both said you could feel what I had always described to you that I had felt when I was nine years old and had planted my seven acres of corn.

I told you then that when I walked between rows of full-grown corn, it felt like I was under the arches of a cathedral, with the dark green stalks loaded with ears of corn bringing a sense of protection and blessing from some kind of higher power. As all of us walked together beneath two rows of our fully-grown corn, I remember you both saying, "I can feel it, Daddy."

I hope all three of you will always be able to keep this awareness of the beauty that surrounds us in all of nature and remember to treasure that blessing. It is a treasure that can't be bought or sold, because, as the Native Americans say, it is a gift to all of us from the Great Creator.

Back in the 1930s, there were no New Age guidebooks telling you how to talk to your plants and animals, but all the neighboring farmers would be sure to make you aware of this nonverbal communication that takes place every day on a farm, with the telepathic conversations the farmers had with every cow, horse, chicken, turkey, duck, and goat, each in their own special language. And eventually, you could learn these languages as well.

If you had animals to take care of yourself, every day during the winter, you shared the warmth of the cows as they stood patiently in their unheated stalls, while you milked them in the chilly mornings. Each of them had their own personalities, and so did all the other animals.

All these memories played themselves back to me as I stood backstage at the Tweeter Center in Camden with Adam, during the early evening of the all-day concert, and stared across the river at the glaring skyline and garish lights of downtown Philadelphia, my place of birth.

As I waited to go on stage to play with Willie and his band, I had a brief astral journey in my imagination. I felt as if I were taking a helicopter ride from the backstage area and soaring over the crowd of one hundred thousand people, to fly a few miles to where our farm used to be. After hovering over it for a few minutes, I then imagined I would fly back to the Tweeter Center in Camden by the banks of the Delaware River, pausing for a moment over the house in North Philadelphia where my grandfather was born. This old house in Germantown is where his father worked as a ship's chandler after serving in the Georgia Rifles during the Civil War and then working his way up north from Savannah, Georgia, to Philadelphia.

Many of the stage hands and people who worked at this Farm Aid concert had the pronounced Philadelphia accents of my relatives who still live there, similar to the more countrified way that people spoke seventy years ago in nearby Feasterville during my childhood there. Random conversations backstage made me think I was in a time warp and back at the farm again.

I had a picture of me milking a cow in the fall of 1937 on the back of my *Southern Stories* CD, as well as in my book *Vibrations*. During the daylong concert when I wasn't playing, I showed the picture to many of the musicians and Farm Aid organizers and activists who attended the event, and it brought gales of chuckles.

As I sat on Willie's bus just before we played the closing set of the concert at 11:00 p.m., Willie and I talked about what we both did as kids growing up in farming communities. Willie grew up in Abbot, Texas. I told him about milking cows by hand when I was a kid.

"I did that too," he said, smiling.

I showed Willie the 1937 photo my father had taken of me for the 4-H club, where I was huddled under my cow on a small metal stool, milking away.

"I look a little older now," I said.

"We all do," said Willie. "But we'll keep on working for the family farmers."

Then Willie talked about the endurance of Farm Aid, since the very first Farm Aid concert in Urbana, Illinois, in 1985. He said that while so many causes seem to come and go, Farm Aid is still here, stronger than ever, and how, during the other 364 days of the year between the annual concerts, the Farm Aid organization continues to help family farmers and receives support from union organizers, environmentalists, ecologists, church groups, educational outreach programs, and small business organizations across the country, as well as communicating with supporters from Canada, South America, and overseas.

In 2006, during a time when both globalization and Corporate Think seem to have engulfed the world, Farm Aid is a joyous reaffirmation of basic values inherent in the struggles of the family farmer. These values are about maintaining high individual standards, tireless work, and respect for the land and all the people on earth who are fed from what is grown on that land.

The familial way of life shared by farmers and their community are ideals put into daily practice that everyone of *every* political persuasion can relate to. Whether you are bedrock conservative or an anarchist, you still need to drink unpolluted water, eat non-carcinogenic food and dairy products, and meat that will not genetically alter you or your children and eventually their children. Support of family farmers and all that they have to offer transcends politics. It has to do with our shared survival. Family farmers EAT WHAT THEY GROW THEMSELVES, AND DRINK THE MILK THEY PRODUCE FROM THEIR OWN COWS.

The information that Farm Aid makes available to the general public shows clearly that corporate farming annihilates the soil by not rotating crops to replenish that soil, while adding poisonous chemicals that pollute water supplies. Added to this toxic cocktail are the hormones and antibiotics fed to the animals to maximize production. Corporate farming has also decimated communities, as well as families, and the values that they maintain. The old-fashioned ideals practiced every day by the family farmers of America are essential for the well-being of all people who live in the cities of our country.

Progress, the catchall justification used by corporate farming to convince us that we will have to pay less for groceries, should not have to force even one acre of land in the United States to become a toxic disaster zone.

It certainly doesn't seem worth the risk of making our children's children become genetically impaired because of untested chemical alterations of milk, meat, and vegetables, all justified as the price we have to pay for high-tech efficiency agribusiness to flourish and give the consumer better bargains. I know this all sounds crazy, but this is what we are told is the reason for adding growth hormones and all kinds of chemicals to produce everything we end up eating. Farm Aid makes us aware of what is happening and gives us a picture of what we can do to halt this destructive pattern by preserving the family farmers who still take pride in what they produce and feel a sense of responsibility to the American public. All of us who come to play for the farmers hope that, as your forebears from Savannah and North Carolina used to say, "We are the honey that draws the flies."

Willie and all those who participate in Farm Aid prove that it is still possible for people of various disciplines to unite in a common cause, work together and make a difference. I remember how both of you and Adam handed out Farm Aid literature at our annual 4-H fair in Putnam County from the vegetable booth where we were roasting corn. We'll do it again next July.

I played the last set and grand finale, performing with Willie and his peerless band, and after saying good-bye to all, packed up at 1:30 a.m. and headed back with Adam to the farm. As we drove down the New Jersey Turnpike, I almost got off at exit 6 to drive by our old place in Feasterville, which was only a few miles away. I wanted Adam to see where my father's farm used to be, even though there is not one inch left of it. Now there are wall-to-wall condos where I once planted seven acres of my own corn patch to sell, along with my sister's homemade lemonade at our roadside stand on Bustleton Pike at the foot of our farm.

I told Adam how lucky I was to have the memories of that time and place, and that maybe what we did at Farm Aid might enable a farmer somewhere to be able to hang on to his farm, and that the next time we were in that part of Pennsylvania, we would drive by and see the old stone house where we once lived, which is now the office space, nestled between ninety-two condos, as if it were the center of a gigantic accordion, with the condos piled up on either side.

But I kept on driving instead, because I had to get up the next morning to resume composing and writing. As we approached New York City, I flashed back to the dreams I had of someday being able to go on that silver train called The Crusader that roared past our farm on the way to a mythical place called New York, a city that I had only seen in the movies, and possibly do something in music some day.

As we passed the Manhattan skyline on the way to the George Washington Bridge to take the highway upstate, I realized again, as I do each day, what a blessing it is to be able to have lived in New York for thirty-seven years and learn all the lessons that New York teaches us all.

Now back for three days, I send love from Peekskill Hollow Farm, as October's fall farewell to summer inches me closer to my big seventy-six this coming November 17. I'm so lucky to have the good fortune to do more work than ever, and to have three such great kids to share my blessings with.

Dizzy Gillespie told me when I played for his seventieth birthday party at Wolftrap that the gig for all of us senior-boppers lucky enough to be going nonstop in our seventies is to be of some use to *others*.

Diz put it this way: "David, in 1951 when we met, you were a kid. Now, you got grey hair. You're getting older. It's time for you to put something back in the pot."

That's something we can all do at any age, all the time, and it is fun trying to do it. That's what I'm doing now, writing this letter to both of you, while taking a break from composing, before heading out to Lowell, MA, this Thursday, Oct 5, for the annual Lowell Celebrates Kerouac Festival.

You are still my two favorite farm gals, even if you have now become prominent city-hillies, and if any of us ever wins the lotto, we can buy a farm with some flat land and grow everything organic the way we did when we were all together.

You are always in my heart.
Daddy

Putnam Valley, NY, Feb 17, 2007
Dear Mari:
As the February cold air seeps through the floorboards here at home at the farm, I

am finishing writing you a short note, which I began writing to you after returning from Lowell just a few weeks ago.

That's when we ended the action packed two-week trip for thirty-five students from the State University of New York in Potsdam, who traveled six thousand miles from upstate NY to San Francisco, Denver, New York, and Lowell as the grand finale in the course created by Dr. Audrey Sprenger, which was called "Jack Kerouac Wrote Here: Crisscrossing America Chasing Cool," sponsored by the State University of Potsdam, New York.

Obviously, our trip with the thirty-five students was much easier to negotiate than Kerouac's sporadic hitchhiking and crazed one hundred-mile-an-hour marathon driving adventures with Neal. And the students got to see some of the treasures of our country, as well as meeting some terrific people. Even with all the changes that have occurred since Jack began his travels sixty years ago, much of the America that he embraced, with its myriad people and places, still remains the same, in spite of the uniformity that continues to diminish our physical landscape and all the beautiful flavors and endless variety of our precious cultural mosaic.

After zipping across the country, the grand finale of the tour to Jack's hometown of Lowell was a real eye-opener for everyone.

From Cotes Market, the old French Canadian store where homemade beans are cooked and where they still make traditional French-Canadian delicacies, to the commemorative park with the stone obelisks set with all his writings, to the mills where his mother worked, to the gravesite, to the Stations of the Cross up on the hill where he went to French school, to visiting his old high school, to the joyous afternoon of poetry and music at the Cafe Paradiso where we honored Lowell Celebrates Kerouac with music and readings, to the tours of the city and other seminars and concerts, the beauty of Lowell and how it inspired Jack and how Jack now inspires Lowell ... all of this was memorable.

The unfailing hospitality of everyone towards this bunch of eager kids made me recall how Jack himself was always someone who would take the time to make others feel that they were appreciated and welcome in his presence.

Now it is great to be back home at the farm in blessed anonymity, working away and enjoying waking up and knowing where I am. I still have dreams of our cross-country trip on the train from Denver to New York, and recall waking in the wee hours, as the Pullman car swayed as if it were hurtling off the tracks. It was so exciting seeing America rolling by out the window of the train, and absorbing the beauty of the countryside at night, accompanied by the sounds of the lonely whistle and clickety-clack of the wheels on the rails, waiting for the sun to rise.

And then, following nonstop frenzied activities day and night in New York City, where I showed the kids where so much has happened artistically in the last fifty years, arriving in Lowell and seeing the look on the faces of the thirty-five young people when they got to this mystical old mill town where Jack grew up in the 1930s, and watching them become immersed in that special feeling that Lowell still has in 2007.

Every time I return from Lowell, I always want to go back there as soon as possible. It is always energizing. Being there makes me look forward to hitting the road again, and in a few days I will, at various gigs of all kinds where I can share with young people the blessings of my life, as well as all my seventy-six years of adventures and what they taught me, which include all the good times, people, and places I experienced during the twelve years that I knew as well as collaborated with Kerouac, as well as so many of the people he wrote about in his books.

Most of these programs I am asked to do today are decidedly non-"Beat" events, held at music schools, festivals, and concerts where those who hire me are not aware of (or interested in) what I was blessed to share with Jack, and the people who hire me are usually equally unfamiliar with the importance of Lowell in EVERYTHING Jack did, but by the time I leave ... they ARE informed.

And I always try to make them aware that Jack was not only a great artist whose work endures on the basis of its own merits, but that he was, among other things, a reporter for so many of the artists of *all* genres of our era, whom history has shown were also much more gifted and hard-working free spirits than the catch-all stereotypical cliché "Beat" implies.

Now, as I finally finish writing you another short, informative, and well-crafted letter, I'm just back from my stint as composer in residence for the University of Tulsa, Oklahoma, one of the many treasures of America that is far enough off the radar to still have a lot of SOUL.

I have been so swamped that I am just now answering some of my mail, since before the Tulsa excursion, I was in Los Angeles, where I went to play an hour and a half musical tribute to two old friends, Jerry Stiller and Anne Meara, who just had a star with their names on it put into the sidewalk for the Hollywood Walk of Fame. I was invited to come and play for the celebration at the reception for them, and fortunately I was free and able to do it.

Fifty years ago, in the summer of 1957, we were all together working for the first season of The New York Shakespeare Festival's free Shakespeare in the Park. Jerry Stiller and Ann Meara (just married, but not yet Stiller and Meara, as they became nationally known later on) were acting in all three Shakespeare plays being done that season, and I was the composer of all the scores for those memorable first productions.

Ever since that first summer, the three of us have remained friends for the past half a century, and I was hired by the television company that produces *King of Queens*, starring Jerry, to come with my trio from New York to surprise Jerry and Annie for a reception honoring them after they had their stars placed into the sidewalk. Their two kids, Ben and Amy, and Ben's wife were there as well, and Jerry sent you his love.

After the near-zero weather of last week at the farm, being in good ol' HollyWeird's balmy days and nights was truly, as they say in Spanish (or *should* say if they don't) ... El change of Pace!!!

Like almost everyone who has been there, I can't help loving downtown Hollywood every time I return. Its total craziness is irresistible. All the hair weaves, plastic surgery, dyed coiffures, capped teeth, and crazed stoned-out looking people in sunglasses stalled in traffic in their convertibles, raggedy palm trees gasping for oxygen through the smog, and the ghosts of old Tinseltown glamour, now as faded a memory as the role played so beautifully by Gloria Swanson as the diva-heroine of *Sunset Boulevard,* remind me how our whole generation was brought up during the Great Depression, and thought of Hollywood and Vine as the mythical magical epicenter of a faraway kingdom of endless pleasure.

You remember, when we lived at the farm, how Artie McCrae and all the guys I knew in Feasterville would work all week, skimp and save every penny and collect bottles, and do anything to be able go to the Saturday matinees at that old movie theater in nearby Frankfort, pooling all our money so that one of us could buy a ticket and then open up a side door to let everyone else sneak in for free (we never did that with you because you were always too ladylike for such nefarious activities) and then we would all wallow in that heavenly dark place of Saturday Matinee Dream Land to be hypnotized as we watched double features until the theater finally closed down that night, oblivious to everything that had ever happened in our lives, as if we were in some sacred mecca, totally taken over by the whole world that Hollywood created for us.

The movies that had scenes featuring the old Hollywood locales seemed as powerful on the screen to us as the Vatican is to worshippers today when they first arrive in Rome and make the voyage to that holy place. I remember how the old hustlers who created Old Hollywood would sometimes appear on screen and address all of us hicks as if they were great world leaders welcoming us to see their movies.

For all of us non–New Yorkers, we were mesmerized, in our hayseed ignorance, by their Brooklyn-tinged oratory as they initiated us into the inner sanctum of the kingdom of Hollywood.

Today, as the global entertainment industry has made even the most plastic and untalented people part of their corporate tasteless forgettable productions, looking back at the shabby remains of what was once the vibrant center of an empire created by cigar-chomping first-generation escapees from the garment district, makes you feel a nostalgia for those trashy days of yore. They provided us with dreams and hopes and escape from hard times, and some really gifted people created enduring works of cinematic art that still remain moving today.

Jerry and Anne are real artists who have been in every medium of entertainment and always give glowing performances and bring joy and excellence to everything they do. They are also warm, loving, loyal friends who never lost their ideals and are as down-to-earth as anyone could be, never spoiled or cynical, always sailing through hard times and success with grace and humor, and spreading kindness to everyone they cross paths with. I am grateful I could be there to play for them as a thank you to two lifetime friends.

After arriving at 4:00 p.m. West Coast time and leaving at 4:00 p.m. the next day, when we were done playing for Jerry and Anne, I returned home to the farm and worked nonstop without interruption until leaving for my three-day round the-clock residency at the University of Tulsa School of Music.

It was a whirlwind marathon of my classical music being performed, as well as soloing at the opening concert for the new Oklahoma Jazz Hall of Fame. The university big band played my music, including my version of "Home on the Range," done with Afro-Cuban rhythms (the *guaguanco* and *comparse*) and all kinds of great jazz harmonies. That's the one you have the recording of with Odetta singing, Ramblin' Jack Elliot yodeling, and my Afro-Cuban band.

I hope that all I did to encourage the young composers, classical players, and jazz and folk players gave them all a new look at cowboyology, since they are the grandkids and great-grandkids of the original cowpokes and cowgals who were part of the old West, so much of which disappeared in Oklahoma when the Dust Bowl of the 30s decimated most families. There are beautiful musical regional accents still here from different parts of the state, and a quiet pride and sense of history that makes it unique.

I also did classes in film scoring, classical composition, screenings of the film *Pull My Daisy,* and some individual time with gifted young composers, instrumentalists, and filmmakers of the future. Now I am finally home again, after being stuck in the airport in Chicago and a motel in New York, due to the ice and snow of a *non*-global-warmed two days of wild weather.

I'm not getting much sleep, but having a wonderful time and hopefully can continue to share some of the blessings I was privy to, when I go to the next place to spread some of the great things I have learned from all the wonderful people who showed me so much, and inspired many in our generation to try to do the best that we could and make some kind of contribution.

I really feel lucky that I have so many events to participate in for this banner year of 2007, as well as new commissions for orchestral and chamber works, a major film score, a world premiere of a new symphonic piece, a new book, and concerts of all kinds coming up this year.

Adam and his band, "The New York Howl," are going to England to tour and Alana, Adira, and Adam are all playing at a festival in Texas and have their own CDs coming out. Am I ever proud of them!!

Soon I can rest on *their* laurels.

With all this crazy activity, I don't have enough time to sit down quietly and figure out how to act my age, but ... I'm working on it!!!

We still have to go to the opera and ballet with the kids, as we always talk about doing, and will do it soon! We all deserve one night off a year!

I send love always.
David

Putnam Valley, NY, April 18, 2007

Dear Mari:

Just made it home from the hills of New Hampshire, after playing the Jazzmouth jazz/poetry festival for the third year in a row. It is growing each year, and I drove back through a monster storm with Eric Mingus, the son of Charles Mingus, who gave me my first job in NYC back in the fall of 1955.

We had a wonderful trip driving through the snow and rain and I had the chance to tell him how playing with him the night before was the completion of another great circle as I could feel the spirit of his father through him, urging me on to play my best. Eric has his own special gifts, and is a terrific poet and totally original as a musician and singer ... a true triple threat.

I also had the chance at the festival to accompany Andrei Codrescu, whose poetry and reading is so natural and musical that I knew exactly what to do just by listening and following him, as I did with Kerouac. Like Kerouac, Andrei sees America and the world through fresh eyes and an open heart. He has a way of bringing everyone into the stories he shares in his poetry, and it was a thrill to play with him, as it was to have Eric Mingus play with me on my set, and for me to play with Eric on his. We had no rehearsal for any of the events we did together. We didn't need to. As I told Eric and Andrei, the mantra for making music with others is, "The more you pay attention, the less you have to rehearse."

There was a whole afternoon program at Jazzmouth where local poets and authors from the ages of ten to seventy-five all read their work. Portsmouth is another unheralded treasure chest of talent and community spirit.

The very first night, I arrived after twelve hours of travel through foul weather, got right out of the car with all my bags, walked up on the bandstand, played with Larry Simon's band, and then spoke at a tribute to my old friend, Sun Ra. He would have done the same thing. We were all used to long rides, bunched up together and finally getting to wherever we were to play and having no time to do anything but unpack and start wailing. And no one ever complained. We were there for the music, and those of us still here today always will be.

Larry Simon's band has been together for years. They are always supportive when backing up readers, in addition to being hot players capable of tearing down the house when they play concerts without readers. It is really gratifying to see young artists like Larry Simon create a festival with such high standards.

Larry organizes this whole event each year, giving the chance to scores of young local poets and musicians to shine. He honors the older artists of our generation as well.

Eric and I talked about the concept of intergenerational interchange, and how his father, Charles Mingus, had done the same thing, creating a virtual army of musicians, composers, painters, poets, and everyday people whom he included in his world, and how I, as a twenty-four-year-old hayseed just arrived in New York in 1955, was now an alumnus of the Mingus school who understands, as Eric himself does, that we have an obligation to pass on what we have learned in a positive and joyous way to new generations.

The snow, rain and sleet were coming down as we talked, but we finally hit the New York State border, after passing Danbury and those foothills that looked like they couldn't decode whether it was actually spring yet, seeming almost embarrassed to be caught in the nude with no snow on the ground and no green grass either. We took the back roads from Carmel, went by the reservoirs onto Peekskill Hollow Road, pulled up to the farm, and just made it over the bridge, which was almost under water. I was home again, even if only for a few days.

I told Eric that I am grateful that every time I leave the house, knowing that whatever I go to do ends up being an illuminating experience, as well as a different one each time. For every place I go, I have the chance to try to add something of value to whomever I am with, and in exchange can learn something new wherever I am. And then after I get back home, I can start to sort it all out.

After Eric left to drive up to his new place outside of Woodstock, I began unpacking and thinking about all the things I am blessed to be doing this year. 2007 is a special year and it sure is good to be around to celebrate it. I thank God that when I applied for a reservation to the Man Upstairs in 1994 to continue to be here for the year 2007, I was able to get a confirmation from Him. I am thrilled to still be here today to be part of many of the fiftieth anniversaries coming up. I'm participating in a bunch of them, so I'm glad that my reservation to still be alive didn't get cancelled!

When we were playing the 1994 Beat conference at NYU, I told my old Seventh Army symphony buddy Midhat Serbagi that 2007 would be the fiftieth anniversary of the publication of *On the Road,* as well as the fiftieth of the first summer of the New York Shakespeare Festival's season in Central Park, for which I wrote the music, and the fiftieth of the first jazz/poetry readings ever given in NYC with Jack and me.

"I want to be around for all these events, Midhat, and you should be too. I did the music for the poetry readings and for the first productions of Shakespeare in the Park in '57 and you were right there with me, playing the viola for those first scores I wrote. You played in the recording for the film score of *Pull my Daisy* and you used to come with me to Lucien Carr's house and play all night when we would have our little jam sessions every time Jack came to town. You should be in all these fiftieth anniversary events too."

"Ah-h-h," said Midhat (in his enthusiastic way). "So what. That's history. If we're still alive thirteen years from now in 2007, we should be doing something new."

"By 2007 it will be new," I said. "A whole new generation will be introduced to a whole level that I suspect will be part of the equation in 2007 that is different than right now. The way things are going today in 1994, the full-greed-ahead syndrome of the 90s is burying a lot of history."

"Well, they can't bury me," said Midhat. "I'm like Rasputin. I'm indestructible."

Thirteen years later, Midhat proved that he is indestructible. Today he is playing better than ever and will be doing a bunch of events with me this year and has a group of his own called "Midhat and Company" that plays concerts featuring many genres of music.

After years of work, in between everything else I do, I have finally finished my latest book, *Upbeat: Nine Lives of a Musical Cat,* which will be birthed and delivered in August of this year. Paradigm Publishers is publishing it, and they will also re-issue *Vibrations* and *Offbeat: Collaborating with Kerouac* in paperback in the spring of 2008. So I'll never have to sign any more copies of these two earlier books of mine if they were stolen from libraries or photocopied, or so beat up from flea markets and rummage sales that you couldn't read half of the pages. After Kerouac gave me the wonderful quote in 1968 to use for the cover of *Vibrations,* it was used only once in the Viking Compass short-lived paperback edition in 1971. Kerouac's quote, "A valuable, readable musicologist's tale," will appear for the first time on the cover of the new edition of *Vibrations* in its new incarnation with Paradigm Publishers in 2008.

For some reason, in 1968, when Macmillan first published *Vibrations,* whoever made the decisions didn't think Jack was important enough to use his quote for the original edition and it has taken four decades to have it finally used this way. But since Moses was in the desert for forty years, I am right on schedule!! And I know that if they permitted loud noises in heaven, Jack would be bellowing with laughter, as he so often did, when he experienced how life's crazy twists and turns ended up taking you right back to where you started from.

So by the spring of '08, I'll have all my literary eggs in one basket, as I do with all my classical music being with the same publisher, C.F. Peters, for the last forty-four years. With my three books in print, I'll have a trilogy which hopefully will serve as a way to honor so many of the wonderful people whom I mentioned in all three books. I hope the sum total of all my experiences, with the stories of triumphs and fiascos, will encourage young artists to hang in there and dare to go for it and *never* give up, regardless of what their career counselors tell them, as they try to convince them that they are incapable of ever doing anything creative.

The world premiere for *Symphonic Variations on a Song by Woody Guthrie* is set for September 29, 2007, in San Jose, California, and I am so happy you will be coming out to hear it. Paul Polivnick will conduct it and he is terrific and has championed my music for years. He will lead the orchestra in the first performance of the piece with Symphony Silicon Valley as their season's opener, and I'm so happy that you, your daughter Jessica, and grandkids can all be there. I hope all the rest of the Amram clan can come too.

Paul really knows how to conduct and studies every note, and knows the music cold *before* the first rehearsal. He did my *Triple Concerto for Woodwind, Brass and Jazz Quintets and Orchestra* with the orchestra in San Jose two years ago, and it was so well received that they want to commission me to write a piano concerto for them for January 2009 for pianist John Nakamura and the orchestra.

As you remember, in the summer of 1948 I was a carpenter's helper when I was in Los Gatos, San Jose, and Palo Alto with my high school sweetheart. I worked for Taylor Made Homes, doing carpentry and driving a truck, and had a chance to play some music that summer in the same area. Now, to come back for a world premiere in San Jose, just a few miles from where I worked that summer fifty-nine years ago, is pretty wonderful. And since the orchestra has just commissioned me to write a piano concerto for them to be premiered in January of 2009, I have work to do.

There are all kinds of exciting events for *On the Road* anniversary celebrations this year. On September 7 I'm doing a huge concert in Lowell with my quintet, and two days later, Fenwick Smith, the flutist from the Boston Symphony, is playing my flute concerto, *Giants of the Night,* in Lowell, led by a great young conductor, Kay George Roberts. As you know, the second movement of the concerto contains two French Canadian folk songs that Jack used to sing to me. He told me that he learned them in Lowell as a boy. I'm also going to England this fall two times, for The British library in London as well as for a festival in Leeds, and across the United States all year long to participate in all kinds of events honoring *On the Road.* I'm also appearing in other concerts celebrating our first jazz-poetry readings in NYC in 1957.

Lincoln Center Library is having me celebrate my seventy-seventh birthday November 17 with a concert of all my Shakespearian related music, including excerpts from my opera *Twelfth Night* and music written for the first productions in the park fifty years ago.

Also this year, my first major film score since the one I composed for Kazan's *The Arrangement* in 1969 is part of a truly great feature-length documentary film called *The Frontier Ghandi,* by Teri McLuhan. She is planning to put out a CD of the entire score as soon as the film is released in theaters. I had to wait forty-two years for a CD of my score for *The Manchurian Candidate* to be released, so I am considerably ahead of schedule for the score for *The Frontier Ghandi.* But as the old saying goes, "all good things come to those who wait" (especially if they can stay alive long enough to be on the scene when the good things finally happen). But there's never really a rush. You, of all people, know that the most important thing to do in your life is just to try and do the best work possible every day. That's the only thing you can really control. And that's what you have always done since you were six years old.

When we were young, we were both lucky to meet people who were committed to excellence and who would talk to us. You were away at school when Dimitri Mitropoulos, to whom I dedicated *Vibrations,* told me in 1948 when he visited Mom in Washington, that the four maxims for a life in music are:

"You have to be in the right place at the right time.

You have to always be ready at the moment to do the impossible if necessary.

You have to respect your audience and your colleagues.

And most important: you have to love the music more than you love yourself."

WHEW!!!

And that's actually the way he lived his life.

Bernstein told me in 1966 why he chose me from hundreds of applicants to be the first-ever composer-in-residence with the New York Philharmonic. He said it was because he thought I had something original to offer. Then he said the following, as he lowered his glasses and looked at me with an intense stare that would snap anybody out of their usual daily routine, "But David ... you have to do more as a composer than just please yourself. You have to add to the repertoire. And you have to find your own way of being an ambassador for music to people of all ages, and make them feel welcome to the many worlds of music we both travel in."

Duke Ellington gave me some great advice in 1972, when I conducted the New York premiere of the symphonic version of *Black, Brown and Beige,* which Maurice Peress orchestrated. When I went to see Duke to bring him a tape of my performance of his piece for him to critique, he told me that when young musicians would ask him for advice on how to excel, his answer was "listen."

Of course, our father was the one responsible for making us the crazed but joyous workaholics that we are today. I know you remember what he used to say, when he was putting in his weekend twelve-hour-a-day nonstop work marathons at the farm in the summer months, after working all week in the city. When we used to complain about the heat or wanted to take a break from working with him and go play ball or jump in the stream to cool off, he would turn off the tractor and after a dramatic pause and a terrifying stare, suddenly seemed to go back five thousand years into an Old Testament mode and say softly, "Remember what you learned from Genesis 3:19 in the Bible in Hebrew from your grandfather. I'll say it in English ... 'By the sweat of thy brow thou shalt earn thy bread.'"

If you and I had earned as much bread as we sweated while working all our lives, we'd both be billionaires. But Pop never indicated that you were supposed to work only for money. He felt that work itself was a noble act. Rather than believing in Art for Art's sake, Pop believed in Work for Work's sake. And that idea of Work for Work's sake made me see later on in life that a dedicated artist works tirelessly to hopefully leave a gift to the world. We were lucky to have such a good example as children.

You have always been a great role model for me, in all the things you do so well in your life, as a translator, an editor, and a well-respected book person at Borders for the past twenty-three years, as well as a pioneer feminist, marathon runner, and outstanding sister, mother, and grandmother. So ... I want to be like you when I grow up. We were both so blessed to have such a wonderful mother and father and you are a reflection of them. I hope I am too.

When I go to reunions of high school classmates and Army reunions, I try to encourage everyone to share the miracle of being alive. So often, after the real treat of seeing old friends, the highlight of these events often seems to end up when everyone is asked to sit around in a circle, and one by one talk about preparing for how to deal with the afterlife. OY VEY! I try to lighten up the atmosphere by telling them, when it is my turn to expound, that since I now believe in reincarnation, I am trying to be a vegetarian in this life so I that I can come back in my next life as either an eggplant or an artichoke. That usually cools everybody out and changes the atmosphere from being like a convention for morticians or undertakers. We all need some well-deserved chuckles. Since the *Divine Comedy* is in part about the sunny side of the street, the New Orleans motto *"laissez les bons temps rouler"* is applicable for all occasions. This old French Quarter slang expression, meaning "let the good times roll," may not be the way proper French is spoken, or how it appears in the writings of Racine, Verlaine, and Baudelaire. But the concept and practice of *laissez les bons temps rouler* means that each of us are responsible for creating our own positive environment, and working towards the creation of that is part of the spiritual path we all have to take to avoid the pitfalls of Whineology, Blameology and Greedology (all of which are curable by laughing).

If there is such a place as heaven, I know we're both on a short list to get a timeshare there. At least I know YOU certainly are assured one with a good view, and even if I'm just allowed to visit you as a sinner on probation, we'll walk through the woods again holding hands as we did in 1938 when there was a brush fire that got out of control and we were lost and you found the way out and led me along with you. And we'll also have the chance to see a lot of old friends up there again in the great jazz club in the sky and have a PARTY!

But for the moment, let's enjoy every precious moment here on earth, putting into practice what Dizzy Gillespie told me I should do, when he invited me to play with him for his seventieth birthday at Wolftrap in 1987. He said "David, I met you down here in Washington in the spring of '51 when you were twenty years old. Now you're fifty-six years old and getting some gray hair. You're older now. It's time for you to put something back into the pot."

That's something we can both do. I know you will do it anyway, because you always have. You have always encouraged everyone you have met to celebrate their life and develop their intellect and character. You practice what you preach because you have always had such fine discipline and such a great work ethic. Hearing you practice the piano at the farm in Feasterville always made me conscious that I should try to be more organized and disciplined and concentrate harder, and not just jam out, rather than practicing my lessons, which you always did. I guess I was always a daydreamer. And in many ways I still am.

I suppose today I am like Uncle David was when he was my age, a crazy seventy-six-year-old, driving that old car of his filled with used books all around the East and telling us when he visited us, "I got so excited driving here. When I was driving up that big hill, I thought, oh boy, I can hardly wait to see what's on the other side of the hill when I get to the top."

He was still a merchant seaman in his heart, long after he had stopped shipping out to sea. He was always searching for that Holy Grail. That's what kept him alive and made him so much fun. I guess I'm still searching too, but I'd really like to settle down again, get married again, and live like a normal person, and I know I will. And if I don't this time, I will in my next life. That's what reincarnation is for.

This Friday I go to Rio Grande, Ohio, to the university there for a barnstorming tour where I can see the Bob Evans model farm again and the old white rickety wooden tower, where they used to hold the Annual National Chicken Flying Contest. Between all my events, I'll have a chance to revisit the electric windmill and the Appalachian Studies Center and Brooks Jones's old home in nearby Jackson. Then after the concerts, readings, and seminars there, I'll scoot back to New York, pick up Adira in Brooklyn, and drive up to Potsdam, NY, to the state university by the Canadian border for concerts and workshops and have some real father/daughter time with her, driving up and back. Then I'll hide out at the farm to work on finishing the symphony.

I hope you know how much I care for you, with as much love in my heart for you as I have for my children. Because of the closeness we all share, whether we are all together or apart, I always know that wherever I am in the world, I am always at home, since home IS where the heart is. And you are proof that sisterhood is powerful.

I send love and fragrant springtime breezes full of 2007 energy to you, all the way to your Upper West Side Manhattan hideout from Putnam County's favorite frequent flyer far-out farmer, your little brother David.

Chapter 9

Fond Farewells: Honoring Six Old Friends

I never wanted to write any of these six memorial tributes, but in 2005, four of these wonderful artists left us, and in 2006, another old friend did as well. They all made such a contribution to our culture, and were such wonderful people to know. George Plimpton, the sixth, passed away in 2003.

I tried to honor each of them in a small way, as a thank you for the joy of knowing them, and as a way of honoring their families as well.

It was a special blessing to be with each of them. We can all rejoice that they left the world so much. They enriched our lives through their work. They were people who maintained enduring friendships, while sharing their art and their humanity with others during their lifetimes. They remain an inspiration to succeeding generations.

Remembering Arthur Miller

The day before Arthur Miller died, I had received a phone call from his house, saying that he was coming home from the hospital. His neighbor in Connecticut, Frank McCourt, called me and said he would visit him the following Monday, and I had hoped to join him as well.

It is difficult to even imagine that he has actually left us. Arthur was not only a great artist, but also a warm and honorable for-real person.

He was a great friend, and really an old fashioned idealist who cared about the world and felt that art, artists, and those who appreciate art were all supposed to ennoble and uplift people and make the world better for being there.

He couldn't stand superficiality or phoniness. He was also a proud man who wanted to be appreciated for being the true artist that he was. He never allowed himself to be put in the position of acting like a publicity hound/celebrity/egomaniac/narcissist, or world-famous and therefore an unapproachable person.

He always acted the way we think gifted and accomplished people should be in their lives. He listened to others, always observed everything around him, and was able to laugh at much of the craziness that the world accepts as being normal.

Because of his complete lack of pretension, he was often uncomfortable when surrounded by jaded, selfish people. He had incredibly high standards for the work he did, but could not bear snobbery in any form. So he avoided trendy chi-chi glitterati events, unless they were raising funds for all of the humanistic causes that he always put himself on the line to help.

In all the times I spent with him when we were not working together in the theater, when anyone on the street or anywhere else came up and spoke to him, he *always* responded in a natural and respectful way.

We first got together in 1963 when he chose me to compose the music for his plays *After the Fall* and then *Incident at Vichy,* both of which were done to open the Lincoln Center Theater.

At that time, we had to use the old American National Theatre and Academy (ANTA) Theater in the Village, because the building uptown at the Lincoln Center complex was still under construction. At night we would hang out in the Village after long hours of rehearsals and listen to jazz, folk music, and Middle Eastern music, and talk about the vibrancy of New York's endless series of unpredictable surprises and energy.

For the world premiere of *After the Fall,* which opened the new theater, he and Elia Kazan had gotten back together again, never mentioning to any of us about their falling out as a result of the McCarthy hearings, and it was a glorious time.

Arthur was great to all the actors and musicians and they all loved him as a soulful person as much as they admired him as a true artist. He often talked to me about how he had been a crooner when, as a teenager, he lived in Brooklyn and worked at the Navy Yard during the Depression. He appreciated performers and was an incredible reader himself when he would narrate his latest new play to the cast on the first day of rehearsals.

When I visited him at his farm, we used to take stuff to the town dump in his old Land Rover, and all the people we ran into there talked to him and liked him, because he never was pretentious or snobbish to them. He loved to do farm chores as well as carpentry and cabinet making, and was proud of the studio which he built by himself for his wife Inge, which he converted and restored from an old abandoned silo.

He also showed me the much more modest studio that he built for himself by hand, where he wrote every day for hours.

"This is the same size as the tiny cabin that I rented when I wrote my early work. I realized then that I didn't need that much space in order to write. I still feel that way."

We used to go to Chinatown and Little Italy when he would visit the city, and sometimes he just rang the doorbell and came by my old one-and-a-half-room apartment on 6th Avenue in the Village. We would go next door to the old Art Foods Delicatessen, owned by Igor Sudarsky and his wife, both Holocaust survivors, and Igor and Arthur would talk about world politics, and everyone's search in this country for reconciling old-fashioned values with the American wide-open possibilities of being whoever you wanted to be and the pitfalls of the go-getter philosophy.

He was happier visiting New York, rather than living there, because the frantic pace made it hard for him to concentrate on his writing, which he did every day. But he often talked of how he loved the old remaining neighborhoods of New York, even though by the 60s and 70s you could see that they were all being decimated by gentrification. He was concerned about this, because he really cared about people, and his plays reflect his understanding of what we all go through every day.

Like Bruce Springsteen, Willie Nelson, and Dizzy Gillespie, his public persona was a 100 percent reflection of what he was like in real life. The only thing the public never shared was his great sense of humor. When you were with him alone in a room, he was so much fun to be with: full of life and always warm.

His shyness in public was because he was a modest person. He became upset when strangers and journalists were only interested in speaking to him in order to obtain gossip about Marilyn Monroe, rather than addressing him in the same honest, respectful way that he addressed others.

He seemed aloof at times because he took what he did in life very seriously and felt that being an artist was really an important lifetime pursuit, not a means for obtaining self-indulgent, cheap celebrity status.

Twenty-five years ago, when my first daughter, Alana, was only a few months old, he insisted that I bring her to a very elegant book-launching party where he and his wife, Inge, were being honored.

"Inge and I want to see her, as well as you and your wife," he said over the phone. "And we need a little Amram to liven things up at the publisher's duplex on Park Avenue. Be sure to bring her."

We were last in touch when he e-mailed me on December 22 about not being able to attend my seventy-fourth birthday party celebration in the Village.

This is what he wrote.

Dear David:
 Some impostor has sent me an invitation to a 74th birthday party over your name. This is a likely story but of course it's impossible since the last time I saw you, you were, I believe, twelve. I am currently a bit under the weather so I can't make it but I wanted to congratulate you and wish you wonderful times ahead.
Love,
Arthur

A few days later, his health took a serious turn for the worse.

It was a blessing as well as an inspiration to know him. He always walked the walk he talked for eighty-nine years, and will be remembered long after we are gone for his enduring work and shining spirit.

We will all continue to have our own lives, as well as the lives of future generations, enriched by studying this great man's own life, and his own timeless plays.

Even when Broadway rejected him for years, he wrote plays and books which are now all being rediscovered. He could have become a billionaire, using his good name to crank out trash for movies and TV, allowing others to actually ghostwrite for him. He described to me this Hollywood factory system of hiring others to do your work with a sense of wonder, not believing that any writer would care so little about their work or themselves that they would allow this to happen. Selling out was never an option for Arthur Miller.

He felt he should set an example for dreamers and visionaries, and he did throughout his long and productive life.

All of us can think about Arthur Miller with pride, because we can see how America is honored throughout the world by the enduring works of one of our own.

He spent his life as an artist who spoke up and spoke out about human rights, the dignity of everyday people, civil liberty and justice for all, and the importance of being an honorable person in all you do in your own life every day.

When we spent time together, he often talked about his own struggles during his boyhood after his family lost everything during the Depression, and how his elders, in spite of their desperate circumstances, emphasized to him the importance of working even harder, of always being kind and loyal to your friends and family, and that even when you reach for the stars you must always remain down-to-earth.

Arthur Miller's legacy is built on ideals which are timeless, and ones that we must all continue to strive for in 2005.

We will all miss him.

February 11, 2005, Putnam Valley, NY

For Hunter S. Thompson

{Note: This obituary was written six months before Hunter S. Thompson's memorial service.}
I first crossed paths with Hunter S. Thompson in 1959 when he was working for the *Middletown Daily Record,* a small paper in upstate NY.

Hunter was staying on the west side of Route 209 in Huguenot, NY. All that was there was a tiny roadside store called the Huguenot Superette. I used to come a mile from where I lived to the store, to get provisions for the week. The Huguenot Superette was almost always empty, and the owner, after months of stony silence, finally spoke to me confidentially one afternoon about seeing flying saucers and saucer people in the field across the road, and how he had never dared to tell anyone, except for two people. Those two people were me and someone else he described as that crazy writer up on the hill in the cabin close to both his store and my place.

That crazy writer turned out to be Hunter, who had moved up north to write and to find work as a journalist. By all accounts, he was doing excellent work for the *Middletown Daily Record,* until he left his job at the paper after attacking and nearly demolishing the soda machine in the building where he worked, when it failed to refund his change.

I was reminded of all this more than thirty years later, when Kentucky poet Ron Whitehead and author and historian Doug Brinkley organized a tribute to Hunter in Louisville in the late 90s. Hunter and Johnny Depp, both Kentucky natives, were to be given awards as Kentucky Colonels.

I was invited to come down to organize a group of musicians I had never met into some kind of tribute band, as well as create all the music for the evening to accompany readers. The unusual group of musicians who had been asked to participate included master songwriter-pianist Warren Zevon, the great Kentucky singer Suzy Wood and her bluegrass band, and Johnny Depp sitting in with us playing slide guitar. None of us in our tribute band knew one another, and everyone showed up at different times all afternoon, so as I was hard at work getting this unlikely ensemble together, Hunter made a grand entrance into the theater.

I heard his familiar staccato bellowing greetings as he roared into the backstage of the theater, dressed like a Viet Cong paratrooper, replete with an Aussie hat, a meerschaum pipe, and a flask of fine Kentucky brew.

"Come back here, Amram, after you rehearse, and we will reminisce," he said.

When we finished rehearsing whatever was possible to plan in advance, I told everyone I would give them signals to go with the spirit of the evening, and that we would have no problem. They all loved Hunter and his work, and were wonderful players.

While the musicians went to get supper, I went back into one of the empty dressing rooms and sat down with Hunter. He told me how excited he was that his hometown of Louisville was honoring him after all these years.

"My mother will be here," he said. "I hope she approves of my behavior. She is a librarian, as you know. She always encouraged me to keep reading all the books I took out as a kid. I guess my early days were similar to Kerouac's. I tried to read practically everything I could get my hands on. I always knew I wanted to be a writer. It is so nice you all came for this. My son will be here too, as well as old friends I grew up with."

It was a real treat to be able to spend some quiet time with him, as he spoke about all the things that had happened during the years since we first met so long ago. As all his friends can tell you, when you were with Hunter in a room alone, he always acted in a completely different way than he did when a lot of people were around.

He was often shy, sometimes reflective, always witty, and genuinely compassionate. I saw, as I listened to him talk, that during all the years, and through the turmoil of his life, he had somehow kept his roots as a southern gentleman, even though in public it was obvious that he kept this hidden from others. He indicated to me that he found out early in life, after leaving Louisville, that graciousness, good manners, and modesty are often perceived by many as being a sign of weakness.

Ironically, he found out that, to his amusement and occasional despair, his wild, crazy, and often outrageous public persona was adored by many, and being a wild man in public allowed him to retain most of himself to draw upon when he retreated to the solitude of writing each day. I think he sensed that if he really allowed others to see him in his moments of gentility and kindness, they would be disappointed or feel that *this* was an act.

That memorable night during the tribute to Hunter in Louisville, there was a mini-marathon of performances, including Johnny Depp reading Kerouac with me accompanying him, musical selections that we hoped Hunter wanted to hear, and a host of speakers all giving their heartfelt speeches honoring Hunter.

During all of this, Hunter stood offstage by the curtain in the wings of the theater, cradling a fog machine taken from the wall backstage, which was supposed to be used in the theater for emergencies to contain fires.

Hunter stood silently, crouched like a commando, clutching the fog machine as he listened intently to the music, the readings, and every word being said about him by all the speakers who came to pay tribute to their native son.

Whenever anyone who was giving their testimonial to Hunter began praising him excessively, Hunter would bound onto the stage, and with perfect theatrical timing, as if on cue, spray them with the machine, filling the whole stage and front rows of the theater with fog, like a production of the famous witches scene in *Macbeth*, until they cut their speech short, all of which was accompanied by gales of laughter and applause from even the most conservative members of the audience.

"This isn't the Academy Awards or a presidential inauguration," he whispered to me backstage, between sprayings. "I'm simply a writer. These windbags have to learn to cut it short and get to the point."

Later that night, after the music was over and the last public speaker had been sprayed, we all went out to celebrate some more. Hunter told me how much Kerouac's work had always meant to him, and he wanted to know how Jack could stand dealing with the pain of instant notoriety after being an overnight success following the publication of *On the Road*. That publication instantly made Jack the last thing any serious writer ever wants to be: an American Celebrity, i.e., a person who is famous for being famous, rather than someone whose work is read and respected.

Hunter, like Jack, always knew since he was a teenager in Louisville that he was a writer and an artist first and foremost, and whatever outrageous events he took part in over the course of his life, he always remained as serious about his work as he was about life itself.

We also talked about music, writing, sports, and our shared love of the South, the beauty of the small towns and farmlands and the old inherent values of what seemed part of a vanishing America, which both Steinbeck and Kerouac had written about.

In the wee hours of the late night/early morning, as we were imbibing some fine Kentucky bourbon, I reminded Hunter of the old Huguenot Superette and the flying saucer-loving proprietor from Route 209.

"I remember him," said Hunter. "Does he still sell the same stale week-old loaves of bread? Is he still there? Is he still alive?"

"He's gone now, Hunter." I said. "He has left us."

"Well, we all have to leave eventually," said Hunter. "Let's have another drink and plan on staying around for a long time. Here's to many more. There is still a lot of work to be done."

Now Hunter has left us, and it is hard to imagine an America or a world without Hunter S. Thompson, here to keep us all in line and remind everyone of the work that needs to be done by all of us.

When he revealed in his writings the dark side of an America that no one else dared to talk about, he was also sharing with us the story of his own idealistic love of America and its glorious history of liberty and free speech, all of which seemed to be in danger of being destroyed by the criminal behavior of Bible-thumping politicians who wrapped themselves in the flag and used the horror of a senseless war to justify their own misconduct.

He believed that truthfulness and honor are the values we should cherish the most, and that pretentiousness and lying should never be ignored or tolerated, especially when indifference and cynicism become the status quo for people we allow to serve us in public office or any positions of responsible leadership in our society.

Hunter said that night, as he did through the years, that the last thing he ever expected was to become famous for what he wrote in 1972, out of desperation and disgust, after seeing firsthand the nightmare of the presidential campaign he covered. He honestly thought that his 1972 reportage would be his swan song as a professional journalist, and instead it made him a star.

"What would have happened if I had liked and admired the people I was writing about in '72?" he said to me that night in Louisville. "I would have remained an obscure journalist, if even that. The whole Gonzo thing is similar to what I am sure Kerouac went through with the Beat thing. Putting a label on someone has nothing to do with their work. I am first and foremost a writer, just as Jack and all the great writers we remember today knew that they were. As a southerner, I was brought up with old-fashioned ideals of what this country was about. I still believe in those ideals and couldn't and never will just sit quietly by when I see our values being trashed and desecrated by lying lizards and thieves!!"

Thanks to Doug Brinkley's brilliant editing of Hunter's letters into a major book a few years ago, Hunter lived long enough to be rediscovered by a new generation as one of the great writers of our time, and a much more important artist than the Gonzo Journalist stereotype, which only defined a part of his impressive literary output.

For his farewell to us, Hunter requested that his ashes be fired from a cannon, and I'm sure that his wishes will be respected. I am also sure that all who will be present at this final ceremony will expect him to leap out with a cigarette lighter to the cannon at the last minute, from wherever he is, to ignite the fuse himself for his final blast off. Hunter never let a good time pass him by.

Long after the final cannon shot has sounded, and his ashes have settled in the mountainside around Woody Creek, Colorado, our children and grandchildren will still be reading those amazing books that he wrote.

At the tribute to Hunter in Louisville, his son Juan told the audience that having Hunter as a dad was an extraordinary experience that he treasured every day. Many of us blessed to spend time with him feel our lives will always be enriched by knowing him every day that we did.

We all should take a moment to send a prayer to him for his spirit, as well as sending our love to his family.

Hunter showed us that none of us have to be afraid, that we must persevere in life, and pay attention to what is happening in the world we live in, just as he did, and that we must dare to speak out and stand up for what we feel in our hearts is honorable, decent, and sensible.

While he now rests in peace, his work will always remind us that we have to remain awake while we are here, and celebrate each precious moment of life.

February 21, 2005, Putnam Valley, NY

For Philip Lamantia

When Nancy Peters e-mailed me on a snowy day in early March of 2005 that Philip Lamantia had passed away, I re-read the e-mail two times, hoping I had misread it.

I was in Lowell, Massachusetts, Jack Kerouac's hometown, in the middle of a snowstorm, where I was performing at the annual celebration of Jack's birthday, presented by Lowell Celebrates Kerouac.

It was also the fiftieth anniversary of Charlie Parker's death.

Earlier that day, I had spoken to a group of students visiting Lowell, Massachusetts, from the University of Denver about what a blessing it was to have known, as well as to have first played with, both Kerouac and Charlie Parker a half century ago when I was their age. Now another great original is no longer with us.

The day before I received the news of Philip passing, I had told all the students about Philip Lamantia, Howard Hart, Kerouac and me presenting the first jazz/poetry readings ever formally held in NYC in the Fall of 1957, first in October at the Brata Art Gallery, then on December 27 at the Circle in the Square Theater, and then at Brooklyn College in early 1958. I told them about the exciting days of early 1957, when Jack introduced me to Lamantia.

At the time Phil was already a veteran of the poetry scene. Lamantia had been one of the featured poets, along with Michael McClure, Philip Whalen, and Gary Snyder, with Kenneth Rexroth as the MC, at the Six Gallery in San Francisco, Oct. 7, 1955, which is where Allen Ginsberg first read *Howl*. Jack Kerouac was there that night as well, but as a cheerleader of sorts, and along with Lawrence Ferlinghetti and others, an enthusiastic member of the audience.

In our readings with music two years later in NYC with Lamantia, Kerouac, and Howard Hart, no matter how insane everyone else's behavior became during the course of our 1957 late night/early morning marathon spontaneous presentations, Philip always remained our anchor, with his mellifluous voice, brilliant delivery, and seemingly effortless elegance.

It was Philip who created the name for the four of us: The Jazz/Poetry Trio, which we used for our public presentations. I think he realized that this way, in case one of the four of us showed up really late, we would still have a trio.

Jack, Howard Hart, Phil, and I all called what we did together poetry/music-music/poetry, long before our first official public appearance at the Brata in October of

1957. When we were all together hanging out, we often gave countless unsolicited performances at coffeehouses, painters' lofts, assorted parties, park benches, and even once on the subway on the way to Brooklyn for a formal reading.

I wasn't only playing jazz when I accompanied poets. I tried to create spontaneous music in many genres, all created on the spot to enhance the music already inherent in the phrasing and nuances of Phil's beautiful poems, as I did when I played with Kerouac.

We never rehearsed. Phil was so musical that it was like playing with a great musician. Phil's poetry tapped into the roots of many sources, replete with the classic styles and rhythms of the great poets of antiquity, as well as the urban street sounds of today, and word/pictures of pastoral moments inspired by his years of travels through the wide-open spaces of the United States, Mexico, and all of the American continent.

Every event we did was unpredictable, spontaneous, full of positive energy, and always fun. When I would talk to Phil over the ensuing years about doing another series with Jack and Howard Hart in NYC someday, he always said, "We should, and I hope we will, but if we don't, we can always know that we were the first to do it in New York."

Philip and I had our final reunion in the spring of 2001, when I was in San Francisco, performing for the showing of the original scroll for *On the Road*. The day after the showing of the scroll, I performed music which I created to accompany Lawrence Ferlinghetti reading his poetry, for a CD/DVD of his *Pictures of the Gone World*. That night, following the afternoon recording at Zoetrope in North Beach, photographer/film maker Chris Felver took me to visit Philip, who had temporarily recovered from the acute depression which had plagued him during much of his life.

That night in the spring of 2001, he was as vivacious, brilliant, and warm as he was the first time we met in early 1957, when Jack Kerouac brought Phil to my old walk-up apartment at 114 Christopher Street to play music, read poetry, and use my phone to call up our various sweethearts.

I reminded Phil how I first heard his voice that night, in counterpoint to Jack's, floating up the stairwell in a gradual crescendo as their nonstop rapping got louder and louder as they trudged up the six flights of stairs to hang out until dawn.

Philip recalled how after I played them some music I had just written, and after they read some poems with music, Jack made a second series of calls at 1:00 a.m. to their friends and admirers to let everyone know that Philip was back in town.

I remember perfectly how I listened that night to Phil and Jack as they rapped nonstop about the collective spirit of jazz and its sociologic effect on the American psyche, about their shared love of Catholicism and Buddhism, about poets past and present from around the world who gave us all mirrors to see ourselves in a fresh light, and about the courage and grace of various athletes, explorers, painters, actors, composers, poets, and everyday folks who dared to follow their hearts and go their own way in life.

As I got to know Phil better, it became clear that Philip seemed to know, even back in 1957, that his work spoke for itself and would always continue to do so. He was a modest person but he had such a great intellect and flawless critical ability that, combined with his enormous knowledge of so many forms of art, Philip knew his work was of lasting value. While he was unfailingly generous in judging the work of others, if one of his own poems didn't meet his high standards, he would keep rewriting it until it did.

Kerouac loved Phil's work as much as he loved Phil's spirit, humor, erudition, and pure appreciation of the beauty of all that surrounded us, which so many people in the 1950s took for granted or ignored. Phil was always ahead of what was supposed to be happening (but still always right on time). He had an understanding of the machinations of the international arts scene that none of us ever did. This was because he had been acclaimed as a child prodigy and hailed as a Surrealist poet while still a teenager, but early on abandoned the whole international literary scene to pursue his own pure path.

We all thought that he was much more than a Surrealist poet, just as we knew that Kerouac was much more than a Beat writer and that Charlie Parker, a true genius, was vastly more than just a bebop saxophone player. Like any significant artist or person of substance, Philip walked his own path, and defied categories. No title could do him or his work justice.

He was and always will be Philip Lamantia, poet extraordinaire. If you ever need to know more about him than that, or wonder now why he has been held in such high esteem for more than a half century, all you have to do is read his poems.

Now he is gone, but through his timeless writings, his voice will always be with us.

I recently discovered an old acetate recording that Phil, Howard Hart, and I made in early 1957, and am transferring it to CD and giving it to Nancy Peters so that she and Phil's estate can let future generations hear what it was like to hear him read his poetry then. Chris Felver filmed us in 2001 at our reunion/jam session at Phil's apartment, to celebrate our continuing efforts forty-four years later. We are giving copies of that to Phil's estate as well.

I always carry a copy of the old black-and-white poster of our 1957 jazz/poetry readings at the Circle in the Square Theater, with Phil, Kerouac, and Howard Hart in my pocket with me. I always tell kids, when they see it, that we all hoped that what we did back then now proves that a thing of beauty *is* a joy forever, and all of us would be happy if our work could in some way inspire them to pursue their dreams, to never give up trying, and to be brave and collaborate with others.

Now, as I do with Jack and Howard, I will always carry, along with the copy of that old poster in my pocket, the memory of the spirit of Philip Lamantia in my heart.

March 16, 2005, Putnam Valley, NY

For Lucien Carr: What Is Born of Spirit Is Spirit

On April 9, I attended a final farewell to my old friend Lucien Carr, held at the Church of St. Luke in the Fields, an old Anglican Episcopal place of worship since the early 1920s, where Lucien's son Simon had arranged for a traditional service.

I was determined to try to be as cheerful as possible as a way of celebrating, as well as paying homage to Lucien's own boundless energy. Like Lucien and Jack Kerouac, who introduced us in the mid-50s, I was and still am a firm believer of living every precious moment of life to the hilt, enjoying all the blessings, and using all the setbacks in a positive way (as post-graduate field research for an eventual degree as a full fledged licensed and accredited Doctor of Hangoutology). Lucien never needed a degree of this kind, because when I met him in the mid-50s, he was already so sophisticated and worldly and so much fun to be with that even while you always felt at home with him, you knew he was always a step ahead and expected you to follow.

When I arrived at St. Luke's and took a seat, I read a part of the program that was given to us before the service. Reading through the various texts helped me to put into perspective something about this great mystery and adventure that we call life on earth.

The service began, and during the Requiem Eucharist celebrating Lucien's life, I was truly moved by hearing the reading of the following two excerpts from John 14:1–6, which was printed as part of the program. It was a portion of the dialogue between Jesus and Nicodemus, the Pharisee, when Jesus explained how it was possible to be born again, after already having had an earthly birth.

"What is born of flesh is flesh, what is born of Spirit is spirit. The wind blows where it chooses, and you hear the sound of it, but you do not know where it comes from or where it goes. So it is with everyone who is born of the Spirit."

The phrase "what is born of Spirit is spirit," leapt off the page for me.

I began thinking not only of Lucien, but of all the other extraordinary people I have been blessed to know in my life, so many of whom had that special indefinable quality that has nothing to do with physical beauty, fame, money, reputation, social position, possessions, or all the other superficial things that can be taken from you in a second. These were the feelings which emanated from truly soulful people, spiritual reverberations that you can feel, that always remain unspoken, yet are still always powerful and nourishing to be around.

I realized that the spirits of people like Lucien, whom I have met around the world, all have a presence that stays with you long after you meet them, and that this strength of spirit has no restrictions due to religion, nationality, or race. It is simply a true plane of existence that has always been here for all of us. This spirit world (which the Lakota people feel is the real one) is definitely a reality, and one that we are all born into, but sometimes forget about, in which case that spirit lies dormant within us, waiting to be nurtured.

Here, in this beautiful old church, we were all together, celebrating Lucien's memory, and suddenly I could feel his spirit, which transcended the ceremony, as it floated around the room for all of us to share, and I could feel Kerouac and others also join us in the room, as we all listened to the heavenly sounds of the choir up in the balcony singing Bach.

During the service, I flashed back a few years to Gregory Corso's memorial, at the huge Catholic church in the Village where he was baptized, where Patti Smith and I played a duet in his memory, and remembered Allen Ginsberg's wild series of memorials, and the memorials of all the other people over the years who were drawn together through the spirit we all shared. I felt that they were all also there with us for this afternoon, but realized that I couldn't go out with them later that afternoon to hang out and reminisce because they were now in a different place, and that now with Lucien gone, there was almost no one left.

It was Lucien who introduced everyone to everyone else, and kept up his friendship with Jack to the very end when most of the old group had given up on him.

When I spent time with Lucien and Kerouac in the mid-fifties, we would always end up our evening adventures by going to Lucien's place whenever Kerouac was in town, staying up till the sun rose, playing music, singing songs, and telling stories of our latest escapades, while his kids would stay up way past their bedtimes, watching and listening to a bunch of crazy, joyous, hyperactive, supposed grown-ups celebrating being together, while Lucien's wife, like a true saint, put up with all of us, making us feel at home and seeming to enjoy the merriment herself.

Now, during the service, I realized that even if Lucien and almost everyone else from that happy time are no longer here, his spirit will always be reflected in the work of so many of us whom he brought together. Lucien always encouraged us to pursue excellence, telling us to always strive to do better than expected when creating artistic work, and hopefully through that work, to enrich the lives of others.

In spite of his vast knowledge of literature, Lucien was not only interested in the work and spirit of his friends who were authors and poets during the vibrant era of the 1950s that later received the dubious catch-all cliche of Beat; Lucien was also interested in and knowledgeable of the enduring work of the musicians, composers, painters, actors, and all the artists who were part of a much larger community, all of whom were united by a merging of each other's spirits, with each one of us contributing something of our own. Being with him made you sense the community that he also celebrated ... open, inclusive, and life-affirming.

At the same time, even in his most gregarious moments, he could spot a charlatan with a special radar that he possessed, which seemed to come from his innate honesty, a quality that helped him to become a major editor for most of his professional life. I am sure that part of his legacy will remain in the hearts of the young people with whom he worked at United Press International (UPI) for several decades. His fellow workers always held him in high esteem, just as his old friends always did.

I looked to my right as the processional came down the aisle, and sitting across the aisle in the church, held in the arms of his beautiful mom, Miia, was Dody Muller's grandson, only nine months old, staring and checking out everyone with his dark eyes. A few years ago, Lucien and his family had all been at Dody's seventieth birthday party, and during a break in the long afternoon, Lucien, Dody, and I all hugged each other and marveled at how lucky we were, in spite of our wild younger days, to have such incredible children, who were all there at the party to celebrate Dody's life.

Dody said to Lucien and to me, "Whatever they say about us in the future, we must have done something right. Look at our fantastic children."

At the service, when Lucien's sons spoke, I was reminded again how remarkable his own kids are.

Four nights before the service for Lucien took place, Dody's daughter Miia, her husband, and her nine-month-old son had come down to the Cornelia Street Cafe in the Village to hear me play. In addition to the music we played, we had readings with music of Kerouac's work, as I had done at Lucien's house for years after the last public performances Jack and I gave together. Dody enjoyed these times at Lucien's as well.

Miia and I talked about Lucien, and how we would be together at the service at St. Luke's to honor his memory, and I told her again how we all hung out with her mom and his then baby-aged kids before she was born. During this, her son seemed to be checking us out as we spoke.

Miia told me at the church that when she and her husband went out to the country after coming to be with us in the Village, that the next morning when they woke up, their son was sitting at the piano for hours playing.

When I greeted him at the reception after the memorial service at the church, he stuck out his hand, as if he was signaling me to play, and I not only saw Dody's spirit in his eyes, I also felt her spirit, right in the room with Lucien's, all while eating some cantaloupe and grapes and talking to Lucien's relatives and old friends.

I decided right then that when he gets a little older, I will tell him stories about his grandmother, Dody, and how she, Lucien, Kerouac, and I all hung out on those very same streets a half-century ago, so that in the year 2079, when he is seventy-four as I am now, he can tell his grandkids what happened way back in the mid-1950s, as well as what happened to him during his lifetime in this new millennium.

Now I know that I can't ever visit Lucien in Washington to go sailing with him, as we had often planned to do, or talk to him on the phone from some funky motel or airport when I am on the road, to tell him about what is happening in 2005 in a far-off place that I know he would love, because he would see the hidden beauty of whatever was there that would be overlooked by everyone else.

Still, wherever I am from now on, I know that I will always be able to feel his spirit, and somehow communicate with him in that special way, as I increasingly do with many others no longer here, who like Lucien, will always have a special place in my heart.

Like most of the remaining hyperactive, workaholic, but still fun-loving members of our era, I always share with young folks the importance of Charlie Parker's immortal recording of his composition *Now's the Time*. When kids tell me that they wish they had been around in the '40s and '50s, I always remind them of the title of Charlie Parker's classic, and that this is the perfect time to be here. Just as Lucien always did, I try to avoid being stranded in the quicksand of nostalgia.

Still, at the memorial for Lucien, and after all that transpired on that lovely spring afternoon at St. Luke's Church, I suddenly became conscious, when reading that phrase, that "what is born of Spirit is spirit," may have been said two thousand years ago but would always remain modern.

Because it is a timeless truth, it is always right on time, as Lucien himself always was, because in that living spirit world, Now is always the time.

April 13, 2005, Putnam Valley, NY

Remembering Ray Barretto

When Ray and I first met and played together in the fall of 1955 at the Monday night sessions at the 125 Club in Harlem, Ray was the only conga player and I was the only French horn player who always showed up.

We used to always laugh because we were surrounded by a small army of great musicians who played what were then considered traditional jazz instruments.

When Ray was complimented for being able to play with anyone and always be perfectly in tune, he would say "I was born with that Latin fire. I'm making that part of jazz."

Saxophonists like Rahsaan Roland Kirk, Wayne Shorter; trumpeters like Art Farmer; and all the members of Mingus's band, of which I was a member, would come up every Monday night to jam, and Ray was always there. He played with everybody, and always knew what to do.

We all loved the way Ray played way back then.

He had a real understanding of how to add to the music, rather than trying to blow everyone else off the bandstand. He was already a true musical artist by 1955, and he always remained one.

He also knew how to inspire others to be that way by his example of always listening and being creative.

In the 70s we both played with our bands, along with Gil Evans's band, at a historic concert for the United Farm Workers at the Felt Forum. Ray's band of young musicians brought down the house.

When I came back from Cuba in 1977, after the concerts we did in Havana with Dizzy, Stan Getz, Earl Hines, and my band, the Cuban musicians were able to come to America for a special concert in NYC at the Lincoln Center.

When I was reunited to play with Los Papines for this series of events in New York, in addition to Tito Puente, Mongo Santamaria, and Candido, Ray Barretto was one of the musicians all the Cubans wanted to meet when they visited here.

By this time, he was known and admired around the world, but he never acted like many people do when they receive recognition. Over the years, it was always a joy to be in his presence, because he remained the same warm gentleman that he was back in '55.

At his birthday party a few years ago, we scat-sang some blues together, making up lyrics on the spot in a song about the 125 Club in Harlem, and how it was when we met fifty years ago.

At another concert in NY, with Clark Terry, when our three bands all played together for the finale, my son was able to sit in and play with Ray's son, as well as with Ray.

Looking at my young son and his own young son, as we all played together, Ray said to me, "There we are, Dave. That's us, all over again."

I know that fifty years from now, my son will still remember that night, because it was a blessing for him to share some of the blessings of Ray's magic, as many of us were fortunate enough to share as well.

Ray's spirit will always remain in all our hearts, and his music will stay as strong and fresh as ever, because it came from his heart. He lived for it and he loved it.

His wonderful family should know that we are thinking of them as we mourn his passing; we're thankful that he was here, and grateful for the years he spent to bring beauty to us all.

He opened up doors, as well as bringing joy for many years to many people around the world.

While he rests in peace, his music is more alive than ever.

February 20, 2006, New York

A Joyous Farewell to George

After spending most of the day stuck in the airport, surrounded by a midwestern November fog, our plane finally took off from Chicago and landed at LaGuardia Airport in New York. I grabbed my bags and drove home upstate to our farm. It was the day of my seventy-third birthday, but I didn't feel like celebrating.

In fourteen hours George Plimpton's memorial service was scheduled to begin at 4:00 p.m., November 18. I slept a few hours, got up, and drove back down to Manhattan.

Like so many others that afternoon, I had come to say good-bye to George. When I walked up to the stairs in front of the Cathedral of St. John the Divine, the steps were filled with people, many of whom, like myself, had grown a little older since the 50s when so many of us met one another for the first time through George.

Several people I didn't recognize at first glance. And many of them didn't recognize me, either. But when we did recognize one another, it was as joyous a reunion as it was a joyous farewell to George.

When I saw Norman Mailer, Kurt Vonnegut, Peter Matthiessen, and a host of other people I have known nearly fifty years, I realized (as they did) that we might not ever all be together again, as we were for so many decades at George's fun-filled get-togethers, where authors, poets, artists, musicians, composers, actors, football players, boxers, bohemians, and society people all got together, and where I would play George's piano for hours and often jam with everyone from Brazil's great Antonio Carlos Jobim to members of the New York Philharmonic until the wee hours.

It was usually after 2:00 a.m. when George would finally sit down at the piano, play his composition that he debuted at the Apollo Theater's amateur night in Harlem, and proudly recall his triumph and the thunderous applause he received.

Seeing so many people from all walks of life at the cathedral was very touching. Many of us sensed, as we greeted one another on the steps outside the cathedral, that this might be a farewell not only to George, but to one another.

When I got inside the cathedral, it was even more mobbed with people I knew from the 50s, many of whom I also didn't recognize at first. Some moved much more slowly now, as they made their way up the stairs and to their seats. But they were all smiling and glad to see one another again and share a few moments to remember George.

The Cathedral of St. John the Divine is magnificent, but it is so enormous, it doesn't automatically exude a healing or spiritual feeling. It needs people to make it smaller and more human. That happened later on, as soon as the gospel choir opened up the program and warmed our hearts with some sanctified wailing music that made you want to get up and dance and holler in the name of the Lord, regardless of which God or Goddess you pray to.

The particular part of the audience where I finally sat down, was by chance a group of what must be the last of the Old New York Society Mohicans. While the rest of the mob of an audience that now filled most of the vast reaches of the cathedral had that typical New York look of a United Nations (which is what makes New York City so fantastic and soulful and always exciting), the section I inadvertently happened to stumble into looked like a New York Stock Exchange Board of Directors meeting, with a lot of extremely reserved men and women, who, in spite of occasional guarded and restrained chuckles, didn't seem the kind of people who could ever be truly appreciative of the free spirit of George. With all his unabandoned wit, grace, boyish sense of adventure, and endless generosity, George was someone who transcended his New York society upbringing to become a wonderful kind of everyman, a genius editor, a brilliant author, an adventurer, and a loving, gracious catalyst for bringing the world closer together.

But as the service progressed, with the excellent speakers and gospel choir singing again, George's mercurial, egalitarian way of embracing everything and everyone in life seemed to change the cathedral into a George Plimpton Saturday night/Sunday morning party.

His spirit seemed to slowly fill the cathedral and it became a warm and inviting place, as it was when I played there with a group of Native American musicians and speakers at many programs we did together during the past few years for their annual Indian Thanksgiving celebrations. By the end of those evenings, the Indians had made the cathedral feel like you were attending a powwow at a ceremonial place of affirmation.

By the end of the service for George, the cathedral became like home, and most of us didn't want to leave, lingering inside talking to one another and greeting old friends. The words and music had changed everything.

Finally it was over and a small group of us were invited by George's lovely wife Sarah to Elaine's. Elaine herself is still the same great down-home lady I knew from the middle 60s from Greenwich Village, when she worked in a bar downtown, close to my old apartment, and hung out with all us crazy folks.

The last time I had been to Elaine's was three years ago, with George, his wife Sarah, my three kids, my sister Marianna, and Helen Kelly and Ed Adler from NYU, who had invited us all for my seventieth birthday in November of 2000.

Here I was, exactly three years later, for a final hurrah for George.

I sat with Mailer (at a tiny table up front by the entrance) for the first time in years. We talked about how in 1955, he drove me uptown to George's (in Plimpton's borrowed red convertible sports car), picking me up from my sixth-floor walkup at 319 East 8th Street, between Avenues B and C, and taking me to George's apartment for the first time. I had been in NY for only three weeks and George had called me (looking up my number in information), having heard that I was back from Paris, where we had met and hung out for a year, and telling me a guy named Norman would come and pick me up, driving a red convertible.

That year, at what became George's weekly gatherings, I made lasting friendships with many people, and many of them who were still alive were at Elaine's to celebrate one more time all the gifts that George had given us.

Later on in the evening, I sat with George's wife, Sarah, and some of her and George's old friends, and told her that my children Alana, Adira, and Adam all hoped that someday we could all visit New York and take her and her kids to the zoo.

With all the heartfelt tributes to George, it seemed (outside of all of us at our table who knew Sarah not just as George's wife) that many had failed to address Sarah and her needs and feelings, as an extraordinary woman and the mother of two five-year-old twins, who now would have to continue her and her children's lives without George by their side. Hopefully, now Sarah and George's first wife, Freddie, and her son Taylor and daughter Medora, will all be able to overcome this loss, have attention paid to their needs, and all receive the love that they deserve.

A few days after George's passing, I had a chance to spend some time with George's son Taylor, who is the kind of son that every father dreams of having. I also had a chance to talk to Taylor's mom Freddie as well, and share memories of wonderful times from long ago.

By the end of the long afternoon and night, there was a sense of completion as we left Elaine's. We had said good-bye to George in the best way that we could, knowing he would want us to celebrate every precious moment of life, as he did. There was no one else like him, and in that celebration that was his life, he touched many other people's lives as well.

All the writers he championed in the beginning stages of their careers, like Kerouac, Terry Southern, William Styron, and Philip Roth, and the *Paris Review* he founded and ran for fifty years, will be a legacy for Sarah, his children, and all of us to be proud of for the rest of our lives.

As the old saying goes ... "There was a man."

November 20, 2003, Putnam Valley, New York

Index

Acca, Claire, 73, 75, 77–78, 80
Accra, Ghana, 43
Actors, 134–135, 152, 302
"Adagio for Strings" (Barber), 117
Adams, Pepper, 196, 205–206
Adler, Ed, 166, 167, 306
Advertising, 234
Africa: behavior toward each other in, 58, 62; decolonization in, 72; music of, 43, 44, 49, 50, 59, 62, 69; as original home, 51. *See also* Kenya
Afro-Cuban music/jazz, 44, 84, 88, 90, 91, 92, 125–126, 129, 139, 283; rhythms in, 87
After the Fall (Miller), 194, 292
Agribusiness, 279
Akbar, Mohammed, 77
Alaska, 188
Ali, Muhammed, 103, 130, 155
Allen, Steve, 239
Amann, Josy, 14, 19
American Indian Movement, 104. *See also* Native Americans
American National Theater and Academy (ANTA), 292
American Symphony Orchestra, 63
Amram, Adam, 39, 249, 255, 260, 267, 269, 270, 273, 278, 284. *See also* Amram, David, children of
Amram, Adira, 39, 105, 107–108, 149–150, 160, 209, 211, 213, 249, 278, 284, 289. *See also* Amram, David, children of

Amram, Alana, 39, 105, 107–108, 160, 208, 246, 251, 272, 278, 284, 293. *See also* Amram, David, children of
Amram, David: acting roles of, 95, 135, 261; in the army, 142, 202, 216; benefits played in, 136; caricatures by, 234, 237, 238, 244; as carpenter's helper, 286; children of, 23, 104, 106, 122, 227, 228, 237, 241, 251, 270, 277–278, 280, 306, 307 (see also *individuals*); as composer-in-residence for New York Philharmonic, 134, 184, 287; compositions of, 3, 4, 6; as conductor, 46, 91, 101, 126–127, 128, 181, 183–184, 186, 273, 287; ESP of, 139, 140, 200; farm in Putnam Valley, NY of (Peeksville Hollow Farm), 92, 280, 285; father of, 4, 132, 287–288; film scores by, 95, 287; first Broadway show composed for, 133; first flight to Africa, 50–56; grandfather of. *See* Amram, Philip; hepatitis illness of, 47; and heritage, family, and respect, 97; inspired by musically, 93; instruments traveled with/played, 12, 21, 49, 56, 57, 83, 153, 155, 258, 259, 273, 275; interviews with journalists in Kenya, 60–61; interview with WEPA, 92–97; letters of, 227, 228–289; made-up songs of. *See* Make-up songs; main premise of his work, 92–93; personal meccas of, 235–236; seventy-fifth birthday tribute/concert, 96, 217; sister of. *See* Amram,

309

Amram, David *(continued)*
  Marianna; traveling necklace of, 2; uncles of. *See* Amram, David; Nahm, Milton; wife of. *See* Amram, Lora Lee; words for aspiring artists, 97
Amram, David (uncle of David Amram), 81, 93, 107–108, 110, 111, 120, 132, 217, 228, 277, 289
Amram, Jose, 92
Amram, Lora Lee, 106, 117, 118, 121, 125, 131, 137, 138, 160, 191; father and brother of, 146, 148
Amram, Marianna, 227, 228, 253, 266. 288–289, 306
Amram, Philip, 277, 278
Amram, Robert, 53
Amram Jam, 219
An American in Paris (Gershwin), 230
Anderson, Dame Judith, 151, 158
Andoh, Adjoa, 266
Angela's Ashes (McCourt), 201
Angola, 41
Anthology of Jewish-American Literature, 50
Aoki (illustrator/photographer), 75, 76–77
Apollinaire, Guillaume, 212
Archuleta, Richard, 104–105, 107
Armstrong, Louis, 57
Arrangement, The (film), 95, 96
Art and religion, 58–59
Aspen, Colorado, 7, 9–10, 24, 26
Aspen Daily Times, 25
Athens, Greece, 179–180, 188
Auerbach, Colleen and Lisl, 29
Austin Symphony, 117, 276, 277
Autobiography for Strings (Amram), 194

Bach, Johann Sebastian, 149, 181, 196, 301
Baker, Julius, 118, 119
Baldwin, James, 228, 269
"Ballad for Red Allen" (Amram), 196
Ballad of the West, A (Bridger), 114
Ballard, Louis, 101, 117, 123
Banks, Dennis, 271
Baraka, Amiri, 169
Barber, Samuel, 117
Barber of Seville, The (Rossini), 127
Barretto, Ray, 205, 304–305
Bartles, Vivian and Joseph, 129, 130
Bartók, Bela, 192, 196, 206, 244
Bashir, Ahmed, 254
Basie, Count, 13, 104, 181

Baudelaire, Charles, 212
Bauza, Mario, 91
"Beat culture: The 1950s and Beyond" (conference), 163
Beat generation, 234, 243, 244, 250, 302; and era of the 50s, 246, 249, 251; words *beat* and *Beatnik*, 246, 256–257
Beatles, 42, 96
Beat Meets East Conference, 221, 232, 233–234, 236
Beethoven House in Bonn, Germany, 247
Beethoven's Ninth Symphony, 46, 56
Behan, Brendan, 201
Belly dance music, 44
Bernstein, Leonard, 130, 134, 136, 160, 183, 184, 185, 287
Berroa, Ignacio, 103
Berry, Chuck, 203
Beyond Treaty, 104
Billy the Kid, 29
Birdland, 63
Birds, 68, 108, 268
Black, Brown and Beige (Ellington), 287
Blake, William, 199
Bluegrass music, 8, 197, 209
"Blue Monk," 64, 103
Blues, 125–126, 129, 180, 188, 221, 260
Bogart, Fred, 37, 216
Bomas dancers, 64. *See also* Masai people/land, Masai dancing
Bonn International Theater Festival, 92, 94
Boone, Pat, 203
Bradley, Ed, 29
Bradstock festival in Long Island, 28, 36
Braga, Portugal, 243–244
Brahms *Requiem*, 46, 56
Brandenburg Concertos (Bach), 149
Brando, Marlon, 103
Braudis, Bob, 11–12, 28, 29, 33, 35
Brazil, 44, 56, 57, 59, 63, 235, 276
Bridger, Bobby, 112, 113–115, 116, 117
Brinkley, Doug, 5–6, 12, 16, 18, 19, 21, 22–23, 28, 29, 164, 165–166, 169, 171, 295, 297
Britten, Benjamin, 130
Broadway theater, 133, 148–149, 155, 160. *See also Harold and Maude*
Bromberg, Dave, 197
Brouwer, Leo, 87
Brown, Georgia, 53
Browne, Nick, 51

Bruce, Lenny, 242
Buddhism, 76, 236, 299
Bull, Sandy, 131
Bunyan, Paul, 29
Burns, Jethro, 188
Burns, Marie, 260
Buta, Steele, 61, 62, 73, 78, 80

Cadenzas, 181
Cage, John, 190
Caldwell, Zoe, 150, 151–152, 153, 155, 158, 159, 160
Camden, New Jersey, 277, 278
Canada, 122, 149, 188, 216, 235, 237, 243
Candido, 304
Carnegie Hall, 47
Carpentier, Geoff, 111
Carr, Lucien, 211, 285, 300–303
Carroll, Joe, 212
Carter, Bill, 27, 32
Carter, Jimmy, 86
Cash, Johnny, 101
Cassady, Carolyn, 266
Cassady, John, 237, 238, 266
Cassady, Neal, 65, 115, 194, 234, 237, 247, 281
Castleman, Charlie, 205
Central America, 56, 90
C.F. Peters (publisher), 187, 286
Chakra (ballet score), 190, 193
Chaluisan, Luis, 91–92, 94
Chayefsky, Paddy, 136
Chengdu, China, 221–223, 232, 235, 260
Chicago Symphony, 183
Chin, Charlie, 199, 200
Christianity, 62, 71, 72, 75, 76, 77
"City of New Orleans" (Goodman), 190
Clancy, Tom, 51–52
Clarence Brown Theater in Knoxville, Tennessee, 151, 153, 159. *See also Medea*
Classical composers, cultural role of, 182–183
Clements, Vassar, 37, 216
Clurman, Harold, 136, 150
Codrescu, Andrei, 284
Colagrande, J. J., 228–230
Concha, Benny, 104, 105, 107
Conductors, 136, 196. *See also* Amram, David, as conductor
Conlin, James, 10
Cook, Jim, 127
Copland, Aaron, 234, 244

Cork Festival (Ireland), 52, 96
Corporate farming, 279
Corso, Gregory, 65, 198, 233, 257, 301
Cowan, Dan, 118
Cowboy movies, 75
Coyote, Peter, 271
Crafton, Randy, 190–191, 192, 193, 194
Creation of the World (Milhaud), 241
Creativity, 57, 178, 179, 183, 187, 188, 213, 224, 225, 226, 228, 243, 248, 250, 251
"Credo" (Amram), 196, 198
Cricket, 252
Crouch, Hondo, 116–117, 118, 132, 215
Cuba, 4, 35, 44, 56, 63, 83–91, 129, 304; Minister of Culture in, 87, 88
Cunnell, Howard, 265
"Custer Died for your Sins" (Westerman song/album title), 73, 99, 112
Custer Died for Your Sins (Deloria), 112

D'Amboise, Jacques, 193
Dameron, Allen, 117
Dances with Wolves (film), 123
Daphne cruise ship, 83, 84, 90
David Amram Collective (Denver), 246
Da Vinci, Leonardo, 185
Deacy, Jack, 51
Deakin, Richard, 173
Death of a Salesman (Miller), 293
Deaville, Darcy, 260
Deloria, Vine, Jr., 73, 112, 113, 123, 132
Democracy, 62, 72
Denton, Texas, 240
Denver, Colorado, 246–251, 276, 281
DePasquale, Bob, 110
Depp, Johnny, 5–6, 8–9, 12, 15, 23, 26–28, 29, 32, 295
Dickstein, Morris and Lore, 164
Dillon, Denny, 138, 141, 144
Ding Darling National Wildlife Refuge, 268
Di Prima, Diane, 211
Dobie Gillis show, 248
Dos Passos, John, 269
Dostoevsky, Fyodor, 248, 249
"Down Home Sunday in the South" (Amram), 216–217
D'Rivera, Paquito, 87, 88, 89, 90, 101
Drugs, 202, 203
DRUM (Determined Red Man's Unity Movement), 107

Drums, African/Native American, 50, 105, 112, 212
Dryden, John, 267
Duggan, Dennis, 18, 51, 113
Dumbek (drum), 21, 49, 152, 196, 273, 275
"Dunkin Donuts" (Amram), 197
Dunleavy, Steve, 17–18
Duologue (CD), 190–191
Dust Bowl, 257, 259, 283
Dvořák, Antonin, 244, 247
Dylan, Bob, 30, 198–199

East African Airlines, 53, 53–55
"East and West" (Amram), 197, 209–210
Ecobelli, Ralph, 118, 120
Edwards, Ben, 151
Egypt, 44
Einstein, Albert, 185
Elegua (Yoruba spirit presence), 89
Eliot, T. S., 212
Ellington, Duke, 7, 93, 110, 248, 273, 287
Elliott, Ramblin' Jack, 117, 189, 194, 195, 283
Ellis, Anita, 194
England, 53, 54. *See also* London, England
En Memoria de Chano Pozo (Amram), 89, 90, 91, 129
ESP communication, 56, 68, 89, 227, 278. *See also* Amram, David, ESP of
Ethiopia, 42
Equis, Jon, 12, 13, 14–15, 16, 19, 20
Evans, Gil, 205, 304

"Fabulous Fifties" (Amram), 196–197, 200, 202–204, 208
Fairbanks Symphony in Alaska, 188
Fanki JuJu Band, 61, 63, 73, 78
Fanon, Franz, 43
Farm Aid, 131, 188, 213, 239, 277, 279, 280
Farmer, Art, 304
"Fate" (Singer), 50
Fear and Loathing In Las Vegas, 23
Feasterville, Pennsylvania, 4, 17, 81, 107, 209, 277, 278, 280, 289; movie theater in nearby Frankfort, 17, 282–283; Wally Freed's gas station in, 179, 254
Feather, Leonard, 88
Feigelson, Yosif, 274, 275, 276
Fellowship of Reconciliation, The, 61
Felver, Christopher, 164, 166, 168–169, 170–171, 172, 173, 272, 299, 300

Ferlinghetti, Lawrence, 168, 175, 212, 234, 272, 298, 299
Fidelio (Beethoven), 127
Fiji Islands, 58
Films, 16, 17, 23, 50, 58, 67, 75, 94, 138, 233, 246; scores by David Amram, 95
Firebird Suite (Stravinsky), 241
Five Towns College in Long Island, 251
Flamenco music, 44
Florida, 268–270, 272–273; Florida International University, 228, 270
Food, 10, 11, 30–31, 51, 54, 65, 66, 97, 170, 171, 177–178, 195, 207, 209, 216, 231, 242, 243, 245, 252, 253, 258, 270, 272, 273, 275; barbeque restaurants in Knoxville, Tennessee, 153–158; of family farmers, 279. *See also* Nathan's Coney Island restaurants
Franck, César, 119, 130
Freeman, Denny, 27, 32, 34
Freestyling, 226, 244. *See also* Scat-raps
"From Cairo to Kerouac, Classics of Jazz and World Music" (concert), 269
Fromholz, Steve, 117
Frontier Gandhi, The (film), 287

Gaillard, Slim, 212
Galway, Sir James, 4, 224–225, 232, 237, 240, 269
Gardener, Mark, 53
Garner, Errol, 276
Garrett, John, 58–59, 60
Gaynor, Janet, 138, 141, 143–144, 145, 149
Gensel, Reverend John, 45, 46, 48
"Georgia," 24
Germany, 92, 94, 202, 237, 247
Gershwin, George, 230, 234, 244
Getz, Stan, 84, 86, 87, 90, 129
Ghana, 43, 49
Giannini, Vittorio, 61–62, 125
Giants of the Night (Amram), 224, 232, 240, 241, 269, 287
Gibney, Alex, 16
Gillespie, Dizzy, 4, 35, 43–44, 49, 50, 63, 91, 99, 129, 192, 211, 219, 220, 234, 240–241, 288–289, 293; in Cuba, 83, 84–86, 88, 90–91; at seventieth birthday party, 280
Ginsberg, Allen, 65, 115, 194, 198, 199, 298, 301
Globalization, 235, 279
Globe Theater in London, 261, 262–263
Goes, Netherlands, 164, 169, 172

Golden Rule, 236
Goldstein, Gerry and Chris, 24
Goodman, Steve, 131, 188–190, 199
Goodrow, Gary, 174
Goodwin, Dick, 117
Gordon, Peter, 140
Gould, Joe, 173
Grapes of Wrath (Steinbeck), 256, 257
"Greasy Spoon" (Amram), 239
Great Depression, 248, 250, 254, 257, 282, 294
Great Rift Valley, 65–66, 72
Green, Mary Woodmansee, 269
Greenwood, Lil, 273
Gregory, Dick, 103
Greymountain, Gus, 73
Guaguanco, 83, 91, 95, 129, 283
Guatemala, 2
Guiness Jazz Festival in Cork, Ireland, 96
Gunga Din (film), 75
Gurus, 76
Guthrie, Arlo, 255, 260
Guthrie, Nora, 255, 259–260
Guthrie, Woody, 96, 202, 237, 257, 260; Guthrie Foundation, 243; Woody Guthrie Folk Festival, 254

Hafid, Ali, 196
Haiku poets, 189
Hamlet (Shakespeare), 261
Hammil, Pete, 18, 112, 113
Hampton, Lionel, 211, 231
Hangen, Bruce, 149
Harold and Maude, 136–149, 160–161; first reading, 138; opening night, 146–147; playwright of, 138 (*see also* Higgins, Colin); producer of, 137, 141–142, 143, 144, 146; special effects for, 141–142, 143, 145, 146–147
Harris, Hilda, 196
Harry the Hipster, 212
Hart, Howard, 169, 211–212, 298–299, 300
"Harumbee," 75
Havens, Ritchie, 103, 111
Hawkins, Jay, 203
Hayes, Tony, 51
Health food, 11. *See also* Food
Heavy metal, 235
Hemingway, Ernest, 85, 232, 247, 269, 270
Henderson, Joe, 196
"Here Come the Anthros" (Westerman), 103
Hernandez, Maria, 94

Hester, Carolyn, 115, 117
Higgins, Colin, 138–140
Hijaz mode, 190
Hill, Charlie, 111, 271
Hilton Head, South Carolina, 269
Hindemith, Paul, 150
Hindi language, 75
Hines, Earl "Fatha," 84, 86, 87, 88, 129
Hingle, Pat, 133
Holladay, Hilary, 247–248
Holland. *See* Netherlands
Hollywood, 50, 94, 95, 282, 283, 294. *See also* Films; Los Angeles
Holmes, John Clellon, 257
"Home on the Range," 283
Homer, 191
Honor Song for Sitting Bull (Amram), 105, 111, 122, 130
Hooper, Troy, 25
Horn and Hardart Automats, 204–208
"Horn and Hardart Succotash Blues" (Amram), 196, 204, 205, 207–208
Howard University, 261
Howl (Ginsberg), 298
Howling Wolf Saloon in Fox, Alaska, 188
How to Talk Texan, 241
Hughes, Langston, 212, 233
Hummel, Johann, 263
Hyman, Earle, 261

Ibbotson, Jimmy, 15, 21–22, 32, 33, 35
Improvisations, 6, 13, 14, 115–116, 152, 168, 186, 190, 194, 201; in eighteenth and nineteenth century music, 181, 184. *See also* Jam sessions; Make-up songs; Scat-raps
Incident at Vichy (Miller), 292
India, 96
"In Memory of Chano Pozo," (Amram), 88. *See also En Memoria de Chano Pozo*
International Theater Festival in Bonn, Germany, 237
Internet, 82, 94, 95, 234, 248, 252
Irakere (Cuban musical group), 87
Ireland, 51–52, 200
Ives, Charles, 126, 234

"Jack Kerouac Wrote Here: Crisscrossing America Chasing Cool," 281
Jacob's Coat of Many Colors, 9
Jacques d'Amboise National Dance Institute, 190

Jam sessions, 13, 14, 15, 60, 61, 86, 87, 88, 129, 130, 135, 200, 231, 234, 242, 265, 276, 300, 304, 305. *See also* Improvisations
Janson, Peter, 60
Japan, 76
Jazzmouth Festival (Portsmouth, New Hampshire), 242–243, 284
Jazz music, 45, 63, 81, 88, 90, 97, 203, 206, 211, 213, 226, 231; first jazz/poetry festival, 242–243; first jazz-poetry readings, 96, 192, 211, 213, 243, 268, 285, 298; jazz/poetry readings, 259, 264, 298–299, 300
Jazz/Poetry Trio, The, 298
J.B. (MacLeish), 133
Jeffers, Robinson, 151
Jefferson, Thomas, 185, 214, 215, 268
Jennings, Waylon, 116
Jewish community in Latvia, 275, 276
Joans, Ted, 51
Jobim, Antonio Carlos, 305
John F. Kennedy Center, 159, 160, 183, 214, 268
Johnson, Joyce, 164, 170, 171, 173, 174, 175
Johnson, Lou, 256, 257
Jones, Brooks, 234, 252, 289
Jones, Elvin, 205
Jones, Thad, 63, 196
Jude, Michael, 16, 20, 35
Juniper, Emma, 7–8, 10, 15–16
Juris, Vic, 103

Katrina hurricane, 217, 271, 274
Katz, Dennis, 195–196, 197
Kaufman, Bob, 211
Kazan, Elia, 133, 136, 150, 292
Kelly, Helen, 166, 306
Kennedy, Rod, 117
"Kentucky Southern Gentleman" (Amram poem), 37–39
Kenya, 4, 43, 44–80; Asian Youth Conference Tea Ceremony in, 75; Colonel Sanders corporation in, 66, 79; international ensemble in, 46, 60, 80; Kenyatta Conference Center, 59, 72; Nairobi, 57, 60, 61; telepathic communication in, 56; visitors to, 58
Kenyatta, Jomo, 43, 57, 72
Kerouac, Jack, 17, 23, 27, 111, 115, 155, 198, 215, 223, 227, 233, 234, 236, 240–241, 242, 246, 266, 269; death/gravestone of, 248; in Denver, 247; and first jazz-poetry readings, 96 (*see also* Jazz music, first jazz-poetry readings); as jazz and scat singer, 199, 211; and Lucien Carr, 301, 302, 303; and Philip Lamantia, 299, 300; quote for cover of *Vibrations* by, 286; and search for the spiritual, 256. *See also* Lowell, Massachusetts, Lowell Celebrates Kerouac; *Offbeat: Collaborating with Kerouac*; *On the Road*; *Pull My Daisy*; "This Song's for You, Jack"
"Kerouac in the British Imagination," 266
Kerrville Music Festival (Texas), 27, 114–115, 116, 117, 190, 256, 260–261, 276
Kerry, John, 28
Kesey, Ken, 169
Key West, Florida, 269–270
Khyber Pass, 20
Kikuyu people/language, 68, 78
King, B. B., 203
King Kong (film) 58
King Lear Variations (Amram), 194
King Pleasure, 212
Kipisgis people, 68
Kirk, Rahsaan Roland, 304
Klein, Estelle, 50
Klein, Stewart, 147
Kline, Franz, 192, 203, 233
Kniaz, Abe, 93
Knoxville, Tennessee, 151–160
Kokopelli (mythical figure), 120, 123, 132
Kokopelli (Amram symphony), 37, 115, 130, 215; dedication in score, 126; first movement, "Lene Tawi," 122, 123, 126, 128–129; opening night, 131–132; rehearsals for, 127–128, 131; second movement, "Mizmor Kaddum," 125, 129; third movement, "Danza del Mundo," 125–126, 129
Kraft, Robert, 183
Kristofferson, Kris, 195
"Kwahare," 80, 81, 82, 115

LaFave, Jimmy, 256, 257, 260, 276
Lakota courting flute, 111, 115, 121, 190
Lakota duck flute (*sheeho*), 121–122. *See also* Lakota courting flute
Lamantia, Philip, 169, 211–212, 298–300
LaNanna, Jimmy (Reverend), 59, 78, 79
Lancaster, Phil, 255
Landesman, Fran and Jay, 53
Landin, William, 260
Language, 93, 94, 96, 104–105, 123, 232,

235, 236, 237, 241, 244, 245, 251, 267, 278. *See also* Swahili
Latin music, 91, 92, 93, 95, 97. *See also* Afro-Cuban music/jazz
Latin New York Magazine, 92
Latvia, 122, 274–276
Lawlor, Bill, 232, 233, 236
Lebanon, 77
Lennon, John, 42
Leonino, Terry, 260
Leslie, Alfred, 172, 174, 257
"Let the good times roll" (New Orleans motto), 288
Lethus Amrami grasshopper species, 108
Leviticus, 75
Levy, Howard, 193
Lewis, Bobby, 136–137, 138, 139–140, 141–142, 142–143, 146, 161
Lewis, Mel, 63
Liepaja, Latvia, 274–276
Lil Greenwood and David Amram: Back to my Roots (CD), 273
Lincoln, Nebraska, 277
Lipuka, Sampson, 61, 64
Literature, 233, 246. *See also* Jazz music, first jazz-poetry reading; *under* Music
"Little Mama" (Amram), 197
Little Orchestra Society (New York), 118
Little Rebellion, A: Thomas Jefferson (Amram), 214, 215
Living in the Now, 227–228, 244, 249, 250, 303
Liv people, 275
Locke, Kevin, 111
London, England, 251–253, 261–266, 287
Lonesome Traveler (Kerouac), 269
Lord, Sterling, 166, 168, 175
Lord Buckley, 212, 262. *See also* Ode to Lord Buckley
Los Angeles, 229–230. *See also* Hollywood
Los Papines, 88, 89, 90, 129, 304
Louisville, Kentucky, 5, 295, 296, 297
Lovett, Lyle, 15, 27, 28, 31–32, 33, 34
Lowell, Massachusetts, 17, 214, 219, 235, 283, 287, 298; Lowell Celebrates Kerouac, 218–219, 221, 237, 238, 247, 280, 281
Luckenbach, Texas, 116–117; Marge the Sheriff in, 215
"Lucy in the Sky with Diamonds, 42
"Lucy" skeleton discovered in Ethiopia, 42
Lumet, Sidney, 136

Lumumba, Patrice, 43
Maa language, 60, 68, 71, 78
Macbeth, Carlyle, 212
McCarthy, Joseph, 202, 292
McCarthy, Kevin, 215
McClure, Michael, 298
McCormack, Ed, 208
McCourt, Ellen, 264
McCourt, Frank, 51, 96, 199, 200–201, 263–264, 291
McCourt, Malachy, 43, 51, 112–113, 199, 200–201, 263
McCrae, Artie, 209, 282
McDermott, Keith, 138, 142, 143, 146
McGovern, George, 5, 28, 29
Machito, 91
MacLeish, Archibald, 133
McLuhan, Teri, 287
Mafia, 17
Mahler's Ninth Symphony, 10, 37, 39
Mahler's *Symphony of a Thousand,* 56
Mailer, Norman, 305, 306
Makem, Tommy, 51
Make-up songs, 45, 78, 79, 187, 188, 195, 211, 226, 229. *See also* Scat-raps
Mal, Karen, 260
Manchurian Candidate, The (film), 50, 95, 96, 229, 287
Manners, 54, 58, 70–71, 236, 253, 295
Mantilla, Ray, 83, 84, 85, 86, 87, 91
Mantovanni, 105
"Man with a Bull Tongue Plow" (Young), 212
Man with a Flower in His Mouth, A (Pirandello), 133
Mariposa Festival in Canada, 189
Markson, David, 112, 113
Marlboro Festival (1960), 131
Marshall, E. G., 214, 215, 268
Martin, Grady, 277
Martin, Nan, 133
Masai people/land, 4, 59, 60, 61, 66–67; Masai dancing, 64, 69, 73, 74
Massey, Raymond, 133
"Mastinchele Wachipi Olowan" 99, 103, 115, 260
Matthews, Dave, 277
Matthiessen, Peter, 305
Maurice the newspaper man (Greenwich Village), 173
Mayan culture, 234

Mayer, Kulwat, 73–74
Mead, Margaret, 80–81
"Mean Dean" (Amram), 196
"Meanderin' in Mandarin" (Amram), 221, 236, 260
Meara, Anne, 135, 282, 283
Medea, 151–160; on Broadway, 160
Meditation, 75, 76
Meer dan Woorden festival (Goes, Netherlands), 164, 170
Meisenbach, Megan, 117
Mellencamp, John Cougar, 277
Menomonee Reservation in Green Bay, Wisconsin, 111
Messina, Frank, 173
Mexico, 111, 234
Mgrdichian, George, 152–153, 196
Michel, John, 16, 20–21, 35
Middletown Daily Record, 294, 295
"Midhat and Company" (musical group), 286
Mighty Sparrow, 212
Miia (daughter of Dody Muller), 302, 303
Milhaud, Darius, 241
Miller, Arthur, 136, 150, 194, 291–294
Miller, Inge, 293
Mingus, Charlie, 63, 87, 96, 182, 202, 254, 265, 284, 285, 304
Mingus, Eric, 284, 285
Mirandesh dialect, 245
Missa Manhattan (Amram), 96, 263–264
Mitchell, Billy, 196
Mitchell, Joan, 233
Mitropolous, Dimitri, 130, 136, 287
Mobile, Alabama, 273–274
"Moby Book" (Goodman), 189
Models (fashion), 252–253
Monk, Thelonious, 63, 103, 192, 220, 234, 276
Monroe, Marilyn, 293
Montreal Jazz Festival, 237
Montreal Symphony, 149
Moore, Big Chief Russell, 109
Moriarity, Sheila, 51
Morrero, Nicky, 91, 99
Mount Tepozteco, 111
Moussa, Roland, 111, 195, 198
Mozambique, 41
Mozart, Wolfgang Amadeus, 91, 124, 131, 247, 263
"Mr. Bojangles," 35
"Mr. Tambourine Man," 30
Muller, Dody, 302, 303

Munvies, Peter, 197–198
Murphy, Blair, 238
Murray, Bill, 27
Music; *gebrauchts musik,* 150; as institutionalized, 107; and the Internet, 95; and literature, 184–185, 201, 211, 212; maxims for a life in music, 287; orchestral/chamber music in 60s and 70s, 186–187; playing music and paying attention, 284; and politics, 84, 87, 92, 184; riffs, 181; as sharing and communication, 3, 227; singing/playing after the beat, 104–105. *See also* Afro-Cuban music/jazz; Bluegrass music; Improvisations; Jazz music; Latin music; Rock and roll; World music; *under* Africa
Musician's Emergency Fund (for Katrina), 217
"My Buddha Angel in Chengdu" (Amram poem), 221–223
"Mysteries of Jewish Music," 276

Nahm, Elinor, 111
Nahm, Milton, 108–110, 111, 132
Nakamura, John, 286
Nashville Symphony, 119, 124, 126, 127, 132, 215
Nathan's Coney Island restaurants, 238, 239
National Public Radio, 118
National Symphony, 93, 214, 268
Native Americans, 2, 48, 56, 71, 73—74, 96, 132, 188, 195, 198, 236, 237, 255, 271, 278, 301, 306; and Respect, Love and Sharing, 105, 109; social songs of, 73, 99, 102, 106, 111, 120; style of group singing, 104–105. *See also* Acca, Claire; *Kokopelli*; *Trail of Beauty*; Westerman, Floyd Red Crow
Nay (musical instrument), 152
Near-death experiences, 150
Neihardt, John G., 112, 113
Nelson, Amy, 260
Nelson, Willie, 37, 131, 188, 213, 239, 255, 277, 278–279, 293
Nero, 185
Netherlands, 4, 163, 164, 168
New Age, 76, 236
New Delhi Airport, 1–2
Newman, Jerry, 212
New Orleans, 4, 44, 224, 225, 235, 264, 288
"New Orleans Horn Man" (Amram), 217–218
New York City, 58, 76, 81, 106, 137, 149, 172, 173, 182, 196, 215, 244, 254, 270, 280, 293; American Indian Community

House in, 71, 123; Bells of Hell bar in Greenwich Village, 51, 114, 199, 263; Brata Gallery, 211, 213, 268, 298; Brooklyn Academy of Music, 100, 149, 167, 193; Brooklyn College, 298; Brooklyn Philharmonic, 91, 100–101, 141, 167; Carnegie Hall, 205, 206; Cathedral of St. John the Divine, 305–306; Circle in the Square Theater, 300; cross-cultural programs in, 100; family dining in, 54; 55 Bar in Greenwich Village, 42; Gaslight Café on MacDougal Street, 195; Harlem clubs, 265, 304, 305; Lincoln Center, 92, 134, 150, 194, 287, 292, 304; Lion's Head Bar in Greenwich Village, 12, 13, 18, 42, 43, 51, 112, 114, 263; Manhattan School of Music, 61; Molly Barnes Gallery, 244; New York Philharmonic, 134, 160, 183, 184, 224, 287, 305; NYU Beat Conference (1994), 166; rents in, 204; Saratoga Performing Arts Center, 121; Shakespeare in the Park, 133, 135, 167, 262, 282, 285; St. Mark's Church on the Bowery in, 166, 167–168; Village Gate in Greenwich Village, 43, 195, 240; White Horse Tavern in Greenwich Village, 228

New York Times, 28–29, 42, 88, 147, 207

Nine to Five (film), 139, 140

Nitty Gritty Dirt Band, 15, 21

Nixon, Richard, 86, 202

No Goodniks, 250

No More Walls (Amram album), 150, 194–195, 197

"NOW's the Time" (Parker), 227, 250, 303

Nunn, Gary P., 24, 115, 116, 117

Oates, John, 15, 16, 32

O'Ceallaigh, Daithi, 263

Ode to Lord Buckley (Amram), 136, 148, 149, 262

Odetta, 60, 101, 195, 283

O'Donnell, Joanne, 51

Offbeat: Collaborating with Kerouac (Amram), 3, 96, 165, 232, 244, 266; genesis of, 163–175; re-issue of, 286

Okemah, Oklahoma, 254, 255–256

Okie (word), 256, 257, 259

Oklahoma Jazz Hall of Fame, 283

Old Testament, 75, 288

On the Road (Kerouac), 6, 166, 167–168, 203, 213, 215, 232, 234, 237, 239, 246, 249, 268, 296; fiftieth anniversary of publication, 285, 287; original scroll of, 265, 272, 299

Oral history, 226, 237, 259

"Oral History of the World, The" (Gould), 173

Orinkas, 59, 69

Ortiz, Simon, 73, 122

Oud (musical instrument), 152–153, 196

Overspecialization, 185

Pacheco, Jose, 268, 269

Paintings/painters, 182, 184, 203, 233, 242, 302

Pakistan, 77

Pandit, Raji, 1–2

Panitz, Murray, 118, 120, 126, 129, 132

Panitz, Myrna, 118–119, 124–126, 132

Papine (Cuban drummer), 89. *See also* Los Papines

Papp, Joe, 133, 135, 136, 167, 190, 262

Paradigm Publishers, 286

Paris, 44, 182, 220, 230–232, 244; Caméléon jazz club in, 231

Paris Review, 307

Parker, Charlie (Bird), 57, 91, 129, 152, 155, 192, 196, 203, 219, 220, 233, 234, 240–241, 271; death of, 269, 298. *See also* "NOW's the Time"

Parton, Dolly, 139

Passagrille, Florida, 268

Past, present, future, 191, 192, 228

Patchen, Kenneth, 212

Pater, Walter, 225, 253

Pauliteiros (stick dance), 245

Pepper, Jim, 101, 123

Peress, Maurice, 287

Perse, Saint-Jean, 212

Perth, Scotland, 52

Peters, Nancy, 298, 300

Pettiford, Oscar, 63, 211, 262

Peyton, Randy, 197

Philadelphia, Pennsylvania, 278; Philadelphia Academy of Music, 110; Philadelphia Orchestra, 93, 110, 113, 117, 118, 119, 120, 121, 132, 183

Phoenix Theater, 134

Pictures of the Gone World (CD/DVD), 272, 299

Pirandello, Luigi, 133

Pittsburgh Symphony, 128, 232

Platt, Amy, 190

Playing the dozens, 179

Plimpton, George, 24, 305–307

Plimpton, Sarah, 306, 307

Plummer, Christopher, 133
Polivnick, Paul, 286
Pollution, 97
Porcupine Singers, 107
Portland Symphony, 149
Portsmouth, New Hampshire, 242–243, 284
Portugal, 95, 243–244
Pozo, Chano, 44, 84, 88, 89
Press conferences, 23, 24–25
Preview audiences, 145
Previn, André, 53
Prine, John, 131–132
"Professor and the Panhandler, The" (Amram), 197
Psalm 133, 75
Pueblo people, 120, 121, 122, 123
Puente, Tito, 91, 304
Puerto Ricans, 94
Pulitzer Prize, 133
"Pull My Daisy," 115, 169, 170, 172, 194, 212, 260
Pull My Daisy (film), 95, 135, 194, 198, 237, 242, 244, 257, 283, 285; Jack Kerouac's narration for, 212
Putnam Valley, New York, 92, 280, 285

Racism, 56, 75, 93
Radnofsky, Kenneth, 149
Rafelson, Bob, 36
Raffi (songwriter), 209
Raphael, Mickey, 37, 131, 215, 216
Ray, Carlene, 197
RCA records, 194, 195, 197, 200, 208, 216
Reardon, Mike, 43
Redbird, David, 111
"Red River Valley," 117, 118
Renaissance, 185
Revé, Elio, 87
Rextroth, Kenneth, 298
Richard II (Shakespeare), 261
Rimbaud, Arthur, 212
Rio Grande, Ohio, 289
Roberts, Kay George, 287
Rock and roll, 203, 231
Rocky Mountain News, 29
Rocky Road Tavern (Okemah, Oklahoma), 256, 257–258
Rogers, Will, 257
Roker, Mickey, 88
Rolling Stone Magazine, 41, 42, 208
Roosevelt Study Center (Middleburg, Netherlands), 163, 166
Rosenkavalier Suite (Strauss), 124, 127

Ross, Annie, 53
Ross, Gayle, 115
Roth, Philip, 307
Rouch, Robert, 140, 141
Rowe, Kenrick, 266
Rumanian Dances (Bartók), 100
Ryan, Mitch, 152

Sacred Run, 271
Safari, 58, 62–63
Sainte-Marie, Buffy, 103, 111
St. Martin in the Fields (London), 263
St. Vincent Millay, Edna, 137, 173, 212, 233
Samoa, 80
Sampas, John, 166
Sampas, Stella, 248
Sampson, Will, 111
Sandoval, Arturo, 87, 88, 89, 90
San Francisco, 271–272, 281, 298
Sanibel Island, Florida, 268
Santamaria, Mongo, 304
Scat-raps, 13, 177, 179–180, 183, 184, 186, 187, 188, 201, 208, 211, 212, 215, 226, 244, 260; on *Duologue*, 191–194; recordings of, 190 (*see also No More Walls*). *See also* Make-up songs
Scavelli, Russ, 270
Scenes for Indian Life (Ballard), 101
Schermerhorn, Kenneth, 37, 119, 121, 124, 126, 127, 130–131
Schwartz, Delmore, 211
Sears, Peter, 271
Seeger, Pete, 202, 255
Seelye, Katherine, 28, 29
Segregation, 179
Serbagi, Midhat, 47, 285–286
Serkin, Peter and Rudolph, 131
Sermon on the Mount, 75, 76
Seventh Army Symphony, 127
Severo, Richard, 88
Sexism, 93
Shakespeare, William, 261, 262. *See also* New York City, Shakespeare in the Park
Shakespearean Concerto (Amram), 194
Shanai (musical instrument), 152, 190, 275
Shawangunk Mountains in Cuddebackville, New York, 7
Sheffield, Lynn, 194
Shekere (African gourd), 89
Shenandoah, Joanne, 103
Shorter, Wayne, 304

Shoshone-Paiute people, 73
Shu Dynasty in China, 234
Signing, 80
Silko, Leslie, 73, 122–123, 123–124, 128
Simac, Charles, 243
Simon, Larry, 242, 284–285
"Sinai Desert Song," (Amram), 275
Sing-alongs, 13–14, 45, 49, 61, 79, 115, 181, 183, 186, 260
Singer, Isaac, 50
Six Gallery in San Francisco, 298
Sky Walking Man-Stick, 190
Smith, Arnold, 88
Smith, Fenwick, 287
Smith, Patti, 301
Snyder, Gary, 212, 236, 298
Socrates, 226
"Son de Palo Volador," 2
Songs of the Soul (Amram), 275
Song swaps, 111
Sons of the Dharma (Kerouac), 166
Sorrels, Rosalie, 13
Soul music, 203
Soundstage (PBS show), 99
South Africa, 41, 74
South America, 107, 108
Southern, Terry, 42, 307
Southern Stories (CD), 37, 216 218, 278
Spain, 95
Spencer, Jake, 173–174
Spiritualism, 76, 236
"Spirituality and the Beat Generation," 270
Spirit world, 56, 301
Splendor in the Grass (film), 95, 96
Spontaneity, 233, 244, 299. *See also* Creativity
Sprenger, Audrey, 246, 247, 248–249, 250, 266, 281
Springsteen, Bruce, 293
Stanford, David, 166
Star Is Born, A (film), 138
State University of Potsdam, New York, 281
Statman, Andy, 197
Steadman, Ralph, 24, 29, 36
Steig, Jeremy, 80
Steinbeck, John, 237, 256, 257, 269, 296
Steinberg, William, 128, 130
Stern, Isaac, 205
Stiller, Jerry, 135, 282, 283
Stillman, Mimi, 269
Stratford Shakespeare Festival in Connecticut, 133

Stravinsky, Igor, 182–183, 206, 241
Street fairs, 99—100, 104
Styron, William, 307
Suazo, Lorenzo, 111
Subway Night (Amram), 196–198, 199, 201–204, 208–209
Sudarsky, Igor, 293
Sun Ra, 284
Sunset Boulevard (film), 282
Swahili, 47, 50, 57, 60, 61, 63, 71, 75, 78, 81, 115
Swanson, Gloria, 282
Sweezey, Jean, 165
Swindle, Michael, 18, 19
Symphonic Variations on a Song by Woody Guthrie (Amram), 96, 243, 251, 255, 286
Symphony in D Minor (Franck), 119, 130
Symphony Silicon Valley, 286
Szell, George, 136

Tablas, 196
Tabuteau, Marcel, 120
Tafoya, Jack, 204–206
Taoism, 236
Taos Summer Music Festival, 110
Tarzan movies, 75
Taylor, Cecil, 169
Taylor, John, 45–46, 56, 58
Taylor, Steven, 199
Taylor Made Homes, 286
Teacher Man (McCourt), 264
Teagarden, Jack, 109
Television, 53, 226, 233, 265, 273
Territory bands of 1930s, 181
Terrorism, 252
Terry, Clark, 304
Texas, 4, 65, 116–117, 188, 213, 214, 216, 235, 237, 241; Texas Women's College, 240. *See also* Kerrville Music Festival
Theater directors, 136
"Theme and Variations on My Old Kentucky Home" (Amram), 6, 7, 8, 15, 23, 24, 26, 32, 33–34
"Theme and Variations on Red River Valley" (Amram), 118, 132, 215, 240, 276
"The New York Howl" (Adam Amram's band), 284
Third World, 71, 74, 80
"This Song's for You, Jack" (Amram), 213–214
Thomas, Dylan, 211, 228
Thompson, Anita, 6, 7, 15, 28, 29, 36

Thompson, Davison, 34
Thompson, Hunter S., 5–39, 41, 216, 294–298; Amram obituary for, 25; ashes fired into space from cannon, 8, 30, 31, 297; and Aspen developers, 10; and Jack Kerouac, 296, 297
Thompson, Juan, 6, 25, 29, 36, 297
Timelessness, 66, 70, 159, 247
Timms, Foster, 14, 16, 20, 35
Tobia, George, 32
Tony Awards, 160
Toronto Symphony, 48, 49, 107
Tower, Joan, 190
Trail of Beauty (Amram), 110, 112, 113, 117, 119, 120, 121, 122; first performance of, 183
Triple Concerto for Woodwind, Brass and Jazz Quintets (Amram), 63, 87, 99, 117, 197, 286
Tuckwell, Barry, 53
Tumkwahey, 105
Turner, Richard, 266
Twelfth Night (Amram opera), 3, 190, 193, 262, 263, 287
Twilight of the Sioux (Neihardt), 112, 113
Tytell, John, 164, 170, 171, 172, 173, 174, 175

Ugly Americans, 234
U Mass Lowell, 247–248
United Press International (UPI), 302
University of Hangoutology, 226, 232, 301
University of Tulsa, 282, 283
Untermeyer, Joel, 211

Vaca, Cabeza de, 268
Valdes, Oscar, Jr., 88, 89, 90
Vancouver Symphony, 149
Van Minnen, Cornelis A. (Kurt), 164, 165, 166, 169, 170
Van Zandt, Townes, 115, 213
Varese, Edgard, 192, 233
Velez, Glen, 190
Venegas, Victor and Ida, 89–90, 103
Vibrations (Amram), 3, 96, 175, 231, 232, 244, 278; re-issue of, 286
Village Vanguard, 63
Village Voice, 18, 42
Visions of Cody (Kerouac), 249
Voice of Kenya (TV show), 77, 79
Vonnegut, Kurt, 215, 305

Wagner, Richard, 119
Wakefield, Dan, 228, 229, 270
Wakschal, Seymour, 118
Walcott, Collin, 196
Waldmann, Anne, 169
Walker, Jerry Jeff, 13, 35, 195, 277
Wallace, George, 259
"Waltz from after the Fall" (Amram), 150
Wamala, Gabby, 62, 64
Wanrow, Yvonne, 111
Washington, D.C., 81, 84, 159, 160, 179. *See also* John F. Kennedy Center
Watergate, 41
Water Music (Handel), 100
Webster, Louis, 111
Weinreich, Regina, 164, 170, 173, 174, 175
Welsh, Johnny, 42, 43, 44, 47, 51
Wen Chu-an (Professor), 232, 233, 236
Wenner, Jann, 29
WEPA, 92–97
Westerman, Floyd Red Crow, 2, 48, 49, 73, 99–100, 103, 104, 105–106, 111, 115, 116, 122, 123, 132, 236, 271; approached by white man dressed as Indian, 101–102
West Indies, 44, 63
Weston, Randy, 51, 101
Wexler, Fran and Barry, 160
Whalen, Phil, 212, 236, 298
Whitehead, Bob, 150–151, 153, 155–156, 157, 158, 171
Whitehead, Ron, 5, 8, 12, 173, 213, 295
Whitman, Sylvia and George, 231
Whitman, Walter, 233, 248, 269
Wichita Falls Symphony, 241
Wilcox, Shelly, 32
Wild animals, 67, 79
Williams, William Carlos, 212
"Will the Circle Be Unbroken," 15, 32, 33
"Will Ya Go Lassie Go," 51, 113
Windber, Pennsylvania, 237
Winnebago dancers, 107
Witchi Tai To, 101
Wolfe, Thomas, 269
"Woman in the Black Beret" (Amram poem), 219–221
Women, 69, 74, 93, 94, 171
Wood, Suzy, 8, 295
Woody Creek, Colorado, 5, 8, 9, 12, 13, 35, 297; Woody Street Tavern in, 16, 17, 19, 21, 22, 24

Woody Guthrie Folk Festival in Okemah, Oklahoma, 254, 255, 258, 261
World Council of Churches, 46, 48, 56, 78
World music, 195, 197, 234, 244, 267, 270
World War II, 246, 274, 276
Wuttunee, Winston, 107, 112

Yarrow, Bethany, 260
Yarrow, Peter, 255
Year on Our Land, A (Amram), 269
Yoruba religion, 84, 89

Young, Jesse, 212
Young, Neil, 277
Youngblood, Pam, 240
Young People's Guide to the Orchestra (Britten), 130
Young Savages, The (film), 95, 96
Yo-Yo Ma, 225

Zamcona, Jorge, 26
Zevon, Warren, 5, 8, 12, 295
Zinmann, David, 197

About the Author

David Amram has composed more than one hundred orchestral and chamber works; written many scores for Broadway theater and film, including the classic scores for the films *Splendor in the Grass* and *The Manchurian Candidate;* composed two operas, including the ground-breaking Holocaust opera *The Final Ingredient;* and composed the score for the landmark 1959 documentary *Pull My Daisy,* narrated by Jack Kerouac. He is the author of the books *Vibrations,* an autobiography, and *Offbeat: Collaborating with Kerouac,* to be reissued by Paradigm Publishers in 2008.

A pioneer of jazz French horn and World Music, he is also a virtuoso on piano, numerous flutes and whistles, percussion, and dozens of folkloric instruments from twenty-five countries. He is also an inventive, funny improvisational lyricist. He has collaborated with Leonard Bernstein, who chose him as the New York Philharmonic's first composer-in-residence in 1966, Langston Hughes, Dizzy Gillespie, Willie Nelson, Thelonious Monk, Odetta, Elia Kazan, Arthur Miller, Charles Mingus, Wynton Marsalis, Lionel Hampton, Johnny Depp, Tito Puente, and many others. Amram's most popular recent works are *Giants of the Night,* a flute concerto commissioned and premiered by Sir James Galway and dedicated to the memory of Charlie Parker, Jack Kerouac, and Dizzy Gillespie, and *Symphonic Variations on a Song by Woody Guthrie.*

Today, Amram continues to compose music while traveling the world as a conductor, soloist, band leader, visiting scholar, and narrator in five languages. He is currently collaborating with author Frank McCourt on *Missa Manhattan,* for narrator, chorus, and orchestra, and composing a new piano concerto. All of his concert music is published by C. F. Peters Corporation.